KW-223-828

Structure and Growth of the Scottish Economy

Planning Regions by Administrative Areas – July, 1971

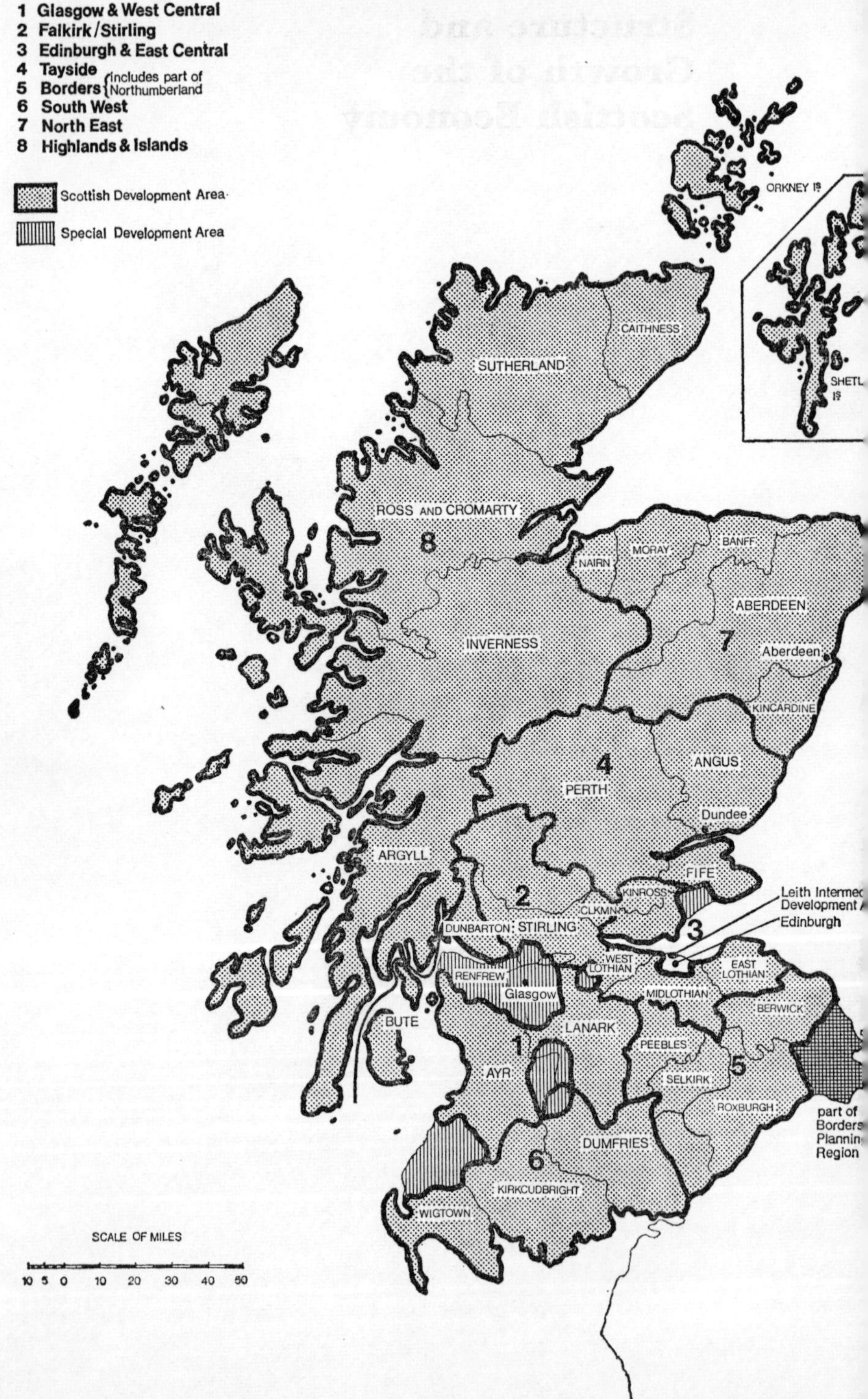

Structure and Growth of the Scottish Economy

Professor T L Johnston
N K Buxton
D Mair
Heriot-Watt University

Collins London and Glasgow

First published 1971

ISBN 0 00 460105X
Printed in Great Britain
C. Tinling & Co. Ltd.

Contents

Contents

Foreword

This is primarily a textbook. It is intended for a variety of consumers. We hope that it will be used by students in Universities and colleges who have studied, or are taking, basic principles of economics, and who wish to relate these to the economy in which they live. It is aimed also at students who are undertaking work for the examinations of the Scottish Council for Commercial, Administrative and Professional Education (S.C.C.A.P.E.). We like to think too that the book may interest the Plain Man (and perhaps the not-so-Plain Woman) who wishes to know more about the Scottish economy, out of a sheer desire for enlightenment or even for more active purposes and pursuits.

Since it is a textbook, we, as authors, do not claim any particular originality for the material or the methods of analysis. If we have succeeded in bringing material together which illumines the Scottish scene in a fresh way, for policy makers and others, we shall be gratified. We are indebted to various authors in the field of regional economics and the Scottish economy who have helped pave the way for us. When these two interests are brought together in one person, as is the case with Dr Gavin McCrone, it will be obvious that we are especially indebted to him for his pioneering work on regional and Scottish economic problems. We have listed at the end of various Chapters the sources which have been particularly useful to us, and which the interested reader may consult for further work, and we hope that other authors will accept that form of comprehensive salute as a token of our thanks.

We are also grateful to officials of Government departments and the compilers of official statistical series for ready assistance. Officers and members of the Scottish National Party have been most kind and helpful in providing material. The Scottish Council (Development and Industry) has also been a fertile source of information. Mr F. S. Taylor, of the Institute of

Bankers in Scotland, helped us with material for Chapter 11. Coming closer to home, Miss Alison Russell has made a vast number of statistical calculations for us, and has dug out material with sense and discrimination, while Mrs Alice Northwood, Mrs Jean Roberts and Miss Moira Telfer have provided swift and expert secretarial assistance. We thank them all. For what is now published as a book we are, of course, completely and jointly responsible.

In such a rapidly changing subject area as applied economics in general, and regional problems in particular, we have obviously had to set a cut-off point beyond which we could not systematically report on and analyse the latest returns. We have tried as far as possible to include information for 1970.

Part I:
Introduction

Chapter 1
The Framework of Economic Analysis

Under the present political structure of Britain, Scotland is an integral part of the United Kingdom. In examining the economy of Scotland in this book we are therefore dealing with the economy of one region within the greater national economy. It has long been recognised that every part or region of a country need not be equally prosperous. Even when unemployment was chronically and generally high in Britain, during the Great Depression of 1929–32, there were marked regional disparities in the extent to which resources of men and machines were standing idle. The present paradox, however, is that we have learned fairly successfully since the second World War how to achieve and maintain full employment of resources in the nation as a whole, yet disparities between regions remain. While no one would claim that the misery of the 1930s is being re-enacted in the less prosperous areas, nevertheless there are disquieting differences between, and even within, regions in unemployment both of people and of other productive potential.

Problems of regional inequalities in employment and income arouse political passions, not least when these are associated with strong regional or national attitudes which stem from historical, cultural or other characteristics. For a variety of reasons and in a number of quarters there is a lively political interest in Scotland's economic performance. In the setting of the British economy as a whole this performance has been unsatisfactory in recent years, and not everyone is comforted by the thought that Scottish economic problems are comparatively modest in the wider international scale of standards of living.

We seek in this book to analyse and understand more systematically the forces which are at work in determining the structure and growth of a particular region within our national economy. When the region is one that has the emotional and ethnic associations identified with Scotland, the analysis becomes at once more stimulating and additionally hazardous. It has to be stated quite firmly at the outset, however, that it is no part of our purpose in this study to make a case for any political policy or philosophy.

As economists, our essential, and professional, purpose here is to take the tool kit of the economist and try to apply it to understanding the forces which have been, and are, at work in shaping the Scottish economy. This involves in the first instance an analysis of the present structure of the economy, and this is the theme of Chapters 2 to 7. The growth of the economy from the standpoint of some of its strategic determinants is taken up in Chapters 8 to 11. Regional economic analysis and policies are set out in Chapters 12 and 13. In Chapter 14 we draw together the threads of the earlier analysis and its implications.

In writing this book as economists, we assume a certain basic interest in, or at any rate no strong antipathy towards, the economist's concern with analysing problems associated with scarce material resources. It may be useful for the reader to have become familiar with the main principles of economics set out in the basic textbooks of the subject. But this is not indispensable. What is essential is that the reader should appreciate that economists have developed a logical set of concepts for reasoning about economic problems.

We shall define our terms as we proceed, but we propose in addition in this introductory Chapter to indicate fairly extensively the tools of analysis which are important and the conceptual framework within which we analyse the economy of Scotland. This should familiarise the reader with the 'apparatus of the mind', or 'technique of thinking' which economists use. At the same time we shall show that there are formidable statistical, as well as analytical, difficulties in handling an economy which is part of a larger national whole.

2 Strategic Concepts

a) The Problem of Choice When resources are scarce, in the sense that not enough material goods and services are available to satisfy all the wants of all the people in a society, there must be some mechanism for determining priorities and for allocating the scarce resources among the competing objectives which people may wish to attain. This involves the key problem of choice, of allocating the resources among alternative uses. Economists have identified the central idea of *opportunity cost* in their attack on scarcity in relation to wants. When we use a resource for a particular purpose we are in essence saying that we have given up, or foregone, the opportunity of using it in some other way to satisfy wants. What we have given up as an alternative is the opportunity cost of the alternative which we do in fact select. If we put resources into growing potatoes in a field, their cost is the alternative crop, say strawberries, which we forego by choosing to grow potatoes.

A related idea is that of *substitution.* When consumers decide how to allocate their scarce income they try to maximise the satisfaction they obtain from their spending; and they will be rational enough to replace items in their spending pattern if they think that some other items will give them more satisfaction. They do this by substituting. Producers likewise will be concerned to produce output in the least costly way, and will replace, or substitute, cheaper for more expensive resources in their production programmes. The rate at which such substitution changes is associated with the concept of *elasticity.* In addition, it is important to notice that the really critical decisions about choice in the use of scarce material resources involve a little more or a little less of a particular resource. It is marginal decisions which are the sensitive ones in the setting of substitution, and the concept of *the margin* is fundamental to the allocation process.

In addition to the conceptual core of opportunity cost there is, of course, a related question about the institutional arrangements for making these decisions. In what ways are decisions about scarcity and wants made? Put bluntly, who decides who gets what, and how much? A wide range of possible arrangements is present. Most countries in western civilisation accept that it is the consumer who is the king pin. He (or she) determines preferences as to the wants to be satisfied, and these are transmitted to prospective producers via the anonymous mechanism of the market. The producers' job is to satisfy these wants by combining scarce resources in the most efficient and least costly way. Even in market economies, however, it is recognised that there is a place for collective decision-making about the use of certain resources for purposes such as defence, public education, and health services.

The growth of the Government, or public, sector of market economies has been very rapid in recent years, as it has come to be accepted that the market mechanism does not always function smoothly, or produce the mix of output that the society is willing to sustain. We shall see at various stages throughout this study that, in recent years, Governments have been very active in our mixed economy in trying to rechannel resources towards geographical areas which market forces have tended to penalise. At the other extreme from the pure market economy, it is possible to think of the decisions about alternative uses of the resources being taken centrally, by some allocative agency, which tells both producers and consumers what the mixture of resources is to be.

b) Micro-economics The problems which we referred to above with reference to the alternative uses for scarce resources have been investigated by economists in their analysis of demand and supply, or what is sometimes termed price theory, or micro-economics. The concepts we identified above are crucial to micro-economics. This book is not about price theory, which shows in a rigorous, analytical way how the millions of decisions about opportunity cost in an economy can be put 'under the microscope' of demand and supply analysis. We are not concerned to show here how demand and supply interact to determine the price of (say) whisky. Obviously, this kind of analysis is important and relevant, since it is the myriad of particular decisions which consumers make about demand—whether to buy, how much, and at what prices—and which producers make about supply—what type and quality of goods to produce, in what volume, with what resources, at what costs and prices—that add up to the broad sweep of regional and national flows within an economy, and indeed between national economies.

We shall largely take for granted here what the price theory textbooks expound at length. *But we ask the reader to bear in mind that scarcity in relation to wants does lead to the discipline of the concepts which we mentioned above.* Consumers with a limited income are assumed to be rational in allocating their scarce resources among competing objectives and making threshold or marginal decisions to this end. Equally, we assume that the producer is rational, that he is trying to achieve some objective, such as the maximisation of his profit. When he employs factors of production—raw materials, industrial plant, labour, managerial skills—we reckon that he is influenced by opportunity cost, and that critical decisions about output, costs and prices will also be made at the margin. We shall not set out this underlying rationale at greater length. Clearly, however, it underlies the pattern of resource use which we analyse in depth in later Chapters.

In Chapter 12, to take an example, we shall be examining the various considerations which businessmen may take into account when they determine the choice of location for the siting of their production facilities. We shall see that the analysis has often tended to emphasise the costs of alternative locations to the exclusion of the returns. In Chapter 13 our discussion of regional policy measures brings out the way in which Government policy has sometimes manipulated various schemes of grants and incentives in order to influence the opportunity costs of individual firms and workers in choosing their geographical base. In our discussion of economic growth in Chapter 9 we shall also be identifying some of the most important concepts in price theory which relate to the *economies of large scale production*, and the *external economies* that producers may enjoy in a particular local or institutional setting.

No one pretends that price theory operates in the real world with a crispness and efficiency that gladden the heart and mind of the purist. We shall lay a good deal of emphasis on the sluggishness which pervades much of the working of the market economy, and we shall show how and why Government has frequently felt it necessary to intervene with a view to modifying or reinforcing 'the laws of markets'. Despite its deficiencies, however, the economic analysis of price theory does provide a logical frame of reference that underpins the use of resources. The mechanism may be imperfect and creaky, and it is not always the case that nice balances are struck by consumers and producers at the margin; but it is most certainly not the case that resources typically are allocated in a random manner. There is more that is rational than random in the way in which resources of land, labour and capital come to be deployed in an economy. This is the continuing message of micro-economics.

c) Macro-economics It is an oversimplification to think that the economic problem is simply one of deciding in some way how all the resources are to be shared out among competing uses. One of the great historical paradoxes of industrial societies has been the failure to ensure that all the production potential available at any one time was being used. We have to distinguish full employment from under-employment. The problem of chronic unemployment generated much of the social bitterness of the inter-war years, and it was this chronic problem that led to the development in economics of the theory of employment which we associate with the name of J. M. Keynes, the great Cambridge economist. It is no accident that we have now experienced a whole generation of consistently full or near-full employment at the national level, and in the international economy.

When we look at the economy of a country as a whole, we become concerned with what is called macro-economics, or *the analysis of aggregates of economic activity*. We look at the economy in the round. While remembering that it is the microcosms that add up to the aggregates, we put aside our price theory microscope and look at the total flows. These relate to categories of economic activity such as total consumption spending, the size of Government spending streams, and capital formation in the economy as a whole. This type of analysis is now as important as micro-economics, and Keynes initiated it in the *General Theory of Employment, Interest and Money* which he published in 1936. The more we know about the factors that determine the total level of activity in the economy the more likely we are to be able to manipulate the economy so that it runs at its full potential. We shall look in greater detail in section III of this Chapter at a simple macro-economic scheme.

Even when we begin to analyse economic forces at the macro end of the spectrum, however, we may frequently be interested in breaking down the aggregates into sub-categories. We may wish to separate out various categories of Government spending in order to identify particular programmes. Obviously, we are particularly concerned here to try to separate out those components of macro-economic flows which relate to Scotland. Perhaps parochially, but understandably, we shall find ourselves seeking to compare the pattern in Scotland with that of The Rest. In certain Chapters, such as the discussion of incomes in Chapter 6, we attempt further sub-division into categories or areas within Scotland.

Whatever the level of aggregation, or disaggregation, at which the analysis of this book is being conducted, we ask the reader to bear vigilantly in mind what has been termed in economics 'the fallacy of composition', or generalising from the particular. For instance, when we look at the structure of production in Chapter 4 we are explicitly trying to look further than a general treatment of industrial production in Scotland. We break down the output mix into industrial groupings which represent particular industrial combinations of factors and distinctive technologies. What is true of one part of the industrial mix may be wildly misleading for others. We have to try and strike a balance between painting a general picture which is not only broad but meaningful, and drawing attention to the minutiae of particular parts of the resource use scene. To take another example, we can say more about incomes in Scotland than simply expressing them as a proportion of U.K. totals. This is the case for disaggregating. In Chapter 4 we show how differences in earnings between old and new industries in Scotland are consistent with the economics of the price mechanism which would suggest that new industries seek to draw labour into them by offering price (wage) differentials which the older industries may not be profitable enough to match. Yet we cannot push this kind of disaggregation to the absurd stage, for our purposes, of listing the wages of particular workers in a certain plant in a specific industry. We shall also see that the groupings of data which we should like to achieve for purposes of analysis may frequently be frustrated by the lack of statistics.

d) Regional economics If micro-economics can be said to be about the study of the particular trees in the national economic forest, and macro-economics the study of the whole forest and its ecology, the analysis of a region such as the Scottish economy suggests an intermediate category, to be likened perhaps to one of the plantations in the forest which has a particular mixture of species of trees that is not necessarily typical of all the plantations in the forest. We have already suggested that there are often severe statistical difficulties inherent in aggregating or disaggregating economic flows to the regional level. Conceptually, too, there is a *lacuna* in the economic analysis of regions. Regional economics, as a special and explicit compartment of economic analysis, is a comparatively new part of the subject, and there is no settled set of regional economic principles.

At first sight, the theory of international trade, which has long been a separate but integral part of economic analysis, appears to provide a handy set of tools for the purpose of regional analysis. International trade is concerned with the movement of goods between nations. No two countries have precisely the same endowment of resources, or factors of production and climate, and particular countries will possess advantages in the production of certain commodities which they are happily placed to produce. Trade may then develop between countries. It is easy to understand that such international trade may arise when one country can produce goods that another could produce only with difficulty, if at all. Adam Smith suggested that it would be technically feasible, but economically nonsensical, for Scotland to become a wine-growing country.

What is not so obvious, but what constitutes the heart of international trade theory, is that countries may all gain from entering into trade with one another even when one country is absolutely superior to the others in its productive efficiency. It is differences in comparative, not absolute, cost which determine the rationale of trade between nations. Hence the term *comparative advantage*. When trade does take place between nations it will be conducted at rates of exchange, or terms of trade, which take account of the size, supply conditions and demand of the trading countries for the commodities being traded, and within the limits set by cost ratios.

This theory assumes that factors of production do not move between the nations entering into trade. Land can obviously not move, and labour has been regarded as immobile because of barriers of language, law and custom. The movement is entirely one of the goods being exchanged in trade. Later versions of this theory have recognised that the movement of goods may have a feed-back effect on the prices of the factors within a country, even if they are immobile.

We can expect that a region, like a nation, will tend to specialise in those forms of economic activity in which its comparative advantage is greatest. We show in Chapter 4, by the use of location quotients, the extent to which the Scottish economy has specialised in particular industries, presumably because her comparative cost advantage has been greatest in them. We can also point to the fact that labour is often rather immobile between different regions of a country.

Yet it is not possible to apply international trade theory without modification to the study of regional economies. One of the traditional criticisms of international trade theory is that it has neglected transport costs, and location theorists claim that no theory of regional economic location can neglect either transport costs or a systematic analysis of the geographical distribution of economic activity. We return to this criticism at greater length in Chapter 12. Another difference between international and interregional analysis is that it is not possible to establish rates of exchange between the regions of a country which has a unified monetary system. Even Federal countries have unified monetary systems. When a country has an adverse balance of trade or payments it will eventually have to take steps to correct the position by altering the rate of exchange between its currency and those of other countries (devaluing), by tariff policy, quotas, or by fiscal measures. Measures could be applied in the opposite direction if the country was running a persistent foreign payments surplus. No such explicit adjustment measures spring so readily to hand for any fundamental disequilibrium that may occur between the regions of a national economy. Not only are balance of payments data unlikely to be available for regions; governments may see no reason to keep each region of the economy in balance with all the others. They may be willing to accept some degree of regional imbalance.

It is possible for a region to lose its comparative advantage, for example, as a result of exhaustion of its natural resource-endowment, or the failure to maintain its comparative efficiency through technological advance. It can develop a persistently adverse 'balance of payments' and experience stagnation, depression and unemployment. We shall be discussing in Chapters 4 and 12 the suggestive analyses of the unfavourable relationships between production structure, incomes, effective demand and unemployment which Professor A. J. Brown and his colleagues at the National Institute for Economic and Social Research have made. As a matter of fact the growing awareness of regional problems and interest in regional policies in recent years has led to many suggestions for improving the balance in a region which is either running a persistent surplus or deficit.

Despite what was said above about the willingness on the part of Governments to accept regional imbalances, adjustment mechanisms have been suggested and applied which are somewhat analagous to international trade measures. Regional taxes and subsidies have been utilised and, to take an example, it has been argued that the Regional Employment Premium (R.E.P.) introduced in Britain in 1967 was a method of trying to devalue, and improve comparative advantage, on a regional basis. Basically, the Premium was intended to lower labour costs and provide a relative improvement in price competitiveness.

e) Resources and technology We conclude this section by drawing attention to some fallacies that occur in the more superficial discussions of resource use. When a country is endowed with a supply of a particular physical resource, it is sometimes argued that the nation should make use of it simply because it is there. We can take deposits of coal as an example to make the point that it is not the mere physical presence of a resource that makes it of interest in an economic sense. The important economic questions in the case of coal concern the alternative fuels that are available, and the costs and returns involved in their exploitation compared to coal. Obviously, the costs of extracting coal will increase—diminishing returns, in the economist's jargon, will set in—when deeper shafts and less accessible seams have to be used. If the resources of men and machines could be applied more economically to generate hydro-electric power, or to produce whisky which is exported in exchange for oil imports, the coal would be better left in the ground. Thus we are not interested simply in stocks of resources as such; *they have to be viable in the setting of the alternative resources available*, and the alternative uses that could be made of factors of production.

This leads us to consider briefly the technological framework of an economy. The economic use of resources at any time will depend on the technologies available. If we do not know how to produce nuclear power this puts an absolute limitation on the choice of alternative fuels available. Much of the effort of scientists and engineers is devoted to developing and seeking to apply new techniques of production which it is hoped to make viable. But it is not enough for technology to become more efficient in a technical sense. New technologies will only be applied in the setting of the alternative use of scarce resources, when they can be shown to be economical vis-à-vis alternative methods, costs and returns involved in producing output. Nuclear power has to show not only technical, but economic, efficiency if it is to be a substitute for other fuels. In our discussion of the structure of production in Scotland in Chapters 4 and 5 we shall see how this technological framework shapes our production possibilities in the economy.

To sum up, the perspective of the economist extends beyond a preoccupation with physical resources and technological possibilities. It is the utilisation of resources in relation to scarcity, and the need to economise in the use of resources which are scarce in relation to wants, that distinguish the techniques or ways in which economists think.

3 Analysing the National Economy

Macro-economic analysis has now developed sufficiently for us to feel fairly confident that we can assess the overall level of demand for output in the economy tolerably close to the potential output of the national economy at any particular time. Within the national picture, however, it is perfectly possible for pockets, islands or regions of under-utilization and over-utilization of capacity to occur. Policies which are successful in the aggregate may be less satisfactory at (say) a regional level. Indeed, it is the very success of these national policies which has made us more explicitly aware of regional disparities.

We can put the point another way. Although the theory of macro-economics is now well-established, it is important not to take it for granted in the setting of this study. By and large the *performance* of the Scottish economy marches in rough step with that of the national economy. The more successful our national economic policy is in running the economy close to its output ceiling, the more the various regions are pulled along in its wake. And vice versa. When national output drops, some regions of the economy may be more adversely affected than others. It is therefore important to have a clear view of the questions and analysis of macro-economics, and in this section we shall set out at greater length the macro-economic aspects of the presentation in the last section.

In analysing the workings of the national economy, we are interested in the following sequence of questions. First, what are the main spending streams and the main spending groups in the economy, and what determines their behaviour? How can we fit together their behaviour into a systematic account of the total spending activity in the economy? Essentially, this can be termed the Keynesian approach to macro-economics. We look at the aggregate demand flows in the economy, and ask how fully demand is matching up to our productive potential.

Second, we have to ask how this productive potential, or our production possibilities, can be augmented. It is not enough to consider that the economic problem is resolved if we analyse the problems of utilising an existing stock of land, labour, capital and organisational skills. We want to ask questions as well about the forces that add to these resources and to the capacity to produce wealth, through population growth, additions to the stock of capital, technological advance, changes in taste, and so forth. This is essentially the theme of economic growth.

Third, we ask how all this activity is to be quantified? What statistical information can be collected, processed and published in order to ensure that the maximum amount of hard information is at the disposal of Government and individual decision-makers? This range of questions has led to the development of national income statistics, or national accounting, as a way of putting statistical flesh on the models of the national economy which macro-economic analysis has constructed.

In the remainder of this Chapter we look at these three themes in turn, first, income determination analysis, second, economic growth, and, third, national income statistics. It will be much easier to grasp the content of some of the later Chapters if we can carry forward from this section the main concepts and framework of ideas. To take an example, the analysis in Chapter 7 of the various expenditure flows in the economy simply brings together income determination concepts and national income statistics for Britain and, wherever possible, Scotland.

a) Income determination analysis In simple income determination analysis for an economy, we try to group spending decisions together in categories which are significant in terms of their motivation and objectives. For example, consumers as a group can be expected to have certain objectives regarding a standard of living, and they seek to achieve the maximum amount of satisfaction through the purchases which they make of final goods and services with the income they have disposable. They also make decisions not to consume, i.e. to save. Consumers as a group, and the decisions which they make, are quite different in character from decisions which business firms make, to add to their productive capacity through capital investment. Their ultimate objective may be to make profits through the production of goods that consumers will purchase; but the whole basis of investment decisions differs from decisions which households make to consume or save their income. Business investment is also notoriously volatile, since so much investment requires a businessman to 'back a hunch' when he plans new productive capacity.

In a simple economy, consisting only of business firms and households, we could see the flow of resources operating in the following way:

1) Money flows from firms to households in return for the factor services, such as labour, which the firms purchase. This money paid for the factor services becomes household income.

2) Money also flows from households to firms in exchange for goods which are bought from the firms. The money paid for the goods becomes the income of firms.

One of the critical features of income flows is that households are unlikely to spend the whole of their income. What is not spent is saved, and the act of saving withdraws funds from the active stream of spending. Income determination analysis distinguishes the propensity to consume and the propensity to save, as concepts which have to be analysed in this income flow process. In particular, it is these propensities in their marginal form which prove to be of great importance for policy purposes. We often wish to know how much of any increment of income is consumed or saved, and we then speak of the *marginal propensity to consume* and the *marginal propensity to save*.

Obviously, an economy with only households and business firms is a drastic oversimplification, and in the real world a good deal of resource use is channelled through the Government, both via its own spending programmes and through its revenue-raising activities which finance these programmes. When we introduce the Government into the picture we find, for example, that household decisions become more complex. Not only may they decide to consume and save. The Government makes decisions for them by taking away a proportion of their income in direct taxation, and by providing certain goods for them itself. Households also pay taxes to the Government indirectly when they purchase goods and services on which indirect taxes have been imposed. It is fairly clear that the whole motivation and purpose of Government differ from those of consumers and businessmen. In Chapter 7 we shall be looking at the controversial subject of the Government's budget in Scotland.

When a country carries on no foreign trade we can speak of a closed economy. In fact, most countries are open economies, in the sense that they engage in trade with other nations. This also affects spending streams in a country. When we purchase imports from abroad these are paid for by remitting funds to the exporting country. Conversely, our exports generate income within this country when foreigners pay us for them. The balance between the two flows has to be taken into account in our final summation of national spending flows.

We can bring all of the active spending streams together in a simple equation and write National Expenditure = Personal Consumption of final goods and services (C), plus Net Investment (I), plus Government Expenditure (G), plus the balance between Exports (X) and Imports (M), i.e.

$$\text{National Expenditure} = C+I+G+(X-M)$$

Total spending constitutes the demand for the output which the economy produces. This output gives rise to the incomes that are received by the various groups, and in turn this income forms the basis of the spending which constitutes the demand for output or production. This is *not* the vicious circle that it may seem at first glance. It is what may be termed the circular flow of income in the economy.

There is nothing in the above analysis of spending flows to suggest that the level of national expenditure will necessarily or automatically gravitate to, and remain at, the level which is just sufficient to ensure that the productive resources of the whole economy are fully utilised. However, one of the most fertile uses which we can make of our understanding of simple income determination processes, and of the interdependence of economic activity which it brings out, is to go on to ask how we may try to change the flows if we do wish to alter the level of resource utilisation. If we wished to expand the economy, for example, we could try to persuade people to consume more (and save less) by cutting direct and/or indirect taxes. Businessmen could be encouraged to spend more on new investment by making the terms on which they borrow easier. Governments could actively expand their spending programmes and cheerfully accept that this might mean a deficit on their own budget. If it was felt that the total spending stream should be reduced measures opposite to the above could be introduced. It is obvious that these measures which could be used to control aggregate spending could also be slanted in such a way as to help not only a national but also a regional policy programme; a reduction in the excise duty on whisky could have many ramifications.

Nor need we content ourselves simply by asking about the direction of change of national spending flows. We can try to estimate the amount of the consequential change in income when we make a spending change, if we know something about the proportion of any increment of income which is consumed (the marginal propensity to consume) and saved (the marginal propensity to save). An addition to spending can have a multiple effect on incomes. If people receive an increment of income we must ask what proportion will be spent and saved. But that is not the end of the matter. The proportion spent will in turn become the income of some person or persons at the second stage, and some proportion of this second stage increment will also be spent. And so on to successive stages. If we assume that at every stage people receiving an increment of income spend the same proportion, we can express the sequence mathematically, in the form of a convergent geometric series, the sum of which is given by the formula $\frac{1}{1-a}$. In economic terms we can substitute for a the marginal propensity to consume. Thus if the marginal propensity to consume is $\frac{9}{10}$ths, the multiple effect of an injection of spending will be 10. This multiple effect is known as *the multiplier*.

This is a very simple but profound concept. In the real world, of course, the working of the multiplier is subject to various time lags and leakages as the process works itself out, and we must content ourselves here with the warning that the multiplier is not a magic wand. If, for example, the capacity of the national economy was being very fully used, it would be absurd to expect an increase in investment or in government spending to produce a significant multiplier effect on the real output of the national economy. If the investment goods industries were working at capacity all that would happen would be that prices would rise.

The multiplier helps us vividly to grasp that economic flows are interdependent. Obviously, it can help us to understand regional and inter-regional as well as national economic interdependence, and the concept of a regional multiplier helps us to understand how impulses can be transmitted and with what amplitude in the setting of regional economies. We shall be looking at the regional multiplier in Chapter 12.

b) The growth in productive capacity The sketch of income determination analysis set out above is essentially Keynesian in character, for it stresses the demand side. In his *General Theory* Keynes was not concerned to analyse economic growth at all, in the sense of asking how we could add to our productive capacity. The problem at that time was one of underutilisation of the capacity that existed to produce wealth. Since the second World War, however, the success with which most industrialised countries have applied the simple analysis of aggregate demand to approximate to full employment has switched the spotlight back to the classical questions of what determines the capacity of an economy to grow and produce more output. Indeed, some economists argue that we have concentrated too much on trying to keep demand at or about the full employment level, and that we have purchased this comparative stability at the price of a slow rate of growth since the War, at any rate in Britain.

Whatever the debate, there is no doubt that growth is once again at the centre of interest in economics, not for the first time. The very title of Adam Smith's famous book—*An Inquiry into the Nature and Causes of the Wealth of Nations*—indicates what he, the Founding Father of the subject, took the grand theme to be. Interest in growth has also been reinforced by the world-wide efforts that are being made to broaden our understanding of economic growth with a view to helping less-developed countries of the world to achieve a 'take-off' into industrialism, which Britain pioneered in the industrial surge of the late 18th century.

Much of the early post-war literature on economic growth stressed the role of capital in economic development almost to the point of a fixation. Recently, however, the approach to economic growth has become much less one-sided, and there is now fairly general recognition that when we look for the well-springs of growth on the supply side we must recognise that all the factors of production have a part to play. The accumulation of capital, the growth of population, the education and training of the labour force, the discovery of new resources, and the introduction of new and better techniques of production will all influence the rate at which the economy can grow. For this very reason growth theory has become less simple, as we understand more about the complexities and the subtle interactions among these factors. For example, we recognise the importance of technology in economic growth, but it is obvious that technology reflects a blend of knowledge on the part of the human factor of production with the capacity to make and use sophisticated capital instruments. Equally, there can be subtle institutional forces at work, say in the harnessing of savings, or the pressures of collective bargaining in the labour market, which affect the expansion of the forces of production in an economy.

Although growth theory tends to emphasise the supply of resources rather than their utilisation through adequate demand levels, it is fairly clear that it is something of an over-simplification to see the demand and supply sides separately. *The whole essence of resource use in economics is interdependence.* In addition to the supply considerations mentioned above, we must reckon that changes on the demand side are also influential as a spur to growth. Changes in the size and composition of the population will influence the structure of demand for output, and the level and distribution of incomes and consumers' tastes and preferences will also put pressure from the demand side on the mix of resources used. Clearly, demand and supply are complementary. The potential of the economy is likely to grow faster if the level of demand is high enough to encourage the capacity to expand, and the expansion in capacity will only prove profitable if there is continuing demand for its output. We shall be examining the sources of growth at much greater length in Chapter 8 and later Chapters.

c) National income statistics The various flows which are identified in national income analysis cry out to be measured. We want to know, for example, how much consumption and saving there is, by how much investment has changed from one year to the next, and so on. Accordingly, there has grown up a whole system of classification for grouping national economic activity in ways that can be measured statistically, and which are also meaningful in the process of income formation in society. The Organisation for Economic Co-operation and Development has prepared a kind of Highway Code for the presentation of statistical information about national income, and this has largely been adopted in the official British publication which is published annually with the title *National Income and Expenditure.*

The national income can be defined as 'a measure of the money value of goods and services becoming available to the nation from economic activity.' Like most definitions this one conceals as much as it reveals, but we can use it as a signpost to distinguish the following essential characteristics of national income statistics.

i) Economic activity has to be defined for purposes of national income statistics. The criterion by which we determine whether an activity is to be regarded as an economic activity is that of market transaction. If goods or a service are bought or sold in a market they are considered to enter into economic activity. However, this general criterion is subject to certain qualifications. Sometimes activities are included which are not the subject of a market transaction, such as the income which a house owner derives from the property he owns and occupies. This is known as an *imputed* value. On the other hand, certain other activities which do not become the subject of market transactions, such as the housework of housewives, are excluded. The important point in national income statistical calculations is to stick to the same classification or conventions over time, so that comparisons can be made from one period to another. The 'Highway Code' mentioned above is intended to standardise such conventions and classifications.

ii) National income must be valued. As suggested above, market prices provide a basis for valuing activities entering the national income stream. National accounts do, however, draw an important distinction between valuing output at *market prices* and at *factor cost*. For certain purposes we may wish to know what it costs, in terms of factor inputs, to produce national output. We cannot always obtain this directly from the prices people pay in markets, since market prices frequently include indirect taxes, such as purchase tax, or may be held down below factor costs by subsidies, for example on agricultural products.

iii) Double-counting has to be avoided. The national income does not consist simply of an aggregate of all the money transactions in the economy which we care to include. In measuring production we try to avoid double-counting, and when we measure spending flows we do not count both the expenditure on final goods and the spending on the intermediate outputs, whose value is included or concealed in the final output value. This means that we either seek to value only final outputs and expenditures, or try to identify separately the *value added* at each stage of the production process. To exemplify on the production side, we do not value both the final purchase price of a car and the inputs of fabricated steel and parts of which it is made up. Either we value the car, or we identify the separate stages of its production, find out the values added (sales minus purchases) at each stage, and add up these intermediate values.

iv) The production of the national income involves the consumption of capital. In the course of the annual production sequence it is obviously necessary to make allowance for the undoubted fact that productive plant and equipment are deteriorating. All investment does not represent a net addition to the productive assets of the economy, since some must be undertaken for the purpose of maintaining the existing stock of capital and equipment which is being depreciated and worn out. An allowance must therefore be made for capital consumption. The gross national product is deflated by deducting from it an estimate of the capital consumed, giving the *net* national product. The word *net* tells us when such an estimate has been made. We shall see in Chapter 9 that the estimation of capital consumption is one of the most difficult tasks in economics.

v) *Transfer payments* must be distinguished from factor payments. In addition to the factor incomes that are generated in the course of productive activity, certain other types of income are received by persons which are not a direct payment for factor services. Income received from government sources in such forms as retirement pensions, sickness and unemployment benefit, and other social security payments and other current grants are termed transfer payments. Much Government activity is concerned with raising revenue which is used to rechannel income to people who are entitled to some form of welfare income, and this is not to be confused with factor incomes such as wages.

vi) *National* income must be distinguished from *domestic* income. This distinction must be made for the whole British economy, not just between Scotland and the rest. We have to take account of the fact that an open economy carries out transactions with the rest of the world. Domestic economic activity, the activity which produces income wholly within the economy, must have added to it the income flows generated by exports and have subtracted from it the income which we pay abroad for imports and other purchases made abroad, in order to arrive at a national total. We shall see in the next Chapter that gross domestic product has proved to be a useful concept in the setting of various attempts that have been made to calculate the national income of Scotland.

vii) National income must be distinguished from national wealth. When we calculate the national income we are trying to quantify the flows of economic activity, appropriately defined, in the course of a period of time, such as a year, or three months. Calculations of national wealth attempt to evaluate the assets of a country at a point in time. A wealth concept is essentially a stock concept, whereas the income, product and expenditure flows in the economy have a time period attached to their measurement.

So much for the bare bones of national income definitions. It is immensely helpful to us in the complex process of calculating the national income that economic activity is interdependent, and we can look at the flows taking place from the standpoint of 1) income, 2) expenditure, 3) product. These are simply three different ways of looking at the same economic activity. This means that we can often double-check a particular statistical measure, which is obtained in the first instance as (say) an income statistic, against the same flow viewed perhaps as a product statistic. Wage income and wage costs are a good example. Building up the income, expenditure, and product picture therefore involves a good deal of tedious and diligent detective work.

Not surprisingly, it is not easy to achieve complete equality among the various calculations, and national income data usually contain residual errors, or balancing items. Statistics are frequently less than complete, or not available in the form in which they are wanted, for purposes of national income calculation. Some statistics, if they are produced at all, are generated for quite different purposes, and it has to be recognised that the generation of statistical data is itself an economic problem, where costs of collection and processing have to be weighed against the uses and benefits.

We endeavour in this study to put statistical flesh on the many themes that we propose to raise in connection with the economy of Scotland. Nevertheless, we shall frequently find that we have to abandon the chase, because statistical material is either lacking or cannot be separated out in a way which gives a clean set of figures for the Scottish component.

For example, until recently one of the major omissions in the statistical coverage of Scotland has been the formulation of any official estimate for national income. Even now many of the component building blocks are simply not quantified. For instance, no figures are available of total investment, total saving, or of capital flows into and out of Scotland. We have only limited knowledge of the size and value of Scotland's overseas trade, and we cannot ascertain either the nature of Scotland's commodity trade balance or her overall balance of payments position.

Sometimes the information which is needed for an assessment of Scottish economic performance is based on sampling enquiries, such as the *Family Expenditure Survey Reports* and *Inland Revenue Reports*. Other statistics are simply derived from *a priori* judgments as to Scotland's likely share of U.K. aggregates, as in the case of defence expenditure. Others still are compiled on a *pro rata* to population basis. Calculations that use index numbers as a means of allowing for the variability of money as a measuring rod have usually to rely on the British index numbers, e.g. of wholesale and retail prices. It is not surprising, as we shall see in the next Chapter, that private investigators have often had to try to fill the gaps in official data, and that their calculations have sometimes to use second-best rather than ideal methods.

On the other side of the medal, we ought to stress that Scotland is better served than any other region of Britain, since there is at least an officially compiled index of industrial production (admittedly covering a restricted range of industries) for Scotland. Further, both the *Census of Production* and *Inland Revenue Reports* provide statistical information for Scotland that is not always available for other regions.

When all is said and done, however, any attempt to build a macro-economic model of the Scottish economy is greatly hampered by gaps such as those which have been mentioned above. In the subsequent Chapters of this book we have therefore to remind the reader at frequent intervals that we are by no means in possession of all the building bricks we should like. Still, enough material is available to make for an interesting journey through the economic hinterland of Scotland. Fortified by the economic framework of this Chapter, let us now turn to our task in detail. We look first at national income statistics, and at various attempts to calculate the Scottish national income. This gives us right away a statistical feel for the Scottish economy.

Reading The following textbooks will be found helpful to the reader who wishes to pursue the themes of this Chapter at greater length:

A. K. Cairncross, *Introduction to Economics*, 4th ed., 1966.
R. G. Lipsey, *An Introduction to Positive Economics*, 2nd ed., 1966.
P. A. Samuelson, *Economics*, 7th ed., 1967.

Part 2:
The Structure of the Scottish Economy

B

Chapter 2
The Measurement of Scottish National Income

The purpose of this Chapter is to examine the ways in which national income is actually calculated. We shall build on the simple concepts and definitions of national income which were set out in Chapter 1, and outline the methods of calculating the British national income, expenditure, and product flows respectively. Naturally, we are concerned not simply to stop at the estimation of figures for the United Kingdom; we also ask whether, and in what ways, the national income of Scotland can be calculated. It is as well to warn the reader at the outset, however, that no official estimate is in fact made of Scottish national income, although in 1971, annual estimates of gross domestic product for the decade of the 1960's have at last been produced by the Scottish Office. For earlier years, and for any lengthy time period, it has, therefore, been left to private investigators to attempt systematic calculation. We shall be reviewing these contributions in the second part of the Chapter.

When we now proceed to look in turn at (*a*) the income shares, (*b*) the expenditure flows, and (*c*) the product value approaches to national income statistics, it is useful to bear in mind the extent to which similar calculations can be attempted for Scotland. We shall see that income and expenditure calculations are particularly difficult for Scotland.

1 British National Income Estimates

a) The income share approach This aggregates for all the residents of a country those incomes that are derived from the current production of goods and services. These incomes, whether individual or corporate, may be described as factor earnings, since they represent the amounts paid to the factors of production, land, labour, and capital, in producing the final goods and services. They are incomes composed of earnings from work and the use of property, or from employment income and profits.

Hence both profits, earned privately or by public enterprise, and rent, defined as the surplus derived from the ownership of land and buildings, must be quantified since both contribute to income.

It is necessary, however, to exclude from the calculation of national income those incomes received by individuals that are not the result of contributions to current production. This form of income, described as 'transfer income', includes such categories as old-age pensions, family allowances and the like. These will have been paid out of factor incomes through taxes and national insurance contributions. They do not derive from the production of final goods and services and therefore fall outside the scope of our definition of national income. It should also be recognised that while national income measures the income accruing to the residents of a country, some of this income derives from abroad. Likewise, some of the income generated by a nation will go to non-residents. As we have seen before, it is the difference between the two that is relevant to the compilation of national income. This 'net income' from abroad, when added to a nation's total factor incomes, gives national income.

The composition of the 'income-share' approach, as presented officially in the annual Blue Books, is outlined below. To give some idea of the magnitude of the separate items involved, values for the year 1969 have been inserted.

Table 2.1 Determination of G.N.P. by Income-Share Method, U.K., 1969 (£m)

Income from Employment	27,174
Income from Self-Employment	3,009
Gross Trading Profits of Companies	4,948
Gross Trading Surplus of Public Corporations	1,461
Gross Trading Surplus of other Public Enterprises	114
Rent	2,601
Less Stock Appreciation and Residual Error	−1,157
G.D.P. at Factor Cost	38,150
Net Property Income from Abroad	451
G.N.P. at Factor Cost	38,601

Source: Central Statistical Office, National Income and Expenditure, H.M.S.O., 1970.

To derive national income, it is necessary only to deduct an allowance for depreciation from the figure for G.N.P. In 1969, capital consumption was estimated at £3,694 million, leaving a national income of £34,907 million.

b) Since national income has been defined as the aggregate value of all goods and services produced by a nation, it may be measured not only by adding the incomes earned in their production (method (a)), but also by aggregating all expenditures on these goods and services. Such expenditures may be undertaken individually, or on a collective basis by the Government, and can be divided broadly into the two categories, consumption and investment. The former consists of expenditure on all types of product, both durables and non-durables. The latter comprises expenditure on goods not for use in current production. It represents investment expenditure either on fixed capital (that is, on buildings, plant, etc.) or on stocks (goods bought in excess of those currently used). Clearly such investment expenditure of whatever type adds to national wealth, so that it must be included in the compilation of national product. To avoid double-counting, only expenditures on final goods and services are calculated.

In an open economy part of a nation's income will be derived from overseas sources. This might take the form of an excess of exports over imports which to the nation represents one form of net investment. The reverse case, in which imports exceed exports, may be regarded as net foreign *disinvestment* since the surplus imports have to be paid for out of the nation's stock of wealth. In addition, income derived from activity or property held abroad is equivalent to exports since it augments total income. Conversely, income paid abroad to other countries is equivalent to imports. As a result, in an open economy, national expenditure $=C+I+G+$total exports and income received from abroad, minus total imports and incomes paid abroad.

The official method of presenting these concepts in the Blue Book, again with 1969 magnitudes, is illustrated below:

Table 2.2 Determination of G.N.P. by Expenditure Approach, U.K., 1969 (£m)

Consumer's Expenditure (*C*)	28,618
Public Authorities' current expenditure on goods and services (*G*)	8,118
Gross Domestic Fixed Capital Formation (*I*)	7,927
Value of increase in stocks and work in progress (*I*)	294
Total Domestic Expenditure at Market Prices	44,957
Exports and Property Income from Abroad	11,986
Less Imports and Property Income paid Abroad	−11,318
Less Taxes on Expenditure	−7,868
Subsidies	844
G.N.P. at Factor Cost	38,601

Source: National Income and Expenditure, 1970.

c) The third approach, that of calculating the aggregate value of all final goods produced within the economy over a given period, represents domestic product. Here, great care has to be exercised to avoid double-counting since a proportion of industrial output for any given period will, as we have seen, not be consumed but rather will contribute towards the production of further goods and services. Essentially, therefore, gross domestic product (G.D.P.) consists of the sum of the values added to a commodity at each stage of production. The concept of G.D.P. takes no account, of course, of the value of imported goods and services, these being part of the domestic products of other countries. Hence, all income received by residents from sources outside the nation are specifically excluded.

Having outlined these different approaches, the relationship between national income, product and expenditure may now be conveniently summarised as follows:

Income or Product	Expenditure
Domestic Product (= Domestic Factor Incomes)	Consumption +Net Domestic Investment
	Domestic Expenditure
+Net Property Income from Abroad	+Exports of Goods and Services and Income from Abroad −Imports of Goods and Services and Income paid Abroad
National Product or Income	= National Expenditure

With these relationships in mind, we can now ask how far it is possible to construct appropriate Scottish estimates. The task of determining Scottish G.N.P. is, however, seriously hampered by the limitations of official data at the regional level. We list below some of the main items, not presently available, that we would need to know to construct firm estimates of G.N.P. for Scotland.

In view of these omissions in the requisite data, a more accurate indication of Scotland's performance might be obtained if the calculation were to be limited from G.N.P. to G.D.P. This is the view adopted by Dr G. McCrone, who has estimated G.D.P. in Scotland over a number of years by calculating the sum of values added in all productive pursuits of the economy. Even more recently, the Scottish Office has produced annual estimates of G.D.P. for the 1960's, calculated from the income side.

Data not presently available for Scotland

Income or Product	Expenditure	
Gross Trading Profits of Companies[1]	Gross Investment	Fixed Domestic Capital Value of Increase in Stocks and work in Progress
Net Property Income from Abroad[2]	Public Authorities' Current Expenditure (particularly on unallocated expenditures like Defence, External Relations etc.)	
	Exports of Goods and Services	
	Imports of Goods and Services	

[1] Even in the newly-produced calculations of Scottish G.D.P. for the 1960s, the Scottish Office has pointed out that estimates of this component are by far the weakest in the compilation of G.D.P. as a whole. For the methods used see the Scottish Office, *Scottish Economic Bulletin,* No. 1, 1971.

[2] The estimation of this item, even for the U.K., is subject to a margin of error of ± more than 10 per cent. See C.S.O., *National Accounts Statistics: Sources and Methods,* H.M.S.O., 1968, p. 42.

The use of G.D.P. for a regional economy such as Scotland possesses certain advantages. It is likely to be more accurate, since in attempting to quantify components of G.N.P. for a regional economy there will be several instances where estimates are derived from ratios (e.g. population, personal income) applied to the national figure. This may well destroy the whole value of the exercise since the region might thus appear to resemble the national economy more closely than is indeed the case. Second, G.D.P. as calculated by Dr McCrone has been built up by the addition of estimates for each industry and sector in the economy. This particular method of compilation provides a useful insight into the economic structure of the region. It also allows meaningful comparisons to be drawn between the structure of the Scottish and U.K. economies.

2 Various Estimates for Scotland

In this section we examine how various authorities have attempted to solve the problems involved in making estimates for Scotland. The basis of these estimates and the methods used will be assessed, and some indication given as to the degree of confidence that can be placed on the figures that are finally achieved. The three approaches are in turn

(*a*) an income estimate by Professor A. D. Campbell;

(*b*) an expenditure calculation by Professor I. G. Stewart; and

(*c*) a product calculation by Dr G. McCrone.

a) An Income Share Estimate Professor Campbell made the first attempt to construct estimates of Scottish national income in his article published in the *Economic Journal* in 1955. His work, based broadly on the 'income-share' approach, was concerned with total income accruing to people in Scotland whether from within the country or outside. Over the period examined, 1924–48, Campbell defined Scottish national income as Scotland's share of U.K. national income. On this basis he was able to conclude that Scotland's national income fell from 9·9 per cent of that in the U.K. in 1924/6 to only 9·4 per cent in 1946/8. Moreover, during the years between 1924–48, real income per head in Scotland varied between 86 and 94 per cent of that in the U.K. and averaged, for the period as a whole, no more than 90 per cent. From the evidence available there had clearly been a decline in the relative importance of Scotland within the U.K. economy. Although providing some insight into the performance of the Scottish economy up to 1948, the methodology of compiling Scotland's national income in this way contains several inherent defects. The problems of disaggregating data for Scotland from global U.K. figures are, in several instances, virtually insurmountable. This applies, for example, to dividing up the interest payable on the national debt, and to apportioning for Scotland a share in aggregate company profits.

b) An Expenditure Estimate In an effort to surmount these difficulties inherent in the 'income-share' approach, an attempt has recently been made by Professor Stewart to quantify domestic product in Scotland from the expenditure side. Since the 'expenditure-mix' is dealt with in greater detail in Chapter 7 below, we shall simply outline here the main features of his approach.

By using material recently made available through Family Expenditure Survey Reports, a measure of consumers' expenditure of a household type was obtained for Scotland. The evidence available for the years 1965–7 suggests that while annual household expenditure might vary widely between Scotland and the U.K. for different individual items, the difference between total household spending in the two areas is insignificant.[1] This, despite the fact that, on average, household incomes in Scotland are estimated to have been between 4–5 per cent below those in the U.K. Clearly, Professor Stewart concluded, total household

[1] In 1965/7 average annual household expenditure in Scotland at £1,162.81 differed by less than one-half of 1 per cent from the comparable U.K. figure of £1,157.89. See *Family Expenditure Survey Reports for 1966 and 1967.*

spending did not respond to the regional difference. Since, however, Scottish households contain on average more people, expenditure *per head* was only 93 per cent of the U.K. average. Total consumer expenditure by household in Scotland for 1965/7 is shown in Table 2.3 below.

No comprehensive information exists for investment expenditure in Scotland. Hence, any estimate for capital formation must be tentative in the extreme. This is particularly true of the private sector in the economy. In this context estimates for capital expenditure by manufacturing establishments obtained from *The Digest of Scottish Statistics* may be added to investment in primary industry and to that in transport, distribution, financial and other services, and private dwellings, so yielding an annual average for the period 1965/7 of some £290 million.[1] For the public sector official documentation is more readily available since information is presented both by nationalised industries and central and local government agencies. Again, annual average investment expenditure in both private and public sectors is shown for 1965/7 in Table 2.3.

A large part of expenditure made by public authorities is identified for Scotland in *The Digest of Scottish Statistics*. From these figures it is possible to distinguish the current from the capital account. To expenditure identified by sectors in the current account, certain unallocated expenditures must be added. Estimating Scotland's share of these unallocated expenditures is a matter of great difficulty, particularly for such items as defence, and for expenditure on external relations. Presently, these can be quantified only by calculating Scotland's share of U.K. aggregates on a *pro rata* to population basis, or by some other such arbitrary method.[2] At the moment, the estimates available for total public expenditure in Scotland on current account differ by fairly wide margins. In a sense, this is not at all surprising since there are different interpretations as to how unallocated

[1] I. G. Stewart, 'Statistics on Expenditures in Scotland', in J. N. Wolfe (ed.), *Government and Nationalism in Scotland*, p. 133. This would appear to conflict with Professor Alexander's figure of £575 million for investment in Scotland in 1967, net of Government investment. See K. J. Alexander, 'The Economic Case Against Independence', in N. MacCormick (ed.), *The Scottish Debate*, p. 140.

[2] On defence, for instance, Professor Stewart uses a figure for Scotland of 7 per cent of total U.K. defence expenditure (see pp. 130–1), obtained from the *Scottish Economic Development Quarterly Report*, No. 11, Nov., 1968. Professor Alexander calculates Scotland's share as 6¾ per cent of the U.K. total (*The Scottish Debate*, p. 137), but figures of 9·4 per cent (based on the population ratio), or of 8·5 per cent (based on the G.D.P. ratio; McCrone, *Scotland's Future*, p. 57) could be just as accurate.

expenditures should be apportioned. Estimates also diverge widely, however, even for that part of public expenditure which is officially identified.[1]

Although they appear almost certainly to understate the position, for the sake of conformity the provisional figures of public expenditure in Scotland compiled by Professor Stewart are used in the Table below.

Table 2.3 Gross Domestic Expenditure in Scotland, Annual Average, 1965–7 (£m)

Consumers' Expenditure	1,950
Capital Formation	600
Government Expenditure	610
	3,160

Source: I. G. Stewart, op. cit., *p. 133.*

The figure shown above for total domestic expenditure in Scotland which, it must be stressed, is a most tentative one, suggests that Scottish expenditure represented approximately 8·7 per cent of the U.K. annual average for 1965–7.[2]

Professor Stewart has undoubtedly made a praiseworthy attempt to throw light upon the size and composition of Scotland's domestic product. Nevertheless, the information necessary to construct reliable estimates from the expenditure side is very deficient at present.

c) A Product Calculation Probably the most accurate existing measure derives from the work of Dr McCrone, who uses an altogether different technique. For the 1950s, McCrone aggregated the values added in all branches of manufacturing, agriculture, mining and the service trades. The resultant total, or gross domestic product, measures the income originating within the region, not that eventually received by inhabitants of the region, which would of course represent gross national product. Such a method depends almost wholly on the availability of *Census of Production* data. Whilst adequate for the 1950s, similar material for the 1960s simply does not exist, apart from the 1963

[1] For 1967, Dr McCrone calculates identified current expenditure by the *central Government* in Scotland as £792 million, with unallocated expenditure, calculated at 8·5 per cent of U.K. aggregates, amounting to £264 million. Professor Stewart, on the other hand, provides a total expenditure, both allocated and unallocated, by *all* public authorities of £661 million.

[2] This compares with a figure of 8·5 per cent for 1965 estimated as Scotland's share of G.D.P. in the U.K. by Dr McCrone. See Table 2.5 below.

Census of Production material published in 1970. In consequence, to obtain a continuous series for G.D.P. in Scotland, estimates for recent years must of necessity, be based on a different approach. We have already noted the difficulties involved in approaching this problem from the expenditure side. Hence, the most reliable G.D.P. figures presently available are those based on the *Censuses of Production*, backed up by estimates calculated through the expedient of summing earnings to factors of production for the 1960s. This is a legitimate but indirect method.

Calculations based on the *Census of Production* may be taken as a fairly accurate indication of Scotland's domestic product. Even here, however, there are problems of apportionment between Scotland and the United Kingdom, particularly in such sectors as transport and communications, public administration and defence, etc. In assessing earnings to factors of production, income from employment and self-employment can be readily compiled, but the analysis runs into difficulties when trying to distinguish Scotland's share of company profits. Here, a purely arbitrary method has to be used.

For purposes of illustration, Scotland's G.D.P. as calculated by the value added approach is shown in Table 2.4 below for 1960. Further, a break-down of total product in the U.K. by main-order groups is presented to allow comparisons to be made.

Table 2.4 Composition of G.D.P. in Scotland and the U.K., 1960

Sector	Contribution to G.D.P. in Scotland	Share of Total G.D.P. in Scotland	Percentage Distribution of U.K. G.D.P.
	£m	per cent	per cent
Agriculture, Forestry and Fishing	113	5·8	4·0
Mining and Quarrying	62	3·2	3·0
Manufacturing	708	36·1	36·1
Construction	125	6·4	6·0
Gas, Electricity and Water	49	2·5	2·7
Transport and Communications	181	9·2	8·6
Distribution	219	11·2	12·1
Insurance, Banking and Finance	44	2·2	2·9
Public Admin. and Defence	122	6·2	5·7
Other Services[1]	340	17·2	18·9
G.D.P.	1,964	100·0	100·0
As per cent of U.K.	8·7	—	—

Sources: G. McCrone, Scotland's Economic Progress, p. 31; Regional Policy in Britain (1969), p. 172.

[1] Includes such items as public health service, rent from ownership of dwelling, local authority education.

At first glance, the composition of G.D.P. in Scotland in 1960 appears to have been very similar to that in the U.K. as a whole. Only in agriculture, etc. and in 'other services' would there appear to be any major differences in sectoral contributions to total product. However, as we shall see in Chapter 4 such a close conformity between the industrial structure of the two regions is more apparent than real. For our present purposes, it is sufficient to make two observations. First, there have been significant changes in Scotland's industrial structure since 1960. Second, it should be emphasised that main-order headings[1] as illustrated in Table 2.4 conceal almost as much as they reveal about industrial structure. Within these main-order groups, there are significant regional differences at the minimum-list heading level.

Since Scotland's G.D.P. for the 1960s has not yet been calculated on the same basis as in the preceding decade, a more vulnerable approach using 'income-share' analysis was employed both by McCrone and more recently by the Scottish Office, based largely on data obtained from Inland Revenue returns and with estimates made for Scotland's share of company profits. McCrone confined his estimates to the first half of the decade whereas the Scottish Office has provided figures for each year of the 1960s. There is, however, a close correspondence between the two sets of estimates. For instance, McCrone has derived figures for Scottish G.D.P. of £2,455 million in 1964 and £2,661 million in the following year.[2] The corresponding figures provided by the Scottish Office are £2,467 million and £2,654 million,[3] in each case a difference of less than one per cent. By virtue of the fact that they are available for every year of the 1960s the figures of the Scottish Office are more suited to our purpose of measuring the structure and growth of the Scottish economy. The main items in these estimates are outlined in Table 2.5.

By combining the estimates available for the 1950s with those calculated from the income side for the decade of the 1960s, a reasonably continuous index of G.D.P. in Scotland can be

[1] The Standard Industrial Classification delineates industries by 'main order' groups. These describe the major industrial groupings (such as Vehicles, Metal Manufacture, etc.) as outlined by the Dept. of Employment for the purpose of presenting their employment statistics. These 'main-order headings' can be sub-divided into numerous component parts ('Vehicles', for instance includes the manufacture of tractors, motor cycles, bicycles, etc. as well as of motor cars). To these components of each main order group the term 'minimum-list heading' is applied.

[2] G. McCrone, *Scotland's Future*, p. 20.

[3] Scottish Office, *Scottish Economic Bulletin*, No. 1, 1971. The figures in the text make no allowance for stock appreciation.

Table 2.5 Scottish Gross Domestic Product,[1] 1960–69 (£m), Current Prices

	1960	1961	1962	1963	1964
Income from Employment	1,308	1,396	1,462	1,520	1,628
Income from Self-Employment	194	206	209	209	219
Rent from Dwellings	67	71	77	83	91
Gross Trading Surpluses	52	58	76	86	98
Gross Trading Profit and Rent from Business Premises and Agriculture	354	351	343	389	431
Gross Domestic Product at Factor Cost	1,975	2,082	2,167	2,287	2,467
As per cent of U.K.	8·6	8·6	8·6	8·5	8·4

	1965	1966	1967	1968	1969
Income from Employment	1,759	1,884	1,960	2,115	2,268
Income from Self-Employment	239	256	263	277	295
Rent from Dwellings	102	112	125	137	155
Gross Trading Surpluses	104	111	115	131	132
Gross Trading Profit and Rent from Business Premises and Agriculture	450	421	432	478	475
Gross Domestic Product at Factor Cost	2,654	2,784	2,895	3,138	3,325
As per cent of U.K.	8·4	8·4	8·4	8·5	8·5

Source: [1]Scottish Office, *Scottish Economic Bulletin.*
[1] No allowance is made for stock appreciation.

obtained. In the Chart below this is compared to a similar index for the U.K. overtime.

In interpreting the Chart it must be borne in mind that, while indices of domestic product in both regions are shown to be rising rapidly, a major part of this expansion can be attributed to inflation. No price series are available for Scotland, so that any attempt to convert Scottish product to constant prices is a hazardous undertaking. Although Dr McCrone has attempted the exercise for the 1950s, so many assumptions are involved that the validity of the resultant index can be seriously questioned.[1] In the absence of a satisfactory price index for Scotland, it is perhaps best to concentrate on current prices, all the more so since we shall be confining ourselves largely to comparisons between Scotland and the U.K. Prices should not vary too widely between parts of one integral economy as they might, for instance, if international comparisons were to be made.

[1] See G. McCrone, *Scotland's Economic Progress*, Appendix 1, p. 171. In the construction of his price index, McCrone used wherever possible the Scottish index of industrial production. Where this was not applicable, Scottish output at current prices was deflated by U.K. price indices, so imparting an obvious 'U.K. bias'.

Chart 1

value of gross domestic product[1] in Scotland and the U.K. 1951 – 1969
(current prices) 1951 = 100

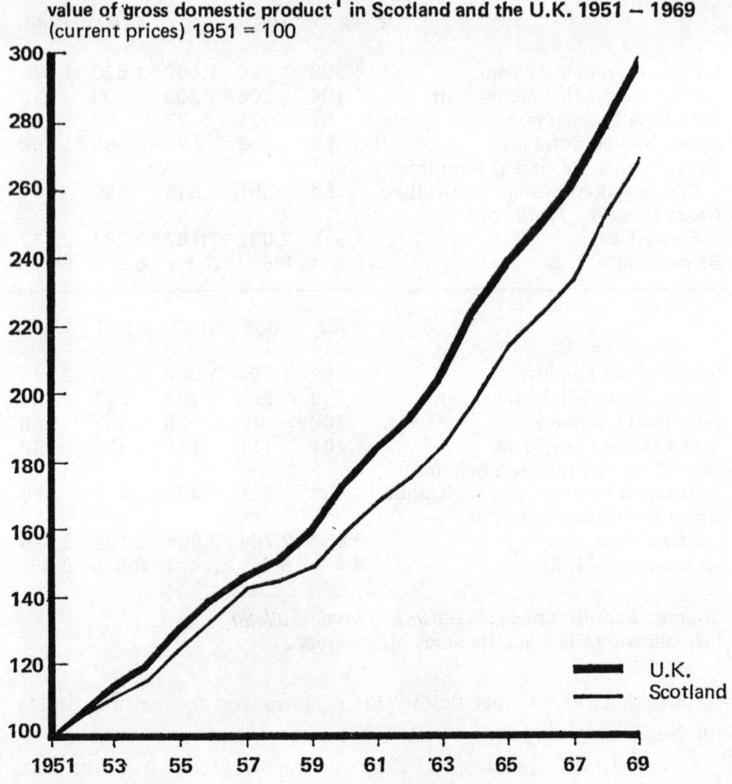

note: [1]excluding any allowance for stock appreciation
sources: G. McCrone, Scotland's Economic Progress, p.31
Scotland's Future p.20
Scottish Office, Scottish Economic Bulletin, No. 1, 1971
Annual Abstract of Statistics

3 Per capita G.D.P. as an indicator of Scottish economic performance If we now concentrate on the product approach at current prices for the remainder of this chapter, a useful insight into the performance and progress of the Scottish economy can be obtained. G.D.P. in Scotland rose from £1,238 million in 1951, 9·3 per cent of the U.K. total, to £3,325 million in 1969, when it accounted for only 8·5 per cent of that in the U.K. Despite the substantial rise of Scottish product in absolute terms, her contribution to the U.K. total fell appreciably over the period. As can be seen from the Chart, the divergence between the two indices was much wider after 1957 than it had been in preceding years. Clearly, there were forces at work in the Scottish economy from the latter part of the 1950s which were retarding the overall rate of progress. We shall be turning our attention to these in later chapters of this book.

Given these aggregate trends, it is likely that living standards in Scotland began to fall relative to those in the rest of the U.K. over the latter part of the 1950s and early 1960s. That this would, indeed, appear to be the case is illustrated in Table 2.6.

Table 2.6 Gross Domestic Product Per Head in Scotland, Selected Years, 1951–69 (£ Current Prices)

Year	Gross Domestic Product per Head	As per cent of U.K.	G.D.P. per Head of Total Working Population in Employment[1]	As per cent of U.K.
	(1)	(2)	(3)	(4)
1951	243	92	542	96
1954	279	91	617	95
1958	342	90	776	95
1960	381	87	853	92
1963	439	87	996	93
1965	510	88	1,144	94
1967	558	89	1,271	94
1969	640	90	1,469	95

Sources: Calculated from *Scottish Economic Bulletin; Digest of Scottish Statistics; Annual Abstract of Statistics; Employment and Productivity Gazette;* G. McCrone, *Scotland's Economic Progress, 1951–60*

[1] Figures for the category Employers and Self-Employed in Scotland are available only from *Census of Population* returns before 1965. Since this group does not change much in numerical terms over the years, estimates based on *Census* data for intervening years are unlikely to be widely in error. These, when added to figures for total employees, gave total working population in Scotland. The appropriate statistics of those unemployed were then deducted to leave the numbers of working population actually in employment. Since 1965, estimates of the total working population in Scotland (i.e, including Employers aud Self-employed) have been made available in the *Employment and Productivity Gazette.*

The figures presented in Table 2.6 do not exactly measure living standards in Scotland in that they do not, of course, include income originating from outside the country. Nor do they take into account price changes. Nevertheless, it is safe to conclude that G.D.P. per head in Scotland (col. 2) fell fairly steadily as a proportion of that in the U.K. during the 1950s and early 1960s. Only by 1965 was that fall firmly reversed, although even by 1969 Scotland had still not regained her relative 1951 position. A somewhat similar trend emerges with regard to domestic product per head of the working population excluding the unemployed. Here, however, the ratio of Scottish figures to those in the U.K. was always higher throughout the period. Again, this ratio fell fairly consistently (see col. 4), reaching a floor in the years 1960–62, but by the end of the period had virtually recovered to the level of 1951.

Evidently, over the period 1951–69, G.D.P. per head of total population in Scotland and of the work-force in employment rose steadily in absolute terms. Yet, for much of this period, expansion was more rapid still in the U.K. as a whole. Between 1951 and 1960 for instance, G.D.P. per head in Scotland at current prices increased by 57 per cent as opposed to a rise of 65 per cent in the U.K. On the other hand we have seen that by the mid 1960s the tendency for G.D.P. per head in Scotland to fall relative to that in the U.K. had finally been halted. Indeed, between 1960 and 1969, the growth of Scottish output per head was somewhat higher than in the U.K. Although at first sight encouraging, this was *not* due to a faster growth in the 1960s of G.D.P. in Scotland. On the contrary, the chart on page 46 shows that the gap between the Scottish and U.K. indices remained wide over this period. In fact, between 1960 and 1969, the value of G.D.P. in Scotland relative to that in the U.K. as a whole remained almost stationary or even showed some slight tendency to fall (see Table 2.5). Hence, the slightly higher growth of product *per head* in Scotland over these years can largely be attributed simply to the fact that total Scottish population was falling as a proportion of that in the U.K.

In analysing the significance of columns (2) and (4) of Table 2.6, it should be borne in mind that, in large measure, the relatively low Scottish G.D.P. per head indicated by column (2) was the product of three factors:

(i) Differences between Scotland and the U.K. in the proportion of total population that fell into the working age group. Here, Scotland was lower than the national average.[1]

(ii) The activity rate in Scotland remained lower than that in the U.K. throughout the period 1955–67.[2]

(iii) Average unemployment in Scotland ran at a rate consistently higher than in the U.K.

Given these influences, domestic product per head in Scotland was almost bound to be lower than in the U.K. as a

[1] The *Censuses of Population* for 1951 and 1961 show that the proportion of the total population of working age in Scotland was 1 per cent and 2 per cent respectively below that of the U.K.

[2] By activity rate is meant the ratio of economically active persons, including those unemployed, to the total population aged 15 years and over.

whole.[1] Column (4) on the other hand, measures only the share of total product per head of the working force actually in employment, this being related to the corresponding figure in the U.K. This serves clearly to reveal the effect of differences in activity rates, unemployment, etc. If the unemployed are excluded from the total working population, and given lower activity rates, domestic product per worker in Scotland constitutes a much higher proportion of the U.K. total. This is not enough, certainly, to explain the difference between Scottish and U.K. G.D.P. per head of population, but enough to account for a substantial part of that difference.

It should be emphasised that total product is not, of course, the only indicator of economic activity. Further evidence exists which shows that Scotland probably fared better in the 1960s than in the preceding decade. This evidence will be investigated more thoroughly in the next chapter. Certain observations are, however, worth making here, in case we may be judged guilty of leaving our discussion of national product on too pessimistic a note. For instance, by 1965, the deterioration of G.D.P. per head in Scotland relative to that in the U.K. had been halted. From that date, the trend of almost a decade was reversed, with domestic product per head in Scotland starting to rise again as a proportion of that in the U.K. As we have seen, however, this resulted not from a faster rate of growth in total Scottish product, but rather from the cumulative effect which net migration from the region had on the size of population. In several other respects, Scottish economic performance could be considered encouraging. Over the 1960s, there were indications that much needed changes were at last taking place in Scotland's economic structure. Several new science-based industries such as electronics and petrochemicals emerged to exercise a significant impact on the economy. To some extent, these have been responsible for the faster rise over the 1960s of labour productivity in Scotland's industrial sector and, in consequence, for the fact that earnings per man employed rose to a level closer to the British average.

In certain respects there was, therefore, evidence of some 'catching-up' on the part of Scotland during the 1960s. However, this has not been sustained, and in the later years of the decade the rate of growth of Scotland's industrial production

[1] Unless, of course, the weight of these factors was offset by a much higher growth in Scotland of labour productivity. In fact, the growth of productivity in Scotland roughly matched that of the U.K. between 1951–60, although there are indications that, thereafter, the Scottish rate did begin to expand more rapidly. See G. McCrone, *Regional Policy in Britain*, p. 160.

began to fall again, relative to that in the U.K., while the unemployment rate continued to cause concern. Scotland's competitive position within the U.K. economy appears once more to be in decline.

References

A. D. Campbell, 'Changes in Scottish Incomes, 1924–49', *Economic Journal*, vol. 65, 1955.
See also his chapter in
A. K. Cairncross (ed.), *The Scottish Economy*, Cambridge 1954.
G. McCrone, *Scotland's Economic Progress 1951–1960*, London, 1965.
Regional Policy in Britain, London, 1969.
Scotland's Future. The Economics of Nationalism, Oxford, 1969.
H.M.S.O., *Report from the Select Committee on Scottish Affairs, 1969–70.*
I. G. Stewart, 'Statistics on Expenditures in Scotland', in J. N. Wolfe (ed.), *Government and Nationalism in Scotland*, 1969, pp. 123–36.
Scottish Office, *Scottish Economic Bulletin*, H.M.S.O.
K. J. Alexander, *The Economic Case Against Independence*, in N. MacCormick (ed.), *The Scottish Debate: Essays on Scottish Nationalism*, London, 1970.
Central Statistical Office, *National Accounts Statistics: Sources and Methods*, London, 1968.

Chapter 3
Other Economic Indicators

The statistics of national product, income and expenditure which are brought together in national accounts provide a comprehensive range of indicators of the performance of the economy in retrospect. However, these statistics are not exhaustive, and other indicators can be studied which throw additional light on the working of the economy. In this Chapter we propose to examine a number of other yardsticks or indicators which enable us to see in a wider setting the conclusions that were drawn in the previous Chapter from an examination of the movements in domestic product. The indicators to be examined here are: (*a*) industrial production, (*b*) the growth of employment and labour productivity, (*c*) unemployment and activity rates, (*d*) earnings, (*e*) personal income, and (*f*) net migration.

The selection of these particular indicators is determined in part by the statistics that are available. Some of them do grow directly out of, and indeed constitute part of the raw material of, the statistics that are compiled in national income accounting. For example, information about industrial production obviously enters into calculations of output; and statistics of earnings and personal income form part of the income streams which are tabulated in the Blue Book on national income and expenditure mentioned in Chapters 1 and 2. Nevertheless, it is useful to take them up separately in this Chapter for more systematic consideration than was possible in Chapter 2.

Some of the other indicators examined in this Chapter do not, however, form part of the statistics of national income directly, although they provide additional sensitive barometers of the health of the economy. The growth of employment and labour productivity, and unemployment and activity rates, are indicators of the functioning of the labour market, and these will obviously work through to national income statistics. But these indicators are analysed in labour market rather than national income publications. Net migration, the final issue taken up here, can be regarded in part as a sensitive indicator which reflects the general state of the economy and its performance.

We shall be returning in later Chapters to some of the indicators which are scrutinised here; for example, in Chapter 6 we look in much greater detail at earnings and income figures. Here the emphasis will be on comparisons of the Scottish position with that of other parts of the U.K., whereas in later sections of the book we shall examine differences *within* Scotland.

Although we are painting, therefore, with a fairly broad brush here, and our set of additional indicators is rather a mixed bag, we shall see that they all tend to transmit similar messages about Scotland's rather sluggish economic performance. This is of course hardly surprising, since some of the indicators are closely related, and there is an over-riding interdependence in the economy, as we brought out in Chapter 1. The general pattern which emerges is that Scotland lost ground in the 1950s within the U.K. economy. After an improvement in the early 1960s she again began to falter, and the indications are that any impetus the Scottish economy might have gained had been lost by the end of the decade. From the vantage point of 1971, it appears that the accustomed *status quo* has been firmly re-established, with Scotland once again lagging behind U.K. growth rates. A closer inspection of the indicators listed serves to confirm this general picture. We look first at trends in industrial production.

a) Industrial Production An official index of industrial production has existed for Scotland since 1948. There is, however, a break in classification in 1958 so that years before and after that date are not strictly comparable. Since 1958 the index has been based on the Standard Industrial Classification, which is used by all Government departments. The indices, available for both Scotland and the U.K., cover manufacturing, construction, mining and quarrying, and the gas, electricity and water supply industries. There are major omissions in coverage such as trade, transport, finance and other service industries. It is important, therefore, not to rely on the index alone when analysing trends in general economic development. Strictly speaking, it is not a measure of general economic performance. The Scottish index, for instance, covers only about 50 per cent of the economic activity making up gross domestic product. Nevertheless, taken in conjunction with other indices of economic development, it can at least be used to show the broad direction of change and gives some indication of the magnitudes involved.

The index for the period before 1958 reveals that Scotland benefitted initially from the prolonged boom enjoyed by the heavy industries up to the early 1950s. As a result, even with resources concentrated in the heavy industrial sector, certain trades such as coal and shipbuilding had found it difficult to meet the demand with which they were faced. At the same time, however, such conditions meant that necessary diversification of industry, and the possibility of creating new types of economic growth, were retarded. That the market environment was changing was clear by the mid-1950s, although only after 1957 did the boom in the heavy industrial trades wholly collapse. From that date, the familiar problem of surplus capacity in these industries emerged, a feature that has remained part of the economy ever since. Taking the decade 1948–57 as a whole, Scotland's rate of growth of industrial production lagged behind that of the U.K. In the former, a growth of 29 per cent over the period compared unfavourably with the 38 per cent achieved in the U.K. The position deteriorated further between 1957 and 1960, so giving a renewed impetus to regional economic policy. As we shall see in Chapter 13, 1960 represented a turning-point in regional policy, with Scotland one of the main areas that was to receive preferential treatment.

Chart 2 below compares the Scottish and U.K. indices of industrial production since 1958.

Over the first half of the decade of the 1960s, the growth of Scottish industrial production kept pace with, and sometimes

Chart 2

indices of industrial production, Scotland and the U.K. 1958–69, 1958 = 100

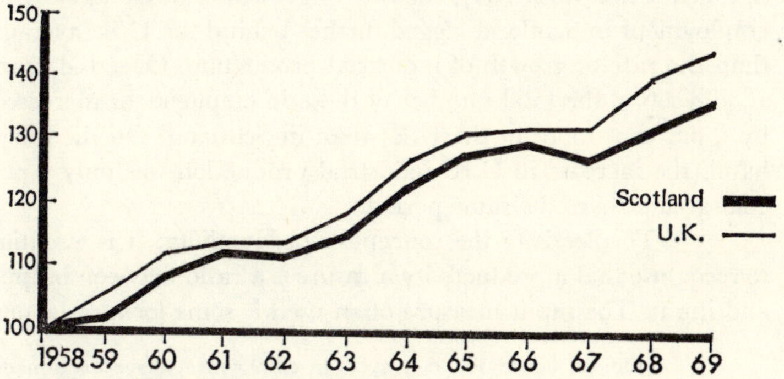

sources: Annual Abstract of Statistics
Digest of Scottish Statistics

even exceeded, that of the U.K. It can be seen from the Chart, however, that this rate of progress was not maintained after 1966. Since that date the gap between the two series has steadily widened again, so revealing as somewhat premature the hopes and claims of a Scottish economic renaissance in the 1960s. It is clear that Scotland still has serious problems to resolve. It has a higher proportion of what are, in fact, declining industries than the rest of the U.K. As a result, the impact of such growth sectors as have developed in the economy tends to be outweighed by the unfavourable influences and drag of declining staples. To secure the same growth rates as the U.K., Scotland would therefore have to achieve a rate of development in the expanding sectors that was *above* the national average. This, in turn, would imply a more rapid rate of structural change in the economy. As we shall see in Chapter 4, such rapid change was not occurring during the 1960s. Indeed it has been neither as rapid nor as comprehensive as would be necessary significantly to raise the rate of growth of output, increase employment opportunities and thereby reduce the net outward flow of population.

b) Growth of Employment and Labour Productivity Trends in the growth of employment reinforce the evidence of the production indices. One of the major weaknesses of the Scottish economy has been its failure to provide additional employment opportunities. The growth of those actually in employment may be measured by excluding from the figures of total employees given by the Dept. of Employment those unemployed.[1] Since 1955, the numbers in work in Scotland have remained stationary or even shown a tendency to decline. In the U.K., on the other hand, a fairly steady rate of expansion was achieved except for the closing years of the 1960s. Indeed it is significant that until 1967, the rate of growth of those actually in employment in Scotland lagged further behind the U.K. average than the rate of growth of industrial production. Over the years 1958–1966/7, the total number of those in employment increased by 5 per cent more in the U.K. than in Scotland. On the other hand, the increase in U.K. industrial production was only 3 per cent greater over the same period.

This leads to the concept of productivity. It is essential to recognise that a productivity measure is a ratio between output and input. The input measure often used is some form of labour

[1] Official figures for 'employees in employment' have been made available in the *Employment and Productivity Gazette* since 1965.

input (man hours, man years, employment). Because it is a ratio, a productivity measure can therefore show an increase or improvement not simply because of changes on the output side, but as a result of changes on the input side. We shall see cases where productivity has increased because labour input or employment has fallen rather than because output has shown significant advance.

Indeed, this explains in part, when we turn to the Scottish scene, why the growth of labour productivity in Scotland was more rapid than in the U.K. as a whole. Simply, Scotland's industrial production was rising more slowly than in the U.K., but her rate of growth of employment was rising more slowly still. To the extent, therefore, that Scotland's better-than-average productivity figures depended on the slow growth of employment and a heavy rate of unemployment, it would be absurd on this basis to claim a higher level of efficiency north of the border. It is surely significant that when, after 1967, the growth of total employment in the U.K. also experienced a fall, figures for labour productivity rose quite suddenly to a level above those in Scotland. In interpreting the labour productivity statistics, therefore, the slow growth of Scotland's industrial production must be constantly kept in mind, allied to the even slower growth of the number in work and a high unemployment rate. These are hardly the indications of a healthy economy.

The trends in the growth of employment and in labour productivity are outlined below for both Scotland and the U.K.

It can be seen from column (1) of the Table below that over the period 1958–68 the numbers actually in work stagnated in Scotland, whilst they showed a significant increase for the U.K. (column (4)). In both economies, a down turn was recorded from 1967, although unlike the Scottish experience, the numbers in work in the U.K. never reverted to the level of the late 1950s.

These movements in employment are partly responsible for the trends in labour productivity shown in columns (3) and (6). To obtain the productivity figures, an index of industrial production was used in conjunction with an index of employees in work. The latter was limited to those sectors covered by the production index. The message of the productivity figures at first sight appears quite clear. Industrial efficiency was rising in Scotland rapidly from 1958 and compared most favourably with that being achieved in the U.K. until the last year or so of the period. To a large extent, however, accepting such an impression unreservedly

Table 3.1 Growth of Employment and Labour Productivity, Scotland and the U.K. Selected Years, 1958–68 (1958 = 100)

Year	**Scotland** Total Employees in Employment (1)	Employees in Employment in Sectors Covered by Index of Industrial Production (2)	Labour Productivity (3)
1958	100	100	100
1960	101	95	115
1964	102	94	132
1966	103	96	136
1967	101	94	137
1968	100	93	143

Year	**U.K.** Total Employees in Employment (4)	Employees in Employment in Sectors Covered by Index of Industrial Production (5)	Labour Productivity (6)
1958	100	100	100
1960	103	99	114
1964	107	99	130
1966	108	101	132
1967	106	97	137
1968	106	96	148

Sources: Calculated from data obtained from the Ministry of Labour Gazette; Employment and Productivity Gazette; Digest of Scottish Statistics; Annual Abstract of Statistics.

would be to misconstrue the nature of this period. The essential characteristics of the decade may be re-stated as follows:

First: Industrial production was rising more slowly in Scotland than in the U.K.

Second: The number of those in work in the sectors covered by the index of industrial production (cols. (2) and (5)) was falling a good deal more rapidly in Scotland than in the U.K. To an extent, this can certainly be attributed to some degree of rationalisation and the continued 'run-down' of the older, declining staples. It also reflected, however, the fact that, despite the renewed vigour of regional policy after 1960, new jobs were not being created quickly enough in Scotland, and particularly in manufacturing, to compensate for the 'shake-out' of labour from the traditional trades. Given, then, the fall in Scotland of those actively in work in the sectors covered by the production index, productivity was bound to rise.

Third: The fact that productivity in Scotland rose more rapidly than in the U.K. can partly be attributed to the fact that the fall in Scottish employment was greater than in the U.K., and more than sufficient to offset the effects of a more slowly rising industrial production.
Fourth: After 1966, there was some change in the respective positions of the two economies. From that date, U.K. employment (col. (5)) began to fall more rapidly than in Scotland. This to some extent explains the rise in labour productivity in the national economy to a level which, by 1968, was well above that in Scotland.

It has not been our intention to suggest that the failure to provide more rapidly growing employment opportunities was wholly responsible for the more rapid rise in labour productivity in Scotland before 1966. Although this certainly contributed, there were other forces at work. Changes were taking place in Scotland's industrial structure during the 1960s. The expansion of certain new capital-intensive industries had a favourable upward effect on productivity figures. These included a growing electronics industry, largely American-owned, established in the Central Belt. Between 1964–8, when employment in the industry almost doubled, a substantial increase was, at the same time, achieved in productivity. The value of output per employee rose from £3,400 in 1964 to £5,300 in 1968.[1] In the early 1960s, too, the Scottish motor-car industry was re-established, and major developments have taken place in petro-chemicals. As part of the re-structuring process, the decline in the heavy industries has continued, particularly in mining, metal manufacture[2] and shipbuilding. The latter has typified the change in environment during the 1960s. Between 1959–69, a total of 12,000 jobs were lost in shipbuilding and ten yards forced to close.

It has been Scotland's experience that the decline in employment in the traditional industries has offset expansion taking place in certain of the more recent lines in manufacturing, and in professional and scientific services. This is highlighted in Table 3.2 below which outlines those industries in Scotland experiencing the greatest rise or fall in employment between 1959 and 1968.

It should be stressed that the industries specified in Table 3.2 are only those in which the movement in employment has appeared most striking. As can be seen, the effects of falling

[1] *The Economist*, 21st–28th February, 1970.
[2] In terms of employment, not output.

Table 3.2 Major Gains or Losses in Employment by Industry, Scotland, 1959–68

Gain in Employment (000)		Loss of Employment (000)	
Food, Drink and Tobacco	7	Agriculture, Forestry, Fishing	36
Electrical Engineering	26	Mining and Quarrying	52
Construction	37	Metal Manufacture	10
Insurance, Banking, etc.	9	Shipbuilding	25
Professional and Scientific Services	69	Textiles	13
Miscellaneous Services	4	Transport	23
Public Admin. and Defence	10	Distributive Trades	19
Total above industries	+162	Total above industries	−178

Source: Calculated from Digest of Scottish Statistics.

employment in the declining trades have to a large extent been mitigated by compensatory rises that have occurred elsewhere in expanding sectors. This has happened to a marked degree in Scotland over the past decade. The result has been that, overall, employment opportunities have neither markedly increased nor decreased in the region. Indeed, this stagnation in the numbers employed and the slow rise of industrial production are of greater moment for Scotland than any increase in labour productivity suggested by a statistical ratio between the two.

c) Unemployment and Employee Activity Rates

The failure of the numbers in work to grow indicates the presence of an under-utilised labour market in Scotland. If this was indeed the case we should expect to find confirmation in the movements of certain other indicators of economic performance. Such confirmation is readily forthcoming in the shape of the greater unemployment and lower than average activity rates consistently experienced north of the border. Changes in unemployment, both in Scotland and the U.K. are outlined for selected years.

Table 3.3 Average Numbers Unemployed as Percentage of those in Civil Work, Scotland and the U.K., Selected Years, 1950–69

Year	Scotland	U.K.	Year	Scotland	U.K.
1950	3·0	1·5	1964	3·6	1·8
1955	2·4	1·2	1965	3·0	1·5
1958	3·8	2·2	1966	2·9	1·6
1960	3·6	1·7	1967	3·9	2·5
1961	3·1	1·6	1968	3·8	2·5
1962	3·8	2·1	1969	3·8	2·3
1963	4·8	2·6			

Sources: Ministry of Labour Gazette Employment and Productivity Gazette.

As can be seen from Table 3.3, Scotland experienced a consistently heavy rate of unemployment over the 1960s, despite the emphasis on regional policy over the decade. Not only was the Scottish rate high relative to that in the U.K., but it was also considerably higher than Scotland had herself experienced in the previous decade. The per annum average in the 1950s had been some 3 per cent unemployed, representing 65,000 people out of work. These figures were comparatively low, certainly in relation to interwar experience and to those of the subsequent decade. Largely responsible was the fact that the staple industries enjoyed a relative prosperity until the mid-1950s. Only thereafter did unemployment rise to reach a level by the end of the decade that was significantly above the annual average for the 1950s. In the 1960s, the number out of work rose to an average of 79,000 persons per annum, or 3·6 per cent of the labour force. Indeed, over the closing years of the decade, the rate tended to be even higher, running at just under 4 per cent per annum. Clearly, this represents a considerable under-utilisation of Scotland's labour resources.

To Scotland's higher unemployment in the 1960s must be added the fact that activity rates were consistently lower during the decade than in Great Britain. Both these characteristics are accompaniments of the fact that the numbers in employment stagnated in the region. The Scottish activity rate (male and female) is compared to that for Great Britain below over the period 1951–68.

Table 3.4 Activity Rates, Scotland and Great Britain, Selected Years, 1951–68

	Scotland	Great Britain	Difference, Scotland from Great Britain
1951	54·9	54·6	+0·3
1953	55·3	54·8	+0·5
1955	55·8	56·1	−0·3
1958	55·5	56·5	−1·0
	. . .	. . .	. . .
1961	56·6	57·0	−0·4
1964	56·9	57·1	−0·2
	. . .	. . .	. . .
1967	56·7	56·8	−0·1
1968	56·4	56·4	—

. . . denotes a break in method of statistical compilation.

Sources: Digest of Scottish Statistics; Employment and Productivity Gazette.

Until 1955, the activity rate in Scotland had been higher than the national average. From that date, the total Scottish activity rate has been consistently lower, although that for males alone fell below the Great Britain level only from 1958. Most significant has been the fact that while the activity rate for males in Scotland has followed a secular downward trend since the 1950s, that for females has been rising, from 35·6 in 1951 to 40·4 in 1968. A growing proportion of the female population in Scotland is becoming actively engaged in economic pursuits. This is almost certainly due in part to the number of newly created jobs becoming available for women in the service trades and in manufacturing industry. The encouragement given to, and the consequent expansion of, such light science-based industries as electronics has increased the opportunity to utilise more fully female labour in the industrial sector.

Taken overall, however, Scotland's progress in the 1950s and 1960s has not been encouraging. Although at the end of the latter decade, a total activity rate had been achieved comparable to that in the national economy, unemployment remained at a level two-thirds as high again as in the U.K. As we have seen above, however, one result of the stagnation in the numbers actually employed has been a rise in labour productivity. This, in turn, has allowed an increase to take place in earnings per man employed. We can now look at trends in the level of earnings and personal income. Chapter 6 will be concerned with a much more detailed examination of the same picture *within* Scotland.

d) Earnings In Chapter 4, section IV, we shall be looking at earnings by particular industries. Here we are concerned with the broader sweep of earnings in industry as a whole. The rise in labour productivity in Scotland has had a most encouraging effect on earnings per man employed in industry. Figures for earnings were first made available on a regular basis by the *Ministry of Labour Earnings Enquiries*. They are now presented for every year by the Dept. of Employment for Scotland and all the other regions of the U.K. They cover, for all regions, the whole of the manufacturing sector and certain other industries for which information is available.[1] An analysis of these statistics shows that over the past decade, average weekly earnings per male manual worker in Scotland, both in manufacturing and in all industries covered, have remained constantly below those in the U.K. Yet, over this period, Scottish earnings have been rising at a faster rate, so that the gap between Scottish and U.K. figures has been steadily closing.

[1] These comprise construction, gas, electricity and water, transport and communication, certain miscellaneous services and public administration.

Table 3.5 below presents average weekly earnings per man employed for Scotland in manufacturing, and in all industries covered, for selected years. In addition, the relationship of these to U.K. earnings is shown in columns (2) and (4).

Table 3.5 Average Weekly Earnings Per Man[1] Employed in Scotland in Manufacturing and in All Industries Covered, and Proportion of these to U.K. Earnings, Selected Years, 1960–9

Year	Average Weekly Earnings Per Man in Manufacturing Industry (Scotland) (1)	As per cent of U.K. (2)	Average Weekly Earnings in all Industries Covered (Scotland) (3)	As per cent of U.K. (4)
	s. d.		s. d.	
1960	270 1	91·1	258 4	91·6
1962	293 9	90·7	285 11	91·4
1964	335 3	92·0	326 2	92·6
1966	398 8	95·1	386 0	95·3
1968	438 4	96·0	430 6	96·7
1969	481 0	97·6	464 6	97·1

Sources: Annual Abstract of Statistics; Digest of Scottish Statistics.
[1] Earnings relate to the weekly average in April of each year for male manual workers aged 21 and over.

As can be seen from Table 3.5, earnings per man in manufacturing in Scotland have remained consistently higher in absolute terms than those in all industries taken together. Nor has the difference between the two narrowed significantly over the decade. *Per capita* earnings in all industries covered have risen only at a marginally faster rate so that the gap between the two has remained in the region of 4 per cent. More important, however, is the fact that earnings have risen more rapidly in Scotland than in the U.K. as a whole. This is made clear by cols. (2) and (4) of the above Table which show that both in manufacturing and in all industries covered the level of earnings per man in Scotland has risen from 91 per cent to over 97 per cent of the national average.

The position is further clarified in Chart II below which shows the growth of weekly earnings per male manual worker in both Scotland and the U.K.

Chart 3 illustrates the extent to which earnings in manufacturing and in all industries covered have risen more rapidly in Scotland. Until 1963, both indices rose roughly in parallel with their U.K. counterparts. From that date, however, Scottish earnings rose much more rapidly so that, as observed, they had reached a level by the end of the 1960s close to the national average. This reflects the increase that had taken place in

Chart 3

growth of average weekly earnings per man employed in manufacturing and in all industries covered, Scotland and the U.K. 1960–69, 1960 = 100

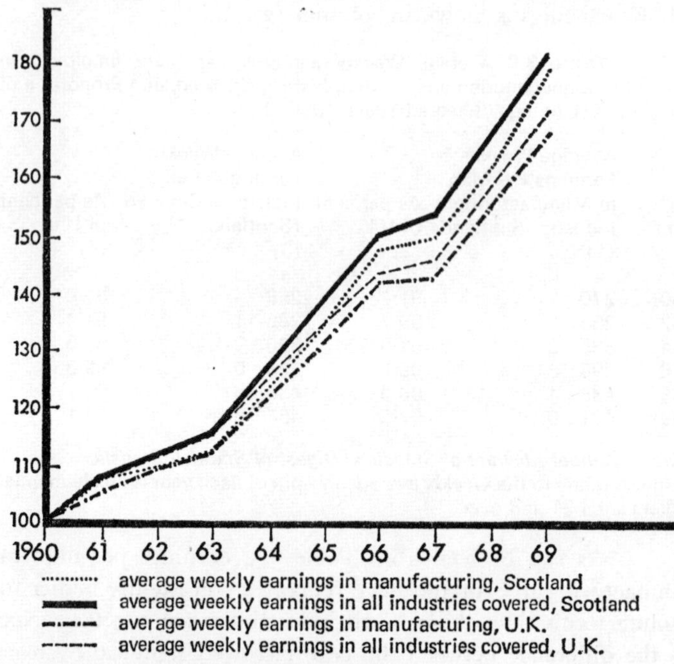

note: male manual workers aged 21 and over
sources: Annual Abstract of Statistics
Digest of Scottish Statistics

average earnings per hour worked by the manual worker in Scotland. The number of hours worked per man had remained roughly similar for both the U.K. and Scotland over the period, so that differences in the length of time worked provide no significant part of the explanation for the difference in the level of earnings between the two regions.[1] On the other hand, *per capita* earnings per hour rose in Scotland from 65·8d in April 1960 to 115·5d in October 1968, an increase of 76 per cent. In the U.K., the increase, from 70·5d to 118·9d, amounted only to 69 per cent. It is this faster rise in earnings per *hour* in Scotland, itself a function of more rapidly increasing productivity in the region, that goes much of the way towards explaining why average weekly earnings should have risen to a level just under that of the U.K.

[1] Indeed, average weekly hours worked per man were marginally higher in the U.K. between 1960 and 1969. See The Scottish Office, *Scottish Economic Bulletin*, No. 1, 1971.

e) Personal Income The more rapid growth of Scottish *per capita* earnings finds no reflection, however, in the movements of *personal* income per head in Scotland. Figures for personal income are available from the *Inland Revenue Reports*. These provide statistics on income which vary considerably from those as measured by G.D.P. in chapter 2. The major difference is that the Inland Revenue figures are not confined to measuring only that income generated within a region. Instead, they are concerned with the income received by the residents of that region, whatever the source. For instance, a part of Scottish income is derived in the form of investment income from companies operating outwith the confines of Scotland. This would be specifically excluded when using G.D.P. as a measure, but it is included within the compass of the Inland Revenue returns. We shall look in more detail in Chapter 6 at different forms of income, and confine ourselves here to the general picture.

The fact is that throughout this present century income per head in Scotland has remained at a level well below that prevailing in the U.K. as a whole. Nor, according to the Inland Revenue statistics, has there been any indication that over recent years Scotland has been able to improve her relative position. On the contrary, during the 1960s *per capita* income in Scotland has fallen as a proportion of that in the U.K. to levels below those existing in the 1950s. In other words, while Scottish income per head has, of course, been increasing in absolute terms over the 1960s, that in the U.K. has been growing faster still. Hence, in relation to the national experience, Scotland has been slipping further behind. This is revealed in Table 3.6 below. The Table shows over a number of recent years, first, the growth of total personal income in the different countries comprising the U.K. and, second, personal income per head of population in these countries expressed as a percentage of that in the U.K.

The indices for the growth of total net income in Table 3.6 show that of all the home countries, Scotland recorded the lowest increase between 1954/5 and 1964/5. Had it not been for the very low rate of growth of income in Wales between 1964/5 and 1967/8, the expansion of income in Scotland would have appeared relatively slow throughout the entire period. The Welsh figure for 1967/8 is astonishingly low,[1] and the consequent

[1] It may be that some sampling error has occurred in the official compilation of the statistics, since the figure for Wales appears to be too low to be wholly acceptable. On the other hand, the figure may be largely a reflection of the sustained run-down in the traditional industries of Wales.

Table 3.6 Growth of Total Net Income[1] in the Separate Countries of the U.K., 1954/5–1967/8. 1954/5 = 100

	1954/5	1959/60	1964/5	1967/8
England	100·0	139·1	196·0	238·5
Wales	100·0	136·2	187·8	201·6
Scotland	100·0	133·6	181·5	211·3
N. Ireland	100·0	144·0	203·6	247·6
U.K.	100·0	138·5	194·4	234·6

Personal Income Per Head[1] in the Separate Countries of the U.K., and Relationship to the U.K. Average

	£	Per cent of U.K.	£	Per cent of U.K.	£	Per cent of U.K.	£	Per cent of U.K.
England	212·0	103·5	286·6	103·7	387·0	103·6	461·7	104·2
Wales	171·7	83·8	231·8	83·8	312·6	83·6	331·6	74·8
Scotland	184·3	90·0	243·2	88·0	328·2	87·8	383·5	86·5
N. Ireland	124·6	60·8	176·4	63·8	241·0	64·5	286·6	64·7
U.K.	204·8	100·0	276·5	100·0	373·7	100·0	443·2	100·0

Sources: Calculated from Inland Revenue Reports; Annual Abstract of Statistics.

[1] Total net income has been adjusted to exclude that accruing to Public Departments, the Forces, and the Merchant Navy.

[2] Total net income per head of total home population in each of the five countries.

fall in income per head in Wales as a proportion of that in the U.K. appears well-nigh disastrous. The retardation in the rate of growth of total net income in Scotland compares very unfavourably with the increases recorded both in England and N. Ireland. As can be seen, each experienced an expansion of income significantly above the national average.

A more important indicator than total income, however, is income per head of the population. Figures for income per head are given in the lower half of Table 3.6. They show that while the growth of total net income had been most rapid in N. Ireland, the absolute figures for income per head in that region remained very low throughout the period. Even by 1967/8, they amounted to less than two-thirds of the national average. On the other hand, whilst income per head in both N. Ireland and England rose as a proportion of that in the U.K. over the period 1954/5–1967/8, the reverse was true for Scotland. Relative to *per capita* income in the U.K., Scotland has in fact experienced a steady decline from the mid-1950s. This proportionate fall in Scottish income conforms with the trends in the level of economic activity earlier outlined for the country. Over the first half of the 1960s, Scotland managed to retain her relative position. Since then, however, she has slipped further back so that, in absolute terms, income per head by 1967/8 was almost 20 per cent below that recorded in England.

Hence, Scotland has, over recent years, experienced the somewhat paradoxical situation of *earnings per man* employed in industry *rising* as a proportion of those in the U.K. at a time when *income per head* has been steadily *falling*. It is not, of course, difficult to reconcile these apparently conflicting trends. The concepts 'earnings' and 'income' are measures of very different variables. Changes in the former may be the product of several factors such as changes in rates of wages, in the number of hours worked, in the proportions of male and female workers in various trades, and extensions by some industries of 'payment by results' systems. On the other hand, the Inland Revenue figures for income, as already observed, represent all income accruing to individuals, whether such income originates inside or outside the Scottish economy. They include income from employment, but also embrace income derived in the form of profits paid to shareholders, the income of employers and those working on their own account, income from rent and so on. Clearly, these different concepts will not display similar rates of change, or even move necessarily in the same direction.

Whilst both have risen in absolute terms in Scotland, the growth of earnings has been such as to narrow the differential between the Scottish and U.K. levels. In contrast, the slow expansion of Scottish *per capita* income has resulted in a widening of the differential. This can be attributed to a number of factors. In the first place, income from the holding of assets in Scotland has always formed a smaller proportion of total income than has been the case in the U.K. as a whole. Hence, there has been a tendency for income per head to be traditionally lower north of the border. Again, it may be that income per head of those self-employed or working on their own account has been rising faster in the U.K. than in Scotland. Further, it must be remembered that the earnings figures quoted in Table 3.5 cover only a restricted range of industries so that there may well be major variations between Scottish and U.K. earnings per head in those trades not included within the scope of the earnings enquiry.

The fact that Scottish income per head has been falling further behind that of the rest of the nation may be added to the growing list of factors indicating that Scotland's growth performance over the past couple of decades has been disappointing. This, to some extent, has determined the heavy net migration that has taken place out of the country, which in turn has inspired the criticism that migration literally does mean a loss of our lifeblood.

f) Net Migration The movement of people, either in or out, can provide a significant indication of a country's economic performance. It is true that some part of such migration may be for entirely non-economic reasons. Strong incentives to move can be political ideology, climate and the like. At the same time, however, prevailing economic conditions will determine a large part of any shifts in population that are taking place. People may move on account of 'pull' factors which attract them to other areas. The attractions of other regions, perhaps in the form of better climate, the promise of better living conditions or more favourable opportunities for economic advancement, may be sufficient to induce people to migrate. Alternatively, 'push' factors may be more important, accentuating peoples' desire to move because of economic depression, lack of suitable opportunities in their existing environment, their experience of political and/or religious intolerance, and other considerations.

Whatever the reasons, it is important to recognise that at any one time a country will experience two-way flows of population. Hence, those who move in must be offset against those who move out, in order to ascertain the degree of net migration that has taken place. If, over a number of years, net migration into a country has taken place, then clearly the population of that country will have increased by an amount over and above the level that purely natural factors (i.e. birth and death rates) would have determined. The reverse is true where a secular trend in net migration out of a country has taken place.

The Scottish experience has always been of the latter type. Indeed, currently one of Scotland's most serious problems is the extent to which she has been losing population. The extent of this loss over the last couple of decades is shown in Table 3.7 below.

Over the whole period, 1951–68, Scotland's total population increased by just under 2 per cent as opposed to an increase in the U.K. as a whole of some 10 per cent. This slow rate of expansion in Scotland was not due, however, to a low rate of natural increase. On the contrary, had Scotland's population growth been determined solely by the trend in natural increase, then her population would have increased by over 12 per cent between these years. The corresponding increase in the U.K., given such an assumption, would have been much the same as was actually recorded, that is, something over 10 per cent. Rather than a slow rate of natural increase, the explanation for Scotland's slower population growth lies in the net loss by migration experienced by the economy.

It can be seen from Table 3.7 that Scotland lost virtually nine-tenths of her natural increase in population through net migration between 1951 and 1968. The loss has been particularly severe over the 1960s when the whole of the natural increase was offset by the net movement of people out of the country. The result was that population growth stagnated between 1961 and 1968. The U.K. presents a very different picture. Taking the period 1951–68 as a whole, a mere 8 per cent of the natural increase was lost through net migration. Since the net loss was so small, population continued to expand, growing by 5 per cent over the 1960s.

Table 3.7 Increase in Scottish Population[1] and Net Loss by Migration, Scotland and the 1951–68 (thousands)

	Scotland				U.K.	
d	Actual Increase of Population	Natural Increase	Net Loss by Migration	Net Loss as Proportion of Natural Increase (per cent)	Net Loss by Migration	Net Loss as Proportion of Natural Increase (per cent)
–61	82	368	286	78	156	6
–8	4	298	294	99	258	9
1951–68	86	666	580	87	414	8

rce: *Annual Abstract of Statistics.*
ires are calculated from mid-year estimates of the home population made available by the trars General.

Concern over the Scottish experience is, however, not confined to the absolute numbers being lost. It is directed also at the *quality* of those moving out of the country. The composition of migrants leaving Scotland, particularly with regard to age-structure, is highly detrimental to the future well-being of the economy. To some extent, this is revealed by the cross-flows of population between Scotland and England and Wales. In Table 3.8 below, migrants moving between the two economies are analysed according to age-structure.

An investigation of the age-distribution of migrants between the two regions shows that Scotland is suffering proportionately heavy losses of people of the most economically valuable type. It can be seen that, between 1961–6, the proportions entering and leaving Scotland were very similar for the age-groups 25–59. Further, the movement, both outward and inward, of the 5–14 age-group, which is largely a function of movements in the former age-range, was again proportionately similar. Where marked differences occurred were in the age-groups 15–19, 20–24,

Table 3.8 Percentage Age Distribution of Migrants between Scotland and England and Wales, 1961–6

Age-Group	Migrants from Scotland to England and Wales (per cent)	Migrants from England and Wales to Scotland (per cent)
5–14	19·4	19·1
15–19	8·3	5·6
20–24	14·3	10·3
25–44	41·8	43·8
45–59	10·6	11·9
60–64	1·9	2·9
65 and over	3·8	6·5
All	100·0	100·0

Source: H. R. Jones, 'Migration To and From Scotland Since 1961', Institute of British Geographers, Transactions and Papers, No. 49, 1970.

and in that classified as 'over 60'. In the former two groups, the proportion of migrants leaving Scotland to move to England and Wales was much heavier than the proportion which entered. In contrast, the reverse was true for the 'over 60' age-group; here, migrants to Scotland formed a much higher proportion than those who left the country.

Precisely the same trends were repeated for Scotland on an international scale. The flow of migrants between Scotland and foreign countries was weighted in a manner similar to that experienced with England and Wales. Again, Scotland was the recipient of a heavier net influx of those in the older age-groups, whilst losing a larger proportion of her youthful population. These trends in migration have obvious implications for Scottish economic development. In essence, Scotland during the 1960s was suffering a much greater net loss, both absolutely and proportionately, of its younger, vigorous population than of its older, retired population.

We have concentrated so far in this section on the heavy net outward movement of population from Scotland. Whilst this is clearly the case, *it is important to recognise that this net loss represents not so much an extremely high rate of emigration from Scotland as a very inadequate rate of immigration.* The number of people moving out of Scotland is not particularly high relative to several other regions of the U.K. Scotland's deficiency has lain in attracting incomers to the country in sufficient numbers to offset those who have moved out. Between 1961 and 1966, for instance, those entering Scotland from England and Wales amounted only to 52 per cent of the flow in the other direction. Again, with regard to overseas countries, Scotland provided 12 per cent of all emigrants from the

U.K. in 1966/7, but only 5 per cent of the immigrants.[1] This is clearly important, since it means that Scotland has been unable to provide the inducements necessary to attract an inflow of migrants. It is a point to which we shall return at greater length in Chapter 10.

Conclusion The main conclusion which we can draw from the evidence of the preceding pages is that Scotland presently stands in some danger of reverting to the same position of 'poor relation' to England and Wales as existed for some time in the past. There are those, indeed, who would urge that Scotland has never been anything else throughout the whole of the 20th century. Yet, there were indications during the 1960s that the position was changing. Particularly over the first half of the decade, the Scottish economy appeared to be making up some of the ground previously lost to the rest of the U.K. Industrial production rose more rapidly, earnings per man employed in industry increased relative to those in the national economy, and there was a distinct reduction in the unemployment rate. Most important of all, changes were beginning to occur in the structure of the economy, with a greater emphasis being placed on emerging, science-based industries whilst older, traditional trades were allowed to run down.

Viewing the entire decade in retrospect, however, it is difficult to be so encouraging with regard to future trends. The growth of industrial production began once more to lag behind the national average over the later 1960s. More significant, the numbers actually in employment stagnated between 1958 and 1968 and the rate of unemployment again rose to disappointingly high levels. Income per head in Scotland, as measured by the Inland Revenue returns, has fallen as a proportion of that in the U.K. since the mid-1950s. It has been the influence of factors such as these that has, in part, determined the heavy loss of Scottish population through net migration. Almost the whole of the natural increase was offset by the net loss of population experienced by the Scottish economy during the 1960s. Clearly both 'pull' and 'push' factors have been at work in determining the rate at which people have left the country. Probably the most important aspect of the latter has been the country's industrial structure. This has changed markedly, as we shall see in the next chapter, over recent years. Yet, the change, as noted earlier, has not been accomplished swiftly enough nor has it been sufficiently

[1] See H. R. Jones, *op. cit.*, pp. 157–8.

comprehensive to absorb the labour displaced by the contraction of certain of the staple industries. Given a slack labour market, a proportion of that labour has sought to find improved opportunities beyond the confines of Scotland.

References

The most important source in future years for trends in the Scottish economy will be the *Scottish Economic Bulletin*, H.M.S.O.

Scottish Statistical Office, *Digest of Scottish Statistics*, H.M.S.O.

Central Statistical Office, *Annual Abstract of Statistics*, H.M.S.O.

Abstract of Regional Statistics, H.M.S.O.

Department of Employment, *Employment and Productivity Gazette*, H.M.S.O.

Statistics on Incomes, Prices, Employment and Production, H.M.S.O.

Board of Trade, *Report on the Census of Production, 1963*, H.M.S.O.

Scottish Office, *The Scottish Economy 1965 to 1970: A Plan for Expansion*, Cmnd. 2864, 1966, H.M.S.O.

Report of the Commissioners of H.M. Inland Revenue, now published annually in two forms—*Report of the Commissioners of H.M. Inland Revenue* and *Inland Revenue Statistics*, H.M.S.O.

General Register Office, *Sample Census 1966, Scotland*, H.M.S.O.

Annual Reports of the Registrar General for Scotland, H.M.S.O.

Scottish Council (Development and Industry), *Scottish Economic Review*.

Glasgow Herald Trade Review, annually.

G. McCrone, *Scotland's Economic Progress, 1951–1960.*

Scotland's Future: The Economics of Nationalism.

Regional Policy in Britain.

H. R. Jones, '*Migration to and From Scotland since 1961*', Institute of British Geographers, No. 49, 1970,

Chapter 4
The Structure of Production

In Chapters 2 and 3 we have examined the conventional statistics of national income accounting and other selected indicators of economic performance. In this Chapter and the succeeding three Chapters we shall be seeking to probe in much greater detail into the structure of Scotland's economy. In other words, we seek to 'disaggregate' the economic flows to a level which is illuminating and to which the available statistics permit. We have seen that economic activity is interdependent, and can be analysed from the product, income, and expenditure sides. We propose, therefore, to follow that sequence. In this Chapter we shall examine the structure of production, and in Chapter 5 we present some case studies of particular industries, to add some flesh to the statistical bones. Chapter 6 takes up the income side and probes this in as much detail as the data allow. In Chapter 7 we take up the expenditure flows and show how these add to our understanding of the picture.

1 To a large extent Scotland's industrial problems at the present time are of a type similar to those that were experienced some 50 years ago. Then, as now, the economy was heavily committed to a relatively narrow range of industries, coal-mining, iron and steel, shipbuilding, engineering and textiles. These were the staple trades which had forged the prosperity of the country during the Industrial Revolution of the late 18th and early 19th centuries. During that period, they had attracted to them the great bulk of the country's factors of production and not only dominated the domestic scene but also made a substantial contribution to Scotland's standing in the international economy. Exports of heavy capital equipment from Scotland, and of labour skilled in the production and use of such equipment, played an integral part in raising the status of the U.K. as a whole to the position of 'workshop of the world' by the mid-19th century.

Precisely because it was so heavily committed to these

few staple trades, Scotland found it difficult to secure a degree of industrial diversification when faced with the growth of foreign competition and the development of substitutes for the products of heavy industry, around the turn of the present century. It was not, however, until the interwar period that the rigidity of Scotland's industrial structure was fully exposed. It was then recognised, too, that Scotland shared, in more acute form, a problem common to the U.K. economy as a whole, namely that of being over-committed to a relatively small group of traditional industries.

In large measure, this same problem still exists today, although more vigorous efforts have been made in recent years to secure necessary diversification. Particularly since 1960, Scotland has been a major beneficiary of the Government's attempts to bring new industry to the 'Development Areas'.[1] With virtually the whole of Scotland designated as such an area, it has been possible to offer major financial inducements to prospective industrialists. To a limited extent this policy has proved successful. This is reflected both in the volume of investment flowing in from outside the region and the increasing number of externally-owned companies that have recently commenced operations in Scotland. These aspects of the broadening industrial base of the Scottish economy are treated more fully in section IV.

The aim of this chapter is, then, to show that on the one hand the Scottish economy still possesses an unfavourable industrial structure. On the other hand, however, a more energetically pursued regional policy over the past decade has been primarily responsible for the introduction of certain new specialisms to the economy. Hence, Scotland is presently experiencing those problems inherent in a period of transition during which a change in industrial emphasis is taking place. Foremost amongst these is the fact that the new employment created by the expanding industries such as electronics, vehicles, telegraph and telecommunications, etc. has so far been insufficient to meet the decline in job opportunities resulting from the run-down of the staple trades. Put another way, the expanding trades have first to compensate for the contraction of the older staples, before they can even *begin* to make any *net* contribution to the expansion of total output or employment. Indeed, we can go a stage further by pointing out that, to achieve the same growth-rates as the U.K., Scotland's 'growth' industries would have to expand at a faster rate. This results, as we shall see in the next section, from the

[1] For a discussion of 'Development Area' policy, see Chapter 13.

fact that these 'growth' industries are still under-represented in the Scottish economy.

The evidence of an unfavourable industrial structure in Scotland is presented in the two following sections. The analysis, which of necessity draws heavily upon statistics of employment, shows first, how the structure of Scottish production *presently* compares with that of the U.K. and second, how that structure has changed *over time*. The impact which recent industrial developments have had on the economy is assessed in section IV. The contribution made to growth, particularly by foreign-owned companies operating in the country, is examined at some depth. In section V, the implications of Scotland's unfavourable economic structure are discussed in terms of unemployment, industrial earnings and migration. It will be shown that a major determinant of the level of economic activity in a region, the level of effective demand, has been adversely affected in Scotland by the nature of the country's industrial structure. The conclusions at the end of the Chapter bring together the principal findings that emerge from the preceding sections.

2 The Present Production Structure A word of caution, about the nature of the statistical data to be used, is in order before we embark on an examination of the evidence relating to the structure of Scottish industry. It is true that Scotland is relatively well served by the extent of statistical coverage on industrial development, at least in comparison to other regions of the U.K. Scotland is the only region for which there exists an index of industrial production. This index, available on a quarterly basis, readily allows a comparison of industrial development in the regional and national economies to be made. In the *Digest of Scottish Statistics*, too, a large volume of miscellaneous information on the output of individual Scottish industries can be found. Even so, the scope of the Scottish data still places serious limitations on any investigation of the region's industrial structure. For instance, as with the U.K. index, that for Scotland covers only a restricted range of the region's economic activity. Indeed, as observed in Chapter 3, it is probable that no more than one-half of the activity making up gross domestic product is represented in the Scottish index.

The other main source of information on output, the *Census of Production*, again covers only a limited range of activity. It provides statistics only for manufacturing industry, mining and quarrying, gas, electricity and water, and construction. Moreover, due to the time-lag between gathering the necessary information and the date of publication, the statistics presented by the Census are, to a large extent, only of historical interest. Neither the Census nor the index of industrial production can, then, provide details of primary industry,[1] transport, finance and other services. In consequence, any comprehensive analysis of the structure of the Scottish economy must depend very largely on statistics of employment. It should be emphasised here that this reliance on employment figures can, of course, give rise to misleading results. A falling level of employment in an individual industry may not, after all, be an indication of depression and decline. On the contrary, it might well be that output per head is rising rapidly, so allowing the industry to release labour for alternative uses. As we shall see in Chapter 5, this is precisely the position in Scotland's agricultural sector. It has also been the experience of both the chemical and metal manufacturing industries in Scotland.

We are now in a position to examine the evidence presented by these different statistical sources on the structure of Scotland's economy. Although somewhat dated, the most recent *Census of Production* returns give some indication of the broad orders of magnitude involved in the composition of output for 1963.[2] They show that the major industries in Scotland, as measured by value of output, were engineering and electrical goods, food, drink and tobacco, textiles, chemicals and those trades associated with paper. In that year, whilst *total* manufacturing output in Scotland comprised almost 8 per cent of the U.K. total, in three industries the Scottish contribution to national output was significantly higher than this ratio. These were shipbuilding, textiles and the food trades. The concentration on the two former sectors is indicative of Scotland's dependence on trades of a traditional nature that have long since lost their dynamic. We shall see in the next chapter that shipbuilding, in particular, has experienced for some time contraction and retrenchment.

With Scotland's industrial structure essentially in a transitional phase during the past couple of decades, too great a reliance on statistics which relate to 1963 would obviously be misleading. For instance, the Census shows that, in that year, the *lowest* contribution made by any manufacturing sector in Scotland

[1] Primary industry is, however, adequately covered by information made available in the *Digest of Scottish Statistics*. Most useful in this context is the index of agricultural production devised for Scotland.

[2] Since this chapter was written, certain preliminary findings of the 1968 *Census* have been made available. These may be found in the *Board of Trade Journal*, 2 September, 1970.

to U.K. output was in the category 'vehicles'. But since that time the position has of course changed. The production of motor cars only began in the early 1960s, but since then British Leyland has commenced operations at Bathgate and the Rootes/Chrysler complex has been making more rapid progress at Linwood. Again details of these developments can be found in Chapter 5. It is also important to remember that the commodity-structure of output in 'vehicles' has been undergoing quite substantial changes. Besides motor-cars and heavy commercial vehicles, the output of the sector ranges from aero-engines manufactured by Rolls-Royce to railway locomotives. In the latter context, the nature of output has been drastically revised, with the production of steam locomotives having virtually disappeared since 1963.

The *Census of Production* cannot take account of such recent changes. Between 1963 and 1969, the total output of the category 'vehicles' expanded by almost one-fifth. Nor is it the only sector which has experienced significant changes since 1963. In the category 'food, drink and tobacco' as a whole, output has remained relatively stable between 1963–9; yet, in the 'drink' branch alone (i.e. whisky) it has grown by over one-third.[1] The other major growth sectors since 1963 have been engineering and electrical goods (29 per cent), metal manufacture (24 pei cent) and chemicals (19 per cent). At the other end of the scale, the output of textiles has stagnated over these same years, whilst that of shipbuilding has actually declined by almost 10 per cent.

In order to take more fully into account such recent developments, statistics of employment can be used to build up a comprehensive picture of the structure of Scottish production. Even here, however, the position is by no means straightforward, since a number of major changes have occurred in the method of compiling the employment data. Changes in the methods of estimating employees mean, for instance that the statistics are not strictly comparable before and after 1964.[2] It is virtually impossible, therefore, to obtain an unbroken run of employment statistics over any length of time. In consequence, the figures for employees must be used with some caution. Even the Department of Employment makes clear that no degree of exactitude is claimed for them. It might also be noted that there are presently available two different series showing employment on a per-industry basis.

[1] This figure and those that follow in the text have been calculated from data made available in the *Digest of Scottish Statistics*.

[2] A more recent change has involved the revision of the Standard Industrial Classification in 1968.

One relates to employees in employment, that is, it shows the numbers actually in work by individual industries. The other presents an industrial breakdown of total employees, whether employed or unemployed. As such, it includes all workers attached to industry. The latter, more comprehensive totals, will be used in this chapter.

The first task must be to obtain some more recent indication of the structure of Scottish production than that made possible by the *Census of Production*. Hence, in Table 4.1 below, the employment structure of both the Scottish and U.K. economies is compared for 1968.

Table 4.1 The Structure of the Scottish and U.K. Economies by Employment, 1968

Sector	Scottish Employment (000)	As per cent of Scottish Total (per cent)	U.K. Employment as per cent of Total (per cent)
Agriculture, Forestry and Fishing	**68·1**	**3·2**	**1·8**
Mining and Quarrying	**49·5**	**2·3**	**2·2**
Manufacturing:	**749·2**	**34·8**	**37·8**
Food, Drink and Tobacco	104·0	4·8	3·6
Chemicals and Allied Industries	34·5	1·6	2·2
Metal Manufacture	47·5	2·2	2·5
Engineering and Electrical Goods	187·0	8·7	9·9
Shipbuilding and Marine Engineering	48·0	2·2	0·9
Vehicles	38·8	1·8	3·5
Textiles	93·2	4·3	3·2
Paper, Printing and Publishing	58·7	2·7	2·7
Other Manufacturing Industries	137·6	6·4	9·4
Construction	**198·8**	**9·2**	**7·0**
Services:	**1,087·3**	**50·5**	**51·0**
Gas, Electricity and Water	32·8	1·5	1·8
Transport and Communications	154·9	7·2	6·9
Distributive Trades	274·3	12·7	12·2
Insurance, Banking and Finance	47·9	2·2	2·9
Professional and Scientific Services	275·4	12·8	11·7
Miscellaneous Services	177·0	8·2	9·3
Public Administration and Defence	125·0	5·8	6·2
Total, All Industries and Services	2,152·9	100·0	100·0

Source: Calculated from the Department of Employment and Productivity Gazette.

By and large, the conclusions initially drawn from the *Census of Production* data are confirmed by Table 4.1. In the manufacturing sector, the category engineering and electrical goods is heavily represented in both the Scottish and U.K.

economies, whilst employment in the traditional industries in Scotland tends to be above the national average. Hence, a larger proportion of Scottish labour is committed to such staples as shipbuilding and marine engineering and textiles, precisely those sectors in which output has either stagnated or declined in past years. Correspondingly, Scotland has obtained an inadequate share of the younger growth industries such as vehicles, and chemicals and allied industries. This dependence on traditional sectors again finds reflection in the higher proportion of Scottish labour devoted to primary and extractive industry. Here, a total of 5·5 per cent of the labour force is employed as opposed to only 4·0 per cent in the U.K.

Apart from this greater commitment to the staple industries, Table 4.1 might suggest that, at first sight, the structure of the Scottish economy was very similar to that in the nation as a whole. In both the regional and national economies, over 50 per cent of the labour force was employed in the service trades, and whilst Scotland was somewhat under-represented in manufacturing industry, this was to some extent compensated by higher than average employment in the constructional trades. As we shall see, however, the structural similarity of the two economies was more apparent than real. An analysis confined only to main-order headings tends to conceal almost as much as it reveals. By disaggregating further, it is possible to distinguish several important structural differences between the Scottish and U.K. economies. This is an issue to which we shall return later in this chapter.[1]

In order to confirm the fact of an unfavourable industrial structure in Scotland, additional evidence may be brought to bear. Hitherto, the discussion has provided only a first insight into the economic structure of the region, in that the degree of concentration on particular industries has been measured simply by comparing employment and output with the national averages. A more precise and sophisticated measure of the structure of Scottish production can, however, be obtained by introducing the concept of a 'location quotient'. The means of devising location quotients for Scottish industry are outlined in appendix I at the end of this chapter. For our present purposes it is necessary only to remember that where the value of the quotient is greater than 1, Scotland has a more than proportionate share of a particular industry. Where it is less than 1, then the converse is true. To allow a comprehensive view to be taken of the economy, the quotients both of main-order headings and of those minimum-list headings

[1] See section III.

that occupy a significant place in the economy have been calculated. The calculations are presented in Table 4.2 below for 1968. The Standard Industrial Classification order numbers have been provided to facilitate the identification of separate trades.

Several interesting findings emerge from Table 4.2. Within manufacturing industry, for instance, the Table confirms that Scotland has a more than proportionate share of several of the textile trades, shipbuilding and of the heavier branches of engineering and metal manufacture. The location quotients of these traditional sectors of industry are all well above 1. At the other end of the scale, Scotland's deficiency in more modern forms of manufacturing is clearly illustrated.[1] The region is markedly under-represented in such branches as motor vehicle manufacture, aircraft, chemicals, electrical machinery and the like. These are precisely the industries which, to a large extent, have been growing most rapidly in the U.K. since the second world war. It is the comparative lack of such growth sectors within Scotland that has been largely responsible for the retardation of the regional economy both before and after World War II.

Table 4.2 also shows that, by and large, an average representation of the service industries is to be found in Scotland. In this sector, where half of the Scottish labour force is engaged, there is no undue emphasis on any particular type of employment or, conversely, any indication of serious deficiency. In primary industry, on the other hand, the results produced by Table 4.2 may at first sight prove surprising. Whilst, as might be expected, the location quotients are high in forestry and fishing, they appear perhaps unduly low in agriculture and coal-mining. Yet in the former over 13 per cent of the total U.K. work-force is employed in Scotland and in the latter some 10 per cent. The low location quotients in each of these sectors may be explained by the fact that Scotland's share of U.K. employment in primary industry as a whole (i.e. the denominator in calculating the location quotient) is so high. Hence, the larger share of Scottish employment in both agriculture and coal-mining, the numerator, tends to be offset in this instance by the magnitude of the denominator. This should not obscure the fact that Scotland is more heavily committed to both these sectors than the U.K.

By using, then, the concept of a location quotient, the impression of a structure of production in Scotland heavily weighted in favour of the traditional branches of industry has been

[1] The one major exception is 'office machinery' in which, as can be seen, Scotland is well represented.

Table 4.2 Location Quotients for Scottish Industry, 1968

Category		Location Quotient
003	Fishing	3·3
002	Forestry	2·6
001	Agriculture and Horticulture	1·1
101	Coal Mining	0·8
102–109	Other Mining and Quarrying	0·5
Manufacturing Industry		
415	Jute	11·2
239	Other Drink Industries	4·4
273	Explosives and Fireworks	4·4
370	Marine Engineering	3·1
419	Carpets	2·8
VII	Shipbuilding and Marine Engineering	2·8
338	Office Machinery	2·8
370	Shipbuilding and Ship Repairing	2·6
417	Hosiery and Other Knitted Goods	1·9
341	Industrial Plant and Steel Work	1·9
214	Bacon Curing, Meat and Fish Products	1·9
312	Steel Tubes	1·6
X	Textiles	1·5
111	Food, Drink and Tobacco	1·5
211–213	Grain, Bread and Flour, Biscuits	1·5
414	Woollen and Worsted	1·4
339	Other Machinery	1·3
313	Iron Castings, etc.	1·2
XV	Paper, Printing and Publishing	1·1
384–385	Locomotives and Railway Track Equipment, Railway Carriages, Wagons, Trams	1·1
XIV	Timber, Furniture, etc.	1·0
311	Iron and Steel	1·0
V	Metal Manufacture	1·0
VI	Engineering and Electrical Goods	1·0
364	Radio and other Electronic Apparatus	0·9
XIII	Bricks, Pottery, Glass, Cement, etc.	0·9
IV	Chemicals and Allied Industries	0·8
271	Chemicals and Dyes	0·8
XI	Leather, Leather Goods and Fur	0·8
XII	Clothing and Footwear	0·7
383	Aircraft Manufacturing, etc.	0·7
361	Electrical Machinery	0·6
VIII	Vehicles	0·6
IX	Metal Goods, Not Elsewhere specified	0·6
381	Motor Vehicles Manufacture	0·5
Construction		
Service Industry		
XXII	Professional and Scientific Services	1·1
XX	Distributive Trades	1·1
XIX	Transport and Communications	1·0
XXIV	Public Administration and Defence	1·0
XXIII	Miscellaneous Services	0·9
XVIII	Gas, Electricity and Water	0·9
XXI	Insurance, Banking and Finance	0·8

Sources: Calculated from Digest of Scottish Statistics; Annual Abstract of Statistics.

confirmed. As we shall see later in this chapter, new developments have been taking place in recent years but it is clear that the Scottish economy still suffers, relative to the rest of the U.K., from an under-representation of the new growth sectors.

3 Changes in Production Structure over Time

Hitherto, our analysis of industrial structure has been conducted purely in static terms, and we have not, therefore determined which sections of Scottish industry have been growing most rapidly and which have been contracting. In this section, we shall concern ourselves with this dynamic element in Scotland's industrial development, that is, with the major changes in the importance of industries *over time*. It will be shown that substantial structural alterations have, indeed, occurred in the economy, although these become wholly apparent only when the statistical data are disaggregated to the level of minimum-list headings.

As a first step towards an understanding of where the principal developments have been taking place, we may consider the degree of change in the broad categories of Scottish industry over the period 1963–8. Perhaps the most significant development has occurred in the *type* of employment now afforded by Scottish industry. Table 4.3 below shows that, over the period considered, total female employment has increased at a time when the number of male employees has been declining.

As can be seen, within this five-year period of the 1960s, female employment increased by 34,000 at a time when the total labour force declined by over 20,000. Over a longer time period, the upward trend in the employment of females is even more pronounced. For example, the number of women actually *in work*

Table 4.3 Changes in Employment by Main Sectors in Scotland, 1963–8

	1963			1968		
	Male (000)	Female (000)	Male and Female as per cent of Total Employees (per cent)	Male (000)	Female (000)	Male a[nd] Femal[e as] per ce[nt] of Tot[al] Emplo[yees] (per ce[nt])
Agriculture, Forestry and Fishing	82	13	4·4	59	9	3·2
Mining and Quarrying	72	2	3·4	48	2	2·3
Manufacturing	498	236	33·7	507	242	34·8
Construction	180	9	8·7	189	10	9·2
Services	555	527	49·8	529	558	50·5
Total Employees	1,387	787	100·0	1,332	821	100·0

Source: Department of Employment and Productivity Gazette.

increased by 12 per cent over the period 1959–69. Over these same years male employees in employment declined by some 5 per cent. Hence, the expansion of female employment, particularly in the service sector of the economy, has offset the fall in male employment and maintained the *total* labour force at a relatively stable level over the 1960s.

The growth in female employment apart, the main trends to emerge from Table 4.3 can briefly be summarised. Between 1963 and 1968, both the primary and extractive industries have contracted rapidly, with the former losing over one-quarter of its labour force and the latter almost one-third. Nor at this aggregate level, would there appear to have been any major expansion in the manufacturing sector to absorb the labour released by these two categories. As can be seen, total employment in manufacturing has increased only marginally between 1963–8, both in absolute and relative terms.

On the basis of these global estimates, it might seem that little change has occurred over recent years in Scotland's manufacturing industry. Such a view would, however, be mistaken. This can be demonstrated by breaking down the aggregate figures presented in Table 4.3. As a next step, therefore, developments in manufacturing are examined at the level of main-order headings. This reveals that significant changes have, in fact, taken place during the 1960s in the composition of employment in Scottish manufacturing industry. The major developments, in terms of expanding and contracting industries, are outlined in Table 4.4 below.

Table 4.4 shows that in no sense has the structure of manufacturing industry in Scotland ossified over the past decade. The most important proof lies in the very rapidity with which the traditional industries have been releasing labour. As Table 4.4 shows, the number of employees attached to shipbuilding, textiles and metal manufacture fell in aggregate by almost 50,000 between 1960–8, or by one-fifth of their combined labour force in 1960. At the same time, however, the Table should also serve to warn us against drawing too hasty conclusions based solely on the evidence of employment statistics. We have already seen in section II that two of the so-called 'declining' industries in Table 4.4, metal manufacture and chemicals, were ranked amongst the most rapidly expanding in the country, as measured in terms of *output*. The explanation of this apparent paradox lies, of course, in the fact that in each of these trades productivity has been rapidly growing. This has allowed both to dispense with a part of their

Table 4.4 Employment in Manufacturing Industry, Scotland, 1960–8

	Increase (+) or Decrease (−) in Employment 1960–8 (000)
Expanding Industries:	
Engineering and Electrical Goods	+30·6
Food, Drink and Tobacco	+ 5·4
Timber, Furniture, etc.	+ 3·9
Bricks, Pottery, Glass, Cement, etc.	+ 3·6
Paper, Printing and Publishing	+ 1·6
Vehicles	+ 1·0
Clothing and Footwear	+ 0·7
Other Manufacturing Industries	+ 0·2
Declining Industries:	
Shipbuilding and Marine Engineering	—20·8
Textiles	—16·1
Metal Manufacture	—10·8
Chemicals and Allied Industries	— 2·9
Leather, Leather Goods and Fur	— 0·7
Metal Goods Not Elsewhere Specified	— 0·7
Total Manufacturing	— 5·0

Source: Calculated from Digest of Scottish Statistics.

respective work-forces whilst, at the same time, output has continued to expand. In no sense, therefore, could either be construed as a 'declining industry'.

To take up some of the slack in employment created both by the contraction of such industries as shipbuilding and textiles, and by the increased efficiency of chemicals and metal manufacture, Scotland has, to some extent, benefitted from the increase in employment opportunities offered by the 'expanding' trades specified in Table 4.4. The Table shows that the great bulk of the growth in employment has occurred in the engineering and electrical goods industry. As we shall see, within the broad framework of this sector, the momentum has derived mainly from those firms engaged in electronics. To a considerable extent, then, growth and decline have tended to offset each other in Scottish manufacturing over the past decade, and the result has been that the volume of employment in the sector as a whole has remained virtually static.

It is when we come to examine more fully the extent to which expansion has taken place in certain lines of Scottish manufacturing that an analysis based only on main-order headings can be misleading. It fails to show precisely which are the trades in the country that have been growing most rapidly over time. In an effort to distinguish these 'growth sectors' more clearly, we can, just as with the analysis in section two, disaggregate manufacturing to the minimum-list heading level. In this way, we are able to appreciate the degree to which change has taken place *within* main-order groups. Table 4.5 below presents employment in certain selected trades in Scotland at the level of minimum-list headings. The Table, covering the period 1960–8, is divided into 'expanding' and 'declining' industries.

Table 4.5 shows that there were, indeed, 'growth sectors' in the Scottish economy. The most notable of these are electronics, motor vehicle manufacture, other drink industries (predominantly whisky) and electrical machinery. Yet, the influence of these trades even within their *own* main-order groups was to some extent offset by declining employment in related branches. One or two examples will suffice to illustrate this point. An obvious case has been the 'vehicles' industry. An expansion of some 12,000 in the labour force of motor vehicle manufacture was almost exactly offset by a decline of similar proportions in the employment of those engaged in the production of railway locomotives, track, carriages, etc. Similarly, rapid expansion in certain branches of the food, drink and tobacco industry has to be considered alongside the corresponding declines in such lines as grain milling, bread and flour, and biscuits.

The major effect that these growth sectors could have on the Scottish economy is, therefore, all but lost. Their expansionary influence has to compensate both for declining branches within their own industry as well as for the contraction of wholly unrelated sectors such as shipbuilding and textiles. As stated at the beginning of this chapter, the growth industries have to make good these declines before they can even *start* to make any positive contribution to the overall growth of the Scottish economy. None the less, the progress that has steadily been made at least provides some hope for the future. In a recent submission to the Secretary of State for Economic Affairs,[1] the Scottish Council was able to point out that, in recent years, several of the expanding trades in Scotland had experienced a rate of growth of employment that was substantially greater than their counterparts elsewhere in the U.K. The result was that whereas in 1959, one person in every 16 in Scottish manufacturing had been employed in these expanding industries, by 1966 the ratio had already fallen to only one person in every 8.

[1] Scottish Council (Development and Industry), *Regional Employment Premium: Submission to the First Secretary of State and Secretary of State for Economic Affairs*, May, 1967.

Table 4.5 Main Changes in the Structure of Employment within Selected Industrial Groups, Scotland, 1960–8

Expanding Industries				Declining Industries			
	1960 (000)	1968 (000)	Per cent Increase (+) (per cent)		1960 (000)	1968 (000)	Per cent Decrease (–) (per cent)
Food, Drink and Tobacco:				**Shipbuilding and Marine Engineering:**			
Other Drink Industries	19·1	25·6	+34				
Bacon Curing, Meat and Fish	11·5	14·6	+27	Shipbuilding	46·4	36·9	−21
Tobacco	2·8	3·5	+25	Marine Engineering	22·4	11·1	−50
Total Employment	98·6	104·0	+6	Total Employment	68·8	48·0	−30
Engineering and Electrical Goods:				**Textiles:**			
Radio and Other Electronic Appliances	9·0	25·5	+183	Spinning and Doubling of Cotton, Flax, etc.	11·5	8·8	−24
Electrical Machinery	9·3	11·7	+ 26	Weaving of Cotton, Linen, etc.	7·0	3·9	−44
Industrial Plant and Steel Work	25·5	29·2	+ 15	Jute	18·0	15·1	−16
				Textile Finishing	11·0	7·3	−34
Total Employment	156·4	187·0	+ 20	Total Employment	109·3	93·2	−15
Vehicles:							
Motor Vehicle Manufacture	6·2	18·4	+197				
Total Employme	37·8	38·8	+ 3				

Sources: Department of Employment and Productivity Gazette; Digest of Scottish Statistics.'

To sum up on the evidence so far presented, we have seen that Scotland possesses an unfavourable industrial structure in the sense that the region is still over-committed to traditional industries that are either growing slowly or in decline. Some degree of industrial diversification has taken place in such lines as electronics, motor vehicle manufacture and certain forms of light engineering. Yet, the full impact of these on the economy has so far been tempered by the loss of employment opportunities in the contracting sectors. It is likely, moreover, that this will continue to be the case for some years ahead. In the next section our task will be to determine the extent to which the situation has been affected by foreign firms coming to this country. It may well be that Scotland's future prosperity will, in large part, depend on her ability to attract an increasing number of such firms to the region.

4 When a country is faced with the necessity of bringing about major changes in its industrial structure, as we have seen is clearly the case for Scotland, there are two avenues of approach open to it. It can seek to restore its economy from within, i.e. its indigenous firms can diversify into new and expanding products and markets, or it can seek to attract new industry from outside to give its economy the necessary diversification and dynamic. The first approach draws on native resources of capital, entrepreneurship and initiative; the second relies on importing these factors. In the event, both have been at work in Scotland since the war. It would indeed have been surprising if there had been no indigenous growth and change, and many Scottish firms have shown that they can respond by diversifying into new products and foreign markets, and by entering into licensing agreements with foreign companies seeking outlets in Britain. Nevertheless, the post-war Scottish economy has received a much-needed impetus from the second source, the import of new resources of capital and entrepreneurship, and we concentrate on these in this section.

It is difficult to be precise about the contributions to post war growth in Scotland from indigenous and external sources. As we have seen in previous sections of this chapter, it has, on occasion, proved necessary to distinguish between growth of output and growth of employment. The first post war *Census of Production* was carried out in 1948. By comparing the growth, in gross sales, of manufacturing industry in Scotland between 1948 and the most recent data with the turnover of foreign firms in Scotland shown in Table 4.6, it appears that something like a third of the growth of sales or turnover has come from foreign firms and two thirds from indigenous firms. Between 1958 and 1968, capital investment by manufacturing industry in Scotland, valued at current prices, has averaged around £113 million per annum. The investment by foreign firms in Scotland up to 1966 was £288 million (see Table 4.6) or on average around £14 million a year since the war. Price changes mean that we cannot compare the period 1945 to 1966 directly with the period 1958 to 1968. But as a rough approximation we may say that investment by foreign firms may account for between 12½ and 20 per cent of annual capital expenditure by industry in Scotland. Foreign firms have made a very important contribution to the growth of employment. *Against a background of virtual stagnation in employment, foreign companies have provided over 100,000 new jobs in Scotland since the war* (see Table 4.6). Established industries have made the major contribution to the growth of output and investment, but without the employment generated by incoming firms there would have been a substantial shortfall in the already indifferent performance of Scottish industry.

A whole new dimension has been added to Scotland's post-war development by the success achieved in attracting new investment and new lines of manufacture from the rest of the U.K. and from abroad. The means of attracting this new industrial investment, whether through industrial development certificates, investment grants or the like, are specifically dealt with elsewhere, in Chapter 13. That an increasing volume of new investment has been moving into Scotland from outside the region is well enough known. Such investment, as we shall see, has been concentrated largely in the new, science-based, light-engineering sectors of the economy. It has had, in its own right, certain significant implications for Scotland. In the first place, it has been necessary for different types of skill to be acquired by a labour force accustomed hitherto to working primarily in traditional industries and using traditional methods. In the more modern forms of light-engineering, skilled labour of the 'operator' and 'technician' type is in heavy demand. Second, the degree of foreign investment in these new specialities has raised questions concerning the degree of 'control' exercised from sources outside the economy. With the increase particularly in investment from the U.S., there have been fears of an 'American domination' of Scottish industry. Such fears are generally groundless since, for the future prosperity of the economy, every attempt should be made to encourage rather than discourage the continuation of outside investment.

The volume of such external investment in Scottish

manufacturing is shown in Table 4.6 below by source of origin. The Table relates to the period up to 1966 and shows, besides investment, the output, employment and number of foreign (including English)-controlled firms which actually manufacture in Scotland.

Table 4.6 Foreign Ownership in Scottish Manufacturing, 1966

Source	No. of Firms	Turnover (£m)	Investment (£m)	Employment (000)
North American	85	247	162	61
English	140	219	119	38
European	3	7	7	3
Total, all sources	228	473	288	102

Source: Memorandum Submitted by the Engineering Industry Training Board, Select Committee on Scottish Affairs, Minutes of Evidence, p. 381.

Table 4.6 shows the extent of outside interests in Scottish manufacturing industry. Foreign-controlled firms were responsible in 1966 for no less than 16·5 per cent of total Scottish turnover and for almost 14 per cent of total employment. The investment of these externally based firms tended to be heavily concentrated in light engineering, particularly in such trades as electronics, business machines and computers, vehicle and aero-engine manufacture and the like. They include such familiar names as I.B.M., National Cash Register, Honeywell Controls, and Rolls-Royce.

As can be seen, the most important contribution to Scottish manufacturing in terms of output, employment and investment came from the U.S. Indeed, American influence has been growing steadily over the past few years, there being, by the start of 1969, 89 U.S. companies manufacturing in Scotland. The great bulk of these were located in the Central Belt to take advantage of the external economies obtaining in the area. This growing 'Americanisation' of Scottish industry over the 1960s can be seen clearly from Table 4.7.

Table 4.7 America's Share of Manufacturing in Scotland, 1964–8

Category	1964	1966	1968
Output (£m)	165	247	366
Output per worker (£)	3,200	4,000	5,000
Exports (£m)	75	118	154
Investment (£m)	106	162	232
Employment (000)	52	61	73

Source: Scottish Council (Development and Industry), Scottish Economic Review, September 1969.

As can be seen, the growth of American-owned companies in Scotland has been very rapid. In considering this expansion, it must be remembered, of course, that the number of these U.S. firms operating in Scotland steadily increased. Even so, between 1964–8 alone, the volume of output, exports and investment all more than doubled, while the employment they generated rose by 40 per cent. Table 4.7 shows that exports commonly accounted for around 45 per cent of the total output of these U.S. firms, a considerably higher proportion than in the rest of Scottish manufacturing. By 1968, indeed, the share of *total* Scottish exports accounted for by American companies amounted to over one-quarter. With the emphasis of the U.S. firms firmly on capital intensive industries, it was, perhaps, to be expected that labour productivity should rise faster than in the rest of Scottish manufacturing industry. Between 1964 and 1968, output per man increased by 56 per cent in American-controlled industry as compared to an increase of only 17 per cent in the rest of the manufacturing sector. When to this increase in productivity is added the fact that the American companies also achieved a substantial rise in employment, their full impact can be properly appreciated.

By 1968, American-controlled business accounted for over 10 per cent of total employment in Scottish manufacturing; for 12 per cent of total output; and for an estimated 27 per cent of the country's manufactured exports. Even this understates the full significance of these firms. The type of activity in which they specialised, examined in Table 4.8 below, meant that valuable demands on the rest of the economy were created for materials, engineering skills and the like. Hence, in the longer term, the indirect effect of these firms is likely to be at least as great as their more immediate consequences. Table 4.8 shows those types of manufacture in which the American influence was greatest.

Table 4.8 makes abundantly clear that American investment and expertise is heavily concentrated in the light, science-based type of manufacturing industry. Indeed, several branches of Scottish manufacturing, including automative machinery and electronics, experienced a major stimulus from American drive and initiative. The growth of the latter trade is dealt with in greater detail in the next chapter. Here, it might be noted that these two branches alone accounted in 1968 for 45 per cent of total American investment in Scottish manufacturing, for two-fifths of the output of these U.S. companies, and for one-quarter of the labour force. These two trades have, indeed, formed the

Table 4.8 Output, Exports, Investment and Employment of U.S. Firms by Type of Activity in Scottish Manufacturing, 1968

Type of Activity	Output (£m)	Exports (£m)	Investment (£m)	Employment (000)
Automative Machinery and Accessories	98·6	36·6	65·0	16·4
Office Machinery	54·0	18·9	39·6	9·3
Instruments and Electronics	49·4	36·0	24·0	12·3
Consumer Durables	36·8	21·0	15·5	12·9
Industrial Equipment	22·0	7·6	12·5	5·5
Industrial Supplies and Services	10·1	3·3	9·7	2·6
Chemicals and Pharmaceuticals	8·7	3·7	5·7	1·3
All Other Products[1]	86·1	27·3	59·6	13·0
Total, All Activities	365·7	154·4	231·6	73·3

Source: Scottish Economic Review, 1969.

[1] This category includes food and drink, watches, clocks, construction equipment, etc.

spearhead of a major American contribution to the reorganisation of Scottish industry that has been taking place.

Finally, it should be emphasised again that the discussion so far has failed to do justice to the full significance of the American contribution to Scottish economic development. Not only are the indirect effects of these American manufactures impossible to quantify, but also the data used hitherto in this section relate only to those companies in the *manufacturing* sector that are actually operative in Scotland. This, therefore, takes no account of U.S. firms involved in *other* spheres of the Scottish economy. Most important, it omits American influence in the service sector, in licensing agreements and in the various interlocking interests between companies. Given the expansion over the past years of U.S. interests in Scotland and the fact that several further companies, not only American but also German and Japanese, have expressed an interest in locating here, it is clear that the next few years will witness a rapid extension of foreign participation in the economy.

5 Industrial Structure and Effective Demand

Despite the impact which foreign, and particularly American, firms have had in Scotland since 1945, their contribution has not been such as to offset the influence of declining traditional industries within the economy. It is not, however, sufficient in itself merely to point to the generally unfavourable nature of Scotland's industrial structure. In order to take the analysis a stage further, we shall attempt in this section to assess what effects this structure has had on the level of Scottish economic activity. We can, in this context, introduce a hypothesis recently advanced by Professor A. J. Brown, who has pointed out that the structure of production in a given region constitutes one of the major determinants of the level of income and hence of effective demand in that region. In turn, the volume of demand will dictate the level of economic activity. It follows, therefore, that regional differences in industrial structure are, through their effects on local demand, to a large extent responsible for differences in regional growth rates. For instance, a region with decided structural advantages will, over time, gain in prosperity. As a result, many of its industries, benefitting via higher incomes from an increased local demand for their products, will display higher growth rates than the same industries elsewhere. Once started, such a process can become self-reinforcing, with factors of production such as labour and capital being attracted in from outside the region. This was typical of growth, for instance, in the Midlands and South-East of England.

In testing this hypothesis for Scotland, we should expect to find, of course, almost the converse of the position outlined above. Far from having structural advantages, we have seen that Scotland possesses a distinctly unfavourable industrial structure. This is in spite of the fact that, as we have ascertained, major changes have been taking place over recent years. The characteristics of the structure of Scottish production are:

(*i*) An undue concentration of resources in industries that have ceased to grow, or are growing very slowly.

(*ii*) Until recently, a comparative absence of new growth sectors.

There is no doubt that these two features have reacted unfavourably on the pressure of effective demand generated within the economy. The evidence on which we are able to base this conclusion can most readily be seen in terms of unemployment, industrial earnings and migration.

a) Unemployment Since the interwar period, Scotland has consistently had a rate of unemployment significantly above the national average. From that time, apart from the boom which followed the second world war, the staple industries in the U.K. have had to contend with problems of surplus capacity, the result of contracting markets both at home and abroad. Inevitably, with the Scottish economy more heavily dependent on these staples, it has experienced in more acute form the resultant problems of unemployment and redeployment. This secular trend in unemployment has, of course, been reinforced by the relatively heavy incidence of cyclical unemployment in Scotland. Again, this derives from the region's dependence on the staples, and particularly on heavy industry such as shipbuilding, engineering and iron and steel. *The capital goods industries show a greater instability over the cycle than, for instance, the consumer goods trades.* In consequence, they are prone to experience, to a greater extent, the unemployment created during the down-swing of the cycle.

Thus the higher level of Scottish unemployment can, in part, be attributed to the region's greater commitment to traditional industries. That this is not, however, the only cause is shown by an examination of Table 4.9 below. In Chapter 3, we presented aggregate figures of unemployment for both the regional and national economies. Here, we break down these aggregates to the level of individual industries. The Table illustrates, for each industry, the proportion of the labour-force out of work in 1968 for both Scotland and Great Britain.

Table 4.9 Industrial Analysis of Unemployment, Scotland and Great Britain, 1968

Category	Scotland	Great Britain
Agriculture, Forestry and Fishing	4·3	2·8
Mining and Quarrying	5·0	4·0
Food, Drink and Tobacco	3·1	1·9
Chemicals and Allied Industries	3·5	1·7
Metal Manufacture	3·8	2·1
Engineering and Electrical Goods	2·6	1·5
Shipbuilding and Marine Engineering	4·0	4·5
Vehicles	1·8	1·3
Metal Goods not elsewhere specified	3·6	2·2
Textiles	2·8	1·7
Leather, Leather Goods and Fur	2·7	1·9
Clothing and Footwear	2·5	1·1
Bricks, Pottery, Glass, Cement, etc.	4·2	2·0
Timber, Furniture, etc.	2·8	1·8
Paper, Printing and Publishing	1·5	1·0
Other Manufacturing Industries	4·1	1·8
Total Manufacturing Industry	2·9	1·7
Construction	6·7	5·9
Gas, Electricity and Water	1·5	1·2
Transport and Communication	3·1	2·0
Distributive Trades	3·0	1·9
Insurance, Banking and Finance	1·9	1·4
Professional and Scientific Services	0·6	0·5
Miscellaneous Services	3·6	2·3
Public Administration and Defence	3·4	1·8
Total, All Industries and Services	3·5	2·2

Source: Calculated from Statistics on Incomes, Prices, Employment and Production; Annual Abstract of Statistics; Digest of Scottish Statistics.

Table 4.9 shows the much heavier incidence of unemployment across virtually the whole range of Scottish industry. The construction trade apart, the unemployment percentages tend to be the highest in the traditional industries—agriculture, metal manufacture, mining and shipbuilding. The last two industries are instances of declining sectors to which Scotland is more heavily committed than other regions of Britain. Agriculture and metal manufacture fall into an entirely different category. In both employment fell, but not output. This places in perspective one of Scotland's fundamental problems. It was pointed out in Chapter 3 that a major weakness of the Scottish economy was the failure to achieve any expansion in job opportunities over the 1960s. This was due not only to the influence of the declining industries but of those that released labour whilst expanding output. In the context of the Scottish economy as a whole, it is much easier as Dr McCrone has pointed out, 'to achieve a satisfactory growth of output . . . than to get an adequate growth of employment.'[1]

The higher level of unemployment in Scotland cannot, however, wholly be attributed to an unfavourable structure of production. In addition to structural deficiencies, Scotland also experienced an unfavourable 'mix' of industries. In Table 4.1 of this chapter we showed that there were substantial differences in the employment structure of the Scottish and U.K. economies, the the former having a much heavier concentration of labour in the staple trades. It follows, therefore, that even if the unemployment rates, industry by industry, were the same in the two economies, Scotland would still have a higher *total* rate of unemployment. This derives from the fact that the region has a greater proportion of labour devoted to industries that have, in both a regional and national context, a relatively high percentage rate of unemployment. Examples such as coal mining, shipbuilding and agriculture spring readily to mind. In this case, then, it is the unfavourable industrial 'mix' that has contributed to the higher general rate of unemployment in Scotland.

The Scottish unemployment problem, created by an adverse structure of production, is compounded, therefore, by an unsatisfactory mix of industries. The effect of this relatively high unemployment across the whole range of Scottish industry is to reduce purchasing power in the economy and thereby to depress the level of effective demand.

[1] G. McCrone, *Scotland's Future*, p. 30.

b) Industrial Earnings The higher proportion of the labour force out of work in Scotland is not, of course, the only influence on the pressure of demand generated within the region. Even for those *in employment*, the level of industrial earnings, although growing recently at a more rapid rate, has remained consistently lower than in Great Britain. We saw this at a more aggregative level in Chapter 3. In Table 4.10 below the earnings of male manual workers are given for selected industries in Scotland and Great Britain.

Table 4.10 Average Weekly Earnings of Male Manual Workers in Selected Industries, Scotland and Great Britain, 1968[1]

Category	Scotland Average Weekly Earings		Scotland Percentage Growth of Earnings 1960–8	Great Britain Average Weekly Earnings		Great Britain Percentage Growth of Earnings 1960–8
Traditional Industries:	s.	d.	per cent	s.	d.	per cent
Iron and Steel	497	9	67	501	2	51
Iron Castings, etc.	454	11	75	467	6	59
Shipbuilding	502	8	85	485	5	73
Marine Engineering	459	3	67	453	0	63
Woollen and Worsted	382	9	65	407	10	59
Jute	379	1	64	379	2	64
Hosiery and Other Knitted Goods	404	11	65	472	10	59
Growth Industries:						
Chemicals and Dyes	476	10	75	484	8	65
Office Machinery	499	6	65	455	2	54
Electrical Machinery	458	2	66	452	3	54
Radio and other Electronic Apparatus	519	11	63	443	11	60
Motor Vehicle Manufacturing	465	4	65	546	5	44
All Manufacturing Industries including the above	458	11	70	472	4	59

Sources: Statistics on Incomes, Prices, Employment and Production, June, 1969; Digest of Scottish Statistics.
[1] Figures relate to October 1968.

Certain conclusions are inescapable from Table 4.10. Most apparent is that, with the exception of shipbuilding, the level of earnings in the traditional industries in Scotland is significantly lower than in the 'growth' industries. Moreover, apart from shipbuilding, earnings in Scotland's traditional trades are relatively lower than in their counterparts in the national economy. Clearly, the experience of the shipbuilding industry in Scotland runs contrary to the general trend. This is explicable in terms of the special forces at work within the industry on the Clyde which have succeeded in raising the level of earnings to a relatively high level. Not least of these has been the achievement of particular unions within the industry in raising the money wages of their members.

The generally lower level of earnings in the traditional industries is entirely consistent with the theory of economic development. Since the interwar years, these trades have, for the most part, experienced a relatively slow rate of growth of output. They have been concerned with problems of rationalisation and with releasing factors of production rather than with attracting them by means of high factor payments. The reverse is true of the expanding industries which, in trying to win away factors of production from other sectors of the economy, have to offer an attractive return to these factors. In such industries, therefore, earnings have to be relatively high in an attempt to attract the particular types of skilled and semi-skilled labour that are required.[1] After all, labour has commonly to be secured not only from other industrial sectors but also from other regions. There is little prospect of obtaining the necessary mobility unless the returns to labour are relatively high.

It was observed in Chapter 3 that a significant feature of the Scottish economy was that the level of industrial earnings had been growing at a faster rate than in Great Britain as a whole. This is confirmed by Table 4.10 which shows that this trend can readily be distinguished in both the old and new industries. As a result, the differential in earnings between the two economies has been steadily narrowing. None the less the fact remains, of course, that the general level of earnings in Scotland has always been consistently lower than in Great Britain. *The main responsibility for this must rest with the greater preponderance of the staple industries and, until recently, the lack of diversification in the Scottish economy*. We have seen from Table 4.10 that earnings in the staple industries tend to be relatively low. The emphasis on these trades in Scotland has resulted, therefore, in a lower level of purchasing power, and hence of effective demand, in the region. In this way, the structure of production has again a direct influence on the rate of growth achieved in Scotland.

c) Migration As we saw in Chapter 3, one of the most significant features of Scotland's economic development during the 20th century has been the net loss of population experienced

[1] See Scottish Office, *Scottish Economic Bulletin*, No. 9, 1971.

through migration. Although always serious, the dimensions of this problem have steadily increased since the second world war. By the 1960s, two features of Scotland's migration were particularly important in terms of future economic development. First, the heaviest losses were concentrated within the working age-limits; the types of skill consequently lost to the economy are examined in Chapter 10. Second, the scale of the net outflow was such that it offset the whole of the natural increase in population during the decade. Inevitably, this heavy rate of net migration from the region meant a loss of aggregate demand. In other words, some degree of purchasing power was lost to the economy with obvious implications for the level of effective demand.

There is no comprehensive statistical coverage of population movements between Scotland and overseas countries. As a result, we confine ourselves here to the population flows between Scotland and the rest of Britain. Even with the survey restricted in this way, however, it is clear that the heavy loss of population from Scotland has been due, in part, to the structure of production in the region. The decline of coal mining and the relatively slow expansion of other traditional sectors have had a significant influence on trends in migration. Over recent years, however, it has by no means been only those in the staple industries who have moved out of Scotland. The higher level of earnings in certain of the expanding industries south of the border has undoubtedly exerted a strong 'pull' on Scottish labour. As can be seen from Table 4.10, the level of earnings in the British vehicles industry and in chemicals looks most attractive when compared with that in Scotland.[1] In addition to the heavy loss of labour, therefore, from such industries as coal mining, metal manufacture and textiles, there has also been in recent years a high rate of net migration from vehicles, chemicals and the food trades.

The latest sample *Census of Population* in 1966 presents information, industry by industry, of those migrants within the working age group who moved between Scotland and England and Wales. From this information, we can distinguish for the period 1961–6 those manufacturing industries in Scotland which have experienced the heaviest net outflow of labour. They are shown separately in Table 4.11 below, with similar details being provided for the primary and service sectors of the economy.

[1] Recently, of course, attempts have been made in motor vehicle production to narrow the differential in earnings between Scotland and England. The Chrysler pay award at Linwood of an average 18 per cent increase in January 1971 can be seen as a step in this direction.

Table 4.11 Industrial Analysis of Migration between Scotland and England and Wales, 1961–6

Category	Net Migration from Scotland	As per cent of Total Net Migration
Traditional Industries:		
Mining and Quarrying	2,650	5·4
Metal Manufacture	2,270	4·6
Metal Goods not elsewhere specified	1,230	2·5
Textiles	1,200	2·4
Expanding Industries:		
Engineering and Electrical goods	4,470	9·1
Food, Drink and Tobacco	1,660	3·4
Chemicals and Allied Trades	1,330	2·7
Vehicles	1,550	3·2
All Other Manufacturing Industry	3,690	7·5
Agriculture, Forestry and Fishing	220	0·4
Construction	4,330	8·8
Services	24,470	49·9
Total, All Industries and Services	49,070	100·0

Source: Calculated from the Sample Census of Population, 1966.

Table 4.11 shows that over the period 1961–6, one-half of the net migration of those within the working age-group occurred from the service sector of the economy. The remaining 50 per cent of migrants came from both the traditional and expanding industries alike. As might be expected, the net outflow was particularly high from coal-mining which has experienced severe contraction in recent years. Amongst the 'expanding' industries, the loss was highest in the category 'engineering and electrical goods', although it should be remembered that this is a main-order heading composed of very different types of activity. It includes a heavy engineering sector[1] which should more properly be regarded as a traditional industry. It is clear, none the less, that migration has served as something of an 'escape-hatch' for labour in both the traditional and 'expanding' industries of Scotland. It is likely that both push and pull factors have been at work. Scotland's emphasis on the staple industries has operated by 'pushing' surplus labour in these trades to possibly richer pastures elsewhere. At the same time, the high level of industrial earnings south of the border, particularly in certain of the newer trades, has been sufficient to 'pull' labour out of even the expanding industries in Scotland.

Whatever the reason for people leaving, the end-result

[1] In the recently revised Standard Industrial Classification, this sector has been isolated and constitutes a main-order heading in its own right.

has been much the same for the Scottish economy. The scale on which the drain of population has been taking place has meant a fall in the level of aggregate demand. The resultant loss of purchasing power has undoubtedly been a major element in Scotland's relatively slow growth-rate over the years.

The conclusion which we can draw from this section is that there exists no single explanation of Scotland's economic problems. None the less, it is clear that the structure of Scottish production has had an important bearing on the relatively poor economic performance of the region since the second world war. We have seen that economic structure played some part in determining the size and composition of each of the three variables—unemployment, industrial earnings and migration. Each of these, in turn, has contributed to a lower level of effective demand in Scotland. The result has been a relatively sluggish rate of growth in the economy, which has compared unfavourably with that obtaining south of the border.

Conclusion

The major conclusion to emerge from this Chapter is that the unfavourable structure of Scottish production which first became apparent during the interwar period still persists today. This has been one of the major determinants of the relatively slow rate of growth of the regional economy. Since the Second World War, the Government's regional policy has been primarily responsible for the more vigorous efforts to diversify Scottish industry. Implicit in the measures applied to the regions has been the aim of lowering unemployment and raising *per capita* income to a level closer to the national average. Judged according to these criteria, the extent to which progress has been made in Scotland has proved disappointing.

Capital and enterprise have been attracted from sources outwith the economy, particularly from America. Certain new industries with a high growth potential, like electronics and motor vehicles, have been introduced. On balance, however, these have not been sufficient to counteract the effects of the declining staple industries, especially in terms of employment. In the next chapter, we examine the role of the expanding, *vis-á-vis* the declining, sectors of the economy in greater depth. Certain of the industries that we have identified as being significant to the Scottish economy have been selected to provide a cross-section of industrial experience since the war. In this way we can appreciate more fully the performance and problems of Scottish industry.

Appendix

To obtain the location quotients of individual industries the following method was adopted:

As a first step, the different industries in the economy were divided into four major sub-divisions, primary, manufacturing, construction and service. The location quotient for a particular industry may then be taken as:

(a) *Numerator:* Scotland's percentage share of total employment in that industry.

(b) *Denominator:* Scotland's percentage share of total U.K. employment in primary/manufacturing/construction/service industry.

By dividing the numerator by the denominator, the location quotient was obtained. Where the value of the quotient was less than 1, Scotland had less than a proportionate share of a given industry. Where the quotient was greater than 1, Scotland had a more than proportionate share.

References

Board of Trade, *Report on the Census of Production 1963.*

Central Statistical Office, *Annual Abstract of Statistics.*

Scottish Statistical Office, *Digest of Scottish Statistics.*

Scottish Office, *Scottish Economic Bulletin.*

Department of Employment, *Employment and Productivity Gazette.*
Statistics on Incomes, Prices, Employment and Production.

Scottish Council (Development and Industry), *Scottish Economic Review.*
The Select Committee on Scottish Affairs, 1969–70, 267, H.M.S.O., 1970.

The Glasgow Herald Trade Review, annually.

A. J. Brown, 'Regional Problems and Regional Policy', *National Institute Economic Review*, No. 46, November 1968.
'Some English Thoughts on the Scottish Economy', *Scottish Journal of Political Economy*, Vol. 15, June 1968.

D. I. Mackay, 'Industrial Structure and Regional Growth: A Methodological Problem', *Scottish Journal of Political Economy*, Vol. 15, June 1968.

G. McCrone, *Scotland's Economic Progress, 1951–1960.*
Scotland's Future: The Economics of Nationalism.
Regional Policy in Britain.

C. E. V. Leser, 'Some Aspects of the Industrial Structure of Scotland', *University of Glasgow, Department of Social and Economic Research, Occasional Papers*, V, 1951.

A. Reid, 'Industrial Investment in Scotland', *Scotland Magazine*, August 1970.

The Economist, 'Scotland: A Sense of Change', 21st–28th February 1970.

Investors Chronicle and Stock Exchange Gazette Survey, 'Scotland', 8th May 1970.

G. C. Cameron and G. C. Reid, 'Scottish Economic Planning and the Attraction of Industry', *University of Glasgow, Social and Economic Studies*, Occasional Papers, No. 6, 1966.

Chapter 5 Industrial Case Studies

Our analysis of the structure of production in the last Chapter was no doubt somewhat clinical, and statistical analysis does not always catch the spirit and the bustle of industry when it is taking its pulse and temperature. It is entirely appropriate, therefore, for us to approach industrial structure from another standpoint, and take a more organic and descriptive view of particular industries in Scotland. In this Chapter we propose to give the reader the feeling of the state of Scottish industry by taking up five industries for further consideration. Obviously, we can only highlight the main features of each one, and we do not pretend to be analysing them in depth. We have selected a mixed bag of staple and new industries, and we do this with a view to enabling the reader to grasp how the fortunes of well-established industries can vary, and how even the newer industries have their problems as well as their considerable achievements.

The industries selected are agriculture, coal-mining, shipbuilding, electronics, and vehicles. These 'case studies' have been chosen as a way of illustrating in a very concrete manner both the problems and the achievements of Scottish industry since the second World War.

The problems have by no means been confined to the traditional sectors of the economy, although it is in them that they have been most keenly felt. Several of the traditional industries—coal, shipbuilding, textiles—have experienced similar difficulties of declining markets, falling output, and surplus capacity. Yet it is important to note that this has not been the experience of all the staple trades. One of the reasons why we have selected agriculture for examination here is that it, like the metal industries, has had a contracting labour force while output and efficiency have increased. We bring out the conflicting fortunes of the various staple trades by examining in turn agriculture, coal-mining, and shipbuilding.

Much of the achievement of Scotland's post-war development has been concentrated in the new growth sectors of the economy, and we take electronics and vehicles as examples. This diversification has involved problems as well as accomplishment. Both electronics and vehicles exemplify the delights, and also the growing pains, of new industries drawn into Scotland by the various incentives deployed in the cause of regional development.

1 Agriculture

The structure of Scottish farming consists basically of a large number of predominantly small holdings engaged in mixed farming. There were, for example, some 55,000 farming units distinguished for Scotland in 1968 and, although a greater specialisation has been developing over the recent past, the great bulk of these still practise a mixed type of farming within which animal production predominates. It should be noted, however, that of the total farming units distinguished, just over 22,000, or 40 per cent, were classified as being 'full-time'.[1] The rest, representing in numerical terms the bulk of Scottish holdings were either 'part-' or 'spare-time' units. Since the great majority of these are extremely small, it is the 'full-time' farms which dominate the acreage of crops and fallow land in Scotland. In 1968, for instance, almost 94 per cent of the crop and fallow acreage was owned by these 'full-time' units.

The size-structure of Scottish farms is broadly similar to that in the U.K. as a whole. Yet, Scotland has, at one and the same time, a higher proportion both of large and very small farms than the U.K. In other words, the distribution of farms in the U.K. was more tightly packed around the mean. A comparative survey, conducted for 1965, will help to clarify the position. Table 5.1 below compares the size-structure of Scottish and U.K. farms for that year.

As can be seen in Table 5.1, large farms are more prominent in Scotland in that they comprise 12 per cent of total holdings in the country and contribute 53 per cent to total output as measured by standard man-days. In the U.K., the corresponding proportions are 10 per cent and 47 per cent respectively. On the other hand, well over one-half of Scottish farms consist of

[1] Holdings are classified into 'full', 'part' and 'spare' time by applying standard man-day factors to every item of cropping and stocking. Hence 'full-time' are those having 250 man-days or more; 'part time' are those having between 100 and 250 man-days; and 'spare time' as those having under 100 man-days.

Table 5.1 Distribution of Holdings and Standard Man-Days[1] Among Size Groups, Scotland and the U.K., 1965

Size Group (Standard Man-Days)		No. of Holdings	As per cent of all Holdings	As per cent of Total Standard Man-Days
Scotland				
Over 1,200	Large	7,100	12	53
600–1,199	Medium	8,800	16	27
275–599	Small	8,700	15	13
Under 275	Very Small	32,200	57	7
Total		56,800	100	100
U.K.				
Over 1,200	Large	41,900	10	47
600–1,199	Medium	66,600	16	26
275–599	Small	96,400	24	19
Under 275	Very Small	201,400	50	8
Total		406,300	100	100

Source: Ministry of Agriculture, Fisheries and Food and Department of Agriculture and Fisheries for Scotland, The Structure of Agriculture, H.M.S.O., 1966.

[1] Standard labour requirements are the annual requirements of manual labour needed on average for the production of crops and livestock, and for maintenance purposes. These requirements are expressed in terms of 'standard man-days' per acre of crops or per head of livestock. Each standard man-day represents 8 hours manual work per adult male worker. The equivalent of one year's work for one man is taken to be 275 standard man-days.

very small units although it should be remembered that a high proportion of these consist simply of Highland crofts.[1] Scotland is in no sense unique in possessing such a large percentage of very small units. As can be seen from Table 5.1 a somewhat similar proportion exists for the U.K. as a whole, and indeed in most European countries. Where Scotland can be distinguished from other regions is in the relatively high proportion of rough grazing, mountain and hill land that exists in the country. Out of almost 16·5 million acres of land in agricultural use in 1968, no less than 12·2 million, or three-quarters, comprised rough grazing land. This type of land, suitable for the most part only for extensive farming, (that is, for the grazing of sheep and cattle) occurs in

[1] Of the 32,200 'very small' holdings in Scotland in 1965, crofts accounted for 45 per cent.

every Scottish county. On the other hand, in the U.K. as a whole, rough grazing constituted little over one-third of the land in use in 1968.

To a large extent, it is this high proportion of rough grazing and hill land that explains why Scottish agriculture receives a proportionately greater volume of agricultural support from the State than that in the U.K. The cost of support from the Central Exchequer to Scottish Agriculture, in the form of price subsidies, production, and improvement grants has risen from £41 million in 1960/61 to almost £50 million in 1968/9. Subsidies in the U.K. on the other hand, amounted to some £240 million at the start of the 1960s and have fluctuated widely over the decade. By 1968 total U.K. subsidies had reached almost £260 million. Consequently, Scotland's share of total agricultural subsidies within the U.K. amounted at the end of the 1960s to roughly 20 per cent. This represented a figure considerably in excess of her share of the value of U.K. agricultural output; in 1968 this was put at only 11 per cent.

The relatively large share of agricultural support received in Scotland in no way implies that the technique and practice of farming are inefficient in the region. Indeed, as we shall see below, the reverse is the case; whether measured in terms of output per man, or yield per acre, most branches of Scottish agriculture are highly efficient. Productivity in farming as a whole, as measured by output per man, was considerably higher than in Germany, France or Italy during the 1960s.[1] At the present time, the industry in Scotland can be depicted as a highly capitalised and efficient sector.

Agricultural efficiency has, in fact, been significantly increased over time, not only in Scotland but in the U.K. as a whole. This can be readily demonstrated. The secular trend in output has been upwards, with the value of Scottish output, as measured in real terms, rising by over one-fifth between 1957/8–1967/8. This increase in output has been achieved at a time when the labour force in agriculture has been falling both in absolute and relative terms. Chart 4 below presents indices both of Scottish and U.K. agricultural production and labour employed for the period 1959/60–1967/8.

The chart illustrates the widely divergent trends of output and employment in agriculture for both Scotland and the U.K. In both economies, as the real value of output rose over the 1960s so the volume of employment declined steeply. The

[1] G. McCrone, *Scotland's Future*, p. 24.

Chart 4

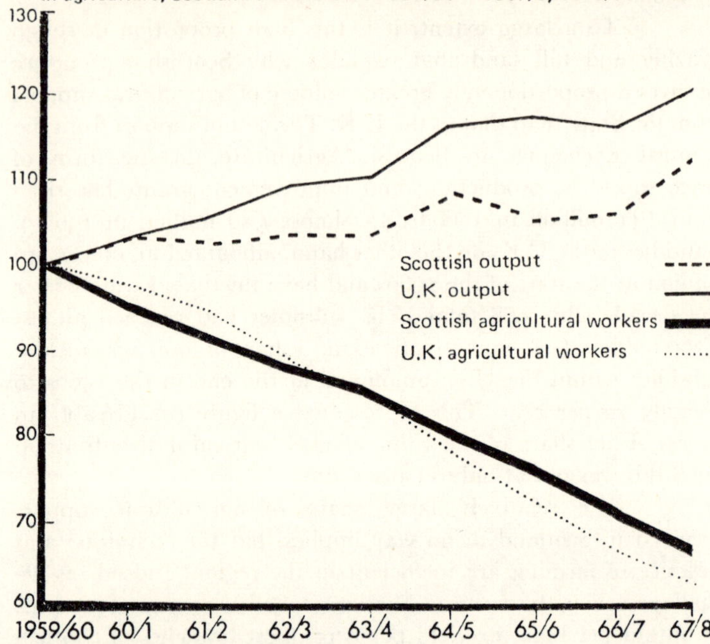

note: The employment figures are obtained from Agricultural Statistics, 1968. They exclude the farmer and wife and are at a level lower than that estimated by the Department of Employment and Productivity.

sources: Digest of Scottish Statistics;
Annual Abstract of Statistics;
Agricultural Statistics, 1968, Scotland;

result was, as we have seen in an earlier section of this chapter, that agriculture's share of the total working force in Scotland fell steadily to reach a mere 3 per cent by 1968. The outcome of these output and employment trends has been a substantial increase in the value of output per man employed in Scottish agriculture. Indeed, in both Scotland and the U.K., the value of *per capita* output rose by some four-fifths over the single decade of the 1960s.

Global figures of output give no indication, of course, of the *composition* of agricultural production in Scotland. The farming sector produces by no means a homogeneous product so that it is virtually impossible to arrive at a figure for the total *volume* of output. The problems of aggregating the tonnage of crops with products such as milk, butter, eggs, meat, etc. are insoluble. Therefore, in order to assess and compare the contribution that each branch of agriculture makes to total output, it is necessary to place a monetary value on the different types of production. In Table 5.2 below, a first step is taken by comparing the value of output in each of the main branches of agriculture in Scotland and the U.K. The Table covers selected years during the period 1959/60–1968/9.

Table 5.2 Value of Output at Current Prices in the Main Sectors of Agriculture, Scotland and the U.K., Selected Years, 1959/60–1968/9

Scotland (£m)

Year	Crops[1]	Livestock[2]	Livestock[3] Products	Total[4]
1959/60	42·5 (24)*	63·9 (37)	62·9 (36)	174
1962/63	52·1 (28)	78·0 (41)	63·1 (33)	189
1965/66	40·1 (21)	86·0 (44)	65·9 (34)	196
1968/69	44·5 (20)	99·2 (45)	71·6 (32)	223

* Figures in brackets show the proportion that each component represents of total output.

U.K. (£m)

Year	Crops[1]	Livestock[2]	Livestock[3] Products	Total[4]
1959/60	410·0 (27)	431·7 (29)	593·5 (40)	1,496
1962/63	500·4 (30)	516·4 (31)	625·5 (38)	1,663
1965/66	536·4 (29)	566·7 (31)	694·9 (38)	1,826
1968/69	555·6 (28)	625·8 (32)	759·2 (38)	1,983

Sources: Agricultural Statistics, 1968; Annual Abstract of Statistics; Digest of Scottish Statistics.

[1] Crops = Cereals, Potatoes, Fruit and Vegetables, Other. It should be noted, of course, that a proportion of this output comes back to farms in the form of feed.

[2] Livestock = Cattle, Sheep, Pigs.

[3] Livestock Products = Milk, Eggs, Other. Certain of the components differ slightly between Scotland and the U.K. in the scope of their coverage (e.g. Eggs, Other). The difference does not, however, materially affect the conclusions reached.

[4] The figures for Crops, Livestock, etc. do not sum to the Total since the latter also includes sundry output and the value of physical changes in growing crops and livestock.

Scotland contributed an average of 11 per cent to total U.K. agricultural production over the 1960s. In 1968, her share of U.K. livestock output was, however, significantly greater than this, amounting to some 16 per cent, whilst the value of Scottish crops and livestock products amounted respectively to 9 and 8 per cent of the national totals. It can be seen from Table 5.2 that livestock was clearly the most important branch of Scottish agriculture, contributing generally over 40 per cent of

Scotland's total output in the 1960s. Over this same period, livestock products comprised roughly one-third of total output, while the value of crops has tended to fall from about one-quarter at the start of the 1960s to approximately one-fifth by the end of the decade. Hence, livestock and livestock products between them account for no less than three-quarters of the value of total gross farm output in Scotland.

This structure of output in Scotland differs significantly from that of the U.K. as a whole. In the U.K., livestock products constitute the most important single sector whilst crop values have been better maintained, forming in common with livestock just under one-third of total output.

In Table 5.3, the output of Scottish agriculture is disaggregated still further to show both the major crops and types of livestock produced. The relationship of these to U.K. totals is again included.

Table 5.3 (a) Principal Crops and Yield Per Acre in Scotland, 1964/8 (annual average)

Crop	Annual Average Output (000 tons)	As per cent of U.K.	Yield Per Acre (cwts.) Scotland	U.K.
Wheat	147·0	4·0	34·8	31·7
Barley	925·4	11·2	30·2	29·0
Oats	462·6	37·3	22·5	24·9
Turnips and Swedes	3,654·6	60·4	21·1 (tons)	19·6 (tons)
Potatoes	1,210·0	17·4	9·2 (tons)	9·7 (tons)

(b) Numbers of Livestock, Scotland and the U.K., 1959–68 (million)

Region	Cattle 1959	Cattle 1968	Sheep 1959	Sheep 1968	Pigs 1959	Pigs 1968
Scotland	1·9	2·1	8·4	7·8	0·4	0·6
U.K.	11·3	12·2	27·6	28·0	6·0	7·4
Scotland as per cent of U.K.	16·8	17·2	30·4	27·9	6·7	8·1

Source: Agricultural Statistics, 1968.

Table 5.3 allows an examination at some greater depth of the composition of Scottish agricultural output. One feature that is not, however, revealed by the Table is that, when all is said and done, the principal crop in Scotland is simply grass. This is natural enough within a mixed farming system where animal production is predominant. *Excluding* rough grazing land, there was, in 1968, some 4·3 million acres of land in agricultural use in Scotland. Of this, 2·8 million acres, or almost two-thirds, were in grass.[1] Of the crops which alternate with grass, barley is now by far the most important in volume terms. This has not always been the case; during and before the 1950s oats comprised Scotland's major cereal crop. Whilst the production of oats has, however, declined continuously from 1950, that of barley has risen correspondingly, so that by 1968 the region was producing over one million tons of the crop.

The principal root crop in Scotland is turnips and swedes, grown primarily as winter fodder for cattle and sheep. Table 5.3 shows that an average of almost two-thirds of total U.K. production was grown in Scotland in the period 1964/8. This is a long way ahead of the next most valuable root, potatoes, which in the same period accounted on average for less than one-fifth of the U.K. total. Whilst these root crops are important to Scotland, it is none the less, on livestock that the reputation of Scottish farming has been based. In breeding, particularly of cattle, Scotland can point to a record of success that is without equal throughout the world. The country is justly famous for such beef-breeds as the Aberdeen-Angus and the Beef Shorthorn, whilst in the context of dairy cattle, the Ayrshire enjoys an equally impressive reputation. As Table 5.3 shows, the total number of cattle has been increasing in Scotland between 1959–68. It is important to note, however, that this is due to the expansion of beef rather than of dairy herds. In 1950 for instance, the number of each type stood at roughly the same level of some 800,000. By 1968, however, the number of beef cattle had risen to almost 1·4 million, whereas the total of dairy cattle had fallen to about 680,000.

The continued prosperity of cattle and sheep farming is of vital importance to Scottish agriculture. As observed, total livestock together with livestock products, presently account for three-quarters of the value of gross farm output in Scotland. Indeed, cattle and milk alone account for nearly one-half. Whether this type of structure can be maintained in view of the proposals recently outlined in the Government's agricultural policy remains to be seen. The Government's objective is to adapt the present system of agricultural support to one relying increasingly on import levy arrangements under which the farmer would get his return from the market.[2] Interim levy schemes on

[1] This total acreage in grass in 1968 was composed of 1·1 million acres in the form of permanent grass and 1·7 million acres in the form of rotation grass—that is, grass crops which alternate with cereals in the rotational system employed by Scottish farming.

[2] *Annual Review and Determination of Guarantees 1971*, Cmnd. 4623, 1971.

certain livestock products and modifications to the existing scheme for cereals have already been proposed. It is expected that full details of such measures will be announced in the near future. The purpose of these interim schemes is to maintain existing high price-levels and so reduce the cost of deficiency payments to the Exchequer. It has been pointed out, of course, that should our application to join the European Economic Community be successful, Britain would adopt the Community's agricultural policy and methods of support.[1]

Finally, the experience of agriculture demonstrates clearly that employment statistics, if used alone, can on occasion give rise to a misleading impression of the level of activity in a particular sector. In certain respects, agriculture, in common with other staple trades has experienced a notable contraction over the past few decades. Employment has fallen substantially: yet, output has continued to expand. Certain specialisms have experienced secular decline—such as the production of oats, and the rearing of sheep and dairy cattle. Others, however, have achieved a notable expansion. A record output of barley was obtained in 1967/8; the numbers of beef cattle continue to increase; and so, too, on a smaller scale, do the numbers of pigs. Hence, far from depression and decline, Scottish farming is on the whole extremely healthy and, relative to several of its European counterparts, most efficient. It is an industry which can be justly proud of the large increases in output per man that it has managed to achieve since the war.

2 Coal Mining

The problems which the modern environment has created for Scotland's staple industries are most clearly illustrated in coal mining. This is a typical example of a high-cost industry which has steadily been losing ground. Since the interwar period, coal has been faced with a constantly diminishing market, the result chiefly of the emergence of cheaper and more efficient substitutes. The availability of oil, electricity, gas and more recently of natural gas has steadily eroded coal's previously held monopoly as a source of fuel and power. The extent of the decline in coal-use in the U.K. is illustrated in Table 5.4. The Table shows total inland energy consumption for the period 1960–9. Faced with these market forces, the number of active pits has fallen rapidly, not only in Scotland but throughout the U.K. Along with this reduction in productive units, both the volume of output and the

[1] *Ibid.*

employment offered by the industry have also followed a downward trend. At the same time, however, production costs in mining have tended to rise. Most of the more easily accessible seams have been exploited some time ago, so that coal has had to be mined at an increasingly greater depth and from increasingly difficult seams.

Table 5.4 Total Inland Energy Consumption in the U.K. (Million Therms)

	Coal, Coke and Other Solid Fuel	Coke Oven and Town Gas	Natural Gas	Electricity	Petroleum	Other
	31,137	3,187	—	3,372	12,385	448
	19,292	4,988	416	6,238	25,628	189
nt change						
69	−38·0	+56·5	—	+85·0	+106·9	−57·8

e: Annual Abstract of Statistics.

Table 5.4 shows that at a time when the direct use of coal and other solid fuel has declined by well over one-third, the consumption of alternative sources of energy has risen substantially. The largest increases over the 1960s have been recorded in the use of petroleum and electricity.

The result has been that for many years past the Scottish coal industry has fought a losing battle with costs. Indeed, in every year since 1950, coal mining in Scotland has made a loss after the payment of interest on capital has been taken into account. In face of these conditions both on the demand and supply side, several different types of remedy have been tried in an effort to revitalise the industry. Of these, the most important was, of course, the complete reorganisation of the industry consequent upon the nationalisation of the mines in 1946. Under the National Coal Board, a programme of rationalisation has been implemented in an attempt to adapt the industry to the post-war environment. Surplus capacity resulting from a decline in demand has been steadily eliminated as shown below in Table 5.5 for the period 1958–1967/8.

Table 5.5 shows the rapidity with which output and employment in the coal industry have declined both in Scotland and Great Britain. Yet, of the two regions, the decline in capacity has been much more significant north of the border. Over the decade 1958–1967/8, the number of mines in operation has fallen by no less than three-quarters in Scotland, as opposed to just over one-half in Britain as a whole. Moreover, Scottish output fell by one-quarter and the labour force by more than one-half. The

Table 5.5 Number of Active Pits, Output and Employment in Scottish and U.K. Coal Mining,[1] 1958–1967/8

Country	1958	1967/8
Scotland:		
Number of Pits	166	47[2]
Saleable Output (ml tons)	19·1	13·7
Wage Earners (000)	82·9	38·9
Great Britain:		
Number of Pits	825	376[2]
Saleable Output (ml tons)	198·8	162·7
Wage Earners (000)	681·1	387·2
Per cent Output Scotland/Gt. Britain	9·6	8·4
Per cent Employment Scotland/Gt. Britain	12·2	10·0

Sources: National Coal Board, Report and Accounts for 1958 and 1967/8.
[1] National Coal Board mines only.
[2] Refers to 1968.

respective proportions in Britain were one-fifth and two-fifths. This more rapid elimination of excess capacity in Scotland has meant that by 1967/8, the region's share of total coal output had fallen to 8 per cent while employment had declined to 10 per cent.

The attempts made to secure a viable coal industry in Scotland have not, however, stopped at the mere rationalisation of the industry. At the same time as surplus capacity was being sheared off, the N.C.B. introduced changes in its pricing policy in an attempt to discriminate in favour of Scottish coal mining. The first such change, implemented in 1962, was initially intended only as a temporary measure. In that year, instead of fixing the pit-head prices of coal at a level common to all coal-producing areas of Great Britain, a special selective regional surcharge was placed on the coal produced by Scottish mines. Given the high price-elasticity of demand for most grades of Scottish coal, this attempt to secure a greater revenue for Scotland's coal industry was to have disastrous longer-term consequences. In the short-term the policy served reasonably well and, far from being a 'temporary expedient', was indeed reinforced by a second special levy in 1966. Later, however, it became clear that these measures had simply precipitated the flight from the consumption of coal in Scotland. Domestic consumers moved all the more rapidly towards alternative forms of fuel, such as gas and electricity, whilst coal-using industries also looked to available substitutes. The gas industry, for instance, accelerated its plans to use oil distillates and electricity has attempted to obtain official sanction to convert increasingly more of its power-stations to oil.

In a further effort to support an ailing industry,

Scottish coal mining has been harnessed firmly to the generation of electricity. Indeed, it has become something of a millstone round the neck of the latter industry, impeding the movement of the power-stations towards greater efficiency. *This has resulted from the fact that, as part of a comprehensive fuel policy, the electricity industry has been forced to consume large amounts of coal, and this in a region where coal is, of course, at its most expensive.* The coal industry is therefore assured of a major market for its product at a time when it would otherwise experience extreme difficulty in securing necessary outlets. The extent to which coal is dependent upon the electricity industry is shown in Table 5.6 below which shows the distribution of coal output for 1969.

Table 5.6 Distribution of Saleable Output of Coal in Scotland, 1969 (000 tons)

Category of Consumer	Tons (000)
Inland Consumption:	
Public Utility Undertakings:	
Electricity	6,219
Gas	640
Railways	12
Total	6,871
Coke Ovens	1,866
Industrial Consumers	1,755
Domestic Consumers	2,153
Collieries and Miscellaneous	951
All Domestic Consumers	13,596
Exports:	
To Rest of U.K.	1,542
To Overseas	15
All Exports	1,557
Total Disposals (Inland Consumption and Exports)	15,153

Source: Digest of Scottish Statistics.

It can be seen from Table 5.6 that of the total inland consumption of coal of some 13·6 million tons in 1969, no less than 46 per cent was absorbed by the electricity industry. When to this is added the consumption of the coke ovens in the iron works, almost 60 per cent of the coal sold in the domestic economy was accounted for by these two outlets. With exports both to the U.K. and overseas comprising only 10 per cent of saleable output, it is clear that the coal industry in Scotland is virtually at the mercy of the electricity and iron and steel industries. The very survival of Scottish coal mining depends on their continued consumption of coal. There can be no doubt, however, that in the present age, coal as the staple of the electricity power stations is something of an anachronism. Better and cheaper substitutes exist, so that the insistence on coal as an input has operated only to the detriment of modern and efficient practice in electricity generation. An immediate improvement in efficiency in the generation of electricity could be achieved by allowing the appropriate fuels, particularly oil, to be used.

The irony of the present situation is that despite rationalisation, a pricing policy which discriminates in its favour, and the partial sacrifice of efficiency in electricity, the Scottish coal industry is still quite incapable of making a profit. Productivity has certainly increased, especially at the coal face, mainly as the result of the substantial advances that have been made in mechanisation. This has not had the effect, however, of preventing a long series of deficits from being made. The increasing proportion of output won by mechanical means and the resultant growth in output per man-shift are shown in Table 5.7 below.

Table 5.7 Proportion of Output Obtained from Mechanised Production Faces and Output per Man-Shift at the Face and Overall, Scotland and Great Britain, 1957–1967/8

Country	Mechanised Coal Face Output as per cent of Total Output (per cent) (1)		Output per Man-Shift at Face (cwts.) (2)		Output per Man-Shift Overall (cwts.) (3)	
	1957	**1967/8**	**1957**	**1967**	**1957**	**1967**
Scotland	15·5	79·8	53·7	97·2	20·0	32·4
Great Britain	23·0	85·7	68·9	113·7	24·9	36·6

Sources: N.C.B., Report and Accounts for 1958 and 1966/7.

As can be seen, there has been a major expansion in Scotland in the percentage of coal obtained from mechanised faces. These are faces where power loading machines operate and on which armoured flexible conveyors are used without the assistance of a separate power loader. It can be seen from column (1) that by 1967/8 the proportion of total output in Scotland which derived from mechanised faces had risen to almost 80 per cent. Although still lower than in Great Britain as a whole, such an increase permitted output per man-shift at the face to rise substantially over the decade 1957/67. By the latter year, output per man at the face in Scotland was still well below that in Britain (col. (2)). None the less, during the decade the *growth* of output per man at the face had been significantly greater in the Scottish pits. Between 1957 and 1967, output per man-shift at the face had risen by over 80 per cent in Scotland as against an increase of only 65 per cent in Great Britain. Much the same trend is reflected by the figures in column (3) for output per man-shift in the industry as a whole. These aggregate figures, which take into account surface workers as well as those at the face, again show that growth has been more rapid in Scotland between 1957 and 1967 than in the national economy. More important, however, is simply the fact that, *in absolute terms*, output per man-shift has remained consistently lower in Scotland than in Britain.

Despite this rapid growth in Scotland both of mechanisation and labour productivity, the progress achieved has not been sufficient to compensate for the extreme difficulties experienced in winning the coal in the region. That is, neither mechanisation nor a higher output per man has been able to reduce the high cost structure of the industry to a level that would enable profits to be made. As observed earlier, the Scottish pits have been unable to make a profit in any year since 1950. The problem, it should be emphasised, has not rested with the proceeds per ton of coal made by the Scottish mines. These are, in fact, higher than those obtained in Great Britain as a whole largely due to two features of the Scottish industry. First, pit-head prices of Scottish coal were fixed, as we have seen, at a relatively high level. Second, fuel policy, by tying coal so firmly to electricity generation, introduced a degree of demand inelasticity that would never have transpired under the full play of market forces. Rather, Scotland's difficulties lie solely with the costs incurred in raising the coal.

These features are brought out in Table 5.8 which presents proceeds, costs and profit/loss per ton of saleable coal in Scotland and Britain for the period 1957–1966/7.

Table 5.8 is presented in current prices, which would

Table 5.8 Proceeds, Costs and Profit/Loss Per Ton of Saleable Coal in N.C.B. Collieries, Scotland and Great Britain, 1957–1966/7

Country	Proceeds	Total Costs	Profit (+) or[1] Loss (−)
Scotland:	s. d.	s. d.	s. d.
1957	84 6	96 0	−11 6
1966/7	109 9	111 0	−1 3
Great Britain:			
1957	82 1	81 6	+0 7
1966/7	100 7	98 5	−2 2

Sources: N.C.B., Report and Accounts for 1958 and 1966/7.

[1] Before charging interest.

account for part of the appreciation in costs that has occurred between 1957–1966/7. Had it not been for the substantial improvements made in mechanisation and output per shift, there can be no doubt that costs per ton would have been even higher by the end of the 1960s. None the less, the trend to emerge from Table 5.8 is clear. The costs per ton incurred in raising the coal from deep and difficult seams are more than sufficient to outweigh the higher proceeds per ton obtained in selling it. As a result, the Scottish mines have consistently operated at a loss, although the extent of the deficit has been diminishing over the years due to rationalisation, and the close relationship maintained with electricity generation. In 1957, the Scottish division of the N.C.B. made an aggregate loss from the operation of the collieries, before charging interest, of over £12 million. By 1966/7, the deficit had fallen to £925,000. In Great Britain, on the other hand, only once, in 1965/6, has a loss been made since the start of the 1950s. In contrast to the Scottish experience, aggregate profits have risen from £6 million in 1957 to £17·7 million in 1966/7.

The continued deficits made by the Scottish collieries despite the improvements in efficiency that have been effected bring into question the whole future of Scotland's coal industry. On purely economic grounds, it seems that coal mining in Scotland would not survive. If it does remain active, it can be due only to social or other such considerations. Energy can, after all, be provided more efficiently by a variety of other means, including atomic power yet to be fully exploited, water power, natural gas and oil burning. At the very least, should Scottish coal mining continue to exist, it cannot for much longer be at the direct expense of electricity.

3 Shipbuilding

Nowhere has change been so dramatic or complete over the last few years as in shipbuilding. Within the past decade, the industry has experienced a revolution both in organisation and techniques of production. The term 'revolution' is used advisedly for the simple reason that nothing short of such a drastic transformation would have been sufficient to save Scottish shipbuilding. Even now, with the recent collapse of Upper Clyde Shipbuilders (UCS), the future is clouded with uncertainty, particularly with regard to shipbuilding in the traditionally famous yards on the upper reaches of the River Clyde. These yards have become the latest victims of the deep-seated difficulties which have affected shipbuilding over the past years. Less than a decade ago, shipbuilding in Scotland was the perfect example of an ailing staple industry, suffering from a combination of its own inefficient practices and unfavourable market forces. It was an industry characterised by the highly individualistic policies pursued by different yards; by a deplorable record of industrial relations; and finally, by a level of orders for new ships that was insufficient to keep the capacity of the yards occupied. Rationalisation and re-equipment of the shipyards were urgently needed. Given the scarcity of new orders and the inefficiency of builders, it was not surprising, however, that the new capital necessary to effect such changes could not be obtained. Late delivery, over-pricing, creeping costs and dogmatic labour attitudes were, it seemed, leading inevitably to the collapse of the Scottish industry.

Nor was it only the competitive ability of Scottish shipbuilders that was in decline. The yards in the U.K. as a whole were steadily losing ground to foreign competitors such as Japan and West Germany. This, in itself, gave cause for concern, but it was by no means all. Of greater significance was the fact that the output both of Scotland and the U.K. was in *absolute* as well as *relative* decline. The gravity of the situation was underlined by the knowledge that this decline in output was taking place within an environment conducive to the expansion of world shipbuilding as a whole. The world's seaborne trade rose from 460 million tons in 1939 to over 2,000 million tons in 1969. To cope with such an increase, a huge expansion in the world's merchant fleet has been necessary. Indeed, between 1959 and 1969, it more than doubled, rising from 8·7 million to 18·7 million tons. Much of this increase was due to the rapid emergence of Japan as the world's foremost shipbuilding nation. Against such a backcloth of growth and expansion, the performance of both the Scottish and U.K. yards has been most disappointing. In Chart 5 below the shipbuilding output of the U.K. is compared with that of certain leading competitor countries for the period 1959–69.

Over the period 1959/60–1968/9, the U.K. output of ships fell by 30 per cent. In consequence, from a position of second largest shipbuilding nation at the start of the 1960s, the U.K. had fallen by the end of the decade to fourth place, behind Japan, West Germany and Sweden. It is true that 1969 was a disappointing year in the U.K. in terms of tonnage launched, so that an unduly pessimistic bias is perhaps imparted to the figures. None the less, the secular trend in the U.K. output has been clear for some time. Over the same period 1959/60–1968/9, tonnage launched rose in West Germany by 27 per cent, by 55 per cent in France and by a staggering 390 per cent in Japan. At a time, therefore, of major expansion in world shipbuilding, the output of the U.K. has run contrary to the general trend.

Chart 5

merchant tonnage launched in leading shipbuilding countries, 1959–69

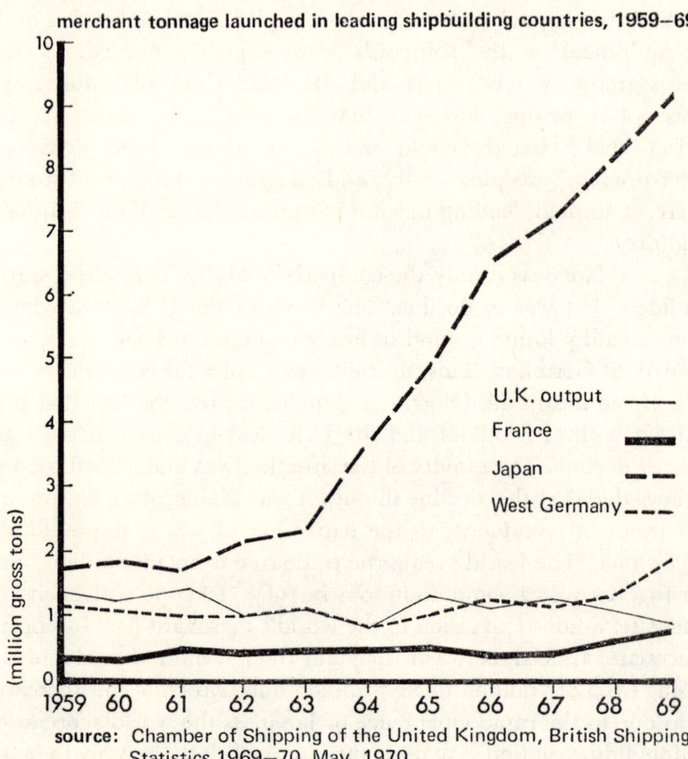

source: Chamber of Shipping of the United Kingdom, British Shipping Statistics 1969–70, May, 1970

The unpalatable truth for Scottish shipbuilding is that, over the 1960s, it secured a dwindling *share* of this rapidly declining U.K. output. Over the decade, the tonnage launched by the yards in Scotland fell by approximately 40 per cent. Their contribution to U.K. output declined, therefore, from 38 per cent in 1959/60 to only 28 per cent in 1968/9. Clearly the competitive position of Scottish shipbuilding has deteriorated over the past years. Within Scotland's shipbuilding industry, the yards on the Clyde predominated despite growing difficulties and the recurrent financial crises which affected particularly the yards on the upper reaches of the river. During the 1960s, the yards on Clydeside contributed on average over 90 per cent of total Scottish output.

From a post-second world war peak in 1955, however, the trend of Clyde output has been almost continuously downwards. This is shown in Chart 6 below.

Chart 6

merchant tonnage launched from the Clyde, 1946/50 – 1969

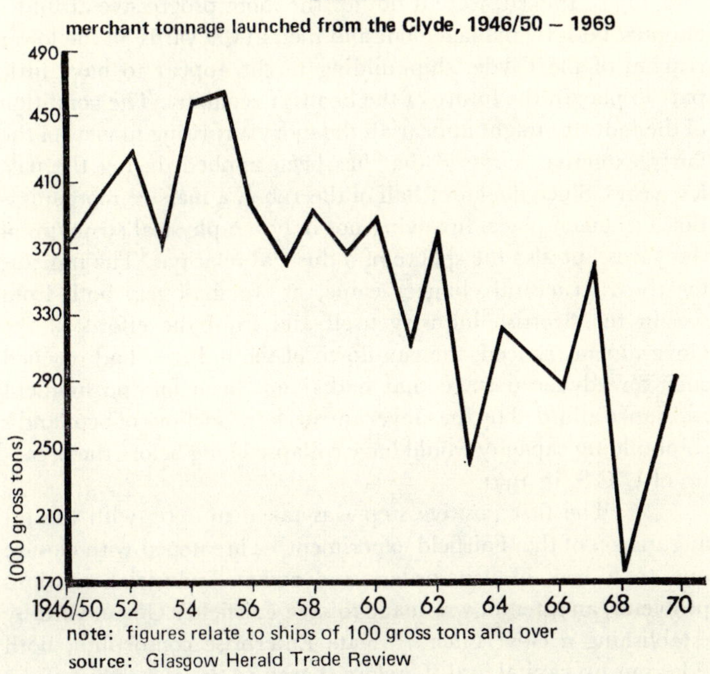

note: figures relate to ships of 100 gross tons and over
source: Glasgow Herald Trade Review

The secular trend in output of the yards on the Clyde emerges clearly from the above chart. As output declined, so a corresponding run-down in the labour force of the industry took place. As observed earlier, output fell by approximately 40 per cent between 1960–69. Over the same period, almost one-third of the labour force was lost to the industry and worse was to follow. As we shall see below, the proposals governing the breakup of U.C.S. will mean approximately 6,000 redundancies out of a work-force in the group of some 8,500. The rate at which contraction on the Clyde has been taking place may be judged from the fact that at the end of 1960, there were 17 shipyards in operation on the upper reaches of the Clyde alone, employing 20,000 people. By the time the U.C.S. redundancies have been effected during the course of 1971, there will be 3 active yards on the upper reaches, employing a total of some 6,500 men. These will comprise the two yards regarded as viable within the U.C.S. group, together with the Yarrow yard which employs about 4,000.

Whichever type of measurement is used, the performance of Scottish shipbuilding has been little short of disastrous since the mid-1950s. Indeed, were it not for the more progressive attitudes adopted both by management and men in the yards on the lower reaches of the Clyde, shipbuilding might appear to have little part to play in the future of the Scottish economy. The condition of the industry might appear all the more surprising in view of the fairly extensive 'surgery' that has been applied during the past few years. Since the latter half of the 1960s, a massive reorganisation has taken place, involving not only the physical structure of the yards but also the sphere of industrial relations. The impetus for these structural changes came, as we shall see, both from within the Scottish industry itself and from the efforts of the Government. Indeed, the run-down of the industry had reached such an advanced stage that had it not been for the frequent assistance afforded by the Government, large sections of Scotland's shipbuilding capacity would have collapsed long before the break-up of U.C.S. in 1971.

The first positive step was taken in 1965 with the inauguration of the 'Fairfield experiment'. Threatened with closure due to a lack of new orders and serious industrial relations problems, an attempt was made to save Fairfield's Govan yard by establishing a Government/Private Enterprise consortium. Both sides put up capital and therefore shared in the ownership of the reorganised company. Along with this fresh input of capital, new work schedules were introduced and, above all, a wholly fresh approach was adopted with regard to the relationship between capital and labour. Traditional management/union postures were realigned. For instance, as part of the new agreement, union representation on the policy-making board was agreed; observer opinion at senior management level was permitted; a full-time shop steward convener was appointed; a central joint council was created to act as a negotiating medium; and finally, major improvements were effected in training programmes, communications and the like. These improvements were all part of a 'new deal' which, it was hoped, would serve as an example for other yards to follow.

In the event, the experiment was probably too far in advance of its time. Traditional attitudes could not be broken down overnight, so that this realignment of responsibilities between management and men failed. The effort to save Fairfields, had, however, been an important first step. It triggered off a new approach both to ownership and to industrial relations. Much of the thinking behind the Fairfield's scheme was incorporated in the recommendations of the *Shipbuilding Inquiry Committee 1965–66 Report* (the Geddes Report). This Report has had a major influence on the subsequent development of the industry. Its major recommendation was that, where appropriate, the industry should be reorganised into larger units of production to allow economies of scale to be secured. In a Scottish context, this was acted upon, although without proper regard, perhaps, for the strength of local loyalties and conflicting interests prevailing on the upper reaches of the Clyde.

The Report recognised that, contrary to the general impression of a depressed and declining sector, shipbuilding could, in fact, more properly be regarded in the 1960s as a 'growth industry'. In an international context, the industry was, during the decade, in a relatively strong position, the result of the expansion in world trade and increased demand for shipping. Hitherto, the problem had been, of course, that an inadequate share of this booming world demand for ships had been secured by U.K. yards. Only by reorganising the structure of production could the industry hope to obtain a larger slice of the growing cake. For instance, within the setting of the Scottish industry, the Geddes committee urged that a combination, formed between yards on the Clyde, would provide the most efficient means of regaining the region's share of world markets.

These proposals of the Geddes committee confirmed much of the already-established thinking within shipbuilding. As a result they strengthened the resolve to bring about some degree of rationalisation of the yards on the Clyde. What might have been, therefore, a turning-point in the industry's development was reached in 1967–8. These years witnessed the emergence of the two large combines which, for a brief interlude, were to dominate shipbuilding on Clydeside. The successful Scott-Lithgow group, which united the interests of those yards on the lower reaches of the river, was formed in late 1967. It was intended that U.C.S. incorporating producers on the upper reaches, should be established in the same year. It was to be a significant omen for the future that the formation of the new company was delayed due to the activities of the Boilermaker's Society and other unions. They were to have signed an employment charter for the consortium by the end of 1967, but in the event, lengthy discussions and delays postponed the signing, and hence the creation of U.C.S., until February 1968. Before assessing the likely future of shipbuilding in Scotland, it will be instructive first to consider briefly the formation and performance of each of these combines.

a) The Scott-Lithgow Group The agreement signed in late 1967 between Scott's of Greenock and Lithgow's of Port Glasgow merged the interests of six concerns on the lower Clyde. Lithgow's brought to the new group their East and Kingston yards and Ferguson Brothers. On Scott's side, their Cartsburn and Cartsdyke yards, together with Scott's of Bowling, were added to the amalgamation. Each of these was a relatively small productive unit but, none the less, their individuality was maintained under the new organisation. The constituent firms could operate autonomously, each being left responsible for the profitability of its own production. At the same time, however, necessary services such as technical and computer resources, buying, marketing, joinery and outfitting were centralised and made available to all parts of the combine. The advantages of this type of structure were, first, that it allowed close management/labour relations to be maintained in each of the separate firms and, second, that as an entity the group benefitted from larger purchasing power and could dictate more firmly the design of the components supplied to it.

From the outset, the aim of the combine was to recover some of the ground lost to Japanese builders. With the latter winning so many of the contracts for super-ships, this attempt to match the competitiveness of Japanese yards has involved Scott-Lithgow's in a heavy programme of capital expenditure. The different yards had to be modernised and the capacity of the berths extended. Unlike the yards on the upper Clyde, the group did not rely upon Government support to accomplish such modernisation. By 1970, over £7 million had been invested in re-equipping the yards, and further plans to increase capacity will on completion carry the combine into the 'big ship league', that is, the building of huge super-tankers and bulk-carriers.

By booking its first order for a 250,000 ton tanker, an order soon followed by a demand for a sister ship, the yards on the lower Clyde have indicated their intention of becoming one of only three centres in Britain capable of building these super-ships. Their emergence into this 'big league' has been carefully planned to come to fruition in distinct stages. The extension of capacity in the first stage has been designed to accommodate bulk-carriers in the 150,000 to 200,000 ton range and tankers in the 200,000 to

250,000 ton class. The second stage, when completed, will allow the combine to build tankers of up to 1,000,000 tons deadweight. The total cost of both stages will amount to just over £10 million. This ambitious project will enable Scott-Lithgow to compete directly with Japanese builders; further, by extending the product-range of the yards in the group it will allow them to meet virtually any type of demand with which they might be faced.

This versatility of output is already reflected in the group's order-book. Like Upper Clyde Shipbuilders, the Scott-Lithgow combine secured over £100 million worth of new orders in 1969. Besides super-tankers, these included naval vessels, refrigerated cargo liners and specialised bulk carriers. Clearly, there has been a welcome return to viability of the yards on the lower reaches of the Clyde. With the sights of the group firmly set on building the giant types of ship, the scene is set for a transformation in capacity and techniques of production over the next few years. It is hoped too that the increase in employment opportunities created by the expansion of the group will be valuable in mitigating, to some extent, the effects of the redundancies caused by the collapse of U.C.S.[1]

b) Upper Clyde Shipbuilders (**U.C.S.**) The Upper Clyde combine was formed in anything but auspicious circumstances in 1968. It amalgamated the interests of five yards—Alexander Stephen, Charles Connell, Yarrow's, Fairfield's and John Brown. Four of these represented yards which, having failed to modernise, found themselves incapable of adapting to present conditions. Between them, these builders had a combined loss of £2·4 million before coming together to form U.C.S. Indeed, of the five, only Yarrow's had been showing a profit and they were, predictably, the least enthusiastic about the prospects of the new company. In 1968, the somewhat optimistic forecast was that it would take approximately four years to turn a loss of this magnitude into a profit.

After its formation, the group experienced, not unnaturally, serious difficulties in attracting the capital necessary to bring about reorganisation and re-equipment. Private investors saw no reason 'to throw good money after bad', so that it was left to the Government, operating through the Shipbuilding Industry

[1] See *Report of the Advisory Group on Shipbuilding on the Upper Clyde*, H.M.S.O., 1971. The hope was expressed in the report that Scott-Lithgow might absorb some 1,000 of those losing their jobs at U.C.S. For further details, see pages 125, 126 below.

Board, to provide the capital so desperately required. At the time of the group's formation, the Government's shareholding amounted to 17½ per cent, the result entirely of its prior involvement with the Fairfield experiment. The subsequent difficulties experienced by the combine in raising capital placed it in dire financial straits before the Government moved in somewhat reluctantly to salvage the operation. By 1970, the Government's stake in the combine had risen to 49·4 per cent but even this was insufficient to solve the problems of shipbuilding on the upper Clyde.

For instance, during its brief life-span, certain major changes had already occurred within the structure of the group. Within a month of being formed in 1968, it was announced that Alexander Stephen's yard at Linthouse, which had not received an order for almost two years, would have to close. This decision meant that only a steel fabrication plant was left in operation at Linthouse and some 2,000 men were made redundant. Again, the Yarrow Co., which had never been a happy member of the group, took the decision to leave, with Government approval, in mid 1970. The Company bought back the 51 per cent shareholding held by U.C.S. and continued to operate, with success, as an independent unit. This highlighted one of the major problems facing the group, namely that from the outset, the yards were an ill-assorted collection with widely differing interests, competitive ability and financial strength. It was, perhaps, unduly optimistic to expect this unwieldly structure to operate as an integrated and efficient unit.

From the beginning, the Upper Clyde group recognised that it had no future in the 'big ship league'—that is, in the building of the huge super-tanker and bulk carriers. There was, too, a notable change in attitude towards building passenger liners for which John Brown's yard had been traditionally famous. The losses sustained by the group in building the Q.E.2 and the £4·5 million liner, *Blenheim*, for Norwegian owners convinced the management that as from 1970, the future lay in building medium-sized specialist ships of up to approximately 100,000 tons. It was appreciated that these specialist vessels were, ton-for-ton, more valuable than the super ship. What was, therefore, termed a 'corner-stone in the re-building of the company'[1] was reached with the launching of the new 'Clyde' design of a versatile cargo, bulk and container ship. This was a standard vessel on which the group pinned a great deal of hope for future orders.

[1] Kenneth Douglas, Managing Director, in the *G.H.T.R.*, January, 1970.

The U.C.S. Collapse

The question to be answered, then, is why was this hope misplaced; exactly what went wrong with U.C.S.? Attention has already been drawn to the fact that from the outset it was an unlikely collection of yards that had been drawn together, with little or no financial strength, out-dated lay-out and equipment and, therefore, with a serious question-mark hanging over their competitive ability in world markets. This inherent weakness was compounded by two further factors affecting the early viability of the company. First, with the formation of U.C.S., it was agreed that the new group would absorb losses from pre-existing contracts, estimated at some £3½ million. In the event, as the Advisory Group was to point out, these losses totalled over £12 million.[1] Second, in the early stages, new contracts were accepted which involved paring profits to the margin. Hence, any increase in production costs through strikes, wage increases or rising material costs could, and did, turn small profits into major losses. Within the first few months of operation, it was estimated that U.C.S. had taken on new contracts which would involve a loss of £4·8 million. In the event, these losses escalated to a total of £9·8 million. On both these counts, therefore, U.C.S. was subjected to a massive drain of some £22 million on working capital which even major injections of public funds could not adequately offset.

Given these initial defects, there can be no doubt that much of the subsequent difficulty experienced by U.C.S. can be attributed to the malpractices both of management and labour. With regard to the former, the most serious shortcoming was the failure to institute proper accounting and cost control procedures. At the time when the liquidator took charge in mid 1971, the most recent accounts, approved and audited, dated back to August, 1968. This made it virtually impossible in the short term to assess precisely what were the total liabilities of the company, eventually established at not less than £32·2 million. For an enterprise that was underpinned by public funds to the extent of over £20 million, the current information available to the Government about the financial dealings and costing procedures of the group must have been remarkably small. Indeed, the failure to evolve a proper financial control system meant that meaningful cash forecasts could not be made.

Finally, management may be faulted for failing to under-

[1] *Report of the Advisory Group, 1971.*

take essential modernisation and rationalisation of the yards. 'No improvement in facilities, no worthwhile investment has been made. Facilities remain as they were before the merger . . .'.[1] In itself this was due, in part, to rapidly rising costs of production which ensured that the funds periodically made available by the State had to be used to avert recurrent crises of liquidity rather than being put to more long term use. As we shall see below, management did little, or perhaps more accurately, could do little, to prevent costs spiralling in this way.

On the labour side of the industry, the tactics employed in the field of industrial relations were, in the longer term, to prove little short of disastrous. It is not the intention here to present a long list of the disputes and unofficial strikes which bedevilled the five yards in the group. Space prohibits. It is sufficient to note that the vast number of unofficial strikes—in one week of August 1968, for example, 4 were taking place simultaneously—has played no small part in contributing to rapidly rising production costs facing the combine. There can be little doubt, either, that management generally adopted the line of least resistance, aware that with perilously narrow profit margins, any prolonged withdrawal of labour could bring the company to its knees. It is quite true that belated improvements in productivity had been made in the yards. Between 1969–71, for instance, productivity in steel output had risen from 11 tons per man per year to 23·6 tons per man per year. Yet, costs per ton of steel remained high since improvements in productivity were generally passed on in the form of higher wages to labour. The danger of such a situation was that U.C.S., with access to public funds, became something of a pace-setter for wage movements in other yards, with no such access, throughout the U.K. The result was to place increasing pressure on other yards such as Swan-Hunter and Scott-Lithgow.

A weak initial structure, timid and inefficient management and the continued exploitation of these two former factors by militant unions have meant that U.C.S. has lurched from one financial crisis to another. It was, to some extent, inevitable that sooner or later a halt should be called to the continued drain of public funds into the company as presently constituted. In just over three years, more than £20 million of public money, in the form of grants and loans, had been invested in the group. It was the request, in mid 1971, for an additional £6 million working

[1] *Report of the Advisory Group*, *1971*.

capital that precipitated the final crisis and the Government's eventual refusal to subsidise for any longer this particular 'lame duck'.

The Consequences for Upper Clyde

The Government's decision to wind-up U.C.S. does not mean the end of shipbuilding on the upper reaches of the Clyde. Clyde. In the first place, Yarrow's remain viable as an independent entity. Second, acceptance of the Advisory Group's proposals means the closure of two yards, the former John Brown's at Clydebank and Charles Connell's at Scoutstoun. These will be disposed of to private enterprise as soon as possible by the liquidator. In place of the existing structure, the Government has proposed that a successor company be created at Fairfield's Govan yard and at Linthouse, and that the existing shipbuilding programme should, as far as possible, be concentrated at Govan. To secure the formation of such a company, the Government has envisaged that approximately £10 million would be necessary, a sum to which it is prepared to contribute, provided that the rest is forthcoming from private enterprise.

Besides the ability to attract sufficient capital, the success even of this limited 'rescue operation' would be dependent upon the fulfillment of a large number of other conditions. These include the acceptance by unions of certain changes in working practice, notably of two-shift daily working; union acceptance of competitive wage rates; the ability to attract satisfactory management; and the production at Govan of standardised vessels. Clearly, the reconstructed company at Govan and Linthouse, the latter being no more than a steel fabrication plant, would require considerably reduced manpower, estimated by the Advisory Group at some 2,500. Given the creation of a new company, by no means presently assured, the break up of U.C.S. would, therefore, entail the crushing loss of some 6,000 jobs, and this in an area of Scotland where unemployment is already relatively high. Nor is this all. It has been estimated that some 15,000 jobs in supply industries are at risk due to the U.C.S. collapse.

By far the most serious aspect of the collapse is, therefore, the effect which unemployment of this dimension will have on Glasgow and surrounding area. It has been emphasised that there will be only 400 immediate redundancies. The rest of the labour force will be phased out gradually as ships already under construction are completed. The position of the work-force as envisaged by the Advisory Group is as follows:

Total Labour Force in June 1971	8,500
Number that might be employed at new Govan/Linthouse company	2,500
Number that might be absorbed by Scott-Lithgow	1,000
Number that might be absorbed by Yarrow plus those retained in work by private interests acquiring U.C.S. facilities from the liquidator	500[1]
Total that might be re-employed	4,000

Source: Report of the Advisory Group on Shipbuilding on the Upper Clyde, 1971.

[1] Not specified in the *Report of the Advisory Group.* The figure given here is simply an indication of possible short-term requirements.

It should be recognised that there is nothing definite or assured about the re-employment prospects of the 4,000 outlined above. If the plan to establish a successor company at Govan/Linthouse is effected, it might still be that 7 out of 10 of the original U.C.S. work-force would be declared redundant. Even on a more optimistic view, with the yards at Scott-Lithgow and at Yarrow's absorbing an additional 1,500 people as suggested above, over one-half of the original labour force would still be out of work. This is the true significance of the break up of U.C.S.

It has been suggested that taking into account the massive unemployment created, both directly and in the supply industries, and the loss of revenue through rates and the like paid by the yards, over £40 million gross trade would be taken out of the Scottish economy.[1] Moreover, between £5 million and £15 million would have to be paid out by the Government in the form of redundancy and unemployment pay and capital would, of course, have to be provided for the suggested new company. All in all, it is clear that Scotland and indeed the nation as a whole, will have to bear a very heavy cost for the decline of shipbuilding on the Clyde's upper reaches.

The Future of Shipbuilding in Scotland

The break up of U.C.S. is all the more important in that along with Scott-Lithgow it has for the past few years dominated the shipbuilding output not only of the Clyde, but of Scotland as a whole. In 1969, for instance, the two groups accounted for virtually all the tonnage launched from the Clyde, the distribution of output being as shown on page 127.

This output in 1969 represented over 90 per cent of total production in Scotland so that the two combines could, with justification, be regarded as virtually synonymous with Scottish shipbuilding as a whole. Inevitably, therefore, Scotland's contribution to U.K. tonnage launched, which in 1969 amounted to

[1] *The Scotsman*, August 3rd, 1971.

	Tonnage (000)	Per cent of Clyde Output
Scott-Lithgow	180·1	59
U.C.S.	120·8	40
Ailsa Shipbuilding Co., Troon	1·7	
James Lamont, Port Glasgow	0·6	1
Fleming and Ferguson, Paisley	0·4	
Total output	303·6	100

Source: G.H.T.R., 1970.

approximately one-third, will decline sharply, with only Yarrow's and possibly a successor company at Govan/Linthouse launching ships on the upper Clyde. Certainly, not all is loss, however, in Scottish shipbuilding. There is a welcome stability both at Yarrow's and at the yards of Scott-Lithgow. By mid-1971, the former had an order book of over £60 million and negotiations for further orders with several foreign countries were fairly well advanced. At Scott-Lithgow's, modernisation has continued rapidly with the building of new covered-in premises at Port Glasgow and with plans taking shape to increase output by 50 per cent within the next two years.

Finally, an additional stimulus, not only to yards in Scotland but also to those in the U.K. as a whole, has been provided by the announcement in August 1971 that shipbuilding credit guarantees are to be increased from £700 million to £1,000 million for British shipowners. Originally introduced by the 1967 Shipbuilding Industry Act, these credit guarantees have proved effective in channelling British demand for ships to British yards. The provision of these guarantees resulted from the fact that in 1966, some 70 per cent of British orders for new ships were placed with foreign builders. The availability of these guarantees had an immediate impact in that within the first nine months of 1968, the year after the Act was passed, over 900,000 gross tons were ordered by British owners from British yards. This compared most favourably with the mere 100,000 tons ordered during the equivalent period of the preceding year. It is expected that the new limit of £1,000 million will be sufficient to cover all home orders placed within the next five years. The announcement will, therefore, provide some encouragement to yards on the Clyde at a time when they are trying to shake off the 'crisis-type' of atmosphere created by the break up of U.C.S.

4 Electronics

The most rapidly growing sector within the Scottish economy since the second world war has been electronics. The growth of the industry is exclusively a post-war phenomenon and, indeed, owes a very great deal to the war itself. It was war-time exigencies that rendered necessary an increased supply of gyroscopic gunsights. The contract for these was given by the Government to the Ferranti firm, based in Manchester. The major bottleneck in any attempt to extend capacity during the war period was scarcity of factor inputs, and particularly of labour, and it was largely to exploit the large and under-utilised labour force available in Edinburgh that the city was chosen as the location for the proposed extension of capacity.

From this original location of Ferranti's in Edinburgh expansion and diversification have taken place sufficient to create at the present time a viable electronics industry in Scotland. The story was by no means, however, one of overnight success. In the post-war years, the Ferranti firm was kept in operation only by means of Government contracts, and employment in the industry fell at one time to little over three hundred. The survival and subsequent expansion of the industry were secured, first, through direct Government assistance and, second, through the incentives made available under a regional policy determined to relieve unemployment in the 'depressed areas'.

With regard to the former, besides placing contracts with the Ferranti firm, the Government selected the Edinburgh plant as a nursery for the training of electronic engineers. By itself, this created the opportunity for valuable 'spin-off' effects to be achieved. Several of those originally trained by Ferranti have subsequently established small plants of their own. In this way, a number of small, specialised producers have emerged, manufacturing items of equipment for Ferranti assemblies, or for markets in the south. The extent to which 'spin-off' has operated in Scotland should not, however, be exaggerated. Although it represents one of the major ways in which industrial growth can take place, as developments in America testify, it has, if anything, been slow to develop in Scotland. None the less, several important examples of growth taking place precisely in this manner do exist. These include Forder & Graham, located at Kelso, Whitwell Electronics, and Precision Machining. Each of these has 'spun-off' from existing Scottish companies.

Besides direct Government assistance and subsequent 'spin-off', the continued expansion of electronics in Scotland has undoubtedly benefitted greatly from the incentives provided under regional policy. Indeed, so successful was the policy that, as observed earlier, 'spin-off' has remained a relatively minor component in the overall expansion of the industry. In other words, self-generated companies within the industry have clearly been the exception and not the rule. Many of the firms attracted to Scotland, particularly those from abroad, are in fact little more than 'foreign production centres which rely almost entirely upon the research and development facilities of the U.S. based parent companies.'[1]

Nevertheless, the location of these plants in Scotland has meant a rapid diversification of the industry and the creation of important secondary or 'multiplier' effects. For instance, both the output and organisation of the Scottish electronics industry have changed radically from those existing only 20 years ago. At that time, Ferranti constituted the sole representative of the industry. By the beginning of 1970, there were over 70 firms in operation, producing an output which varied from computers, telecommunications and instruments to components and other electrical or electronic devices.

The secondary effects of this growing sector within the Scottish economy have been fairly obvious. In the first place, although these are science-based firms with a relatively high capital input, they have none the less helped to reduce unemployment and increase purchasing power, particularly in the Central Belt of Scotland. From a floor of little over 300 during the industry's post-war struggle to survive, employment has risen to over 30,000 in 1970 and there appears little reason to doubt that it will continue to grow. Second, the very nature of the output of electronics is indicative of the fact that strong linkage effects can be exercised by the trade. A shortcoming of the structure of the Scottish industry has been, however, that these linkages have not been confined to Scotland. Indeed, for the most part, they have 'leaked' to other parts of the U.K.

In order to appreciate this, it must be recognised that there are, in essence, three distinct categories which, taken together, comprise the electronics industry. The production of electronic equipment and instruments, which may be regarded as falling into the first category, inevitably creates a demand for, or has a 'secondary' impact on, those in category two, who supply the components and sub-assemblies necessary to the production of firms in category one. Finally, a third category consists of what might be termed the 'services' sector. This group provides the professional and scientific services such as those supplied by the

[1] *Investors Chronicle and Stock Exchange Gazette*, 'Scotland', 8th May 1970.

industrial consultants, sales agents, data processing experts and the like. Of these three categories making up the electronic industry, only the first is strongly represented at the present time in Scotland. Clearly, the success and prosperity of the two latter groups are dependent upon the demand derived from the continued expansion of the first. Should a recession occur in category one, this derived demand would cease to exist, so creating a 'chain-reaction' effect through the rest of the industry.

Whilst there has been a proliferation of firms within Scotland in category one, development in the other two groups has remained disappointing. Hitherto, Scotland has not provided a market strong enough to induce the suppliers of components (category two) to set up plant in the region. Much the same is true, as we shall see below, in the context of the motor vehicle industry. *This is the one weak element in the structure of the Scottish industry.* It is the only factor in the foreseeable future which appears likely to inhibit further expansion. At the moment, sub-contracts for components such as castings, switches, mouldings and registers have still to be placed in the Midlands and South-East of England. Unless there is an increase in the number of firms generated within Scotland itself, through 'spin-off' or other means, the lack of external economies for Scottish plant engaged in the commercial side of the industry may hinder development.

Given the slow progress made in the components and services side of the industry, the rapid expansion of the branch concerned with electronic equipment and instruments (category one) might at first sight appear surprising. This paradox can, however, be resolved when two factors are taken into account. First, Scotland has very definite attractions to offer prospective entrepreneurs: and second, the nature of output of the components firms means that they do not have to be in immediate proximity to those engaged in category one of the industry. We shall examine briefly each of these factors in turn.

The positive attractions by which firms in the first category of the industry have been induced to Scotland are first, financial inducements offered as part of regional policy, second, the existence of surplus trainable labour, and third, the availability of good land and sites suitable for industrial development, together with an adequate communications network. It is here that the 'new towns', able to offer such 'tailor-made' facilities as locations and factories have made a substantial contribution. Finally, there must exist technical training and educational facilities. In this context, the research conducted by Burroughs showed that their new Glenrothes plant was within 90 minutes drive of seven universities. This is an important consideration in a field where there can be no doubt of the practical value of maintaining close links between the industry and the research work and facilities available within the universities.

The fact that such expansion has not been reflected in the components branch of the industry can largely be attributed to the extremely high value of the components themselves. This makes any differential in transport costs and time between a location in Scotland and one in the Midlands of England somewhat less significant. In other words, transport costs constitute a relatively small proportion of the value of output. As a result, components firms can profitably remain in the south to take advantage of the readily available external economies rather than establish an offshoot in Scotland.

Finally, it might be noted that it is virtually impossible to give an adequate quantitative assessment of development in the Scottish electronics industry. Statistical data on any comprehensive scale are almost entirely lacking. Some ten years ago the Scottish Council (Development and Industry) predicted that by 1970 approximately 20,000 people would be employed in this branch of Scottish industry, yet the actual number finding employment at the start of the year stood at 37,000, almost double the predicted total. Again, whereas there was only one firm in Scottish electronics twenty years ago, the number had risen to over 70 at the start of 1970, a major expansion in such a comparatively short-time period. Indeed, the rate of growth in Scotland has been substantially above that achieved elsewhere in Britain. For instance, in the one category 'radio and other electronic apparatus' alone, the Scottish Council's submission to the First Secretary of State in 1967 showed that between 1959 and 1966 the expansion of employment in Scotland amounted to 145 per cent, compared with only 40 per cent in Great Britain. This rapid growth-rate has subsequently been maintained so that electronics presently stands as Scotland's principal growth industry and a source of considerable hope for the future.

5 Vehicles

One of Scotland's potential growth sectors is motor vehicle production. The industry had to be re-established in Scotland after the second world war since, of the Scottish firms created during the formative stages of development prior to 1914, only one, Albion Motors, survived. In many ways, the pattern of development in motor vehicles has been similar to that in electronics. Both are essentially post-second world war phenomena; both stemmed directly from the policies pursued by the Government of bringing new industries to the depressed areas; and both experienced serious teething-troubles so that grave doubts were expressed at different stages in their development about their chance of survival in a Scottish environment. But, most important of all, *expansion in each sector has been seriously hindered by the failure of secondary or 'supply' industries to develop in Scotland.* Hence, the servicing of these growth industries with necessary components has remained largely a prerogative of manufacturers located in England. To date, this 'second-phase' development has simply not gathered momentum in Scotland. This has been the chief cause for concern about the future well-being of these 'growth sectors' in the Scottish economy.

It was in 1961 that Government pressure for the creation of new growth industries in Scotland resulted in the location of the British Motor Corporation near Bathgate. The plant specialised in the manufacture of heavy trucks and agricultural tractors, the objective being to produce 1,000 trucks and 750 tractors per week. Two years later, in 1963, a further encouraging development was the opening of Rootes' plant at Linwood, specially designed to produce a new range of small cars. From this total specialisation on the Hillman Imp, the Linwood factory has, in subsequent years, diversified largely due to a change in consumer preference away from the smaller type of vehicle to the larger family saloon.

It is not the intention here to embark upon a lengthy discussion of why these concerns, far from achieving any overnight success, almost collapsed within the first few years of their operation. Sufficient to say that it simply proved impossible to build new factories, instal expensive equipment, and then expect to have a labour force that could within a few months rival the skill and experience of workers in the Midlands and South of England.[1] The major problem undoubtedly lay with the adapting and training of labour in Scotland to cope with assembly-line techniques. Much of the labour that was drawn upon represented men released from the declining staple industries in the region—coal, engineering and shipbuilding. In large measure, these were skilled men but they were wholly unaccustomed to motor vehicle production. It is certain, therefore, that in the initial stages the large problem of training such labour to the standards required

[1] See J. F. C. Thompson, 'A Statistical Review of the Vehicle Industry in Scotland', *Scotland Magazine*, July 1968.

was seriously under-estimated. As a result, it proved impossible in the short-term to achieve a level of productivity in the Scottish industry sufficient to compensate for relatively high overheads and transport costs.

Besides the problem of labour adaptation, the industry in Scotland and other parts of the U.K. suffered from the periodic financial squeezes that had to be introduced as part of general British economic policy. The result was that during the 1960s, production schedules had to be cut, short-time working introduced and the labour force allowed to run down. Difficulties such as these resulted in something of a revolution in the organisation of Scottish motor vehicle production. Rootes' Linwood plant was taken over by the Chrysler Corporation of America and the organisation re-named Chrysler (Scotland) Ltd. Similarly, B.M.C.'s complex at Bathgate was absorbed by the Leyland group, which already had a foothold in Scotland, having taken over Albion Motors in 1951. The output of B.M.C. and Leyland was largely complementary in that the former specialised in trucks at the lighter end of the scale (up to approximately 16 tons) whilst Leyland dominated the heavy range in Britain.

These organisational changes have placed the Scottish vehicle trade on a sounder footing, although the industry has yet to make any significant contribution to the general level of activity in the economy. Yet, at both Linwood and Bathgate, there have been developments that portend well for the future. At Linwood, for instance, Chrysler has yet to make profits but, undeterred, has continued to invest heavily in plant and equipment. In consequence, between 1963, when the factory opened, and 1970 it is estimated that an amount approaching £50 million has been invested in the Rootes/Chrysler complex. Most important, expansion and reorganisation at Linwood have equipped the plant to accommodate the medium-powered range of cars in the Chrysler group. The result has been that the entire production of the 'Arrow' range of cars (that is, those of the Minx type), previously shared with Coventry, has been transferred to Scotland. Linwood now constitutes a fully comprehensive manufacturing plant. It produces cars right from the sheet steel to the final product, at the rate of some 1,500 vehicles per week. Half of this output presently comprises the different types of 'Imp', the rest being made up of cars in the 'Arrow' range. In addition, 95 per cent of all the body panels for Chrysler models are manufactured at Linwood, plus a high proportion of other components such as gearboxes and back axles.

At Bathgate, a similar move to a more comprehensive type of production has taken place. Organisational changes within Leyland Motors (Scotland) Ltd. have meant that virtually all activities associated with the plant—finance, engineering, production and marketing—will soon be undertaken in Scotland. For instance, the whole of Leyland's tractor operation is now concentrated at Bathgate. On the truck side, all operations are now Scottish-based with the exception of marketing, which is still conducted in the Midlands. Hence, at Bathgate a fully integrated manufacturing plant, rather than a mere assembly line, has been created in recent years.

The other Leyland plant, Albion Motors at Scotstoun, has continued to specialise in heavyweight trucks in the higher price ranges. A high proportion of its output consists of buses destined for the export market. Indeed, of Albion's total output of trucks, exports account for approximately 50 per cent. In common with the Leyland plant at Bathgate, Albion's has benefitted from the economies of scale achieved through commercial integration. It is able, for instance, to make use of Leyland engines but, in turn, it provides gearboxes and axles not only for its own vehicles but also for other commercial vehicles throughout the Leyland group. There has emerged, therefore, a valuable cross-feed of inputs, precisely the type of economy that the Scottish motor industry so desperately needs in order to become an economically viable proposition.

In view of the degree of reorganisation and integration that has taken place in Scottish motor production, the industry has now the equipment and capacity substantially to increase its output of vehicles. There is still, however, one major bottleneck in this potential growth sector. As with electronics, there is still a decided lack of component suppliers in the Scottish region, despite the fact that a far greater number of the manufacturing activities have been transferred to Bathgate and Linwood. The development of component firms has simply not 'taken-off' in Scotland so that the secondary employment that might have been generated has not fully materialised. For instance, it was estimated in 1968 that at Bathgate some success had been achieved in this direction. Since 1966, the manufacture of some 400 components, previously made in Birmingham, had been transferred to the Scottish plant. Despite these efforts, no less than £18 million worth of material had still to be brought up from the south of England. Products such as castings, seats, bearings and electrical apparatus are not, as yet, manufactured at Bathgate.

At Leyland's Albion plant the position, far from improving, has actually deteriorated over recent years. In 1958, Albion obtained 22 per cent of its supplies from within Scotland. By 1968, this proportion had fallen to only 10 per cent.[1] Precisely the same problem is experienced by Chrysler's plant at Linwood. Here again, a relatively high degree of dependence on the Midlands for components has meant that the Scottish plant has suffered from disproportionate costing in this respect. It is clear, therefore, that all sections of motor vehicle manufacture in Scotland suffer from the distinct shortage of producers capable of making within the region the necessary high-precision types of component. Hitherto, neither the Bathgate nor the Linwood factories has been able to pay their way in Scotland. If the full potential of the motor vehicle sector is to be realised in the region, this deficiency of component suppliers will have to be overcome in the near future.

References

Scottish Statistical Office, *Digest of Scottish Statistics*, H.M.S.O.

Scottish Office, *Scottish Economic Bulletin*, H.M.S.O.

Central Statistical Office, *Annual Abstract of Statistics*, H.M.S.O. *Abstract of Regional Statistics*, H.M.S.O.

National Coal Board, *Annual Reports and Accounts*, H.M.S.O.

Department of Agriculture and Fisheries for Scotland, *Agricultural Statistics, Scotland*, H.M.S.O. (annually).

Ministry of Agriculture, Fisheries and Food and Department of Agriculture and Fisheries for Scotland, the *Structure of Agriculture*, H.M.S.O., 1966.

Department of Agriculture and Fisheries for Scotland, *Scottish Agricultural Economics*, H.M.S.O. (annually).

Scottish Council (Development and Industry), *Scottish Economic Review*.

The Glasgow Herald Trade Review.

S. Paulden and W. Hawkins, *Whatever Happened at Fairfields?* London, 1969.

K. Gibbs, 'The Clyde Enters the Big-Ship League', *Scotland Magazine*, October 1970.

K. J. W. Alexander and C. L. Jenkins, *Fairfields: A Study of Industrial Change*, London, 1970.

Report of the Advisory Group on Shipbuilding on the Upper Clyde, H.M.S.O., 544, 1971.

[1] J. F. C. Thompson, *Scotland Magazine*, 1968.

J. F. C. Thompson, 'On the Brink: A Statistical Review of the Vehicle Industry in Scotland', *Scotland Magazine*, July 1968.

W. Irvin and D. Stark, 'Anatomy of Clydeside', *Scotland Magazine*, February 1965.

Electronics Weekly, 'Scotland Expands in Electronics', 14th August 1968.

Chapter 6
Income and Wealth

This is primarily an introspective Chapter. We were able in Chapter 3 to identify trends in earnings and personal income in Scotland compared to the rest of the United Kingdom, as part of a broad survey of significant indicators of economic performance. Here we begin by setting out the differences in aggregate net income between countries of the U.K., whereas in Chapter 3 we looked at an index of total income but were primarily concerned with *per capita* income data. The Chapter then goes on to break down the available information about income, largely from Inland Revenue sources, and shows (a) *per capita* differences in income between Scotland and other regions *within* England, and (b) the differences that prevail *within* Scotland in income levels and trends. We shall also try to look in more detail than we did in Chapter 3 at the various categories of personal income, such as earned and investment income, and see how these differ between Scotland and other parts of the country. Finally, the Chapter throws up some significant differences in asset holding between Scotland and the rest of the U.K.

1 Total Income

A comparison of the size and composition of income and wealth in Scotland with those of other regions within the U.K. must rely largely on the returns of the Inland Revenue. This remains true despite the fact that statistics on Scottish income can be obtained from a number of other sources. One such source is to derive income in the way that was attempted in Chapter 2, by calculating gross domestic product *per capita*. The figures so obtained are, however, of little value for comparative purposes because of the severe limitations of the official data at anything below a national level. As a result, whilst figures on income as used in national accounting practice can be constructed for the separate countries comprising the U.K., it is not possible to compile similar figures for sub-regions of those countries. This renders impossible any comparisons between Scottish income as obtained through national accounting procedure and that of regions within England. Nor can inter-regional comparisons within Scotland itself be made.

Another source of information on income is the Department of Health and Social Security's *Annual Analysis of Earnings*. It is probable, however, that these are not as reliable as the Inland Revenue returns; nor are they as comprehensive in coverage. In the first place, the figures of the Department of Health and Social Security are based on a relatively small sample of population registered for national insurance purposes, amounting to one-half of one per cent. This may be sufficient for comparisons between standard regions, but any further regional breakdown means that the errors involved assume considerably greater importance. Hence, the figures are not suitable for comparisons between sub-regions of Scotland. Second, the statistics refer not to total income but to gross earnings. They comprise, therefore, only one of the items used by the Inland Revenue in determining total income. Much the same criticisms can be levelled at income figures derived from the *Family Expenditure Surveys* of the Department of Employment. When broken down to a regional level, the sample size on which these Surveys are based makes the results most unreliable.

These problems can be avoided to some extent by using Inland Revenue statistics. The latter make comparisons possible both between and within countries, though a number of qualifications must be borne in mind when using these statistics. First, the Inland Revenue returns cover income as computed for tax purposes;[1] second, they embrace all incomes over £275 that were reviewed by the Inland Revenue for tax purposes; third, the income figures are based on a systematic stratified sample—the 1964/5 sample, for instance, included some one million, out of approximately 21 million incomes;[2] finally, as distinct from national accounting procedure, all income accruing to U.K. inhabitants from whatever source is included within the scope of the returns.

Inland Revenue figures are, then, the best available for

[1] Certain minor grades of income will therefore, be excluded since they are exempt from income tax. This includes, for instance, the first £15 of Savings Bank interest, certain National Insurance benefits, etc.

[2] The most recent Inland Revenue figures on income, relating to 1967/8 are based on a much smaller sample of 110,000 out of almost 28 million incomes.

our purposes; but they must still be used with great caution. They are estimates derived from samples and are therefore subject to sampling errors. With this in mind, total net income in Scotland over the past decade may be compared to that in other U.K. countries.

Table 6.1 Total Net Income[1] in the Separate Countries of the U.K. 1959/60–1967/8

	1959/60		1967/8		
Country	Total Net Income (£m) (i)	As per cent of U.K. (ii)	Total Net Income (£m) (iii)	As per cent of U.K. (iv)	Absolute growth of Income 1959/60–1967/8 per cent (v)
England	12,310·1	85·3	21,115·4	86·4	72
Wales	608·5	4·2	900·9	3·7	48
Scotland	1,257·7	8·7	1,989·6	8·1	58
N. Ireland	249·4	1·7	428·9	1·8	72
U.K.	14,425·7	100·0	24,434·8	100·0	69

Source: Inland Revenue Reports.

[1] Adjusted to exclude income accruing to public departments, the forces and merchant navy.

The Table shows (col. v) that over the past decade, the growth of total income in Scotland has been disappointingly low. The result has been that as a proportion of U.K. income, total Scottish income has fallen from 8·7 per cent in 1959/60 to 8·1 per cent in 1967/8. Table 6.1 also shows that the growth of income in both England and N. Ireland was above the national average over the period. In absolute terms, however, total income was so low in the latter country that it comprised less than 2 per cent of that in the U.K. as a whole over the decade.

2 Regional Income Comparisons

It would be fair to say that broad global comparisons such as can be made from Table 6.1 tend to conceal as much as they reveal. Comparing income in Scotland to that in the U.K. or to that in England as a whole is of limited significance. Properly considered, Scotland is one amongst many regions of the U.K. Hence, a more useful standard against which Scottish income might be measured is the income-level obtaining in the several regions south of the border. In addition, some idea of approximate living standards in the separate regions can be secured by expressing such income in *per capita* terms. This is done in Table 6.2 below where Scottish income per head is compared to that in the various regions of England for 1967/8.

Table 6.2 Income per Head of Total Population[1] by Regions of the U.K., 1967/8

New Standard Regions	Income Per Head (£)	As per cent of U.K.
London and South-East	543	123
East Anglia	400	90
South West	418	94
West Midlands	462	104
East Midlands	427	96
North-West	415	94
Yorkshire and Humberside	428	97
Northern	354	80
Total England	462	104
Wales	332	75
N. Ireland	287	65
Scotland	384	87
U.K.	443	100

Sources: Calculated from *Inland Revenue Statistics, 1970; Annual Abstract of Statistics.*

[1] Total net income expressed as a proportion of total home population. Income figures exclude payments to public departments, the forces and the merchant navy.

Several interesting features emerge from Table 6.2. The income figures provide some indication of the relative living standards in the separate regions, although it must, of course, be emphasised that price-levels may differ in different regions. The figure for income per head prevailing in London was outstandingly high. The only other region in which *per capita* income exceeded the U.K. average was the West Midlands. As can be seen, most of the regions in England were fairly close to the U.K. figure with the one exception of the Northern region. Here, income per head amounted in 1967/8 to only 80 per cent of the U.K. average. The Northern region was, indeed, the only part of England in which *per capita* income was exceeded by that in Scotland.

On the other hand, it could be pointed out that the region 'London and the South-East' is something of an exception. This region apart, the level of income per head in Scotland was not too dissimilar from that prevailing in several of the other English regions. The same could not be said, however, of income per head in N. Ireland and Wales. As was observed in Chapter 3, the Welsh figure should be treated with great caution, but even so, it can be seen that the level of *per capita* income in both countries was substantially below the average for the U.K. Indeed, income per head in Ireland amounted to little more than half the level prevailing in London and the South-East of England.

It should be stressed that, as important as the absolute level of income in the separate regions, are the trends in income growth over the past few years. Here, the trend in Scottish income confirms the conclusion reached in Chapter 3 that, at best, Scotland was marking time relative to the rest of the country over the 1960s. According to Dr McCrone, the level of Scottish income per head at the beginning of the decade was not far below the majority of English regions. Indeed, overall, it surpassed that in four of the regions which he specified, namely N. Ireland, Wales, the Northern region and the South-West region.[1] Since then the more northerly regions have fared badly.

In relation to *per capita* income in the U.K., Scottish income has remained stagnant between 1959/60–1967/8 whilst that in the Northern region of England has declined from 87 per cent to 80 per cent of the national average. In contrast, income per head in the South-West has risen substantially over the same period to a level that is now well above the Scottish figure. From 80 per cent of the national average in 1959/60, income in the South-West had reached 94 per cent in 1967/8. It is clear, then, that the growth of Scottish income has been disappointing. Not only is the absolute level of income now exceeded in all but three of the standard regions of the U.K., but also there has been no indication over the past decade of any narrowing of the income-differential between Scotland and the nation as a whole.

3 Income Differences within Scotland

So far, we have treated Scotland as a homogeneous unit, discussing total income and income per head in the whole of the region. It is instructive, however, to make a further break-down of the country to the level of areas and counties. This serves several purposes. First, it enables us to discover whether there are marked variations in the geographical distribution of income within Scotland. Second, an analysis of income per head in the different counties and areas of Scotland over the past few years will enable us to ascertain how living standards in the different parts of the country have changed over time. Most relevant in this context is to determine which areas have enjoyed the most rapid growth of income per head and which types of economic activity appear to

[1] G. McCrone, *Scotland's Economic Progress*, p. 78.

have had the most stimulating effect on the growth of *per capita* income. Table 6.3 below presents a regional break-down for Scotland of total income and income per head of population for the years 1959/60 and 1967/8.

Table 6.3 shows quite clearly that marked regional variations do, indeed, exist in the distribution of income in Scotland. As can be seen, by far the largest share of total income accrued to the county of Lanark. Midlothian, the county which, in absolute terms, received the next largest share had a total net income in 1967/8 amounting to less than one-half of that in Lanark. At the other end of the scale, total income was lowest throughout the period 1959/60–1967/8 in the areas of Clackmannan and Kinross, and Argyll and Bute. This might largely have been expected in view of the very small size of the former and the predominantly agricultural base of the latter.

In addition to having by far the largest share of total income in Scotland, Lanarkshire also had an income per head of population which grew to a level significantly above the Scottish average in the course of the 1960s. Indeed, over the decade the county experienced one of the most rapid rises in *per capita* income of all Scottish regions. To a large extent this is an indication of the success achieved by the county in re-diversifying its economy, with the recent emphasis particularly on the electrical and instrument-making industries. Since 1945, the area has, in fact, absorbed approximately one-fifth of total new industrial investment in Scotland.[1] Table 6.3 shows that besides Lanarkshire, the other most prosperous parts of the country were the counties of Midlothian and Renfrew. Both had *per capita* incomes well above the average for Scotland as a whole.

Perhaps providing a greater insight, however, into the efficacy of regional policy is the extent to which income per head has increased in the different regions over the decade. The most rapid growth occurred in the north of Scotland. *Per capita* income virtually doubled in the area Caithness, Inverness, etc. and a rapid rise was also experienced in the Aberdeen, Moray, Banff, Nairn region. Nor was this increase the result of any substantial decline of population in either area. Indeed, over the 1960s, the fall in population was marginal, amounting in each to not much more than 1 per cent. Clearly, then, changes in population-size are in no sense an adequate explanation for the large increases in income per head experienced. With regard to the former area, the greatest influence has almost certainly been exercised by the nuclear power

[1] *The Economist*, 21st–28th February 1970.

Table 6.3 Total Net Income and Income Per Head of Population by Regions of Scotland, 1959/60 and 1967/8

Area	1959/60 Total Net Income (£m)	1959/60 Income per Head (£)	1959/60 Income per Head as per cent of Scottish average	1967/8 Total Net Income (£m)	1967/8 Income per Head (£)	1967/8 Income per Head as per cent of Scottish average
Aberdeen, Banff, Moray, Nairn	93·5	215·8	89	152·7	361·9	94
Angus and Kincardine	77·4	252·7	104	115·1	380·1	99
Argyll and Bute	14·2	200·8	83	19·3	271·6	71
Caithness, Inverness, etc.[1]	39·6	180·8	74	76·7	351·2	92
Ayr	79·6	230·4	95	108·2	309·0	81
Berwick, East Lothian, etc.[2]	34·7	223·6	92	50·4	331·7	86
Clackmannan and Kinross	11·6	238·2	98	16·5	334·0	87
Dumfries, Kircudbright and Wigtown	34·1	226·4	93	49·1	340·5	89
Dunbarton	40·2	220·4	91	51·5	235·2	61
Fife	71·2	218·6	90	97·5	301·5	79
Lanark	403·0	246·8	101	683·8	439·0	114
Midlothian	167·5	288·2	119	282·4	477·2	124
Perth	29·9	237·5	98	39·0	312·8	82
Renfrew	99·9	295·2	121	153·7	430·2	112
Stirling	46·2	236·7	97	64·4	321·1	84
West Lothian	14·8	156·8	64	29·2	280·5	73
Total Scotland	1,257·7	243·2	100	1,989·6	383·5	100

Sources: Calculated from Inland Revenue Reports; Annual Reports of the Registrar General.

[1] Also includes Ross and Cromarty, Orkney, Sutherland and Zetland.

[2] Also includes Peebles, Roxburgh and Selkirk.

installation at Dounreay and the consequent introduction of a relatively large number of highly-paid civil service staff. In addition, the Highland Board has achieved some success in attracting new enterprise to the region, sufficient, perhaps, to have an influence on living standards. The Aberdeen region, on the other hand, has benefitted from the growth of its food-processing and light engineering industries. All in all, it has been apparent that over the past decade the traditionally wide differential between *per capita* incomes in the north and south of the country has narrowed considerably. The gap in income per head between the first four regions specified in Table 6.3 and the remaining more southerly counties was of the order of 13 per cent in 1959/60. By 1967/8, this gap had narrowed to only 8 per cent. It is quite probable, too, that given the continued energy and foresight of the Highland Board and the efforts of the North-East to attract new industrial development, this trend will continue in the future.

So far, we have concentrated largely on the high-income areas and those in which income has grown most rapidly over recent years. There is, of course, another side to the picture which has yet to be considered. According to Table 6.3, living standards at the beginning of the 1960s would appear to have been lowest in West Lothian and the primarily rural areas of Caithness, Inverness, etc. and Argyll and Bute. By 1967/8, however, expansion had been such in the northern area that income per head had risen from 74 per cent to over 90 per cent of the Scottish average. In contrast, although Argyll and Bute experienced an increase in income per head of over one-third during the 1960s, the increase in Scotland as a whole had been well over one-half. As a result, the area had further lost ground in a Scottish context, having in 1967/8, one of the lowest levels of *per capita* income in the country.

Perhaps the two most remarkable cases in Scotland were those of West Lothian and Dunbarton. In the former, income per head of population remained at a relatively low level throughout the 1960s. This was due to the 'run-down' of such traditional industries in the area as coal and shale, added to the fact that the major new industrial development, vehicle manufacture, had little influence on general income-levels in the region in the period examined. Indeed in 1959/60, living standards in the county had been by far the lowest of any area in Scotland.[1] Thereafter, West

[1] It might be, of course, that the levels of income per head in certain of the individual counties which have been aggregated together were lower still. Unfortunately, the Inland Revenue provides no separate details for these counties.

Lothian experienced a greater than average rise in income per head over the 1960s, so that by the end of the decade living standards were higher than in several other regions. The experience of Dunbarton, on the other hand, was almost exactly the reverse. Between 1959/60–1967/8, the level of *per capita* income hardly grew at all, with the result that by the latter date, living standards in the county had slumped to a level lower than any other area in Scotland. To a large extent, this reflected the closure of several of Dunbarton's main employment-giving industries. As a consequence, the rate of unemployment in the area remained relatively high.

From this regional break-down of income per head in Scotland, we can appreciate which regions enjoy the highest living standards, and which have been most successful in raising their income-levels over recent years. It may be that the economic policies pursued in these areas and the types of activity in which they specialised could, in some measure, be applied to less fortunate parts of the country. On the other hand, it is obvious that the type of enterprise suited to certain parts of the country might be wholly inappropriate for others. It would, for instance, be hard to envisage a thriving motor-assembly plant located in the far north of Scotland.

4 Categories of Income

Whilst the preceding analysis has revealed some striking regional differences within Scotland in *per capita* income levels, it is now necessary to carry the investigation one stage further. Table 6.2 above showed clearly that the level of income per head in Scotland was relatively low when compared with other parts of the U.K. Indeed, by 1967/8, it was lower than in all but one of the standard regions of England. A highly relevant question, therefore, in a Scottish context is which were the *types* of income in which this country was so deficient? To answer this, we must take a closer look at the structure of Scottish income. Obviously, personal income derives from many different sources, including employment, profits, property, etc. By comparing these different components of income in Scotland on a *per capita* basis with those for the U.K., we should be able to highlight those categories in which the share accruing to Scotland appeared unduly low.

In Table 6.4 below, the structure of income per head of population is compared in the separate countries of the U.K. for the year 1967/8.

As can be seen from Table 6.4, Northern Ireland has

Table 6.4 Structure of Income Per Head of Total Population in the Separate Cou[ntries] of the U.K., 1967/8 (£)

Income Category	England	Wales	Scotland	N. Ireland	U.K.
Profits and Professional Earnings	34·5	31·8	33·9	33·1	34·3
Salaries	133·6	73·0	81·7	73·4	124·1
Wages	214·4	172·1	195·7	133·0	208·3
Net Earned Income[1]	435·6	319·1	357·0	275·0	418·1
Rent and Other Income from Land	3·2	2·4	0·8	2·6	2·9
Interest, Dividends and Other Investment Income	26·7	15·6	26·0	12·0	25·7
Net Investment Income	29·9	18·0	26·8	14·6	28·6
Total Net Income[2]	465·5	337·1	383·8	289·6	446·7

Sources: Calculated from Inland Revenue Reports Annual Reports of the Registrar General.

[1] The constituent parts do not sum to the total since certain minor components of net e[arned] income, such as wife's earnings, etc. have not been separately distinguished.

[2] These figures are slightly different from the total income figures given by country earlier [in this] chapter and in Chapter 3. This is due to some small discrepancies in the Inland Revenue sta[tistics] when breaking down income into its component parts.

both the lowest earned income and investment income per head in the U.K. At the top of the scale, both these categories are significantly above the U.K. average in England. The Scottish case is somewhat different. The Table shows that the major reason why Scotland has had a generally low *per capita* income lies in the relatively low level of *earned* income accruing to the country's residents. On the other hand, investment income per head of population, although below the national average, was only marginally so, and accounted for only a small part of Scotland's smaller income per head *in toto*. In 1967/8, for instance, earned income per head in Scotland amounted to only 85 per cent of the U.K. average and to 82 per cent of that in England. The corresponding figures for investment income per head were 94 per cent and 90 per cent. Nor is this in any sense a phenomenon new to the later 1960s. Dr McCrone found much the same results for the years 1959/60, when *per capita* earned income in Scotland amounted only to 87 per cent of that in the U.K. while investment income comprised 92 per cent.[1]

We must therefore look mainly to earned income in seeking reasons for the relatively low level of Scottish income per head. Within this category, Table 6.4 shows that profits and professional earnings in Scotland were relatively high and approximated fairly closely to the U.K. figures. Where the major part of the discrepancy arises is with regard to income from employment.

[1] G. McCrone, *Scotland's Economic Progress*, Table 2, p. 78.

Here Scotland, in common with both Wales and Northern Ireland, fell far short of the levels obtaining in England. It might be expected that wages-income in Scotland, calculated on a *per capita* basis, would be somewhat lower than the national average in view of the traditionally lower rates of payment prevailing in the country. In addition, it should be remembered that Scottish unemployment rates were relatively high and activity rates low during the 1960s. As a result, the number actually in work stagnated at a time when they were rising in the U.K. as a whole. Quite simply, a lower proportion of Scotland's labour force was in work and earning income by means of employment, and wage-income per head of the total Scottish population was therefore bound to be lower than in the U.K. In the event, however, the margin of difference in 1967/8 was not very great. Income per head from *wages* in Scotland, at 94 per cent of the U.K. average, was not the major reason for the country's relatively low employment income and hence generally lower living standards.

To a large extent, the answer to Scotland's relatively low *per capita* income lies with the category 'salaries'. Here, Scotland compared most unfavourably both with England and the U.K. as a whole. Per head of population, salary-income amounted to a mere 61 per cent of the level prevailing in England and to two-thirds of that in the U.K. in 1967/8. Consequently, if we can explain why the proportion of income derived from salaries was so low in Scotland, we will at the same time have advanced a good deal of the way towards explaining the relatively low level of Scottish *per capita* income as a whole.

Several reasons may be suggested for Scotland's inferior *per capita* income from salaries. First, as with wages, the fact that Scotland had a lower proportion of her total working population in employment would be likely, other things being equal, to affect salary income. Second the proportions differ of relatively high paid *head-office* staff amongst the salary earners, where Scotland is at a decided disadvantage. The ownership of a large proportion of Scottish industry is either based in London and the south, or is American controlled. Indeed, in 1968, of the value of total turnover of all firms operating in Scotland, more than one-tenth was accounted for by American-owned companies. Given this large degree of control resting outwith the country, the proportion of highly-paid head-office staff in Scotland is likely to be relatively small. This is certain to have an unfavourable influence on the level of salary-income earned per head of total population in the country.

Third, salaries tend to be lower in Scotland for comparable posts, at least in the private sector, than they are elsewhere in the U.K. Finally, and most important, is the fact that Scotland has simply a lower proportion of salaried personnel than is the case south of the border. The sample *Population Census of 1966* reveals, for instance, that the percentage of professional workers, employers and managers to the total economically active and retired males aged 15 and over was 12·1 per cent in Scotland. In England and Wales, on the other hand, the ratio was 15·1 per cent.[1] Clearly, because Scotland has relatively fewer salaried people, there will be repercussions on the level of *per capita* income of the total population.

While it was the level of *earned* income in Scotland that primarily explains the country's relatively low living standards, other forces were also at work. As observed earlier, the broad category of net investment income per head of population in Scotland came fairly near to the U.K. average. Yet, when this total investment figure is disaggregated, it can be seen that there existed marked differences in composition between Scotland and the rest of the U.K. Scottish *per capita* income from interest, dividends and other investment was relatively high and, indeed, exceeded the national average. On the other hand, income from property was extremely low; *per capita* income from this source was below that of any of the regions specified in Table 6.4. To some extent this reflects the slightly smaller proportion of private housing to let in Scotland when compared with England and Wales. Moreover, the greater age and hence poorer quality of private housing to let north of the border results in a low level of rents.[2] It is, therefore, income from property that depresses total investment income per head in Scotland to a level below that obtaining in the U.K. as a whole.

In sum, the lower level of *per capita* income in Scotland stems from the fact that the levels both of earned and investment income fell below the national average. Primarily responsible for the difference, however, was *earned* income, and within this category, the relatively low level of income derived from *salaries*. We have also seen that the level of income per head varied quite

[1] Calculated from General Register Office, *Sample Census 1966, (Scotland)*, *Economic Activity Tables*, H.M.S.O., 1968.

[2] Approximately three-quarters of unfurnished private rented property in Scotland dates from the period before 1900. This is a much higher proportion than in England and Wales and, obviously, renders Scottish property much less desirable. Hence the relatively low level of rents in the Scottish region.

markedly in the different regions of Scotland. The most affluent areas comprised Lanarkshire, Midlothian and Renfrewshire. In the two former counties, *per capita* income has grown rapidly during the past decade, although not as rapidly as in the Caithness, Inverness, etc. area where it virtually doubled between 1959/60–1967/8. The lowest living standards are to be found in those areas which have suffered most from the run down of traditional trades and from various closures of main employment-giving industries. The counties of Dunbarton, West Lothian and Fife came under this category. In addition, Argyll and Bute remains a traditionally low-income area, dependent largely upon primary industry.

5 Total Assets

Moving from income to a consideration of total wealth in Scotland is a most hazardous undertaking. Whilst the income figures have to be used with caution, those on total wealth are tentative in the extreme, so making it impossible to reach hard and fast conclusions. Much of the data necessary to an assessment of the nature and distribution of wealth in Scotland is simply not available. As a result, estimates have to be constructed for many of the different components of wealth, these varying in their probable degree of accuracy.

One such set of estimates has recently been compiled by Dr L. C. Wright, these being based on the number and value of estates at death assessed for death-duty purposes, with the addition of sample figures for estates below the death-duty exemption limit of £5,000. According to these statistics, Scotland experiences in a more extreme form the uneven distribution of wealth-ownership common to Britain as a whole. For instance, 11 per cent of those people with a total wealth of £40,000 or more were located north of the border in 1965. This is a somewhat greater share than might have been expected. On a *pro rata* to population basis, Scotland should have had something in the order of 9–10 per cent in 1965. At the other end of the scale, a mere 7 per cent of those whose wealth amounted to less than £5,000 lived in Scotland.

The origins of this uneven pattern of wealth distribution in Scotland are rooted in the past. Dr Wright attributed the relatively high proportion of those with large wealth-holdings to the profits made either from the land or from heavy industry in the era before 1914. The low proportion with wealth of less than £5,000 might, in part, be attributed to a factor for which

Scotland is traditionally famous—thrift. The relatively small numbers in this wealth-range would appear to indicate a high propensity to save on the part of the Scottish people.

This uneven distribution of Scottish wealth apart, there are some grounds for believing that within the separate wealth groups, *individual* holdings of assets in Scotland are, on average, higher than in Great Britain. An investigation of the holdings of selected financial assets shows that the total of these assets is absolutely and, on a population basis, proportionately smaller than in Great Britain. Yet, although proportionately smaller, this tends to be offset by the fact that there are relatively fewer people in Scotland holding such assets. In consequence, the value of these assets, when expressed on a 'per wealth-holder' basis is higher than in Great Britain as a whole. This is brought out in Table 6.5 below, which compares for certain selected assets, Scottish and British holdings on a per wealth-holder basis.

Table 6.5 Estimated Holdings of Selected Assets per Wealth-Holder, Scotlan[illegible] Great Britain, 1965 (£)

	1960		1964		1965	
Assets	Scotland	Gt. Britain	Scotland	Gt. Britain	Scotland	Gt. B[illegible]
National Savings, Bonds, T.R.Cs	565	396	712	401	632	406
Deposit Accounts	623	711	741	747	770	953
Building Society Deposits	1,449	1,386	1,909	1,300	1,906	1,628
Equities	5,319	5,430	7,906	5,342	9,479	5,367

Source: L. C. Wright, op. cit., *p. 145.*

As can be seen, individual Scottish holdings of national savings and bonds, equities and building society deposits were generally higher than in Great Britain. Indeed, the thrift of the lower income groups, already remarked upon, has resulted in Scotland being a disproportionately heavy investor in low interest forms of Government savings. Perhaps the Scot is not such a rational miser after all!

To conclude this chapter on Scottish income and wealth, it is constructive to compare the holdings of total wealth and assets in Scotland with those in Great Britain. In Table 6.6, estimates are presented of the magnitudes of the various components of wealth for both regions. In this way, it is possible to determine those types of holding in which Scots have tended to specialise and, correspondingly, those in which the country appears under-represented.

Table 6.6 Wealth and Asset Holdings, Scotland and the U.K., 1965

Type of Asset	Scotland (£m)	Assets as per cent of Gross Wealth in Scotland	U.K. Assets as per cent of Gross Wealth in U.K.
Financial Assets:			
Banking and Official	1,811	28·5	19·4
Insurance, Pension, Building Society	1,011	15·9	16·4
Companies	1,314	20·7	18·2
Other Financial Institutions	716	11·3	11·2
Total Financial Assets	4,852	76·3	65·2
Fixed Assets:			
Home Ownership	644	10·1	22·8
Value of Consumer-owned durables	650	10·2	9·1
Land	129	2·0	2·4
Miscellaneous	48	0·8	0·6
Total Fixed Assets	1,507	23·6	34·8
Gross Wealth	6,359	100·0	100·0
Liabilities:			
Mortgages outstanding	86		
Consumer Credit	250	U.K. Gross Wealth 83,087	
Debts, etc.	268	U.K. Total Liabilities 10,538	
Total Liabilities	604	U.K. Net Wealth 72,549	
Net Wealth	5,754		

Source: Calculated from L. C. Wright, op. cit., p. 146.

As can be seen from Table 6.6, Scots had a decided predilection for financial assets. More than 76 per cent of the value of gross wealth in Scotland was held in this form, as against only 65 per cent in Great Britain as a whole. This, allied to the markedly smaller proportion in Scotland, *vis-à-vis* Britain, of house-ownership, has undoubtedly retarded the growth of Scottish wealth. Property since 1945 has been the fastest growing of all assets. Table 6.6 shows that the value of fixed assets in Scotland amounted to a little under one-quarter of the country's gross wealth. In Britain, more than one-third of wealth was held in this form. This discrepancy can be almost wholly attributed to house-ownership. The value of house-ownership in Scotland in 1965 amounted to a mere 3 per cent of that in the U.K.

Hence, since the second world war, total wealth in Scotland has not grown as rapidly as might have been the case. The ownership of houses has contributed only a very small fraction of that in the U.K., while at the same time Scots appear to have placed undue emphasis on the holding of relatively low interest forms of financial assets. As a result, in 1965, total gross wealth in Scotland comprised only 7 per cent of that in the U.K., a proportion significantly lower than might have been expected on a *pro rata* to population basis.

References

H.M.S.O., *Report of the Commissioners of H.M. Inland Revenue.*

H.M.S.O., *Report from the Select Committee on Scottish Affairs 1969–70: Economic Planning in Scotland*, 267, 1970.

Select Committee on Scottish Affairs 1969–70: Minutes of Evidence . . . Appendices and Index, 267–1, 1970.

G. McCrone, *Regional Policy in Britain.*

Scotland's Future: the Economics of Nationalism.

Scotland's Economic Progress, 1951–60.

B. E. Coates and E. M. Rawstron, 'Regional Variations in Incomes', *Westminster Bank Review*, February 1966.

P. J. Devine, 'Inter-Regional Variations in the Degree of Inequality of Income Distribution: the United Kingdom, 1949–65', *Manchester School*, June 1969.

L. C. Wright, 'Some Fiscal Problems of Devolution in Scotland' in J. N. Wolfe (ed.), *Government and Nationalism in Scotland*, Edinburgh, 1969.

Chapter 7
The Expenditure Mix

In this Chapter we are concerned with breaking down aggregate spending in Scotland into its main component parts. We saw in Chapter 1 that models of national economic activity seek, on the expenditure side, to classify streams of spending which are significant both with respect to their motivation and their objectives. National income statistics try to fit data to these categories of spending.

The size, composition, and movements in these components of national spending are important in the theory and policy of income determination. For example, government spending can be readily used to change the level of activity, and this will have multiplier consequences. Government policy may also try to affect the spending of consumers (and their saving) by changing direct tax rates, and also by the choice of taxes which are levied on goods and services (indirect taxes). In addition, it follows that the greater the statistical information we can assemble about the expenditure mix the more we can try to quantify, on the basis of simple income models, the likely effects of any changes in private and/or public spending flows.

In a Scottish context, much of the information which is necessary to obtain a firm statistical grip on these components of total expenditure is not available, and many of the items of total spending undertaken both by individuals and the Government have to be estimated. An even larger gap is our inadequate knowledge of (X–M), the nature and value of Scotland's trade balance. We noted in Chapter 1 that no official estimate of the country's trading account has ever been attempted.

At a time when there is widespread interest in assessing the economic strength of a possibly independent Scotland, and the issue of Scottish Nationalism has emerged as a matter for serious analysis and consideration, the lack of such statistical data on expenditures can be particularly frustrating. For Scotland, we should like to know the size of the contribution that each component of expenditure makes to the total. Does the 'expenditure mix' in the regional economy of Scotland differ significantly from that in the national economy of the United Kingdom? What is the size of the regional multiplier operating in Scotland? Much as we should like to answer these questions, on both theoretical and policy grounds, we cannot give precise assessments at present. For the reasons already given it is not possible to value Scottish exports and imports (X−M). We have therefore to confine ourselves to the components of gross domestic product. In the sections that follow we shall consider in turn the major expenditure components—Consumption, Investment, and Government spending—in as much detail as the limited data allow. The final section of the Chapter deals with the highly controversial question of the 'Scottish Budget'. The separate 'Budget' estimates compiled by various authorities will be analysed in an attempt to assess, not only their reliability, but also their relevance to the debate about an 'independent' Scotland.

2 Consumption

Consumption spending forms the largest single spending stream in national economies. After all, most people engaged in economic activity are employees, and they typically spend most of their disposable income on goods and services. What they do not spend is saved, saving being defined as the disposable income which they do not consume.

Information on consumption is far from adequate. There are a few scattered reports on expenditure for individual items but, these apart, reliance has to be placed on the Department of Employment's *Family Expenditure Surveys*. These surveys, now conducted annually, were initially concerned with the expenditure patterns of private households in the U.K. More recently, however, additional information has been collected involving the characteristics of each household and the income of its members. Although such data are extremely useful, each survey is based upon such a small size of sample that the conclusions drawn must necessarily be tentative.

The most recent survey for 1967/8, for example, is based upon an effective U.K. sample of 10,400 households, of which only 69 per cent fully cooperated. Further, like all estimates based on samples, the *Expenditure Surveys* contain sampling errors which are likely to be largest when average expenditure for small groups of households is being computed or when calculating expenditure for items infrequently purchased. To the extent that the income and expenditure patterns of the households in the effective sample which did not cooperate differed from those cooperating in the survey, then the final results of the survey will be affected. It was found, for instance, that the proportion of households without children in the non-cooperating group was slightly higher than in those households which did participate. Finally, with all the *Expenditure Surveys*, it should be borne in mind that there are certain inherent weaknesses in the figures. Expenditure on alcoholic drink and tobacco are consistently under-estimated, probably because householders reveal what they consider their expenditure on such items *should* have been rather than what their expenditure actually was. On average, it would seem that spending on alcohol is under-estimated by approximately one-half and that on tobacco by one-fifth. Much the same is true both of expenditure on meals taken outside the home and on items of confectionery such as chocolates, sweets and ice-cream. No corrections are made for these types of error so that, once again, the figures finally derived must be used with discretion.

Bearing these qualifications in mind, a comparison of the results produced by the *Family Expenditure Surveys* over the 1960s produce some interesting results. Table 7.1 below compares annual average income and expenditure per head of population for both Scotland and the U.K. in the two periods 1963/5 and 1967/8.

The first point to note from the Table below is that surveys for the two periods specified are in substantial agreement. As one might expect, both show that absolute expenditure per head in Scotland was highest for food, clothing and footwear and transport, whilst income paid in the form of tax amounted to approximately one-half of the expenditure shown under 'other payments recorded'. Again, both reports produce similar results in that they show expenditure per head in Scotland to be above the national average for fuel, light and power, clothing and footwear, and tobacco. Expenditure on alcohol, on the other hand, falls into a somewhat different category. Whereas in the most recent survey, *per capita* spending in Scotland was clearly above the U.K. average, in the 1963/5 report it was significantly below the national level. It is most probable that for the earlier period, the Scots seriously under-estimated their expenditure on this item. On the other hand, it could simply be that people in Scotland have dramatically increased their expenditure on alcohol over recent years. This hardly seems likely.

Table 7.1 Average Annual Income and Expenditure Per Head of Population, Scotland and the U.K., 1963/5 and 1967/8

	1963/5			1967/8		
	Scotland (£)	U.K. (£)	Ratio of Scotland to U.K. (per cent)	Scotland (£)	U.K. (£)	Ratio of Scotland to U.K. (per cent)
Average Income	355·1	404·9	88	463·5	508·0	91
Average Expenditure:						
Housing	27·2	38·6	71	36·5	51·0	72
Fuel, Light and Power	22·6	22·1	102	26·7	26·3	102
Food	92·7	98·7	94	110·0	113·1	97
Alcoholic Drink	12·7	13·7	93	18·0	17·5	103
Tobacco	22·1	19·4	114	24·6	22·2	111
Clothing and Footwear	33·2	32·3	103	40·0	37·2	108
Durable Household Goods	22·1	21·3	99	27·3	27·6	99
Other Goods	19·0	24·2	79	26·0	30·4	86
Transport and Vehicles	32·4	40·5	80	45·6	53·9	85
Services	30·7	38·8	94	35·3	40·3	88
Miscellaneous	1·4	1·4	100	1·3	1·4	93
Total All Above Expenditure	315·1	345·0	91	391·2	421·0	93
Other Payments Recorded:						
Tax	32·1	36·7	88	47·8	55·7	86
National Insurance	13·3	14·0	95	17·1	17·8	96
Mortgages, etc.	3·1	13·8	23	5·7	27·8	21
Pension Contributions, Life and Sickness Insurance, etc.	12·9	13·8	94	18·0	18·2	99
Other	7·8	9·0	87	7·6	10·6	72
Total	69·2	87·3	79	96·2	130·1	74

Source: Calculated from Family Expenditure Surveys. The figures given in these sample surveys on a household basis have been converted to a per capita basis.

At the other end of the scale, it can be seen that while expenditure per head on housing was low in Scotland relative to that in the U.K., expenditure on mortgages, included under 'other payments recorded', amounted to a mere one-fifth of the U.K. level. This reflects the relatively low level of owner-occupation in Scotland and, correspondingly, the high proportion of subsidised housing in the country. The latter may be attributed to the fact that local authority housing in Scotland is more heavily subsidised than in England and Wales since tenants are supported by means of the local rates as well as through the central exchequer. It is also interesting to note that for both periods shown in Table 7.1, the tax burden in Scotland is relatively low, this despite the fact that the absolute amount paid in taxation forms a fairly large part of the individual's total expenditure. Figures on income tax will, of course, depend on the prevailing level of income and how that income is distributed. It is, therefore, to be expected that in Scotland, a low-income area, the burden of income tax would be well below the national average.

One of the major advantages of the *Family Expenditure Surveys* should be that they allow a rough estimate to be made of the size of regional savings. Such an estimate would be extremely valuable since it would demonstrate the extent to which different regions could generate funds capable of being invested. Much of a region's savings are, of course, likely to be invested outwith the region while much of the investment actually taking place within it derives from altogether different areas. Nevertheless, an estimate of regional savings would then make it possible to determine whether a given region saves more than it receives in terms of 'outside investment' or *vice-versa.* It is unfortunate that the data presently made available by the *Expenditure Surveys* make any such estimate of regional savings virtually impossible.

At a regional level, the *Expenditure Survey's* calculations both of income and expenditure may be subject to so large a degree of error that savings, considered as the difference between the two, (a residual), might be grossly inaccurate. It is certainly the case, for instance, that the income figures compiled by the surveys do not accord with those given by the Inland Revenue. The former appear not only to be higher, but also to follow a different trend.[1] Moreover, an unqualified acceptance of the *Expenditure Survey's*

[1] The Inland Revenue figures show *per capita* income in Scotland to be declining as a proportion of that in the U.K. between 1964/5–1967/8. See Chapter 3, Table 3.6. The figures of the *Expenditure Surveys* tend to be higher in absolute terms, and *rising* as a proportion of the national average.

statistics would lead to the curious conclusion that 'dissaving' was taking place throughout the U.K. in 1967/8. This result is derived by subtracting tax and national insurance contributions from the total income figure given by the *Expenditure Survey* in order to acquire 'disposable income'. Once total expenditure and other items recorded are deducted from disposable income, any surplus remaining can be classified as 'savings'. Such a calculation produces a negative total or 'dissavings'. This is precisely the result that McCrone found from an investigation in earlier years.[1] He found that for every region in the U.K. total expenditure exceeded disposable income, the difference being most marked in London and the south-east of England.

It would seem, therefore, that it is not presently feasible to calculate the extent of regional savings from the *Family Expenditure Survey* reports. This is most regrettable since it means that this important concept for regional economics must remain largely indeterminate, for example as an aid in estimating income changes when economic policy changes are being examined. In general, however, the surveys do provide a useful guide to the levels of expenditure on individual items. For Scotland, they substantiate the evidence concerning the relatively low number of owner-occupied houses in the country and the high level of spending on such items as tobacco, clothing and footwear, etc. Nevertheless, it is worth repeating that the information provided must be used with caution, particularly at the regional level, where sampling errors are likely to be greatest.

3 Investment

As with consumption expenditure, so information about capital spending in Scotland is far from comprehensive. In the case of central authority spending, certain types can only be estimated for Scotland, largely because expenditure undertaken to benefit the U.K. as a whole cannot be accurately allocated to particular regions. Capital expenditure undertaken by the central Government or local authorities in the form of overhead capital have been specifically excluded from this section, and will be dealt with in section IV of the Chapter. We shall concentrate here only on those sectors of the economy for which reasonable estimates of investment can be supplied. Since for certain industries, such as transport and distribution, there is a complete dearth of regional data we shall be dealing essentially with the volume and composition of private investment in manufacturing

[1] G. McCrone, *Scotland's Economic Progress*, pp. 93–4.

industry and the level of expenditure in certain of the nationalised industries for which information is readily available. This latter category comprises mining and quarrying, and the gas, electricity and water supply industries.

With regard even to private investment in manufacturing, statistical coverage in Scotland compares unfavourably with that for the U.K. as a whole. The U.K. figures of manufacturing investment are available on a quarterly basis; are disaggregated by main industrial groups; and finally, are broken into three types of asset, 'new building work', 'plant and machinery' and 'vehicles'. The material for Scotland, on the other hand, is available on a yearly basis, is not broken down by industry and can be obtained only with a two-asset breakdown, 'new building work', and 'plant, machinery and vehicles'. In order to obtain information on capital expenditure *by industry* in Scotland, reliance has to be placed wholly on the *Census of Production* reports. These, whilst extremely useful, are available only at five-yearly intervals. Even more unfortunate, the delays in publication commonly associated with these reports renders the figures obsolete before they can serve any practical purpose. For instance, the results of the 1963 Census only became available late in 1970.

The official figures for investment in Scotland, published annually, are shown in Table 7.2 below. Although quoted originally in current prices, they have been converted to constant (1963) prices by means of the same price index as is used officially to deflate the corresponding quarterly figures for the U.K.[1]

In absolute terms, real investment in manufacturing in

Table 7.2 Capital Expenditure on Plant, Machinery and Vehicles in Scotland, 1960–8, Constant (1963) Prices

	Scotland (£m)	U.K. (£m)	Scotland as Proportion of U.K. (per cent)
1960	76	819	9·3
1961	90	957	9·4
1962	89	874	10·2
1963	75	792	9·5
1964	79	898	8·8
1965	90	989	9·1
1966	107	1,043	10·3
1967	95	1,042	9·1
1968	112	1,070	10·5

Sources: Digest of Scottish Statistics, April, 1970; A. Reid, op. cit., p. 33.

[1] See A. Reid, 'Manufacturing Investment in Scotland', in *Scotland Magazine*, Vol. 14, No. 8, August 1970, pp. 32–7.

Scotland rose only by 47 per cent over the period 1960–8. It can be seen, however, that relative to investment in the U.K., Scotland's share increased by just over 1 per cent over these same years. Even this probably casts an unduly favourable light on the level of investment achieved in Scotland, since the annual average level of expenditure in Scottish manufacturing amounted to 9·4 per cent of that in the U.K. between 1960–64; between 1964–68, the average was still only 9·6 per cent of the U.K. level. Clearly, there has been no significant improvement in Scotland's relative position over recent years, despite the financial incentives offered to companies under 'Development Area' policy.

In order to get behind these aggregate figures for investment in Scottish manufacturing, data made available by the *Census of Production* may be used. The *Census* provides a breakdown of investment by industry, and it is therefore possible to isolate precisely those sectors in which capital expenditure appears deficient in Scotland when compared to U.K. levels. In Table 7.3 below, capital expenditure in manufacturing is presented for Scotland by individual industries for the two years 1958 and 1963. In addition, the level of expenditure in certain trades outside the manufacturing sector is included in order to allow some comparison of investment in different types of industry.

It can be seen from Table 7.3 that a large proportion of Scottish investment was still going into the heavy industrial trades. The three categories metal manufacture, engineering and electrical goods, and shipbuilding and marine engineering accounted for no less than 42 per cent of total investment in manufacturing in Scotland in 1958 and for 36 per cent in 1963. In addition, capital expenditure in mining and quarrying remained heavy. In 1958, investment in Scottish mining amounted to over one-fifth of that in the manufacturing sector and even in 1963 the proportion was still one-tenth. The 'heavy' trades were, then, still absorbing a major share of Scotland's capital resources in 1963. Unfortunately, it is not possible to be precise about the contemporary situation in view of the absence of more up-to-date statistics, but it would seem reasonable to suppose that, although still heavy, the share of investment absorbed by these trades has continued to fall.

Whilst there is still likely to be a decided imbalance in the distribution of capital expenditure in favour of the heavy industries, certain features of Table 7.3 might be deemed encouraging to the long-term well-being of the Scottish economy. It can be seen, for instance, that in both 1958 and 1963 Scotland was devoting a relatively larger share of her capital resources to the

F

Table 7.3 Capital Expenditure in Manufacturing Industry,[1] Scotland, 1958 and 1963

Industry	1958 Expenditure (£m)	As per cent of Total Expenditure in Scotland (per cent)	U.K. Expenditure as per cent of Total (per cent)	1963 Expenditure (£m)	As per cent of Total Expenditure in Scotland (per cent)	U.K. Expenditure as per cent of Total (per cent)
Food, Drink and Tobacco	11·2	15·5	11·0	16·0	17·3	13·3
Chemicals and Allied Industries	13·4	18·5	23·4	10·7	11·6	13·5
Metal Manufacture	9·5	13·1	15·3	14·1	15·2	14·0
Engineering and Electrical Goods	15·5	21·4	15·7	15·2	16·4	16·9
Shipbuilding and Marine Engineering	5·3	7·3	2·4	3·6	3·9	1·6
Vehicles	1·0	1·4	7·1	9·6	10·4	10·0
Metal Goods not elsewhere specified	1·3	1·8	3·5	1·8	1·9	4·4
Textiles	4·3	5·9	5·6	5·9	6·4	7·0
Leather, Leather Goods and Fur	0·1	0·1	0·2	0·1	0·1	0·2
Clothing and Footwear	0·5	0·7	0·9	0·6	0·6	1·1
Bricks, Pottery, Glass, Cement, etc.	2·1	2·9	3·8	3·7	4·0	5·0
Timber, Furniture, etc.	0·7	1·0	1·2	1·7	1·8	1·7
Paper, Printing and Publishing	5·3	7·3	6·9	7·5	8·1	7·6
Other Manufacturing Industries	2·1	2·9	2·9	1·9	2·1	3·6
All Manufacturing	72·4	100·0	100·0	92·5	100·0	100·0

Industry	1958 Expenditure (£m)	1958 Scotland as per cent of U.K.	1963 Expenditure (£m)	1963 Scotland as per cent of U.K.
Mining and Quarrying	15·8	14·8	8·9	9·2
Gas, Electricity and Water	47·6	12·9	61·0	9.3

Source: Board of Trade, Report on the Census of Production 1963, H.M.S.O., 1970.

[1] Includes estimated figures for small firms not required to complete returns and for unsatisfactory returns.

lighter expanding trades of food, drink and tobacco, and paper, printing and publishing than was the case with the U.K. Perhaps most significant, however, was the large increase between these years in investment in the category 'vehicles'. By 1963, expenditure had risen to almost £10 million, this representing a larger share of Scotland's total investment in manufacturing than was the case for the U.K. as a whole. Of this investment in 'vehicles' four-fifths took the form of new plant and machinery.

The distribution of expenditure in the private sector can be carried a stage further by comparing investment by industrial groups in each of the regions of the U.K. This serves to place the Scottish investment performance firmly in perspective. In Table 7.4 below, the investment undertaken by the different regions of the U.K. within each industrial group is expressed as a proportion of total U.K. investment in that industrial group.

Amongst other things, Table 7.4 presents a breakdown of manufacturing investment for the separate countries of the U.K. It shows that across the whole range of manufacturing industry, capital expenditure in England amounted to virtually four-fifths of the U.K. total, that in Scotland roughly to one-tenth, whilst the remaining one-tenth was made up of investment in Northern Ireland and Wales. The Table also brings out the overwhelming predominance of investment in the South-East of England. As can be seen, expenditure in this region was the highest of any in the U.K. in six out of the eight industrial groups specified. The South-East region apart, the volume of total investment in Scottish manufacturing also lagged behind that of Yorkshire and Humberside, the West Midlands and the North-West region. In other respects, the evidence of the Table reinforces the conclusions drawn earlier. For instance, it can be seen that Scotland's share of U.K. investment in the chemicals industry was disappointing, and, relative to other regions of the U.K., expenditure also appeared deficient in textiles, leather and clothing and in the category 'other manufacturing industries'. In only one industrial group, food, drink and tobacco, did Scotland's share of U.K. investment rise above the level of one-tenth. Here, Scotland's expenditure was the third largest of all U.K. regions, behind that only of the South-East and North-West regions.

All in all, the volume of Scottish investment is much as might have been expected. Over the early 1960s Scotland's share of G.D.P. in the U.K. amounted to some 8–8½ per cent. Hence, her share of capital investment in 1963 amounted to a level slightly in excess of the G.D.P. ratio. In order to raise Scotland's

Table 7.4 Regional Distribution of Capital Expenditure in Manufacturing, 1963: Figures Expressed as Proportion of U.K. Expenditure in Each Industrial Group

Region	Food, Drink and Tobacco	Chemicals and Allied Industries	Metal Manu-facture	Engineering, Ship-building and Metal Goods	Vehicles	Textiles, Leather and Clothing	Paper, Printing and Publishing	Other Manufac-turing Industries	All Manu-facturing Industries
North	2·9	16·7	7·3	5·9	0·4	3·8	0·9	3·7	5·8
Yorkshire and Humberside	8·9	8·0	32·2	7·9	3·4	19·2	6·9	7·8	11·9
East Midlands	4·6	2·9	6·3	5·9	2·0	15·0	4·0	5·9	5·6
East Anglia	5·9	1·1	0·1	1·7	1·4	1·2	3·3	1·8	2·0
South-East	24·6	21·3	6·0	34·0	41·9	8·2	42·6	32·7	26·2
South-West	7·5	3·8	0·4	3·3	4·8	3·1	6·2	4·6	4·0
West Midlands	11·4	3·2	19·6	15·2	22·7	5·9	5·7	14·6	12·9
North-West	17·0	22·4	5·3	11·4	9·6	24·1	16·9	16·2	14·6
Total England	82·8	79·4	77·1	85·3	86·3	80·6	86·4	87·4	83·0
Wales	2·6	10·6	13·1	2·8	3·9	4·0	3·1	4·2	5·7
Scotland	11·7	7·7	9·8	8·8	9·4	7·7	9·7	6·8	9·0
N. Ireland	2·9	2·2	—	3·1	0·4	7·7	0·9	1·5	2·3
Total U.K.	100·0	100·0	100·0	100·0	100·0	100·0	100·0	100·0	100·0

Source: Calculated from Report on the Census of Production, 1963.

proportion of U.K. national product, a corresponding increase would have to take place in investment, particularly in those 'growth' industries where capital spending is presently deficient. It is, of course, much easier to postulate the desirability of such an increase than actually to achieve it. Despite all the incentives provided under regional policy, investment in Scottish manufacturing has hardly risen as a proportion of that in the U.K. over the 1960s. It remains to be seen whether the new measures introduced in 1970 to govern investment will prove more effective.

4 Government Expenditure

It is possible to obtain information on the bulk of public expenditure from official sources. The *Digest of Scottish Statistics* makes available for every year data derived from the Treasury on identified public expenditure in Scotland. Such expenditure includes that undertaken by the central Government, local authorities and the nationalised industries. Moreover, details are provided both of identifiable current expenditure and gross domestic fixed capital formation. Perhaps most important, however, is the fact that a full breakdown of expenditure is presented for individual categories, so permitting trends in the distribution of public expenditure to be observed over time.

There remains, of course, a fairly substantial category of 'unidentified' public spending in Scotland. This is expenditure normally undertaken to benefit the U.K. as a whole, so that it proves virtually impossible to allocate it accurately to particular regions within the nation. Typical examples are expenditure on defence, maintaining external relations, and the servicing of the national debt. The problems involved in allocating Scotland's share of this type of expenditure have already been dealt with in Chapter 2. They are investigated in even greater detail in the next section of this chapter which deals with the issue of the Scottish budget. In the context of the budget, estimating Scotland's probable share of unidentified expenditure becomes a matter of some importance. Clearly, the volume of such spending in Scotland could be of crucial importance in determining whether, under independence, the Scots could 'balance the books'. Here, however, we shall content ourselves merely with acknowledging the existence of such unallocated expenditure. Its exclusion from the analysis of this section can be readily justified. So arbitrary are the methods of allocation used and so large, therefore, are the possible margins of error that the estimates finally obtained might serve only to confuse and even distort the findings derived from an investigation of *identifiable* public expenditure in Scotland.

The Treasury estimate of Scotland's budgetary position, discussed below in section V, relates to the period 1967/8. This being the case, we shall examine the distribution of public spending in Scotland for the same year in order to maintain comparability. The Treasury figures for public expenditure in Scotland in that period are shown below. They include the spending of the central Government, local authorities and public corporations, but specifically exclude debt interest, the capital expenditure of the nationalised industries and those items of expenditure in Scotland which cannot readily be distinguished.

In 1967/8, identifiable public expenditure in Scotland amounted to almost 12 per cent of that in Great Britain. The distribution of such expenditure in Scotland serves to confirm much that we already know about the economy. For instance, as might have been expected, proportionately more is spent north of the border on the promotion of local employment, the provision of investment grants and regional employment premiums. All of these are part of the inducements provided under 'Development Area' policy. To this extent, then, Scotland has certainly received 'preferential treatment' compared with other regions of Great Britain. Moreover, since agriculture, forestry and fishing occupy a relatively larger part of the Scottish economy, Scotland was the recipient of a greater share of support in each of these three sectors. The implication is, of course, that any independent Scottish exchequer would have to face a relatively heavy burden of support for primary industry: either that or allow food prices to be determined purely by market forces. Whichever method was adopted, the onus would be on the Scottish people, in their role as taxpayers or as ordinary consumers, to meet a mounting expenditure on foodstuffs.

Above all, perhaps, Table 7.5 emphasises the peculiar position of Scottish housing. As already observed, the Scots are much more heavily dependent on subsidised housing than is the case in England and Wales. Hence, in 1967/8, 15 per cent of identifiable public expenditure in Scotland went into housing as opposed to less than 10 per cent in Great Britain as a whole. On the other hand, it might be noted that a significantly larger share of public spending in England and Wales was devoted to education other than Universities, to health and welfare and social security benefits.

A still more valuable insight into the nature and distri-

Table 7.5 The Distribution of Identifiable Public Expenditure in Scotland and Great Britain, 1967–8

Service	Identifiable expenditure in Scotland (£m)	As per cent of total identifiable expenditure in Scotland (per cent)	Identifiable expenditure in Gt. Britain as per cent of total (per cent)
Civil Defence	2·6	0·2	0·2
Roads and Public Lighting	63·2	4·8	4·8
Airports	2·9	0·2	0·2
Ports	5·3	0·4	0·3
Promotion of Local Employment	12·7	1·0	0·3
Investment Grants	43·2	3·3	2·7
S.E.T. additional payments	10·7	0·8	1·2
Regional Employment Premiums	13·0	1·0	0·3
Research Councils	7·0	0·5	0·7
Agricultural Support	46·4	3·5	2·3
Agricultural Services	5·4	0·4	0·7
Fisheries	2·3	0·2	—
Forestry	14·5	1·1	0·3
Housing	196·9	14·9	9·5
Environmental Services	83·0	6·3	6·9
Libraries, Museums and Arts	4·2	0·3	0·6
Police	24·8	1·9	2·5
Prisons	3·8	0·3	0·3
Other Law and Order	11·4	0·9	1·2
Education other than University	186·4	14·1	15·0
Universities	41·8	3·2	2·6
Health and Welfare	172·5	13·1	14·6
Children's Services	40·4	3·1	3·5
Social Security Benefits	272·7	20·7	24·7
Financial Admin. and Common Services	25·2	1·9	2·2
Other Services	27·1	2·0	2·3
Total	1,319·4	100·0	100·0

Source: H.M. Treasury, Estimates of Central Government Revenue and Expenditure Attributable to Scotland for the Financial Year 1967–8, H.M.S.O. 1969.
— Negligible.

bution of public spending in Scotland can be obtained by expressing identifiable expenditure on a *per capita* basis. This serves clearly to distinguish the major differences in the distribution of such spending between Scotland and Great Britain. Table 7.6 below presents a breakdown of public expenditure per head in Scotland and the order of difference existing for each category between Scotland and Great Britain.

In Table 7.6, the 'service' categories are ranked according to their importance in terms of absolute *per capita* expenditure.

Table 7.6 Identifiable Public Expenditure Per Capita, Scotland, 1967–8

Service	Per Capita Expenditure (Scotland) (£)	Difference in Per Capita Expenditure, Scotland and G.B.[1] (per cent)
Social Security Benefits	52·6	+ 3
Housing	38·0	+48
Education other than University	35·9	+14
Health and Welfare	33·3	+10
Environmental Services	16·0	+12
Roads and Public Lighting	12·2	+19
Agricultural Support	8·9	+46
Investment Grants	8·3	+33
Universities	8·1	+33
Children's Services	7·8	+ 8
Other Services	5·2	+ 8
Financial Administration and Common Services	4·9	+ 8
Police	4·8	− 9
Forestry	2·8	+77
Regional Employment Premiums	2·5	+74
Promotion of Local Employment	2·5	+73
Other Law and Order	2·2	−18
S.E.T. Additional Payments	2·1	−18
Research Councils	1·4	− 5
Ports	1·0	+49
Agricultural Services	1·0	−34
Libraries, Museums and Arts	0·8	−58
Prisons	0·7	+ 5
Airports	0·6	+25
Civil Defence	0·5	+22
Fishing	0·4	+85
Total	254·4	+19

Source: Calculated from H.M. Treasury, op. cit.,

[1] The plus sign indicates a greater *per capita* expenditure in Scotland; the minus sign that expenditure fell short of that in Great Britain.

Thus the list is headed by expenditure on social security benefits, housing, education other than University and so on, these being the categories where expenditure is most heavy. It should be noted from the outset that total *per capita* expenditure in Scotland in 1967/8 was almost one-fifth higher than in Great Britain. This, however, represents only the volume of public expenditure that the Treasury claims to be able to identify. It is a figure, therefore, that omits expenditure which cannot easily be allocated; yet even on these terms, it is a figure with which the S.N.P. would take issue.[1]

For our present purposes, however, we may accept the Treasury's estimates. By expressing these on a *per capita* basis

[1] See section V of this Chapter.

certain conclusions emerge very different from those previously expressed. As can be seen, the volume of expenditure per head of population was highest on the social services, housing and education. On the other hand, apart from the support afforded to fishing and forestry, the distribution of *per capita* expenditure differs most radically between Scotland and Great Britain in those sectors where the region is afforded preferential treatment under 'Development Area' policy. With regard to regional employment premiums and the promotion of local employment, for instance, the volume of public spending per head of population in Scotland exceeds that in Great Britain as a whole by over 70 per cent. *Per capita* expenditure on investment grants, too, is one-third as high again as in the national economy. Clearly, there are major differences in how public money is spent in Scotland as compared to the rest of Britain. To keep matters in perspective, however, it should of course, be remembered that on each of these items the absolute level of *per capita* expenditure is relatively low.

In addition to the incentives provided under regional policy, public expenditure per head in Scotland was significantly above that in Great Britain for the categories of primary industry and housing. As we have observed, primary industry is more important in the Scottish economy and therefore receives a proportionately higher volume of financial support. Expenditure on housing, on the other hand, is so high because of the low level of owner-occupation in Scotland and the consequent reliance on housing subsidised by the State. In only a restricted number of cases is *per capita* expenditure lower in Scotland than elsewhere. For instance, it can be seen that public spending per head is lower in Scotland on police services, the maintenance of law and order, and the arts. As might be expected, too, expenditures on additional payments under the Selective Employment Tax (S.E.T.) were relatively low in Scotland. One of the features of S.E.T. was that manufacturers had the employment tax refunded by the exchequer, together with an additional payment or premium which was intended to encourage the movement of labour into the manufacturing sector. Given the fact that the labour force in manufacturing was proportionately smaller in Scotland than in Great Britain as a whole, it is not surprising that the expenditure incurred in S.E.T. additional payments was also smaller.[1]

[1] It should be noted that this premium is now available only for workers employed in manufacturing in Development Areas. The whole subject of S.E.T. is discussed more fully in Chapter 13, in the setting of regional policy measures.

All in all, there appears to be little doubt that Scotland benefits to a greater extent than other parts of Great Britain from public spending. In terms of support for primary industry, expenditure per head was significantly higher in Scotland. A relatively high proportion of Scottish housing was subsidised through the central exchequer. Most distinctive, perhaps, was the element of support derived under regional policy, and manifested in the relatively high *per capita* spending on investment grants, regional employment premiums, and promotion of local employment. It must be emphasised, however, that these conclusions are based on the figures produced officially by the Treasury. These, and indeed the whole nature of Scotland's budgetary position, are in dispute. Let us now consider this controversial subject in greater depth.

5 The Scottish Budget

Until the 1930s it was accepted that the State, like the individual, had to ensure that its expenditure did not run in excess of revenue. Mr Micawber was the epitome of the conventional wisdom for individual happiness, and it was held that the same applied to the State. A major objective of Government economic policy should be a balanced public budget. It was the world crash, however, in the 1930s and the pioneering work of Keynes and other economists, for example in Sweden, which compelled a revision of this dogma. The policy of balancing the Government's budget annually had meant that the Government restricted its spending during a depression because its tax revenues were also falling at such a time. Conversely, when revenue began to rise during the upswing in economic activity Government spending could also increase or taxes be cut in order to maintain a balance between its own income and expenditure.

This policy meant that Government simply accentuated and reinforced general patterns within an economy. Only in the 1930s did the benefits of a 'counter-cyclical' fiscal policy begin to gain recognition, both in the theory of aggregate economic analysis and in the setting of Government public works programmes. Instead of falling into line with everyone else, the new economics argued that the Government should attempt to stabilise the economy by running counter to private behaviour. More broadly, the Government should not give priority to balancing its own books but to ensuring that a level of economic activity was attained which was consistent with the objectives of economic policy. The balanced budget had ceased to be an end in itself.

At a time of inflation or balance of payments deficit caused by an excess of demand for goods and services over supply, the Government nowadays aims at a budget surplus, i.e. an excess of revenue over expenditure. This can be achieved by drawing more revenue out of the economy through taxation than it has fed in, via current Government expenditure. The effect will be a decline in the economy's purchasing power and a consequent fall in effective demand. On the other hand, when the economy is experiencing a period of depression and the national economic engine is not running at full potential the Government can run a deficit on its own account. Expenditure then exceeds revenue, so creating more demand for output, more employment and higher levels of real activity.

Since the second world war, the major problem facing British Governments has in fact been full employment, inflation, and periodic balance of payments crises. As a result, policy has generally aimed at achieving a budget surplus, in keeping with the analysis outlined above. It is quite conceivable, therefore, that England, Scotland and Wales have *all* contributed more in tax than they received in terms of public expenditure. If this, indeed, was the case, then in no sense could any one of them be said to be subsidising the others. Attempting, however, to determine the budgetary positions of the individual countries comprising Great Britain is a task fraught with difficulties. We have already noted, in a Scottish context, that many of the constituent parts necessary for budgetary analysis are incapable of being satisfactorily quantified. This includes, for instance, such major components as income and corporation tax on the revenue side, items such as defence, external relations, etc. which comprise part of current expenditure, and loans and allocated expenditure on capital account.

The aim of drawing up a budget for Scotland is not, of course, to determine whether the country could be self-supporting under independent rule. Clearly this is an issue not in dispute, since Scotland presently stands as one of the most economically advanced nations in the world. She is much more capable of supporting herself than many countries that are now independent. The major question is not *whether* Scotland could support herself but *what* her standard of living would be under independence.

On the basis of their estimates, several authorities would argue that long-term living standards would be bound to fall. Separate estimates of Scotland's budgetary position, each showing an overall deficit, have been calculated by the Treasury, Dr McCrone and the *Scotsman* newspaper. Professor Alexander lends his weight to their point of view in his paper outlining the economic case against separation. All are agreed that Scotland is to some extent 'subsidised' by the U.K. central exchequer. Independence would, therefore, imply that in order to maintain the same level of expenditure in Scotland either taxes would have to be raised, or more borrowing would have to be undertaken. The obvious consequence would be some lowering of living standards.

Amidst such unanimity of opinion, the only note of dissent is sounded by the Scottish National Party. Their budget estimates for 1967/8 show Scotland in surplus and therefore independent of any 'subsidy' from the rest of the U.K. At the same time, the nationalists hotly dispute the methods by which the official estimates of the Treasury were compiled. Claims are made of 'deliberate underestimation' and of figures being 'concocted in an attempt to justify the Chancellor of the Exchequer's claim . . . that Scotland could not stand on her own feet'.[1] We shall confine ourselves in the pages that follow purely to the economic content of the debate and to a consideration of the reliability of the various estimates that have been made of the Scottish budget.

Table 7.7 below presents the Treasury's estimates for 1967/8. Although every effort was made to distinguish specifically Scottish receipts and payments, a large number of assumptions still had to be made in arriving at the figures presented. In consequence, these are to be taken as 'indicating broad orders of magnitude rather than precise accounting statistics'.[2]

In 1967/8, the U.K. central Government had a surplus of current revenue over current expenditure.[3] For Scotland, the above estimates show a deficit on current account of £140 million. When to this is added an estimate of Scotland's deficit on capital account, the country's total borrowing requirement rises to £476 million. This represents the amount that would have to be borrowed from the private sector, over and above taxation and other revenue, in order to finance expenditure. According to the Treasury, then, there can be little doubt either that the Scottish budget was in deficit or that, given independence, living standards would inevitably suffer. It is quite prepared to concede, however, that in several of the constituent parts of the budget there may be a fair margin of error.

[1] S.N.P. Research Department, *Who Says We Need Subsidies? The Treasury's Scottish Budget Analysed*, November 1969.

[2] H. M. Treasury, *A Scottish Budget.*

[3] For the U.K. as a whole, nearly one-third of total capital expenditure in 1967/8 was covered by the surplus of current receipts.

Table 7.7 Treasury Estimate of the Scottish Budget, 1967/8

Current Account

Current Revenue		As per cent of U.K.	**Current Expenditure**		
Income Tax	274	7·2	Identified Government Expenditure		
Surtax	18	7·5	Grants to Local Authorities		-
Profits Tax	3	9·4			-
Corporation Tax	85	7·0			
Less Transitional Relief	−3				
	377	7·2			
Taxes on Expenditure	341[3]	9·2			
Motor Vehicle Duty	21		**Allocated Expenditure**		
S.E.T.	30	6·4		Population Ratio[1]	Per Inc Ra
Stamp Duties	6	6·1			
I.T.A. Advertising Levy	1				
National Insurance	175	8·9	Defence	222	
Gross Trading surplus	15		External Relations	20	
Rent	2		Other Services	4	
Interest on loans	83	12·7	Debt Interest	111	-
Miscellaneous Receipts	10			357	
	684	9·2	Total Current Expenditure	1,201	1,
Total Current Revenue	1,061	8·3	As per cent of U.K.	10·3	9
Total Surplus (+) or Deficit (−) on Current Account				−140	—

Source: H.M. Treasury, A Scottish Budget.
[1] On the basis of a 9·4 per cent Population ratio.
[2] On the basis of a 7·7 per cent Personal Income ratio.
[3] This figure has been revised by the Treasury from that given in the Treasury's *A Scottish Bu* By error receipts from hydrocarbon oil duty were over-estimated by £10 million. This in a revised figure for total current revenue of £1,061 million instead of the £1,071 million Treasury's paper. See *Report from the Select Committee on Scottish Affairs*, H.M.S.O., 267, p. 27.

Capital Account

tal Receipts		Capital Expenditure:	
s on Capital	37	Identified Government Expenditure	141
		Grants to Local Authorities	19
		Grants to Public Corporations	2
		U.K. Expenditure Allocated at 9·4 per cent	16
		Loans to Local Authorities, Public Corporations, etc.	195
		Total Capital Payments	373
Surplus (+) or Deficit (−) on Capital Account			−336

The most important of these on the revenue side concern taxes which are centrally collected so that totals for Scotland cannot separately be obtained. One example is corporation tax, where the basic estimate is of tax assessed on Scottish companies. Many companies, however, operate throughout the U.K. The Treasury attempts to get round this problem by including in the estimate tax on profits earned by Scottish companies operating outside the country, but excluding the tax on profits made by English companies operating in Scotland. Income tax presents much the same problem since, clearly, the tax paid by Scottish employees operating south of the border will be assessed and collected outside Scotland. Again, therefore, allowance has to be made for this in assessing the tax revenue contributed by Scotland to the central exchequer. We shall see below, in a consideration of the S.N.P. case, how inappropriate the Nationalists regard the magnitude of these 'allowances' made by the Treasury to their basic estimate.

On the expenditure side, the bulk of Government expenditure in Scotland can be identified. Controversy exists, however, over that part of expenditure undertaken to benefit the U.K. as a whole. Under this category come expenditure on defence, external relations, financial administration and the like. It is virtually impossible to apportion the expenditure on such items to any particular part of the U.K. since the benefit derived is of a wholly national character. Perhaps the most appropriate method is simply to allocate such expenditure either on a *pro rata* to population basis, or according to a given ratio with the U.K., such as G.D.P., personal income or the like.

Given the difficulties inherent in constructing estimates for the various components of revenue and expenditure, it is not at all surprising that such disagreement exists over the nature of the Scottish budget. This disagreement is highlighted in Table 7.8 below which compares, again for 1967/8, the findings of Dr McCrone and the S.N.P.

As can be seen from the Table, McCrone's estimates, based on a population ratio, place the total borrowing requirement in respect of Scottish transactions in 1967/8 at £87 million (Current Account) + £130 million (Capital Account), a total of £217 million. The S.N.P. calculations, on the other hand, lead to an altogether different conclusion. Their estimates show a *surplus* in respect of Scottish activities of the following magnitude:

+£159 m. (Current Account)
−£138m. (Capital Account)
+ £21 million.

It should be noted that both the totals of McCrone and the S.N.P. *exclude* expenditure on loans. Were such expenditure to be included, then the final conclusions reached by the former would not be dissimilar from those presented by the Treasury. For many constituent parts of the budget, however, McCrone's figures stand roughly midway between the more extreme positions adopted by the Treasury on the one hand and the S.N.P. on the other. For instance, the Treasury estimate of total current revenue contributed by Scotland in 1967/8 amounted to 8·3 per cent of that in the U.K. as a whole. McCrone has the proportion somewhat higher at 8·8 per cent, and the S.N.P. higher still at 9·3 per cent. A major part of the discrepancy rests with the categories income and corporation tax, and with taxes on expenditure. In each of these, there is certainly room for some debate.

With regard to income tax, the Treasury estimate of the amount that can be attributed to Scotland was constructed as follows:

	£m.
Amount physically collected in Scotland	238
Scottish share of investment income	26
Allowance for tax paid by Scottish employees assessed in other parts of the U.K.	10
	274

The major controversy arises from the last of these items, the amount allowed for taxes paid by Scottish employees but collected outside the country. According to calculations made by the Scottish Nationalists, for instance, 29·5 per cent of Scottish employees are assessed for income tax purposes as living in England.[1] If, therefore, the figure for income tax actually collected in Scotland (£238 million) is increased by 29·5 per cent, then the resultant total is £308 million. To this must be added £26 million as Scotland's share of investment income, so giving an aggregate sum of £334 million. This is considerably in excess of the £274 million estimated by the Treasury.

The margin of error in the estimate of corporation tax is likely to be even greater. As observed earlier, it is very difficult to determine how far U.K. companies, based in England, earn

[1] For a discussion of the basis for the Treasury's estimate of £10 million and of the reliability of the Scottish Nationalists' figure of 29·5 per cent, see the examination of Treasury representatives by the Select Committee on Scottish Affairs, *Minutes of Evidence, Appendices and Index*, H.M.S.O., 267–1, 1970, pp. 89–94, 506–8.

Table 7.8 The Scottish Budget Estimates of Dr McCrone and the S.N.P., 1967/8

Current Account

Current Revenue

	McCrone	S.N.P.
Income Tax	308	330
Surtax	23	20
Profits Tax	3	3
Corporation Tax	101	115
Less Transitional Relief	−6	−6
	429	462
Taxes on Expenditure	358	393
Motor Vehicle Duty	22	23
S.E.T.	39	30
Stamp Duties	6	6
I.T.A. Levy	—	—
National Insurance	185	185
Gross Trading Surplus	1	—
Rent	9	—
Interest and Dividends	82	74
Miscellaneous Receipts	8	22
	702	724
Total Current Revenue	1,131	1,186

Current Expenditure

	McCrone
Identified Current Expenditure	638
Grants to Local Authorities	178
	816

Allocated Expenditure

	Population Ratio[1]	G.D.P. Ratio[2]	
Defence	224	203	
External Relations	31	28	
Debt Interest	111	100	
Other Services	36	33	
Total Current Expenditure	1,218	1,180	1
Total Surplus (+) or Deficit (−) on Current Account	−87	−49	+

Sources: G. McCrone, Address Delivered to Scottish Economic Society, 1969.

[1] Based on a 9·4 per cent population ratio.

[2] Based on an 8·5 per cent G.D.P. ratio.

Capital Account

pital Receipts:	McCrone	S.N.P.	Capital Expenditure	McCrone	S.N.P.
es on Capital	37	37	Identified Government Expenditure	149	175
			Grants to Local Authorities	18	
			Grants to Public Corporations	—	
			Total Capital Expenditure *Excluding* Loans	167	175
al Surplus (+) or Deficit (−) on Capital Account				−130	−138

their profits in Scotland and, correspondingly, the extent to which Scottish companies earn their profits in England. A purely arbitrary figure of £13 million was allowed by the Treasury as the *net* contribution made by Scottish companies making profits in England. This was added to a figure of £72 million, representing the actual corporation tax assessed in Scotland. A total of £85 million therefore results as the Scottish contribution made to total current revenue by corporation tax. Yet the Treasury readily concedes that this figure may be subject to a margin of error of between £10 million and £15 million. This is because the 'net excess' of Scottish corporation tax assessed in England is so indeterminate.[1] Conceivably, then, the Scottish revenue derived from corporation tax could amount to £100 million, although the Nationalists have the figure higher still at some £115 million.[2]

Revenue derived from income and corporation taxes in Scotland has been examined in some detail simply to illustrate the possible margins of error contained in presently existing estimates. It is true that these are probably the most controversial items on the revenue account. None the less, even with the official Treasury estimates, it is accepted that the figure for total current revenue in Scotland in 1967/8 is subject to a margin of error of ±£32 million.[3]

On the expenditure side, both the Treasury and McCrone reach virtual agreement with regard to total current expenditure, calculated on a *pro rata* to population basis. Both have public expenditure in Scotland at over 10 per cent of that in the U.K., a figure well above the population ratio. Their estimates are, however, at odds with the calculations made by the S.N.P. According to the Nationalists, Scotland's share of current U.K. expenditure amounted to no more than 8·8 per cent in 1967/8. Whilst there appears to be disagreement even about the size of identified current expenditure, the major controversy on this side of the account arises from the items included under 'allocated expenditure'. It is here that the Nationalists accuse the Treasury of changing its methods of calculation in mid-stream. Whereas in the compilation of previous estimates, the Treasury had concentrated on Government spending actually *in* Scotland, the estimates for allocated expenditure refer to benefits *attributable to Scottish residents*. Hence, as noted earlier, expenditure on defence is not the amount of money spent in Scotland for defence purposes but

[1] For evidence on this issue, see the Select Committee on Scottish Affairs, *Minutes of Evidence*, pp. 90–93.

[2] See Table 7.8.

[3] Select Committee on Scottish Affairs, *Minutes of Evidence*, p. 96.

simply a monetary value of the extent to which the Treasury deems Scotland to have benefitted from total U.K. defence spending.

On the defence issue, the S.N.P. may well have a reasonable case. It was pointed out in Chapter 2 that the most recent official figure for actual expenditure on defence in Scotland amounted to 6·75 per cent of the U.K. defence budget in 1967/8. On this basis, spending on defence in Scotland would amount to £152 million rather than the £222 million quoted by the Treasury. The other major discrepancy within allocated expenditure on current account concerns debt interest. The Nationalists claim that the precise degree of Scottish responsibility for interest on the national debt would be a matter for negotiation. Since they regard most of the debt as having been incurred through major capital expenditure south of the border, they estimate a reasonable debt commitment would be some 50 per cent of Scotland's population share. The figure so determined, however, falls a long way short of the Treasury's estimate of Scotland's commitment (see Tables 7.7 and 7.8).

However general expenditure is allocated, whether on a population basis or according to some other criterion, both the Treasury and McCrone are in agreement on one fundamental issue, namely, that total current expenditure forms a much higher proportion of the U.K. total than is true of current account revenue. Depending upon the assumptions used, the deficit on current account, in absolute terms, ranges from the Treasury's £140 million, calculated on a population basis, to McCrone's £49 million, estimated on a G.D.P. ratio. The S.N.P., on the other hand, reach an altogether different conclusion. Since they estimate current revenue as constituting a much higher proportion of the U.K. total than the other two series, and current expenditure a much lower proportion of equivalent expenditure in the U.K., they are able to produce an overall surplus on Scotland's current account of £159 million.

The capital account poses no serious problems since all three estimates reach fairly similar conclusions. On the receipts side, all are prepared to accept the Treasury's figure for taxes on capital, whilst estimates for capital expenditure, excluding loans, are also very close to each other. In consequence, Scotland's overall deficit on capital account, exclusive of loans, amounted apparently to between £130–£140 million. Taking, therefore, both the current and capital accounts together, only the Scottish Nationalists manage to find an overall surplus for Scotland, of some £21 million. McCrone places the total deficit at over £200 million, whilst according to the more extreme Treasury view Scotland's borrowing requirement would have been £476 million. It must be remembered, however, that this latter estimate includes expenditure on loans, specifically omitted from the other two series.

In a sense, the conclusions reached by McCrone and the Treasury appear more realistic. That Scotland's budget, overall, was in deficit would seem appropriate. Under a progressive tax system, it is likely to be the case that Scotland, one of the poorer regions of the U.K., received assistance from the rest of the nation. According to both the Treasury and McCrone this was precisely what happened. Revenue was being transferred to Scotland from other parts of the nation, although they differ, of course, on the extent of the transfer taking place. Using the official Treasury figures, a calculation of the Scottish contribution per head of population towards total U.K. revenue shows that it is well below the U.K. average. In 1967/8, the Scottish contribution amounted to £212 per head, compared to the £238 per head contributed by residents of the U.K.[1] In other words, Scotland was contributing less per head of population to actual current expenditure on central services than England and Wales. On the other hand, public expenditure per head of population, including loans to local authorities, public corporations, etc. undoubtedly favoured Scotland. Expenditure per head amounted to £303 north of the border, compared to only £265 in the U.K. as a whole. Hence, on this evidence, more was certainly being spent in Scotland per head of population than was being contributed in terms of revenue.

As Table 7.8 illustrates, however, the S.N.P. estimates would deny the validity of such conclusions. According to the Nationalists, the Treasury's implication that Scotland was being subsidised to the extent of some £476 million in 1967/8 is wholly misleading. Even if the Treasury figures are accepted at face value, they include loans worth almost £200 million. These loans, as the Nationalists point out, are in no sense a 'subsidy' since, of course, they must be repaid with interest at some future date.[2] To interpret, as several commentators have, Scotland's borrowing requirement of £476 million as a subsidy is, then, unacceptable since, even if accurate, well over 40 per cent of this

[1] These figures, and those which follow on expenditure per head, should be used with great caution. They refer to both the current and capital accounts and include all items quantified in Table 7.7, several of which have already been computed on a *pro rata* to population basis. It should also be noted that in the expenditure figures, loans to local authorities, etc. have been included in the calculation.

[2] See D. Simpson in the *Scotsman*, 15th November 1969.

sum consists of loans. It would clarify matters, in the Nationalist view, if these loans made to local authorities, public corporations and nationalised industries were omitted altogether from the calculation of central Government expenditure. In the first place, interest is payable to the Government on the loans received and in the second, there is no particular reason anyway why these loans had to come from the central Government. Yet, whilst it is argued that loans should be excluded from the expenditure side, the Nationalists have, apparently, no hesitation in including interest paid on these loans on the revenue side.

Another of the major issues emphasised by the S.N.P. is that, of the allocated expenditure attributed to Scotland, an inadequate share is actually *spent* within the country.[1] Although the central Exchequer claims that such expenditure is undertaken for the benefit of the Scottish people—in the form of defence, maintaining external relations, etc.—it neither improves conditions nor provides work and employment within Scotland itself. This argument is, however, weak on several counts. First, allocated expenditure, upon which the Nationalists concentrate, amounts to only a small proportion of total expenditure. Moreover, the effects of public expenditure are not limited merely to the region in which the grants or spending takes place. Economic activity can be stimulated by public spending over a much wider area than the single region. In other words, there may be important 'spill-over' effects experienced by areas and by sectors other than those in which the initial expenditure took place. Although, therefore, defence contracts and the like may not actually be placed with Scottish firms, it could well be that, nevertheless, Scotland benefits considerably from such expenditure. To insist that such contracts be placed in Scotland when more economical suppliers might exist elsewhere would, from a given amount of public expenditure, result either in less equipment and/or facilities being provided, or in these being of poorer quality than would otherwise have been the case. Clearly, such a policy would not be in Scotland's long-term interests. Nor would it be consistent with an efficient use of scarce resources, the ultimate economic test, which was highlighted in Chapter 1.

Finally, it should be emphasised that until we are provided both on the revenue and expenditure side with more accurate and reliable statistics, it will not be possible to reach

[1] See S.N.P., '*Who Says We Need Subsidies?*'; D. Simpson, 'Independence: the Economic Issues' in *The Scottish Debate* (ed. N. MacCormick), p. 151.

any firm conclusion about the budgetary position of an independent Scotland. Attention was drawn earlier to some of the more important assumptions and estimates that have to be made on both sides of the account. As long as there is still room for such large margins of error in the composition of the estimates, the economics of an independent Scotland will remain a matter for debate. The Nationalists clearly have some grounds for criticism in pointing to the existing confusion between public expenditure in Scotland and what is spent by Government agencies in Scotland; between expenditure in Scotland as opposed to the benefits which may be gained by Scottish residents from public spending; and, since budgetary policy is most likely to be determined by the balance of payments, to the lack of any official data on the nature of Scotland's trade balance.

In the event, however, it may be more important to recognise that an independent Scotland would face a wholly different set of priorities from those presently existing. Given these changed priorities, the nature of public spending today is, in many respects, irrelevant to what it might conceivably be like in an independent Scotland.

References

Department of Employment, *Family Expenditure Survey Reports*, H.M.S.O., annually.

Board of Trade, *Report on the Census of Production, 1963*, H.M.S.O., 1970.

G. McCrone, *Scotland's Economic Progress, 1951–1960.*

Scotland's Future: the Economics of Nationalism.

A. Reid, 'Manufacturing Investment in Scotland', *Scotland Magazine*, August 1970.

H.M. Treasury, *A Scottish Budget: Estimates of Central Government Revenue and Expenditure Attributable to Scotland for the Financial Year, 1967–8,* October 1969.

S.N.P. Research Dept., 'Who Says we Need Subsidies? The Treasury's Scottish Budget Analysed', November 1969.

K. J. Alexander, 'The Economic Case Against Independence', in N. MacCormick (ed.), *The Scottish Debate: Essays on Scottish Nationalism*, London, 1970.

'Scotland's National Balance Sheet', *Scotland Magazine*, May 1968.

D. Simpson, 'Independence: The Economic Issues' in N. MacCormick (ed.), *The Scottish Debate: Essays on Scottish Nationalism.*

'The *Scotsman*' *newspaper*, 4th July 1968.

Part 3: Components of Growth in the Scottish Economy

Chapter 8
Elements of Economic Growth

In this and the next three Chapters we shift our perspective on the Scottish economy. So far in this study we have been looking at the *structure* of the Scottish economy and showing how this is made up when we study it from the production, income and expenditure sides. In this Part we propose to look at the important forces which underlie the development through time of an economy. An important part of economic analysis is concerned with the growth in the capacity which economies have to produce wealth. Interest in this particular part of economics has undoubtedly waxed and waned in the past. Adam Smith placed economic growth firmly in the centre of his scheme of things, and stressed division of labour, specialisation and exchange as key mechanisms which made possible the growth in output. He gave a clear indication of the spur to growth which a large market could provide when he pronounced that 'division of labour is limited by the extent of the market'.

Early 19th century economists, such as David Ricardo and Thomas Malthus—often called the classical economists—were much less optimistic than Smith in their outlook on the working of economic forces, and in their hands economics became rather a gloomy subject, inspiring the famous jibe by Carlyle about the respectable professors of the Dismal Science, Political Economy. Malthus and Ricardo tended to stress the obstacles in the path of growing output. When one appreciated how powerful was the biological propensity of the human race to reproduce itself, and the difficulties which had to be overcome in order to wrest more food from the limited supply of cultivable land, there was in their view no cause for cheery optimism about the economic problem. Ricardo in particular became preoccupied with a study of the forces that determined the shares which the various factors of production received of the output of the economy, rather than with the analysis of the growth of output itself.

The powerful analysis of the working of the capitalist form of economic system which Karl Marx made around the middle of the 19th century can perhaps be described as one form of theory about economic growth. Marx, however, was obsessed with the theme that capitalist production was bound to become excessively concentrated and to destroy itself through the class struggle to which it would give rise. His object was to show how a new type of society and economic system would inevitably develop in the form of a Dictatorship of the Proletariat. By the late 19th century economics had, however, survived the Marxist onslaught well enough to become particularly concerned with the refined analysis of price theory and the perfection of rather a static technique of analysing economic problems. Many of the strategic concepts which were identified in Chapter 1 were sharpened and refined in this setting. When it did show any strong interest in the laws of motion of an economic system economics tended to stress cyclical fluctuations, and the boom and bust of the business cycle. The underlying long-term growth of the production potential of economic systems was rather taken for granted as a natural tendency.

As we have seen, macro-economic analysis of a new kind was developed by Keynes in the 1930s, when he became impatient with the inter-war years of stagnation and depression, and the evident inability of the existing corpus of economic analysis to explain how we could pull the economy out of the slough and get it growing again as a sturdy, self-sustaining process. His analysis was not concerned with identifying the capacity of economies to grow, but with the problem of ensuring that existing productive potential was being used to the full. Most countries have been pretty successful since the war in stabilising their economies at, or about, the full employment level in which Keynes was especially interested, and it is therefore not surprising that in recent years there has been a reawakening of interest in studying the forces that determine the productive potential of an economy and its growth through time. This is true not only of industrialised but of less developed economies as well.

Growth theory is very much the New Frontier of modern economic analysis, distinguished by the clash of elegant theories, which are frequently mathematical in form, but marked also by other approaches which stress the organic, almost biological, characteristics of the growth process in an economy. Undoubtedly, it is now generally recognised that both quantitative and qualitative factors have to be taken into account when we try to understand the complex processes by which an economy expands. It is not enough, for example, to look at the growth of labour supply as one determinant of growth, but to take account of the qualities of education and training of labour and of the institutional characteristics, such as collective bargaining arrangements, which affect its utilisation in economic activity. There is as yet no settled theory of growth. What we propose to do in this Chapter, therefore, is to set out some of the main elements that are undoubtedly in the mainstream of the analysis and discussion of growth, and use these as a framework for the succeeding Chapters in which we shall discuss the theme of growth in the Scottish economy.

2 Growth Measurements

We look first at some of the important considerations to be borne in mind when measures of economic growth are being studied. Economic growth can be defined and measured in terms of the growth of a country's national income over time. As we have seen in earlier Chapters, it is essential to define precisely what is meant by national income. A net measure is preferable to a gross measure, since the net measure of output or income will have made allowance for capital consumption, or that part of production which goes merely to replace and maintain the assets of machinery and capital goods which are being used up continuously in the course of production. It is also necessary to distinguish, over time, changes in real national income from changes in money national income. If money national income were to double, but so too were the general price levels in the economy, real national income would obviously be unchanged. As we know, money tends to be an unstable, and also a depreciating measuring rod, and accurate comparisons of the growth of national income over time can only be made after due allowance, through the use of index numbers, for the instability of this measuring rod.

Next, aggregate increases in real net national income must be distinguished from *per capita* changes. If population were to grow faster than real national income, net income per head of the population would fall. Again, we should try to distinguish the important difference between an increase in national income which arises from more intensive use of the existing production capacity and the growth which is secured by adding to that productive potential. It may be difficult to disentangle the two, since changes may be taking place in productive capacity, via new investment, even when an economy may be experiencing a temporary recession. Nevertheless, economic growth over the 'long haul' is likely to be greater if we at least avoid chronic under-utilisation of our productive capacity at any time.

Lastly, it is common to report economic growth in terms of growth in output per man hour, or per person employed. This is a very convenient measure; but we must notice that there is a vast difference between measuring output in terms of labour input, as such a measure does, and saying that it is the labour input alone which has caused the growth in output. The main problem in understanding the determinants of growth is precisely that of disentangling the contributions which the various factors of production make. Simple production theory teaches us that the factors are joint inputs, while at the same time they are also partial substitutes for one another. What can we say about the contributions which the various factors make? We shall look first at some of the simple concepts, and then ask how far it is possible to quantify the separate contributions of the different factors of production.

3 Relationships between Factor Inputs

Adam Smith was inclined to see in the growth of the population and labour force of a country both a source and an indication of economic growth. The classical economists were at once more rigorous in their analysis and much gloomier about the interaction between land and population. Taking rather a simple view of capital, as consisting of a stock of circulating capital which was used primarily to pay the wages of the workers, they saw the economic process as one in which the labour force interacted with the fixed supply of land. As more labour was used in production in conjunction with a fixed supply of land they saw production becoming more difficult, and the increments of output from the land smaller. There would be diminishing returns from the land as more of the variable factor, labour, was applied to its cultivation. Because the population had such a strong biological propensity to reproduce itself, economists like Malthus saw that there would indeed be a pressing need to try to produce more from the land. The constant clamour for food could only be satisfied by working the hard-pressed land more intensively and extensively.

The implications of this simple diagnosis were twofold. First, workers would compete by the very force of their numbers, and would through competition depress the level of real wages to a subsistence minimum. Second, the law of diminishing returns was seen as a brake on economic progress. Developments in industrial society have not in fact matched up to the predictions which Malthus made about a burgeoning population, though it is of course true that population pressure is still a problem if we take into account the economies of less-developed countries. As to diminishing returns, the principle is recognised as valid. Indeed, although it was first enunciated with reference to the addition of variable labour inputs to a fixed supply of land, later analysis has shown that the principle has more general validity. What has been of interest historically, however, is that the tendency for returns to diminish has been one of the great spurs to invention, innovation and technological advance.

As suggested, we can apply the technique of varying inputs to other factors of production besides land. If, for example, capital were to be treated as a variable input, and labour as a fixed input, we could equally expect that the increase in capital per worker would lead eventually to diminishing returns for every additional unit of capital set to work along with the fixed supply of labour. Put another way, the ratio of capital to output (C/O) would rise, as output would not grow in proportion to the growth in the stock of capital. We shall see in a moment that technological innovation can make a profound difference to any simple conclusion about this C/O ratio.

In the real world, we find that labour and capital both tend to increase, and there is evidence to support the following three propositions about the interaction of labour and capital in production. First, the ratio of capital to labour (C/L) has tended to rise. After allowing for the replacement of capital and for the growth in the labour force through time, there has been an increase in the amount of capital which each worker has had at his disposal. Historically, there has obviously been an improvement in the quality of capital at the disposal of the worker as well.

Second, the labour force has not simply grown in size. There have been qualitative improvements as labour has become better educated and trained. Thirdly, improvements in technology have taken place which have offset the tendency suggested above for the capital/output ratio to rise. Just because of the existence of diminishing returns when the stock of resources and technology are given, there has been strong pressure to try to develop new techniques of production. Historically, the C/O ratio has tended to be stable rather than to increase, and this is due, at least in part, to technological advance.

Some of these concepts have been put together in modern

growth theories. One model developed by Harrod envisages that there is a natural rate of growth which can be interpreted to mean the annual percentage increase in the supply of labour. By this is not simply meant additional numbers of workers, but also improvements in the efficiency with which labour is used, through technological development. If the economy is to grow in a balanced way Harrod suggests that capital and output must also grow at this same natural rate.

Putting all these strands together, we can see that, as economies grow, capital is likely to increase in quantity and improve in quality, the labour force not only grows but improves its skills and efficiency, while technology constitutes a subtle blend of human talents and inventiveness finding outlets in new and more sophisticated forms of productive equipment. Growth takes place through an increase in the quantity of factors and through improvements in productivity per unit of input of each factor.

The contributions of labour, capital, and technological advance to growth can thus be identified conceptually and also historically. Is it possible to assess the relative importance of these various elements in the growth process? A large amount of statistical work has been done in recent years in an effort to provide some numerical answers to this question, particularly in the United States. One of the pioneers of this approach, Edward F. Denison, has examined why growth rates differ in different countries, and he also contributed an important analysis of the sources of growth in Britain to a major study of the British economy which was published in 1968 by a group of American and Canadian economists, working under the aegis of the Brookings Institution in Washington. It is useful to use Denison's analysis here, for not only is it highly suggestive but it has the merit of detachment and objectivity in appraising the British scene. We shall set out the framework in a British context, and then use it as a lead in to our assessment of growth in Scotland.

4 Growth Factors in Britain

The first problem which has to be resolved in trying to identify the significance of any one factor's contribution to growth is that of establishing weights for the various factor inputs. If we leave aside technical change for a moment, and suppose that labour supply grows by 1 per cent per annum and capital at the rate of 3 per cent per annum, we can ask whether we are entitled to conclude that output will grow at a rate corresponding to the average of the two, i.e. at 2 per cent per annum. The answer depends on the shares, or weights, which the factor inputs in question have or are given. As a matter of fact, the contribution of labour to product is much greater than that of capital. Labour usually contributes about $\frac{3}{4}$ to the product, and receives a similar proportion of the income shares, while about $\frac{1}{4}$ of output goes to capital as the interest and profit share. Labour should therefore carry three times the weighting of capital in our simple example. If we then apply these weights output will grow annually at the following rate:

$$\begin{aligned}\tfrac{3}{4}\times 1 \text{ per cent (labour input)} &+ \tfrac{1}{4}\times 3 \text{ per cent (capital input)}\\ &= \tfrac{3}{4} \text{ per cent} + \tfrac{3}{4} \text{ per cent}\\ &= 1\tfrac{1}{2} \text{ per cent.}\end{aligned}$$

Put another way, if the return which capital receives amounts to a quarter of the total product, an increase of 1 per cent in the stock of capital will be held to have accounted for $\frac{1}{4}$ per cent of the growth of the total product.

Denison estimated that in the period 1950–62 the earnings of labour averaged 77·8 per cent of the national income, and incomes from capital, including stocks, dwellings, and property income from abroad, received 22·2 per cent. It was then assumed that labour represented 77·8 per cent of the total input of factors of production, and that a 1 per cent increase in the input of labour alone would accordingly raise total product by 0·778 per cent. By the same token, a 1 per cent increase in capital of all kinds would raise output by 0·222 per cent.

From 1950 to 1962 national income in the United Kingdom grew by 2·29 per cent per annum. If this annual rate of increase is put = 100, the relative contributions of the factors to growth in Britain during the period can be seen from the table on page 192.

The top part of the Table shows how changes in the *total amounts* of particular factors used to produce national output provided sources of growth. The calculations underlying such assessments are inevitably complex, and sometimes controversial. Not all economists feel comfortable, for example, about any attempt to add together such a heteregeneous mass of factor inputs as different forms of capital. As the Table indicates, the quantification of the labour input is much more than a simple counting of heads.

In addition to the changes that take place in the total quantities of factors used in production, we have also to take

Table 8.1 Sources of Growth of Total Real National Income in the United Kingdom 1950–62

	Percentages of Total Growth	
A. Labour Input		
1. Employment	21·8	
2. Hours of work	−6·6	
3. Age-sex composition	−1·7	
4. Education	12·7	26·2
B. Capital Input		
1. Non residential structures and equipment	18·8	
2. Inventories or stocks	3·9	
3. Dwellings	1·7	
4. International assets	−2·2	22·3
C. Land	0·0	0·0
Total Factor Input		48·5
D. Advances of knowledge		33·2
E. Economies of scale		15·7
F. Other sources of growth		2·6
Total Output per Unit of Input		51·5
Total Contribution of Growth		100·0

Source: 'Britain's Economic Prospects' R. E. Caves and associates. Brookings Institution 1968, p. 235.

into account, however, that *each* unit of input may be used more efficiently. Changes in output per unit of input also affect growth, and these stem from improvements in technology, in managerial and business organisation which may generate economies of scale, and so on. There is no doubt that it is extraordinarily difficult to separate out the unique contribution of some of these factors; there is usually a ragbag of 'residual factors'. The lower part of the Table shows that changes in output per unit of input, accounted for rather more than half of the growth.

Some of the individual items in the Table are worthy of comment. The number of hours worked has been an adverse factor, and the Brookings study was quite critical of the British practice of reducing labour input via longer holidays and shorter hours. Not surprisingly, the major contribution among the capital inputs was that of non-residential structures and equipment, which is rather a cumbersome way of describing the reproducible or physical capital employed by businessmen. Only two items made any significant contribution in terms of output per unit of input, advances of technology, which was the largest single contributing factor, and economies of scale.

In a sense, advances in knowledge are measured as a residual obtained by deducting from the total growth of national income the estimates which can be made for the specific factors such as labour and capital. Included in advances of knowledge are such elements as changes in the health of workers, changes in the skill and initiative of managers and entrepreneurs, changes in government services that affect productivity in the private sector (as, for example, the work of the Department of Employment in industrial training, outlined in Chapter 10), and changes in the legal and other institutional obstacles to the efficient use of resources. Quite an array! The direct promotion of the advance of knowledge by means of scientific research is another possible element, but one which is extremely difficult to measure, as we shall see in Chapter 9.

As the size of markets increases, gains from economies of scale can be an important source of improvements in productivity. When he estimated the contribution of this source to Britain's economic growth, Denison took account of the fact that the larger the size of existing markets, the smaller the likely gains from existing economies of scale as markets expand. The 1950s was the decade in which Britain passed into the era of high mass consumption. It brought British patterns of consumption much more closely in line with those of the United States. Much of the increase was in durable consumer goods such as cars, washing machines, refrigerators, television sets and so on, where substantial gains from economies of scale are possible by adopting American methods of production. These techniques would not have been possible until a sufficiently large market came into existence. This factor may have contributed something like one sixth to growth in Britain as a whole.

In the wider setting of the Brookings study as a whole, we can draw attention to some of the other features of growth in Britain which help to set the scene for our discussion of Scotland. Since the second World War, economic growth in Britain has tended to be very sluggish compared with most other industrialised countries, and Governments have often been criticised for the recurring balance of payments crises and the stop-go policies which these have engendered. Yet Brookings reminds us that in the long time-scale of our industrial history, the *absolute* rate of growth of the economy since the war has been higher than ever before. It is our *relative* position that has caused concern. Moreover, the Brookings study did not convict British Governments of running seriously erroneous policies of demand management through monetary and fiscal adjustments. On the whole, much of their critical appraisal of the economy is reserved for those more qualitative factors which are so difficult to measure but which are of immense significance for the efficiency with which the supply of our resources is deployed. The quality of management, labour utilisation, technical and professional education and training are some of the disquieting features singled out for comment.

In an international setting, the Brookings study also drew attention to the relatively unfavourable experience which Britain has had in the addition to the amount of the supply of basic factors such as capital and labour. The stock of capital per worker in Britain, for example, is low by the standards of other major industrialised countries. Additions to that stock in the form of capital investment have also been low. The obvious role of capital formation is to sacrifice some part of current output in order to create capital goods and add to the capacity to produce output. An economy which devotes a relatively small part of its resources to capital investment must then anticipate slow growth in the future. One of the dilemmas of British Governments has been the shortage of spare productive capacity in the economy when expansion of demand was allowed. The Brookings study sheds interesting light on the subtleties of the disquietingly low investment ratio in Britain. It does not see the explanation in a shortage of liquid funds for investment, but rather in the lack of confidence which businessmen have in frequent policy changes, and the lack of expertise which they show in appraising their investment projects. The attitude of labour to new investment, through the existence of restrictive practices, is also held to be a deterrent to investment. In terms of the C/O ratio, the amount of capital required to produce output is raised if labour adopts restrictive practices; and attitudes to shift-working may prevent capital from being fully utilised when it has been purchased. Here we see the subtle intermingling of capital and labour in economic performance which does make growth theory such a complex area.

The growth of employment in Britain has also compared unfavourably with other European countries, and the prospective growth of the labour force in Britain up to 1980 is likely to be extremely modest. One other feature of labour supply, which reflects Britain's early industrialisation, is that many European countries have benefited since the war from the transfer of labour out of agriculture into manufacturing industry. This process took place much earlier in Britain, and productivity gains from this source are not available to us. This slow growth in the quantity of labour clearly raises important issues of quality, both in the educational and training setting.

The education of the British labour force was improving in the 1960s more rapidly than it had done in the previous decade. We shall be looking at this with particular reference to Scotland in Chapter 10. Education is a very important determinant of labour quality and income. But the lead-time between the educational process and economic pay-off may be long. The full benefits of additional education are spread over the whole working life of the individual.

Conclusion

This brief examination of the nature and relative size of the sources of growth has not purported to be a theory, but we have at least been able to indicate some of the dimensions and elements of the growth theme. This enables us to go forward to the succeeding Chapters with at least some awareness of the significance of the elements we shall discuss. In Chapter 9 we examine the role of capital accumulation in the progress of the Scottish economy, and also look at the significance of economies of scale and of the advance of knowledge. A considerable amount of information is available on the various dimensions of labour, and in Chapter 10 we look at the contribution of human resources to the growth of output in terms of population dimensions, education and training.

Since our concern with economic problems in modern economies is invariably expressed through the mechanism of money we endeavour in Chapter 11 to look at the significance of financial institutions in the Scottish economy. This is important not only in general terms, but for any understanding of the institutions that are available for channelling and harnessing savings. Our emphasis on financial institutions does not of course mean that these are the only ones that are important to economic progress. We have to recognise that there are subtle questions of attitude, motivation and institutional behaviour at work in the process of economic activity. As Denison's work brings out, many of these are, however, difficult to quantify. We have had to be selective. It would no doubt have been fascinating to seek to assess the contribution of the Protestant Ethic to the growth of industrial societies in general, and the Scottish one in particular. But we have drawn a line at that. Our institutional coverage is therefore restricted.

Recommended Reading

Miles Fleming, *Introduction to Economic Analysis*, Minerva Series, George Allen and Unwin, 1969, Chapter 31.

Richard E. Caves and Associates, *Britain's Economic Prospects*, George Allen and Unwin, 1968 (The Brookings Study).

Chapter 9
Capital, Economies of Scale, and Advances of Knowledge

In the previous Chapter we distinguished the relative importance of the main factors that contribute to economic growth in the United Kingdom. In this Chapter and the next we shall examine these factors more closely and try to establish how far it is possible to say something meaningful about them in a Scottish context. Capital, economies of scale, and advances in knowledge will be treated in this Chapter, while we take up human resources in Chapter 10. The sequence is accordingly somewhat different from that adopted by Denison, in part because rather more material is available about the human factor than about some of the other growth factors now to be discussed.

1 Capital

Capital comprises the stock of productive assets from which output is derived. This capital stock represents many types of asset—plant, machinery, and buildings in the various sectors of the economy—and this stock will obviously have been acquired or built over a period of time. The problems of measuring and valuing this stock of very heteregeneous assets are clearly enormous, particularly when it is remembered that prices change over time, technology develops and the assets do wear out in the course of their lifetime. Capital is consumed in the course of production, but it is extremely difficult to put a precise valuation on capital consumption of productive assets in the course of (say) a year. It is fairly clear that a stock of new assets is likely to be more valuable than capital of more ancient vintage. Yet an old asset which has been 'written off' for accounting purposes may still be making an active contribution to the economy as part of the stock of productive assets from which output is being generated.

A moment's reflection shows that the economist cannot always use with confidence the data relating to assets and depreciation as these are found in the balance sheets of companies. Assets are frequently valued at original or historic cost, and the whole stock of assets is obviously not of the same vintage. Likewise, depreciation rules reflect conventions for dealing with the age structure of assets, not their 'real' contribution to resource use in production. We can then have the following curious situation. If an asset is considered to last, for purposes of valuation, only as long as the length of time used to depreciate it, the stock of capital may be under-estimated in a real sense once the asset has been written down in accounting terms. By the same token, this will mean that capital consumption in real terms has been over-estimated.

Information about the stock of capital and gross and net additions to the stock is clearly indispensable, if economists are to undertake any reasonable assessment of the forces of growth which stem from the role of capital in production. It is only comparatively recently that official estimates of capital stock and capital consumption have been published in the United Kingdom, and no data have been published for gross capital stock in Scotland. However, it is possible to make further progress in Scotland than in any other region of the United Kingdom with the assessment of *additions* to the stock of capital from year to year. The purpose of this section is to pursue this question in a Scottish setting. In doing so, it is important to bear in mind that some part of current investment may be going merely to replace outworn capital. In the absence of comprehensive information about the capital stock, we cannot read too much into the gross figures for additions to the stock through the investment that occurs from year to year.

Figures are published in the *Digest of Scottish Statistics* of capital investment by manufacturing industry in Scotland, although this accounts for only one fifth of fixed capital formation. For Census of Production years, such as 1958 and 1963, the investment figures are obtained directly from the Census. For intervening years, the Board of Trade carries out a sample survey to produce estimates of capital formation. These figures suffer from the twin defects of being measured at current instead of constant prices, and of being gross figures, in the sense that they contain no allowance for capital consumption. As industry in Scotland will, in the main, buy similar types of plant and machinery in the same markets as firms throughout the country, it is not unreasonable to use the same price indices for capital investment in Scotland as those used nationally. Equally, the rather arbitrary assumptions which underlie estimates made of capital consumption may also be applied to Scotland.

The figures of capital spending by manufacturing industry have already been set out in Table 7.2 of Chapter 7, and need not be reproduced here. They are expressed in real terms, and show that between 1960 and 1968 capital expenditure in Scottish manufacturing industry increased by almost 50 per cent.

A recently published study by Heriot-Watt University indicated that house construction costs are considerably higher in Scotland than in England and Wales, and it may be that industrial buildings are similarly more expensive. Scotland's share of industrial building may therefore be more accurately presented by comparing the areas built rather than the costs incurred. This is done in Table 9.1.

Table 9.1 Industrial Building in Great Britain and Scotland 1960–8: Area completed in million sq. ft.

	Great Britain	Scotland	Scotland as per cent of Great Britain
1960	48·6	4·1	8·4
1961	53·4	3·5	6·6
1962	45·5	5·2	11·4
1963	34·1	3·9	11·1
1964	32·1	3·9	12·1
1965	38·0	4·3	11·3
1966	37·2	6·5	17·5
1967	34·0	6·0	12·6
1968	38·6	4·1	10·6

Source: Abstract of Regional Statistics.

In recent years, Scotland's share of gross domestic capital formation has varied between 8·8 per cent and 10·5 per cent for plant, machinery and vehicles and between 6·6 per cent and 17·5 per cent for industrial buildings.

Agriculture is another sector in which it is possible to gauge the extent of fixed capital formation. Around 3 per cent of the nation's total fixed capital formation is in agriculture and around one eighth of this expenditure takes place in Scotland (see Table 9.2).

In recent years, the Treasury has adopted the practice of providing an analysis of total public expenditure which reflects the basis on which public expenditure programmes are decided.[1] Since 1963/4, the *Digest of Scottish Statistics* has published data of

[1] For fuller details, see National Income and Expenditure 1969, p. 104.

Table 9.2 Capital Expenditure in Agriculture in the United Kingdom and Scotland 1960—8: (£ million at current prices)

	U.K.	Scotland	Scotland as per cent of U.K.
1960	145	18·4	12·7
1961	157	19·8	12·6
1962	152	20·4	13·4
1963	167	21·2	12·7
1964	170	20·4	12·0
1965	171	21·1	12·3
1966	171	21·9	12·8
1967	185	25·2	13·6
1968	211	23·5	11·1

Source: Digest of Scottish Statistics National Income and Expenditure 1969.

identifiable public expenditure in Scotland, analysing it into current expenditure and gross domestic fixed capital formation. The comparative figures for the United Kingdom and Scotland are presented in the following table. As has already been indicated in Chapter 7, there are certain items of expenditure such as defence and transport and communications which cannot be allocated on a regional basis; these are omitted from the table. The capital expenditure of the nationalised industries is treated separately in Table 9.4.

Table 9.3 Gross domestic fixed capital formation in the public sector in the United Kingdom and Scotland: (£ million)

	Annual average expenditure 1963/4 – 1968/9		
	U.K.	Scotland	Scotland as per cent of U.K.
Roads	248·0	29·0	11·7
Technological Services	53·7	3·3	6·1
Housing	653·2	109·7	16·8
Environmental Services	262·7	39·1	14·9
Education	199·3	35·1	17·6
Health and Welfare	117·8	12·9	10·9
Other[1]	126·3	19·7	15·6
	1661·0	248·8	15·0

Source: National Income and Expenditure; Digest of Scottish Statistics.
[1] Includes employment services, agriculture, libraries, museums, police, prisons, fire service.

As the table shows, fixed capital formation in the public sector in Scotland has in general been well above any proportional allocation on the basis of population. In part, this reflects the undertaking given in the White Paper on Central Scotland in

1963 and repeated in the White Paper on the Scottish Economy in 1966, to achieve a substantial improvement in infrastructure, particularly in Central Scotland. Increased expenditure on roads, services, schools and so on was seen to be a necessary part of the effort to promote a faster rate of growth in Scotland. Of the cuts in Government spending announced since 1966, as part of the measures to correct the balance of payments, it is fair to say that investment in the Development Areas has suffered least.

The relatively high level of expenditure on education can be explained in part by the fact that Scotland has a *relatively* larger proportion of her population in the younger age groups and also an above average proportion of university students. In Chapter 10 we shall examine in more detail the growth of pupil and student numbers in Scotland and the associated capital investment in schools, colleges and universities. Housing is another element of public expenditure where Scotland's share of the national total is high. This is undoubtedly the result of the much higher proportion of houses built in Scotland by local authorities and government agencies such as the Scottish Special Housing Association. Environmental services and roads also indicate higher levels of expenditure than would be justified on a straight population basis. It might be argued that a formula other than population might be more appropriate in the context of roads and environmental services. Scotland, after all, comprises something like 40 per cent of the land area of the United Kingdom. On this basis Scotland might merit an allocation of expenditure under roads and environmental services considerably greater than on a *per capita* basis. Scotland, for example, has 28,800 miles, or 13 per cent, of the total road mileage in the United Kingdom. The final item of expenditure requiring some comment is technological services, where Scotland's share of expenditure appears low by any criterion. The regional imbalance in expenditure on research and development is the major contributory factor to Scotland's small share. This subject is discussed more fully in section 4 of this chapter.

In addition to the fixed capital formation in the public sector, it is also possible to compare capital expenditure in Scotland by the nationalised industries and public corporations against the national totals.

Overall, Scotland's share of capital expenditure by the nationalised industries and public corporations is more or less in line with her share of gross domestic product. There are certain points, however, to be borne in mind when studying this table.

Table 9.4 Capital expenditure by the nationalised industries and public corporations in the United Kingdom and Scotland

	Annual average expenditure 1963/4–1968/9 £ million		
	U.K.	Scotland	Scotland as per cent of U.K.
Coal	79·3	8·8	11·1
Gas	168·0	9·1	5·4
Electricity	625·0	63·3	10·1
Steel[1]	59·4	6·2	10·4
Inland transport	130·3	9·7	7·4
Air Transport	47·3	1·0[2]	2·0
Post Office	246·0	19·2	7·8
	1355·3	117·3	8·7

Source: National Income and Expenditure 1969; Digest of Scottish Statistics.

[1] 1967/8 and 1968/9 only.

[2] Includes B.B.C. and I.T.A.

In Chapter 5 it was pointed out that output and employment in the coal industry in Scotland have been declining rapidly in recent years. One might expect, therefore, to find a similar fall in capital expenditure. Over the last six years, investment by the National Coal Board in Scotland has in fact been remarkably stable, varying between £8 and £10 million each year. The explanation is that while a considerable number of uneconomic pits have been closed during the last 10 years, new, large, modern pits have been opened up. An increasingly large proportion of coal output is being concentrated in such new collieries as Bilston Glen and Monktonhall in Midlothian and Seafield in Fife, where the coal reserves are large and where the most modern equipment can be installed. The proportion of output which is power-loaded in Scottish collieries rose from 63 per cent in 1964 to over 85 per cent in 1969. Over the same period, productivity increased by 30 per cent as a result of the substitution of capital for labour. A substantial level of capital investment will be required in coal mining even if output continues to fall, if only to ensure further increases in productivity.

At first sight, investment by the gas industry in Scotland may appear low. Since 1965/66 fixed capital formation in the gas industry in the United Kingdom has trebled, mainly as a result of the introduction of natural gas. Conversion to North Sea gas and the consequent installation of pipe lines began first in England, but capital expenditure by the Scottish Gas Board has now begun to show an appreciable increase over its previous level. As the process of conversion is extended more widely throughout Scotland, fixed capital formation in Scotland will rise, relative to the national total.

Investment in the electricity industry has been at a high level during the 1960s as new power stations have been built to overcome the shortages in generating capacity which emerged in the early 1960s. In its new power stations at Cockenzie, near Edinburgh, completed in 1968 and at Longannet, near Alloa, to be completed in 1971, the South of Scotland has doubled its generating capacity. It has also a substantial commitment to nuclear generation in its Hunterston power stations on the Ayrshire coast. With the completion of the Cruachan pump-storage scheme, the North of Scotland Hydroelectric Board envisages no further significant additions to its capital investment in hydroelectric schemes. The most recent major addition to its capacity has been the oil-fired power station at Carolina Port in Dundee and it is shortly to commence construction of a nuclear power station in Banffshire. The growth of demand for electricity has slackened somewhat in recent years, but a high level of investment will still be required to replace out-dated generating capacity.

Only since re-nationalisation in 1967 has capital investment by the steel industry appeared in the public sector. Two years' figures are an insufficient basis from which to draw any conclusions. In the longer term, the decision by the Secretary of State for Scotland in 1970 to give approval to a deep water iron ore terminal at Hunterston on the Firth of Clyde should the British Steel Corporation put forward such a proposal, may presage a high level of investment in Scotland during the 1970s by the steel industry.

The low level of investment in Scotland under air transport is explained by the fact that purchases of new aircraft by B.E.A. and B.O.A.C. appear in the national figures but none of this expenditure is allocated to Scotland.

To sum up, it is possible on the basis of data currently available to analyse gross domestic fixed capital formation in Scotland for agriculture, manufacturing industry, a large part of the public sector and for the nationalised industries and public corporations. Gaps still exist, of which the largest are dwellings, the distributive trades and service industries. Nevertheless, for items covering over 60 per cent of gross domestic fixed capital formation in the United Kingdom in 1968, it is possible to produce comparable estimates for Scotland. The Government's statistical services in Scotland have recently been strengthened and it may be that with greater resources it will be possible to produce a reasonably comprehensive set of figures for Scotland. If that were achieved it would then be possible to attempt to estimate gross capital stock in Scotland.

2 Economies of scale

Adam Smith put forward in his *Wealth of Nations* the central proposition that 'division of labour is limited by the extent of the market'. One of the major features of the growth of industrial economies has been the expansion of markets, both domestic and international. With this expansion in markets has come the opportunity for individual firms to grow, and enjoy the economies of producing on a larger scale. As firms grow, for example in industries producing durable consumer goods, it is possible for them to experience cost-reducing advantages associated with mass production. Unit costs of production fall. Higher levels of output allow technically more efficient methods of production to be used; a higher degree of division of labour becomes possible as well as the recruitment of more specialised staff; large firms may enjoy advantages in negotiating discounts for bulk purchases of raw materials and supplies. In short, there are economies of purchasing, production, marketing, and management. Such increasing returns to scale are not of course inexhaustible, and one of the reasons for the persistence of small firms is that larger firms may encounter certain diseconomies of scale associated with large size, such as heavy administrative overhead costs.

If we ask what evidence is available in Britain about economies of scale, the answer must be that the data are limited. As far as Scotland is concerned, the presence of economies of scale has to be inferred from other evidence, rather than measured directly.

A number of different ways of measuring economies of scale can be distinguished, though it should be noted that none of these is very satisfactory on its own, and corroborating evidence may be required from other sources. The following are worth noting:

a) Analysis of cost data of firms of different sizes

By studying the cost records of firms of different sizes in the same industry it should be possible to establish whether average costs fall with increases in output. The drawback to this method is that very few firms manufacture a single product. Most produce a range of products and the mix of products will almost certainly differ between firms. Also lack of uniformity in accounting practices regarding costs can make comparison difficult.

b) The use of engineering data Production engineers are frequently called upon to estimate costs of production at different levels of output, assuming the most efficient method of production is used appropriate to each level of output. Other costs as well as production costs are also estimated at different levels of output. Information of this kind does appear, particularly in technical journals, but not in a sufficiently systematic fashion to make this a comprehensive basis of analysis.

c) The 'Survivor Principle' This method studies the size distribution of the firms in an industry at two periods of time. A comparison is made of the most popular size of firm at each date, and the method is based on the argument that the firms with the lowest costs will be those who have survived into the next time period.

d) Analysis of the return on capital of firms of different sizes If economies of scale exist in an industry, then the large firms will typically have lower costs than the smaller firms and will, therefore, earn higher profits or higher rates of return on capital. As with method (a), variations in accounting practice regarding the definition of profits and the valuation of assets limit the usefulness of this method.

Method (d), however, formed the basis for the one systematic attempt which has been made to measure the existence of economies of scale in Scotland. In 1961 Hart and MacBean published a study of productivity, profitability and growth in Scotland compared with the United Kingdom as a whole. While their study was concerned with examining the regional variations, if any, in productivity, profitability and growth, and the implications for the location of industry, it is possible to infer from their study certain tentative conclusions about economies of scale.

A first comparison was made on the basis of the profitability of Scottish companies quoted on the Stock Exchange. Comparing this data with corresponding data for all United Kingdom quoted companies, Hart and MacBean found that between 1953 and 1959, the Scottish companies earned a return on capital of 20·4 per cent against 20·9 per cent for U.K. companies as a whole. A difference of only 0·5 per cent is negligible.

Use of quoted companies as the basis of comparison means that the conclusion is limited to companies large enough to have a stock market quotation, in other words larger companies, with which we tend to associate economies of scale. Such companies, however, earn about 70 per cent of the profits in manufacturing industry. Our particular interest is to observe whether the largest Scottish companies are big enough to achieve the available economies of scale. Hart and MacBean's study suggests that the contribution of economies of scale has been no less important for the Scottish economy, judged by the return on capital.

As a further test of the similarity of profit performance of Scottish and U.K. industry Hart and MacBean took a random sample of 50 quoted Scottish companies and matched each of them with an English company of the same *size* from the same industry. Analysing these 50 Scottish and 50 English companies over the nine years from 1950 to 1958, produced 450 observations from each country. The average rate of profit for the Scottish companies was 16·3 per cent and for the English companies 16·6 per cent. Again, the difference between these two figures was insignificant and permits the conclusion that when comparing company profitability of similar firms and industries in Scotland and the United Kingdom as a whole, profitability is much the same.[1]

By itself, Hart and MacBean's analysis does not prove that industry in Scotland has achieved economies of scale comparable to those for the country as a whole. What it does indicate is that if differences in economies of scale do exist, they are not sufficiently great to exert any marked downward effect on the profitability of Scottish industry.

While economies of scale are associated with the growth in size of the individual firm, we use the term external economies to identify cost reductions which a firm enjoys as a result of the activities of other firms in the industry, or the nature of the environment in which the firm operates. Often external economies are associated with concentration of firms in an industry in a particular geographical area. The manufacture of motor cars in the Midlands has led to the development of specialized engineering skills in both labour and capital, the development of allied educational and training facilities, and specialized local com-

[1] That Hart and MacBean's conclusions were essentially correct was confirmed by G. Fisher in the *Scottish Journal of Political Economy* 1962. Fisher applied much more extensive and rigorous analysis to Hart and MacBean's figures, but arrived at essentially the same conclusions.

mercial expertise, such as service facilities, banking and credit services. Many of these economies would not accrue if the industry were scattered over a wide area.

We shall see in Chapter 11 that one of the concepts which Governments have used in regional analysis and policy is the 'growth point', one of whose purposes is to establish an environment of public facilities which introduce a framework of external economies. The evidence of external economies in the context of the Government's growth area policy for Central Scotland has been assessed by Cameron and Reid. They concluded that Central Scotland is too small and too well developed for such a policy to have much effect in inducing firms to grow faster as a result of external economies. Something like 75 per cent of the population and 90 per cent of the manufacturing industry of Scotland are located in the Central Belt. No part of Central Scotland is more than one hour's drive from the two major urban centres of Edinburgh and Glasgow. Both centres provide specialised maintenance and professional services which are easily accessible to all parts of Central Scotland.

Central Scotland is a geographically compact area with a good road network and a high density of population. It would appear probable that all parts of Central Scotland experience, in more or less equal measure, the external economies arising from transport facilities or labour supply.

External economies are uniformly available throughout Central Scotland. The longer established, or more fully developed an industry, the greater the potential external economies are likely to be. The introduction of the motor industry into Central Scotland in the early 1960s is, as we saw in Chapter 5, an example where external economies have not been fully developed. The limited range and restricted scale of output in the motor industry in Scotland have been insufficient to attract significant numbers of components suppliers from their traditional locations in the Midlands; nor have they been sufficient to induce any great number of Scottish firms to expand or diversify into component manufacture for the vehicles industry. The vehicles manufacturers prefer to transport the greater part of their components from their traditional sources of supply, and thereby they are enjoying only limited external economies.

By and large, the evidence on economies of scale so far as Scotland is concerned is rather inconclusive. Generally speaking, the evidence suggests that Scotland may have experienced economies of scale of the same magnitude as the country as a whole. But one can point to instances, vehicles, for example, where undoubtedly further economies, particularly external economies, could be achieved by increases in output.

3 Advances in Knowledge

Advances in knowledge or technical progress have proved a major source of economic growth not only in the United Kingdom but in most industrialised countries. The following table illustrates the estimated contribution to the growth of Gross Domestic Product of changes in the labour force, the stock of capital, and 'technical progress' or advancement in knowledge in a number of countries.

Table 9.5 Estimated Contribution to Growth of Gross Domestic Product of Increases in Labour Force, Capital Stock and Technical Progress in a number of Countries

	Annual per cent rate of growth of			Estimated per cent contribution to growth of		
	Labour	Capital	G.D.P.	Labour	Capital	'Technical Progress'
United Kingdom						
1949–59	0·6	3·1	2·5	0·4	0·9	1·2
France						
1949–54	0·1	2·9	4·8	0·1	0·9	3·8
1954–59	0·2	3·9	4·1	0·1	1·2	2·8
W. Germany						
1950–54	1·8	4·8	8·3	1·3	1·4	5·6
1954–59	1·4	6·9	6·6	1·0	2·1	3·5
Belgium						
1949–54	0·6	2·4	3·6	0·4	0·7	2·5
1954–59	−0·1	2·7	2·3	−0·1	0·8	1·6
Netherlands						
1949–54	1·4	4·0	4·9	1·0	1·2	2·7
1954–59	1·1	5·5	4·1	0·8	1·7	1·6
Canada						
1949–59	2·1	7·1	4·3	1·5	2·1	0·7
Japan						
1950–58	2·4	10·6	7·9	1·7	3·2	3·0

Source: Aukrust 'Productivity Measurement Review', February 1965.

Only in the Netherlands 1954–9, in Canada 1949–59 and in Japan 1950–8 is the growth contribution of capital stock greater than technical progress. This finding is broadly in line with Denison's analysis of the factors contributing to growth in the United Kingdom which we looked at in Chapter 8. To a certain extent, advances in knowledge must be treated as a residual, or as an amalgam of factors, whose precise contribution to growth cannot be measured exactly. Important amongst these is investment in measures designed to promote greater efficiency in the use of capital and investment which leads to the discovery and production of completely new products and processes. This expenditure is known as research and development or, more commonly, R and D.

There are several stages in this process which must be clearly identified. The first is invention. By invention is meant the creating of a new idea or technique. Following invention is the phase known as innovation, which is the application of an invention to an actual process of production. The time lag between invention and application may be long—years, decades or even centuries—and this is known as the period of development. Not all invention leads to innovation. Costs of development may be many times the cost of the original invention.

Research activity, i.e. the pursuit of new products and processes may fall into three categories. *Basic (or pure) research* is undertaken for the sake of advancement of knowledge without any specific committment to an industrial or commercial objective. This type of research is generally undertaken in universities, Government laboratories, and non-profit making research institutes. Second, *applied research* is directly concerned with the discovery of new scientific knowledge which has specific industrial application. This type of work is undertaken in the research laboratories of private firms or research associations, which are formed by voluntary groupings of firms with common technical interests and are supported in part by Government grants. Thirdly, there comes *development*, which means the translation of research findings and scientific knowledge into commercially viable new products and processes. Again, this is a process which is carried out within industry although in certain industries, such as aircraft, a large part of development costs may be met by the Government.

If technical progress or advances in knowledge are an important element of growth, and if technical progress can be promoted by increased expenditure on R and D, this raises the important question as to whether there is a direct relationship between growth and R and D. Will a country by spending more on R and D automatically generate a faster rate of growth? Unfortunately, the answer to this question is by no means clearly established. Among countries outside the Communist bloc, the United States spends by far the greatest amount of money on R and D. When allowance is made for the differences in cost levels between the two countries the R and D effort of the United States is perhaps five times greater than that of the United

Kingdom, yet the United Kingdom ranks second behind the United States in *per capita* expenditure on R and D. The United States spends more than twice the amount spent in total by the United Kingdom, France and W. Germany. As well as large differences in the total amounts spent there are also large differences between countries in the ways R and D is allocated. Considerably more than half the expenditure in the United States is for military and space research: France spends about 50 per cent on military and space research and the United Kingdom around 45 per cent. Countries like West Germany, Belgium and the Netherlands spend 10 per cent or less in this direction. Even so, the amount spent by the United States on civil research far outstrips the effort of any Western country.

Will this great disparity in R and D expenditure mean that the United States will far outstrip all other countries in terms of growth? The evidence to date does not support this view. It is of course important to introduce a time lag between R and D expenditure and any anticipated increase in growth, to allow the results of R and D to manifest themselves. Allowing a time lag of five years between R and D expenditure and its effect on growth, there is no evidence during the 1950s and early 1960s to support any direct association between the two. Between 1955 and 1964, the average compound rate of growth of output per man in the United States was 1·9 per cent. This was only 10 per cent greater than the average percentage increase in growth of R and D in the years 1950–9. For the United Kingdom, the rate of growth of output per man was 50 per cent greater than the rate of growth of R and D: in West Germany, France and Japan growth of output per man grew between seven and fourteen times faster than the growth of R and D.

Increased efficiency in the use of capital, or technical progress, is important for the growth of an economy. The stimulus to this increased efficiency should not be conceived in terms of what each country spends on its own R and D. The spread of knowledge is international. There are well-established means whereby new technology is disseminated throughout the world. The fact that a country does not devote as large a proportion of its resources to R and D as do others does not imply that it need necessarily be technologically backward. Provided it has the means of applying the fruits of R and D in its own industrial environment, a country does not require to rely exclusively on the outcome of its own R and D efforts to promote growth.

In 1967–8 the United Kingdom spent £962 million

on R and D, equivalent to 2·7 per cent of gross national product. Whilst second only to the United States in the amount spent on R and D, the United Kingdom earns one of the lowest rates of return on this expenditure in terms of the economic growth generated. R and D may be regarded as a necessary, but not a sufficient, condition for growth. The highly qualified manpower and the costly physical resources it commands have alternative uses and impose heavy opportunity costs. It is possible to impede growth by spending more on R and D. The United Kingdom's resources are too limited to operate effectively in all fields of

Table 9.6 Location of Research Establishments in the United Kingdom 1968

	Private Sector					
	Industrial firms		Other private establishments		Research associations	
	No.	per cent	No.	per cent	No.	per cent
North of England	35	4·9	2	2·0	1	2·2
Yorkshire and Humberside	46	6·4	3	2·9	8	17·4
North West	79	11·0	4	3·8	2	4·4
West Midlands	82	11·4	2	2·0	5	10·8
East Midlands	40	5·5	—	—	6	13·0
East Anglia	14	1·9	5	5·0	1	2·2
South East	325	45·2	79	77·4	20	43·4
South West	40	5·5	2	2·0	1	2·2
N. Ireland	7	1·0	—	—	1	2·2
Wales	11	1·5	2	2·0	—	—
Scotland	41	5·7	3	2·9	1	2·2
United Kingdom	720	100	102	100	46	100

	Public Sector					
	Government establishments		Universities and polytechnics		All research establishments	
	No.	per cent	No.	per cent	No.	per cent
North of England	5	2·1	5	6·2	48	4·1
Yorkshire and Humberside	6	2·4	8	9 9	71	5·9
North West	14	5·8	8	9·9	107	8·9
West Midlands	9	3·7	8	9·9	106	8·9
East Midlands	4	1·7	5	6·2	55	4·6
East Anglia	16	6·6	2	2·4	38	3·2
South East	133	54·9	22	27·1	579	48·6
South West	12	4·9	5	6·2	60	5·1
N. Ireland	5	2·1	2	2·4	15	1·3
Wales	5	2·1	8	9·9	26	2·2
Scotland	33	13·7	8	9·9	86	7·2
United Kingdom	242	100	81	100	1,191	100

Source: Buswell and Lewis, op. cit.

R and D, but a policy of concentration of effort into fields of technology where the scientific and market growth potential is good, could have beneficial effects on Britain's growth prospects.

What of the regional distribution of Britain's R and D effort? Little was known until recently about this question, but Buswell and Lewis have provided an analysis of the regional distribution of R and D establishments in the United Kingdom which gives a valuable measure, even allowing for the possibly substantial variations between establishments in the amounts spent and the numbers of staff employed.

The immediate observation from the table is the heavy concentration of all forms of research activity in the South East of England. Just under half of all the research establishments in the country are in that region; around two-thirds of all private research establishments; well over half the Government establishments; over 40 per cent of the research associations, and more than a quarter of the universities and polytechnics. No other region accounts for more than 10 per cent of the total, and only in the West Midlands and Yorkshire and Humberside are there sizeable concentrations of research associations. Outwith the South East, Scotland is the only region with a significant number of Government research establishments. Apart from the National Engineering Laboratory at East Kilbride, which is the national focal point for research into mechanical engineering, and the Atomic Energy Authority research establishment at Dounreay, most of the other Government research establishments in Scotland are small in scale and highly specialised in character; much of the emphasis of Government research in Scotland is directed towards agriculture, forestry and fishing. The only research association located in Scotland is the Jute Research Association in Dundee.[1] It is for this reason that the level of capital formation under the heading 'Technological Services', noted earlier in Table 9.3, is so low.

The factors behind the overwhelming domination of the South East in the field of research are not far to seek. The high standard of transport and communications associated with London for both domestic and overseas travel; the high proportion of science-based industries like aircraft, aerospace, radio, electronic and electrical industries already located in the region; the large number of head offices of major companies in the South East, and

[1] The government has recently decided to withdraw financial support from the Research Associations, which may lead to the closure of the Jute R.A.

the unrivalled facilities of London for specialised scientific information, have all contributed greatly. Bearing in mind that the Government contributes around 50 per cent of the total cost of all R and D, ease of access to and from Whitehall has been an important factor governing the location of research establishments in both the public and private sectors. Conversely, of course, as the major sponsor of research, the government can exercise a degree of control over the location of research. The location of the National Engineering Laboratory at East Kilbride is an example of the Government's discretion in this field.

Scotland's 7·2 per cent share of the total number of research establishments is almost certainly an overstatement of the money spent and the numbers employed on R and D. It may well be that Scotland commands only around 5 per cent of the nation's R and D resources, both human and financial. While it would be difficult to argue that this under-representation of R and D has been a direct cause of Scotland's slow rate of growth, it has undoubtedly had a retarding effect. The heavy concentration of highly qualified and highly paid manpower in one region of the country has meant impoverishment of the others. The single most influential factor conditioning the location of a research establishment is the need to recruit, retain and develop a team of scientists and technicians of the appropriate quality. Such people are highly mobile and highly selective in their preference of area in which to live. Their demands for good schools, good quality housing and access to cultural facilities have to be met by potential employers.

As we shall see in Chapter 13, the Government has accepted the view that it is in the interest of the country as a whole that there be a more uniform spread of economic activity. The location of industrial research is one of the most obvious aspects of regional disparity, not just between Scotland and the United Kingdom but between the South East and every other region of the country.

There has been considerable experimentation in the United States in setting up science parks. Major research facilities have been established at such locations as Stanford in California, Ann Arbor in Michigan and along Route 128 in Massachusetts. The conditions under which such science parks have thriven include proximity to institutes of higher education and industry with an established high R and D content, suitable industrial estate facilities, access to transport and communications facilities of a high standard, and supporting facilities and environment which are attractive to the type of staff who will live and work on such science parks.

4 Summary

The growth of an economy depends to a large extent on the growth of the stock of capital at its disposal, on the technical efficiency with which it uses this capital and on the size of the markets it serves. In none of these respects is it possible to carry out a comprehensive analysis of Scotland's performance. From the analysis of gross domestic fixed capital formation in the manufacturing sector we have seen that investment by industry in Scotland is, generally speaking, at least on a par with the country as a whole; in terms of industrial buildings it is somewhat higher. It is dangerous to infer too much from the figures of gross capital formation. It is important to know something about the age structure of the stock of capital and how much of current investment is going merely to replace outworn capital. It may be that as a consequence of her early start in the Industrial Revolution, and her over-dependence on traditional declining industries, Scotland's stock of capital is relatively elderly. A higher level of gross capital formation than is indicated by a simple population or output basis may well be required, simply to maintain the stock of capital intact, far less to provide for growth in the stock of capital.

Much the same considerations apply in relation to capital formation in the public sector. Again, under most headings investment in Scotland has been higher in recent years than would be justified on a straight population basis. In part, this is a consequence of government regional policy which since 1963 has aimed deliberately at attaining a higher level of investment in infrastructure, particularly in Central Scotland. Again, without some knowledge of the age structure of capital in the public sector, it is dangerous to infer that a generally higher level of gross capital formation means that Scotland is in some way getting more than her 'fair' share or is being subsidised by the rest of the country. A higher level of gross capital formation again may be required simply to maintain the net capital stock intact.

The argument is sometimes put forward that industry in Scotland is too small and relatively inefficient. No direct evidence is available from *Census of Production* data as to the size structure of Scottish industry compared with the national pattern. While it may be possible to identify particular industries or firms in which further economies of scale are possible in Scotland, in overall terms there is no evidence to suggest, at any rate from the early 1960s that Scottish industry is inefficient by national standards. The profitability of Scottish industry is similar to the profit performance of all British firms.

There is considerable evidence that there is an under-allocation of R and D resources in all regions of the country except the South East. While it is difficult to establish any close relationship between the amount a country spends on R and D and its rate of growth, it can be argued that the United Kingdom would benefit from a more efficient re-allocation of its R and D resources.[1] The multiplier and spin-off effects of a redeployment of R and D resources to regions such as Scotland could be substantial. The arguments for such a redeployment have been argued cogently but so far with limited success by the Scottish Council (Development and Industry). There are locations in Scotland, particularly around Edinburgh and the new towns, which could be conducive to the growth of R and D.

References

R. J. Nicholson, *Economic Statistics and Economic Problems*, McGraw-Hill, 1969, Chapter 6.

B. R. Williams, *Technology, Investment and Growth*, Chapman and Hall, 1967.

Richard Caves and Associates, *Britain's Economic Prospects*, George Allen and Unwin, 1968, Chapter 6.

National Accounts and Statistics: Sources and Methods, H.M.S.O., 1968, Chapter 12.

National Income and Expenditure, 1969, p. 104.

The Economies of Large Scale Production in British Industry, Cambridge University Press, 1965.

P. E. Hart and A. J. MacBean, 'Regional Differences in Productivity, Profitability and Growth', *Scottish Journal of Political Economy*, February 1961.

G. C. Cameron and G. L. Reid, *Scottish Economic Planning and the Attraction of Industry*. Oliver and Boyd, 1968.

B. R. Williams, *Technology, Investment and Growth*, Chapman and Hall, 1967, Chapter 9.

Buswell and Lewis, 'Geographical Distribution of Industrial Research Activity in the U.K.', *Regional Studies*, October 1970.

Memorandum to Minister of Technology, Scottish Council (Development and Industry), 1965.

[1] When it left office in June 1970, the Labour government had just published a Green Paper on its proposals for a major re-organisation of R and D in the public sector.

Chapter 10 Human Resources in Scotland

We have already seen that labour input has been increasingly recognised as a major source of economic growth. For the United Kingdom, Denison estimated that labour input has accounted for over a quarter of growth between 1950 and 1962. Indeed the contribution of changes in employment and improvements in education to total growth would have been as high as one third if it had not been for the reduction in hours of work and the unfavourable age-composition of the labour force.

It is only comparatively recently that economists have begun to appreciate again the contribution which labour can make to economic growth. Adam Smith was perfectly clear on the subject. In his definition of fixed capital he included

> 'the acquired and useful abilities of all the inhabitants or members of society',

and went on to say that

> 'The acquisition of such talents, by the maintenance of the acquirer during his education, study or apprenticeship, always costs a real expense, which is a capital fixed and realised as it were, in his person. Those talents as they make part of his fortune, so do they likewise of that of the society to which he belongs.'

In this Chapter we shall seek to follow the example set by Adam Smith and endeavour to identify and measure the 'talents' of the Scottish people as a whole and of important elements within it. In the contemporary jargon, we speak of 'human resource development', and our task here will be to identify its main dimensions.

Human resource development has been defined by Harbison and Myers as the 'process of increasing the knowledge, the skills and the capacities of all the people in a society. In economic terms it could be described as the accumulation of human capital and its effective investment in the development of an economy.' Obviously, there are many ways in which human resources can be developed. Education plays an important role from primary through secondary school and on to colleges of various kinds and the universities. Nor does the process finish with the completion of formal education. Industrial and vocational training are important aspects which have been increasingly recognised in Britain since the Industrial Training Act was passed in 1964. People may also seek to further their knowledge and skills themselves by formal or informal means. In developing countries in particular it is also recognised that better medical and public health facilities and higher standards of nutrition can do much to improve the quality of human resources.

We have already seen in Chapter 3 one of the disturbing and negative characteristics of human resource utilisation, namely unemployment. Scotland clearly under-utilises her stock of manpower when unemployment remains so intractably high, and policies to reduce unemployment are an obvious part of an 'active manpower or human resource policy'. In this Chapter, however, our primary concern is with the demographic, educational and training aspects of Scottish experience of human resources. Highly qualified manpower is generally regarded as a strategic component of the supply, and we shall pay particular attention to it.

We distinguish two aspects of human resources. The first is the *stock*, that is the numbers of people with various skills, abilities and attributes who go to make up the existing pool or stock of human resources in an economy. The second is the *flow* into or out of this pool. This will have such dimensions as the influx of young people who have completed their formal education at school, college or university, the balance between immigrants and emigrants, and the upgrading of the skills of the existing labour force through training and retraining.

1 Demographic Features

Although the relationships between the growth of population and the growth of national income are by no means clearly established, it is nevertheless important to consider the size of the stock and flows of population. Economists and demographers are still a long way from defining such elusive concepts as the minimum and maximum populations of a country, far less the much more debatable concept of an optimum population. In most countries, there will be a wide range of population over which it will not be possible to say whether population is having a retarding or accelerating effect on economic growth. For certain countries, such as India, it is almost certainly the case that a reduction in population would permit a faster rate of growth. For a country such as Scotland, with an almost stationary population, we have as yet no evidence to relate the slow rate of economic growth with the slow growth of population.

At June 1969, the home (or *de facto*) population of Scotland was estimated at 5·2 million, an increase of only 0·2 per cent over the population at the last census in 1961. Table 10.1 shows the population of Scotland at each census taken this century. The inter-censal changes have been calculated and compared against the inter-censal changes for England and Wales.

Table 10.1 Census Population of Scotland and England and Wales 1901–61

	Thousands					
	1901	1911	1921	1931	1951	1961
Scotland	4,472·1	4,760·9	4,882·5	4,843·0	5,096·4	5,179·3
Inter-censal change per cent		+6·5	+2·6	−0·8	+5·2	+1·6
England and Wales	32,528	36,070	37,887	39,952	43,758	46,105
Inter-censal change per cent		+10·9	+5·0	+5·5	+9·5	+5·4

Source: Digest of Scottish Statistics; Annual Abstract of Statistics.

Between the censuses of 1901 and 1961, the population of Scotland grew by 16 per cent: over the same period the population of England and Wales grew by 42 per cent, or two and a half times faster. The most up-to-date figures show the population of Scotland in an even more unfavourable light (see Table 10.2).

Scotland's population has been stagnating in recent years while the population of England and Wales has continued

Table 10.2 Population of Scotland and England and Wales 1965–9

	Mid Year Estimates Thousands					
	1965	1966	1967	1968	1969	per cent change 1965–9
Scotland	5,203·9	5,190·8	5,186·6	5,187·5	5,194·7	−0·2
England and Wales	47,688	47,985	48,301	48,593	48,827	+2·4

Source: Digest of Scottish Statistics; Annual Abstract of Statistics.

to increase by an average of 0·5 per cent per annum. What are the reasons for this stagnation? To answer this question we must look at the flows into and out of this stock. These flows are of two types—(a) a natural increase flow and (b) a migratory flow. Both flows have inward and outward components.

a) Natural Increase For the natural increase flow, the inflow is the number of births and the outflow the number of deaths. Scotland has experienced a substantial inflow from natural increase because the number of births has always been greater than the number of deaths.

Table 10.3 Births and deaths in Scotland 1901–61

	Thousands				
	1901–11	1911–21	1921–31	1931–51	1951–61
Births	1,306	1,185	1,005	1,849	959
Deaths	763	824	652	1,347	619
Natural Increase	543	360	352	502	339

Source: Digest of Scottish Statistics.

On the basis of natural increase, the population of Scotland would have grown by over 2 million this century, whereas the recorded increase was just over 700,000. We shall examine the reasons for this discrepancy shortly.

There is evidence that the rate of natural increase in Scotland is now slackening (see Table 10.4).

Table 10.4 Births and Deaths in Scotland 1961–9 (Thousands)

	Births	Deaths	Natural Increase
1961/2	103·1	64·0	39·1
1962/3	103·2	65·0	38·2
1963/4	103·4	61·1	42·3
1964/5	103·0	62·4	40·6
1965/6	97·5	64·3	33·2
1966/7	98·1	60.0	38.1
1967/8	94·9	63.0	31.9
1968/9	92·9	62.6	30.3

Source: Digest of Scottish Statistics.

While the number of deaths has varied from year to year between 60,000 and 65,000, the number of births has been falling steadily since 1963/64 and in 1968/9 was 10,000 below the level of 1960/1. There has been a corresponding effect on natural increase which has fallen from over 40,000 a year to around 30,000. Since 1911, the rate of natural increase of population in Scotland has been greater than in England and Wales although the margin has narrowed considerably in recent years.

Next, we look at the two components of the natural increase flow separately. The generally accepted methods of assessing fertility are by means of either birth or fertility rates. The birth rate which expresses the number of births per 1,000 population is rather a crude assessment of fertility; the fertility rate which expresses the number of births as a ratio of the number of women in the child-bearing age group 15–49 years is a more sensitive measure.

Table 10.5 Birth and Fertility Rates in Scotland and England and Wales, Selected Years, 1951–68

	Crude Birth Rate per 1,000 population		Fertility Rate: Legitimate births per 1,000 married women 15–44		Fertility Rate: Illegitimate births per 1,000 unmarried women 15–44	
	Scotland	England and Wales	Scotland	England and Wales	Scotland	England and Wales
1951	17·8	15·5	131·5	105·4	8·6	9·8
1956	18·6	15·7	137·4	108·2	8·6	11·4
1961	19·5	17·6	146·0	123·7	11·1	16·5
1966	18·6	17·7	137·4	123·9	15·2	21·5
1967	18·6	17·2	137·2	120·6	16·8	22·6
1968	18·3	16·9	134·8	118·1	17·8	22·7

Source: Registrars General.

Both Scotland and England and Wales experienced a peak in legitimate post-war fertility in 1947—the famous 'bulge'. Through the 1950s the Scottish legitimate fertility rate rose from 131 per 1,000 to 142 per 1,000 and was always above the rate for England and Wales. The early 1960s saw another surge in fertility: in England and Wales a peak legitimate rate of 128·2 per 1,000 was reached in 1964: in Scotland the rise was even greater, reaching 147·6 per 1,000 in 1964. Fertility now appears to be on the wane and is currently falling at about the same rate both nationally and in Scotland.

Mortality, the other element of our natural increase flow, can be measured in the form of a death rate, i.e. the number of deaths per 1,000 population. Although the picture of mortality given by death rates may be influenced by differences in age structure between populations, for our present purposes a straight comparison of death rates between Scotland and England and Wales is sufficient.

Table 10.6 Death Rates in Scotland and in England and Wales, Selected Years, 1947–68

Crude death rates per 1,000 population	Scotland	England and Wales
1947	13·1	12·3
1951	12·9	12·5
1956	12·1	11·7
1961	12·3	11·9
1966	12·3	11·7
1967	11·5	11·2
1968	12·2	11·9

Source: Registrars General.

Two features emerge from the above table. First, there is little evidence of any significant change in death rates since the end of the war, and second, the death rate in England and Wales is consistently below the Scottish rate.

The consequences of the fertility and mortality features of the Scottish population can be summarised by a measure known as the net reproduction rate. This rate indicates the number of girls which a group of women will give birth to during their lifetime at current fertility and mortality levels for each age group. If this rate is above 1 this implies a natural increase: if below 1 a natural decrease. The net reproduction rate in Scotland fell below 1 in the inter war period, leading demographers of the time to forecast a falling population. Since the war it has always been above 1, although in recent years it has tended to fall, as the following table shows.

Table 10.7 Net Reproduction Rate in Scotland

Selected Years 1939–68	
1939	0·932
1947	1·281
1951	1·099
1956	1·228
1961	1·365
1966	1·347
1967	1·336
1968	1·308

Source: Registrar General for Scotland.

In summary, we have seen that Scotland has had a healthy rate of natural increase of population and that there has been a substantial net inflow from this source into the stock of population. Why, then, is it that Scotland's population has only grown at a fraction of the rate that the size of the natural increase would have warranted?

b) Migration Flows The answer is that the migration flows into and out of Scotland have been predominantly in an outward direction and have to a very large extent eroded the gains recorded from natural increase. When looking at natural increase, we were able to distinguish the inflow in the form of births and the outflow in the form of deaths. Unfortunately, until very recently it has not been possible to identify the migration inflows and outflows separately. The data available to the Registrar General for Scotland only allow him to estimate the net migration flows, i.e. the difference between the inward and outward movements. In the Sample Census taken in 1966, questions relating to previous residence were asked which have allowed estimates to be made of the size and composition of the inward and outward migratory movements; these we shall look at shortly.

Table 10.8 Natural Increase and Migration: Scotland 1901–61

			Thousands		
	1901–11	1911–21	1921–31	1931–51	1951–61
Natural Increase	543	360	352	502	339
Actual Increase	289	122	−40	253	83
Net Migration	−254	−239	−392	−220	−282
Overseas	N.A.	N.A.	−330	−10	−140
Rest of U.K.	N.A.	N.A.	−60	−210	−142

Source: Digest of Scottish Statistics.

Between the censuses of 1901 and 1961, Scotland experienced a *net* loss by migration of 1·4 million. This does not mean that 1·4 million people left Scotland. What it means is that 1·4 million *more* people left Scotland than came into Scotland. We have no means of knowing how many people came in and how many left, nor what kind of people they were. In the period between 1951 and 1968, 92 per cent of Scotland's natural increase was lost through emigration. Between 1921 and 1931 the loss by emigration was greater than the gain from natural increase, and this experience has been repeated in recent years as is shown in Table 10.9 below.

The problem of containing Scotland's migration losses has now become a major feature of Government regional policy. The extent and gravity of Scotland's migration imbalance were revealed recently in a study carried out by the Scottish Economic Planning Board.[1] Among the principal findings were these:[2]

[1] For a discussion of the composition and function of the Scottish Economic Planning Board see Chapter 13.

[2] See The *Scotsman*, 29th January 1970.

Table 10.9 Natural Increase and Migration: Scotland 1961–9 (Thousands)

	1961/2	1962/3	1963/4	1964/5
Natural Increase	39·1	38·2	42·3	40·6
Actual Increase	9·6	4·2	−1·7	−2·4
Net Migration	−29·5	−34·0	+40·6	−43·0
Overseas	−9·0	−13·0	−16·6	−21·0
Rest of U.K.	−20·5	−21·0	−24·0	−22·0
	1965/6	**1966/7**	**1967/8**	**1968/9**
Natural Increase	33·2	38·1	31·9	30·3
Actual Increase	−13·8	−6·9	−1·1	5·3
Net Migration	−47·0	−45·0	−33·0	−25·0
Overseas	−25·0	−29·0	−20·0	−14·0
Rest of U.K.	−22·0	−16·0	−13·0	−11·0

Source: Digest of Scottish Statistics.

(a) Since 1951 Scotland has experienced a level and rate of net loss more severe than any other part of Britain, the total net loss being greater than for all the northern regions of England and for Wales put together.

(b) Despite one of the highest regional rates of natural increase, Scotland has achieved less than one fifth of the rate of population growth of Great Britain as a whole between 1951 and 1968.

(c) While Wales and the northern regions of England have lost on average just over one third of their natural increase by net emigration between 1951 and 1968, Scotland has lost 92 per cent.

(d) Between 1961 and 1966, Scotland experienced the highest rate of net emigration in Western Europe apart from Malta.

(e) Significant statistical relationships exist between the level of net emigration to the rest of the U.K. and the difference in the percentage level of unemployment in Scotland and Great Britain; between net emigration to the rest of the U.K. and the differential in earnings levels in Scotland and those in the U.K.; economic opportunity and housing conditions were also found to be exerting strong influences.

These findings show that Scotland's emigration problems are serious by national and international standards—in a class of their own, says the Planning Board report. The solutions will be found in improving economic and social conditions in Scotland. Apart from the scale of the migration loss, it is also important to consider its direction. Migration is analysed by movements to other parts of the United Kingdom and movements overseas. Information presented in Chapter 3 has allowed us to look at the internal movements within the United Kingdom, but we have very little knowledge about the movements overseas. One source of information is data collected by the immigration authorities in certain overseas countries. One country to which many Scots have emigrated is Canada, and Table 10.10 below shows for some recent years the number of British immigrants.

Table 10.10 Immigrants Admitted to Canada by Country of Last Permanent Residence

	U.K.	Scotland	England	Wales	N. Ireland	Scotland as percentage of U.K.
1961	11,870	2,578	8,499	91	688	21·7
1962	15,603	3,505	10,950	187	951	22·5
1963	24,603	6,074	16,562	201	1,743	24·7
1964	29,279	6,698	20,481	236	1,847	22·9
1965	39,857	8,363	28,820	682	1,934	21·0
1966	63,291	16,077	43,567	1,192	2,400	25·4
1967	62,420	14,953	43,481	1,263	2,044	24·0
1968	37,889	7,302	28,623	449	1,477	19·3
1969	31,977	5,426	24,556	490	1,491	17·0

Source: Registrar General for Scotland.

Scotland's population is presently about 9·5 per cent of the United Kingdom total. On that basis, emigration to Canada from Scotland in the 1960s has been two to two and a half times greater than would have been expected on a simple population ratio. The proportion of all British emigrants going to Canada has risen from less than 20 per cent in 1964 to nearly one third in 1967.

The conclusion we arrive at is that Scotland's stock of population has been growing only very slowly because the inward flow from the side of natural increase is being offset by an almost equally large outward migration flow. It should not be thought that there is no connection between these flows. We have observed that the rate of natural increase has been falling in recent years as has the net reproduction rate, and that the reason has been a fall in the number of births. A major reason for the fall in the number of births has been the erosion of Scotland's reproductive capacity by this continuing emigration. It has been estimated by the Registrar-General for Scotland that a net migration loss of 1,000 in a year costs about thirty births in each year for the next ten years, about twenty in each of the following five years and a decreasing number in subsequent years. The net migration loss of 47,000 in 1965–6 alone will cost Scotland at least 17,000 births over the next fifteen years.

The final feature of Scotland's demographic structure we must look at is the number of dependents in the population. Dependents are defined as people who by virtue of age make no contribution to national output. Children under 15 and people over the statutory retiring ages are classed as dependents. If the proportion of dependents in a population is increasing, the burden of supporting these dependents, either directly or indirectly, will fall on proportionately fewer producers. While such a burden may well have adverse effects on the growth of income per head dependents need not be regarded entirely as a burden. This is particularly true of young dependents, for on a long view an increase in their number holds out the confident expectation of an increase in the stock of producers. As we have suggested above, this increase in the young stock may, however, be eroded in part via emigration.

Table 10.11 Composition of Population: Scotland and U.K. 1901–69

	Percentages					
	1901	1911	1931	1951	1961	1969
Scotland:						
Under working age	33·4	32·3	26·9	24·6	25·9	26·2
Working age	60·2	60·8	63·7	62·9	60·7	58·9
Over working age	6·4	6·9	9·4	12·5	13·4	14·9
United Kingdom:						
Under working age		30·8	24·3	22·6	23·2	24·0
Working age		61·9	65·3	63·8	61·8	60·3
Over working age		7·3	10·4	13·6	15·0	15·7

Source: Digest of Scottish Statistics; Annual Abstract of Statistics.

As a consequence of both higher fertility and mortality levels, Scotland has always tended to have a higher proportion of young dependents and a lower proportion of elderly dependents compared with the national average. Although dependents have accounted for a larger proportion of the population than in the United Kingdom as a whole, the overall effect has been for Scotland to have experienced a proportionately larger flow of young people entering the labour force.

2 Scotland's Stock of Human Resources

With this examination of the main dimensions of Scotland's population behind us, we now turn to examine the quality of the stock of human resources in Scotland. It is not enough simply to 'count heads'. Earlier, it was said that emphasis would be placed on studying those aspects of human resource development which were associated with 'high level' manpower. It is now time to define more closely what we should understand by this term. Any definition of human capital or high level manpower is bound to be arbitrary, but we shall follow the definition used by Harbison and Myers in their study of the economic implications of human resource development. High level manpower comprehends the following categories:

(1) Entrepreneurial, managerial and administrative personnel in both public and private establishments including educational institutions.

(2) Professional personnel such as scientists, engineers, architects, doctors, lawyers, economists, accountants, journalists, etc.

(3) Qualified teachers, i.e. those with a minimum of twelve years of education themselves.

(4) Subprofessional technical personnel such as nurses, engineering assistants, technicians, senior clerks, supervisors of skilled workers, the highest levels of skilled craftsmen, skilled clerical workers.

(5) Top-ranking political leaders, trade union leaders, judges, officers of the police and armed forces.

The reason for concentrating attention on this distinguished but rather mixed bag of people is that they are, in general, the type of people who fill the strategic occupations in modern societies. From them is drawn the leadership for economic, social and political activities. The importance of human capital acting in conjunction with physical capital has already been stressed. But while dams, power stations, factories, steel mills and so on can be constructed in a few years, it takes ten to fifteen years to develop managers, engineers and administrators to operate them. To this 'lead time' should also be added the twelve years or more of full time education which such people will normally have experienced.

For Scotland, we can come reasonably close to Harbison and Myers' definition of high level manpower from the occupational analysis which is an integral part of the Census of Population. In the following table, which is based on a 10 per cent sample taken as part of the 1961 Census, all persons employed in Occupation Order XXIV, Administrators and Managers, and in Occupation Order XXV, Professional and Technical workers (this Order includes the medical, legal, teaching, scientific and engineering professions as well as skilled workers such as draughtsmen and artists) have been amalgamated with persons defined as self-employed, employers and managers, foremen and supervisors in all other industries and occupations, to give a definition of high level manpower.

From Table 10.12 we see that in Scotland the stock of

Table 10.12 High Level Manpower in Scotland and England and Wales in 1961

	Scotland		England and Wales	
	Number	Per cent	Number	Per cent
No. XXIV:				
istrators and Managers	41,950	1·1	601,160	1·7
No. XXV:				
sional and Technical Workers	188,760	4·9	1,880,090	5·3
mployed, Employers, Managers, Foremen				
ıpervisors in the following categories:				
y Industries (I and II)	61,830	1·6	382,320	1·1
Nos. III–XVIII:				
'acturing and Construction	67,150	1·7	754,210	2·1
Nos. XIX to XXVII:				
e and Other Industries	132,450	3·4	1,855,170	5·2
	492,140	12·8	5,472,950	15·4
er workers	1,827,710	47·2	16,221,520	45·4
mically inactive aged 15 or over	1,551,010	40·0	14,003,770	39·2
Population aged 15 and over	3,870,860	100·0	35,698,240	100·0

: H. Lind, Regional Distribution of Educated People in Britain, Scotland, October 1969.

what we have defined as high level manpower was, in 1961, proportionally rather smaller than in England and Wales. The two groups, administrators and managers and professional and technical workers, account for 6 per cent of Scotland's over fifteen population and for 7 per cent in England and Wales. With the exception of the primary industries, there is a higher proportion of high level manpower in England and Wales than in Scotland in each of the categories identified in the table. The reason for this imbalance is not far to seek. The centre of government in the United Kingdom is in London, as is a large proportion of the head offices of British industrial, commercial and financial organisations. London, therefore, exerts a strong gravitational pull on the type of person whom we would regard as falling into the definition we are using of high level manpower.

While Table 10.12 has given us one measure of high level manpower, it suffers from the defect of including large numbers of self-employed, particularly small farmers and shopkeepers not all of whom would be regarded as high level manpower in the sense in which we are using the term. Nor does it provide any inter-regional comparison within the United Kingdom apart from a Scotland, England and Wales comparison. The National Institute of Economic and Social Research has recently conducted a large scale study of the regional economies of the United Kingdom. One aspect studied was the regional distribution of educated people. The basis of the analysis was people with a Terminal Age of Education (TAE) of 20 years or more, i.e. people with education of university standard or its equivalent. The regions of Great Britain seem to fall into three categories. At the top, with a very high proportion of educated people, are the South East and Southern England, that is to say, regions with a considerable dependence on London. There is an intermediate category, consisting of two southern English regions, Eastern and South West, and Wales and Scotland. Finally, there is a category with a very low proportion of educated people, consisting of all the northern English regions and the Midlands.

Table 10.13 People with T.A.E. 20+ as a Percentage of Regional Population over 15 in 1961

	per cent of adult population	
Regions:	Male	Female
Southern	4·8	3·4
London and South East	4·7	3·3
Wales	4·1	3·3
South West	4·0	3·1
Eastern	3·9	2·9
Scotland	3·7	3·3
Midland	2·9	2·3
North Midland	2·8	2·2
North	2·8	2·5
North West	2·8	2·3
East and West Ridings	2·6	2·2
Great Britain	3·6	2·8

Source: Lind, op. cit.

By this measure, Scotland's stock of educated manpower is proportionally higher than the average for the country as a whole and considerably better than for large parts of England. Despite the economic difficulties which Scotland and Wales have experienced each has a far higher proportion of educated people than does the booming Midlands.

The age structure of the well-educated population is important. It makes a great deal of difference to a region's economic potential to know whether its educated people are young with a full working life ahead or whether they are mainly older people close to retirement. London, Southern and South East England, the regions with the highest proportions of well-educated people, also have by far the highest proportions of educated under the age of 35. While these regions have proportionally more people in all age groups, it is in the younger age groups that their dominance is particularly marked. Scotland, on the other hand, has exceptionally low numbers in the 20–29 age group but thereafter shows large gains. A possible reason suggested by N.I.E.S.R. is that there may be an influx of educated people to Scotland in the 30–44 age group.

We can widen our perspective on Scotland's comparative position by looking at the international studies of human resources which Harbison and Myers conducted, using 1960 as the benchmark. They examined a number of countries at different stages of economic development in order to identify differences in their level of human resource development. They measured human resource development from a number of aspects:

a Stock of high level manpower Three measures of the stock were used: the number of teachers at the first and second levels of education, the number of engineers and scientists, and the number of doctors and dentists—all expressed per 10,000 population.

b Measures of educational development These were expressed in terms of the enrolment ratios of pupils at the first and second levels of education adjusted to take account of variations in the length of schooling at different levels, using the U.S.A. as the yardstick.

c The orientation of higher education This measure expressed the numbers of students at universities and other comparable institutes of higher education in faculties of science and technology and in faculties of humanity, arts and law as a proportion of total student enrolment.

Finally, two measures of the level of economic development, *per capita* G.N.P. and the proportion employed in agriculture, were included along with measures of the resources allocated to education in terms of the proportion of national income spent on education and of the demand for education in terms of the proportion of the population in the age group 5–14.

Harbison and Myers' analysis for the advanced countries of the world is given in Table 10.14. We have inserted in the table estimates for Scotland which we made by using the measures mentioned above. On this basis, the United Kingdom ranks sixth in the world and Scotland, on our calculations, seventh. Scotland's human resources would appear to be more fully developed than those of Japan, France, Canada, the U.S.S.R., and West Germany.

Combining the various measures we have looked at above, it seems reasonable to conclude that, overall, Scotland's stock of high level manpower, however defined, may be rather smaller than that of the country as a whole. Nevertheless, Scotland

Table 10.14 Human Resource Development in Advanced Countries

	Composite Index[1]	Per Capita G.N.P. $	Per cent of Population in Agriculture	Stock of High Level Manpower			Measures of Educational Development enrolment ratios				Orientation of Higher Education		Expenditure on Education. Per cent of Nat. Income	Per cent of Population in age group 5–14
				Teachers 1st and 2nd level	Engineers and Scientists	Doctors and Dentists	1st level unadjusted	1st and 2nd level unadjusted	2nd level unadjusted	3rd level unadjusted	Science and Technology	Humanity Law, Arts		
Denmark	77·1	1057	24	60·5	49·9	15·5	69	91	30·5	6·9	20·4	17·5	2·9	18·1
Sweden	79·2	1380	20	79·5	63·5	13·1	74	89	38·7	8·1	30·4	48·8	3·2	16·3
Argentina	82·0	490	25	88·1	12·5	17·5	68	70	32·0	10·0	14·9	36·1	2·5	19·5
Israel	84·9	726	17	103·7	Not available	27·5	80	86	46·4	7·7	42·3	50·4	3·0	19·9
West Germany	85·8	927	23	49·3	42·8	20·0	68	84	55·3	6·1	24·7	29·2	3·6	14·7
Finland	88·7	794	46	96·4	Not available	9·0	69	86	52·7	7·2	25·1	42·1	6·3	19·2
U.S.S.R.	92·9	600	50	65·2	48·1	16·7	67	79	33·9	11·8	45·3	7·6	7·1	20·0
Canada	101·6	1947	13	88·9	45·5	17·0	86	92	54·6	9·4	25·9	45·6	4·5	19·5
France	107·8	943	26	69·7	35·4	12·1	76	94	58·8	9·8	32·1	46·1	3·0	15·3
Japan	111·4	306	39	75·3	Not available	13·5	62	96	79·4	8·4	22·1	26·6	5·7	22·7
Scotland	114·3	1137	7	61·3	15·8	14·4	67	77	69·8	8·9	43·2	41·3	4·0	16·6
United Kingdom	121·6	1189	5	64·2	33·2	11·5	68	81	82·1	7·9	33·5	34·5	4·2	15·2
Belgium	123·6	1196	12	Not available	35·0	12·0	70	90	78·1	9·1	23·2	16·4	5·6	13·5
Netherlands	133·7	836	19	81·0	37·1	12·4	63	86	68·2	13·1	36·6	26·4	5·2	19·0
Australia	137·7	1316	13	62·1	Not available	13·0	78	96	72·2	13·1	27·6	23·4	2·2	15·0
New Zealand	147·3	1310	16	77·8	Not available	17·0	84	97	66·3	16·2	21·2	35·6	3·7	19·1
United States	261·3	2577	12	135·1	61·7	18·0	88	104	95·3	33·2	22·7	Not available	4·6	18·4
Mean	115	1100	23	80	42	15·4	73	89	59	11	28	32	4·2	18

Source: Harbison and Myers: 'Education, Manpower and Economic Growth', page 48.
[1] Composite Index = Column (9) plus 5 times Column (10).

does appear to be well-endowed as compared with large parts of England. On an international scale, the evidence of some ten years ago suggests strongly that Scotland is one of the leading countries in the world in terms of the development of her human resources.

Having established that Scotland possesses a well developed stock of human resources we must now turn to examine the flows entering and leaving this stock. These flows have a number of dimensions, including the numbers and quality of young people starting and completing their formal education, young people entering employment for the first time, the gains and losses through migration of people with differing skills and abilities, and the training or retraining of those who already form part of the established stock of human resources. Each of these dimensions will be considered in the remaining sections.

3 Inflows from Education

The relationship between the demographic features of Scotland's population and their educational implications is clearly shown in Charts 7 and 8. Chart 7 shows actual live births in Scotland from 1935 to 1968 and estimated live births to 1990. The reader should of course bear in mind that forecasts of population are extremely difficult to make, and can only be carried out on the basis of certain assumptions. These assumptions have to be revised periodically to take account of the most recent mortality, fertility and migratory trends which the population is exhibiting. The assumptions currently being used show that the present fall in births will be reversed shortly, may level off in the late 1970s, and thereafter rise to reach a level of over 110,000 per annum, last reached just after World War II.

The actual and projected numbers of births are translated into numbers of pupils in Chart 8. As well as taking account of the projected increase in the number of births, the forecast of the number of pupils also allows for the raising of the school leaving age to 16 in 1972/3. There has been a steady increase in the number of pupils since 1958. This is expected to continue to 1974 (inflated by the raising of the school leaving age); thereafter the numbers are expected to level off until the mid 1980s, by which time the anticipated increase in the number of births from 1980 onwards will start to influence the number of primary pupils.

These forecasts are, of course, tentative, but they do indicate that on the basis of present assumptions Scotland can look forward to a steady increase in the inflow of young educated people into the stock of human resources. As this chapter has already shown, human resource development is not just a question of numbers. The quality of people is vitally important. As economists, we have no means of assessing the genetic implications of improvements in a population. What we can do, however, is examine the end products of our educational system and see if we can observe any improvements in educational standards. Let us now look at this.

Chart 9 shows the number of passes in the Ordinary and Higher Grades of the Scottish Certificate of Education examinations since the current regulations were introduced in 1962. While the number of candidates passing in at least one subject at the Ordinary grade has only risen slowly, there has been a marked increase in the number of candidates passing in at least one subject at the Higher grade. This increase may be taken as one instance of an improvement in quality. But it is not in itself irrefutable proof of a significant quality change. Are the passes which pupils are gaining in subjects which are geared to the changing demands of society and employment?

Judged by the changes that were made in Scottish education in the course of the 1960s the evidence of a quality improvement seems fairly convincing. Many new subjects have been introduced, syllabuses have been reorganised, old subjects revised, and new methods of teaching and learning introduced. Moreover, there has been considerable progress in the development of education with an explicit vocational purpose.

About 60 per cent of the young people in Scotland enter employment for which some form of further education or training is required. As in primary and secondary education, further education is a field in which substantial changes are taking place. Up to the end of World War II, little attention had been paid in Scotland to the full development of further education courses for operatives and craftsmen. Most of the instruction was in evening class centres which were used as secondary schools during the day. In the decade 1950 to 1960 great strides forward were made in the provision throughout Scotland of technical colleges capable of offering the widest range of courses. There has been a continual increase in the provision of facilities for students to attend courses either by day-release, block-release, sandwich or full-time classes. Chart 10 shows that the number of full-time students in vocational courses in further education has more than doubled in the 1960s. This has been accompanied by a substantial rise in the number of students released by employers during working hours to attend

Chart 7

live births in Scotland

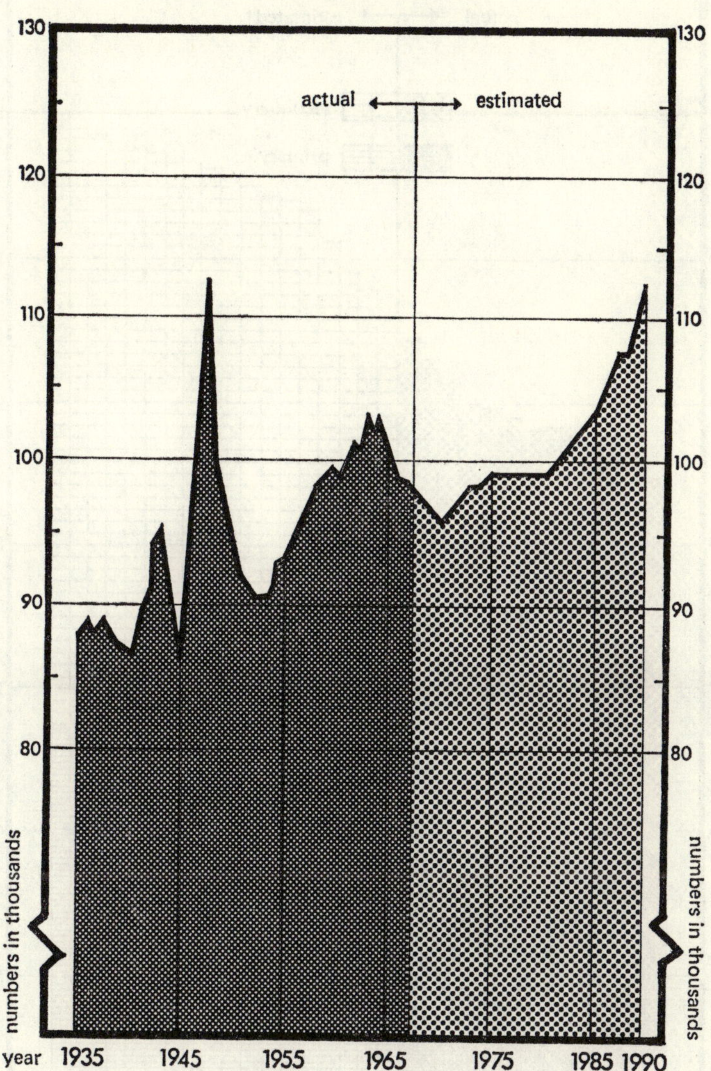

Assumed future births depend, in part, on the level of migration. For the births depicted here, it is assumed that migration will fall from around 33,000 in 1969 to 21,000 in 1975 and to 16,000 a year from mid-1981 onwards. This assumption is subject to revision in the light of changing trends and the effects on migration of Government policy and other factors.

source: Scottish Education Statistics 1969

Chart 8

pupils (including special school pupils) in education authority and grant-aided schools — January of each year

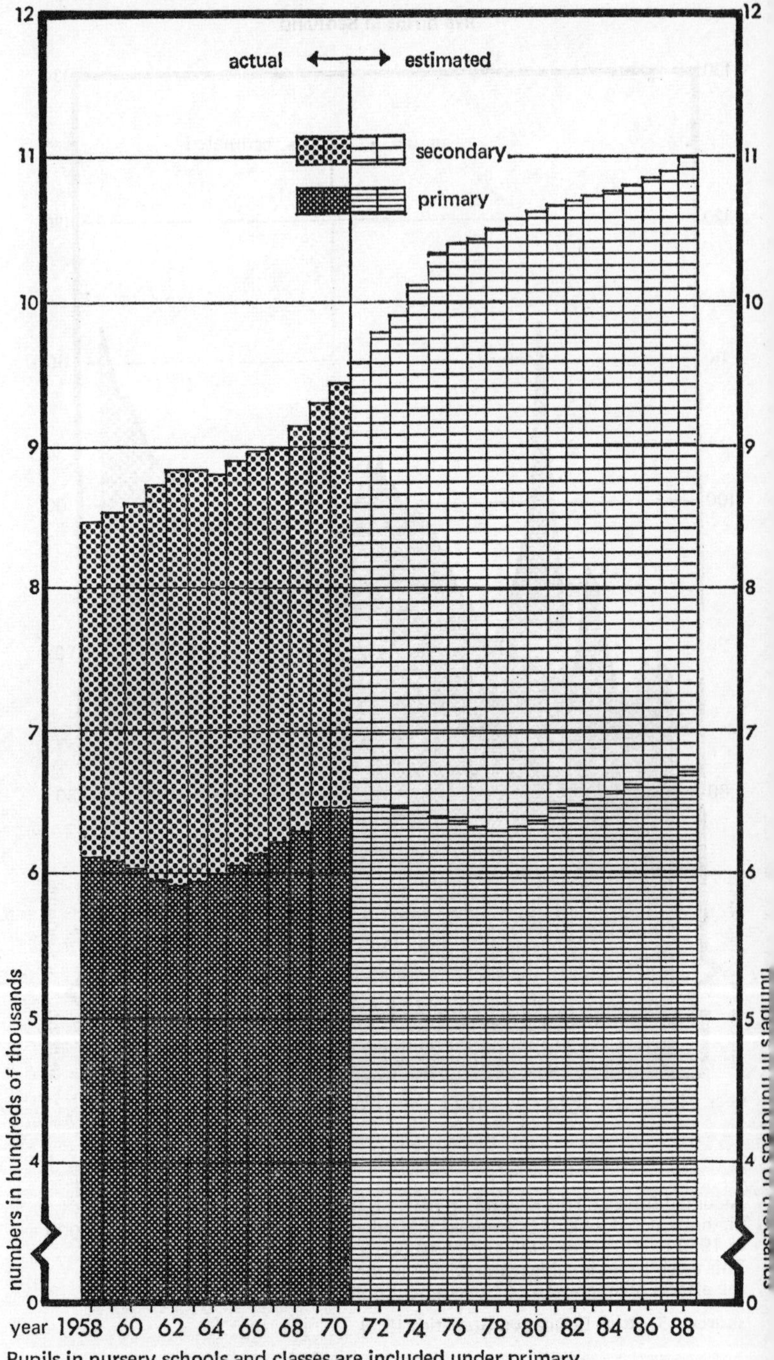

Pupils in nursery schools and classes are included under primary

source: Scottish Education Statistics 1969

courses in Central Institutions or Further Educational Centres. Developments in technical education have accelerated since the introduction in 1964 of the Industrial Training Act.

Developments in further education have not been confined to technical subjects. The Scottish Council for Commercial, Administrative and Professional Education (S.C.C.A.P.E.) was set up in 1961, and since its formation there has been an enormous increase in the number of commercial education courses provided in Scotland. In 1963 the Council sponsored syllabuses and examinations in 29 subjects; by 1970 this number had risen to 128. S.C.C.A.P.E. is also closely involved with a number of Industrial Training Boards in the organisation and provision of appropriate courses.

Lastly, we turn to the enormous changes in the educational system which have taken place in the universities and other institutions of higher education in recent years. The Robbins Report, published in 1963, provided a tremendous filip to higher education, since its main thesis was that the demand for such education should lead, and supply should follow. Great Britain began the 1960s with 120,000 students in 23 universities; by the end of the decade there were 232,000 students in 44 universities. Scotland in 1960 had 18,500 students in four universities; she ended the decade with 38,000 students in eight universities. The Robbins targets for expansion have been exceeded. Scotland has always offered proportionately more places in universities relative to population than England and Wales. With around 9½ per cent of the population, Scotland provides over 16 per cent of the places in British universities.

These developments in primary, secondary and higher education have placed large demands on the economy in terms of both finance and manpower. Chart 11 shows the growth in money terms since 1959/60 of current and capital expenditure on education in Scotland by local authorities and central government. The very large increase in capital expenditure by the Scottish Education Department and the University Grants Committee is particularly noticeable. The item of expenditure which has grown least—current expenditure by education authorities—has more than doubled over the decade and even allowing for price increases represents a substantial increase in real terms.

When we compared the development of Scotland's human resources with those of other countries, we observed (Table 10.14, Column 4) that the stock of teachers at first and second levels of education in Scotland was rather lower than for

Chart 9

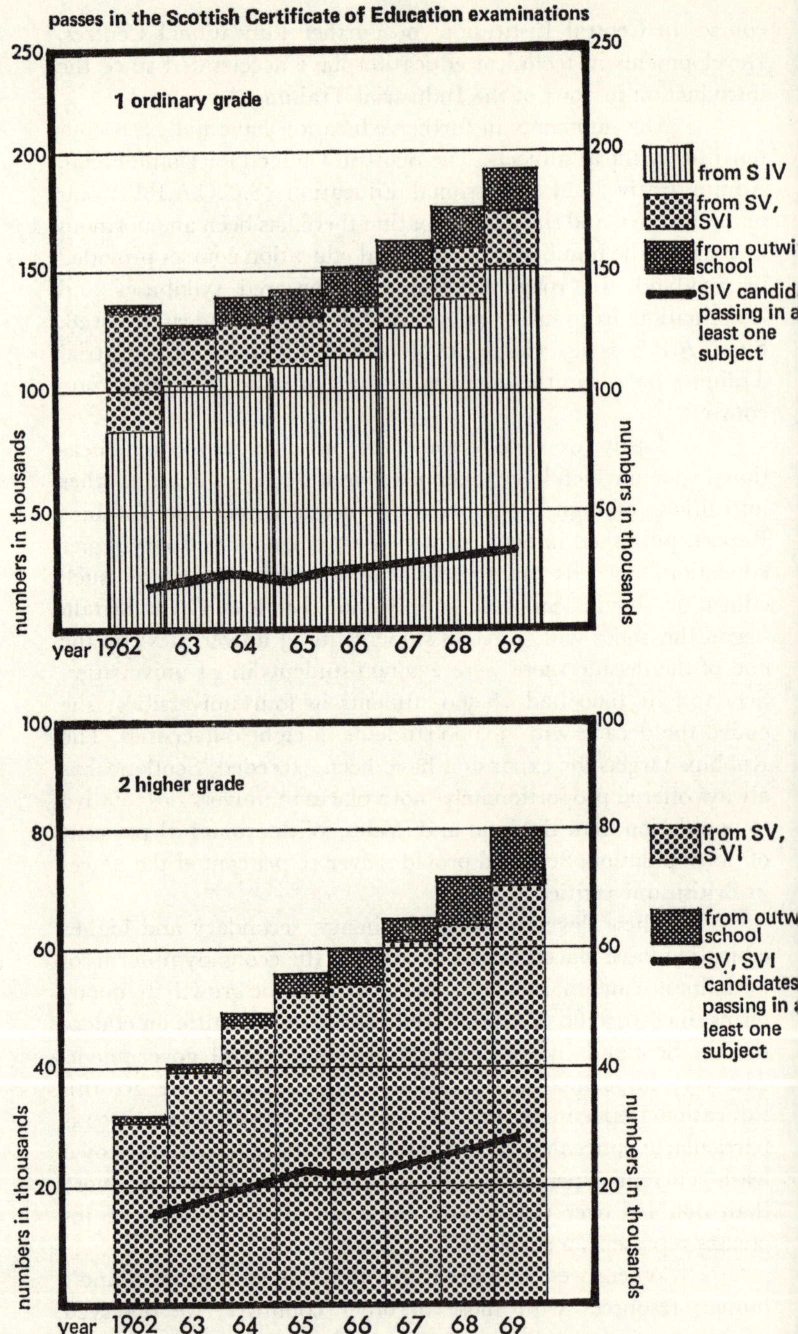

source: Scottish Education Statistics 1969

Chart 10

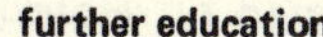

further education

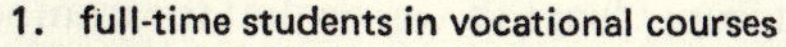

1. full-time students in vocational courses

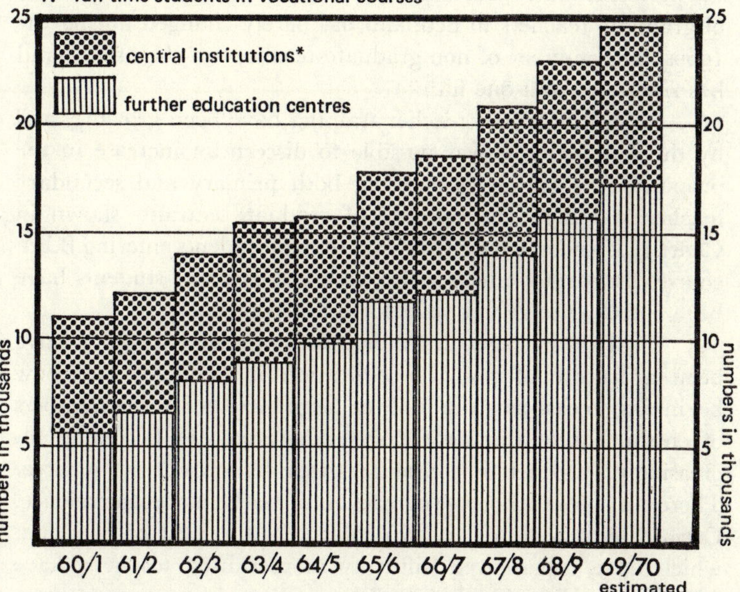

2. students in vocational courses released by employers during working hours

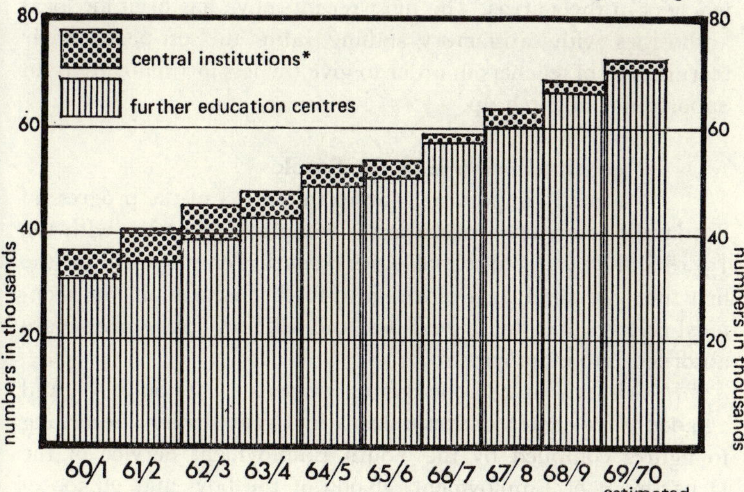

*Students at the former Royal College of Science and Technology are excluded for each of the years shown. Students at the former Scottish College of Commerce are included up to and including session 1963–64 and at the former Heriot-Watt College up to and including session 1964–65.

source: Scottish Education Statistics 1969

the United Kingdom as a whole and among the lowest for the group of developed countries. The data in Table 10.14 relate to the period around 1960, and from Chart 12 we see that the number of graduate teachers in Scotland has barely changed during the 1960s. The number of non-graduate teachers on the other hand has risen by about one fifth.

Entrants into teacher training have been growing, and by the late 1960s it was possible to discern an increase in the proportion of graduates entering both primary and secondary teacher training. The number of graduate entrants shown in Chart 13 is understated by the exclusion of students entering B.Ed. courses from 1965 onwards. Between 200 and 250 students have been enrolling in recent years for B.Ed. degrees.

The shortages in the numbers of teachers, which have been a feature of post-war education in Scotland, are now beginning to ease as a result of the large increases in the numbers of entrants into training colleges. Shortages are becoming increasingly localised in character either by subject or by area. There is a chronic shortage of teachers of mathematics and science. Certain local authorities, particularly in the west of Scotland, which have experienced difficulty in recruiting teachers, have followed a policy of offering differential or bonus payments to teachers in their areas. The most recent move has been for local authorities with satisfactory staffing ratios to 'soft-pedal' their recruitment of teachers in order to give the less fortunate areas an opportunity to catch up.

4. Absorption into the Stock

Equally important is an examination of the progress of Scotland's youth once education is completed. Starting with the 15, 16 and 17 year old school leavers entering employment for the first time, we shall then move on to further education, the technical colleges and the univerisites, and ask how young people are absorbed into employment.

In 1969, 483,000 young persons—254,000 boys and 229,000 girls—entered employment in Great Britain, according to figures compiled by the Youth Employment Service of the Department of Employment. 28,000 of the boys and 26,500 of the girls entered employment in Scotland. Nationally, the boy entrants accounted for 1·8 per cent of all male employees and the girl entrants for 2·6 per cent of the female employees. In Scotland, the proportions were somewhat higher, being 2·1 per cent for boys and 3·2 per cent for girls.

Chart 11

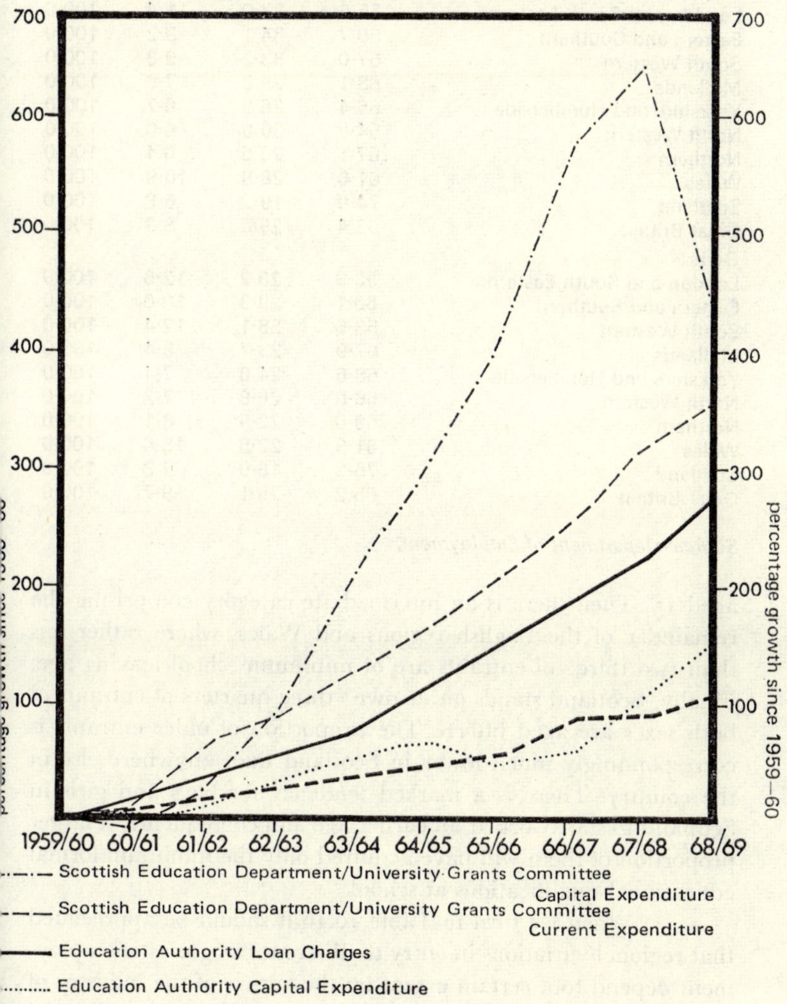

Table 10.15 shows the age distribution of entry into employment analysed by regions of Great Britain. The regions fall into three categories. First, there are the regions of Southern England where less than 60 per cent of boy and girl entrants are

Table 10.15 Age of Entry into Employment 1969

	Percentages Age at Entry			
Boys:	15	16	17	Total
London and South Eastern	55·6	33·0	11·4	100·0
Eastern and Southern	56·7	34·1	9·2	100·0
South Western	57·0	33·2	9·8	100·0
Midlands	63·1	29·3	7·6	100·0
Yorkshire and Humberside	66·4	26·9	6·7	100·0
North Western	64·0	30·0	6·0	100·0
Northern	67·1	26·5	6·4	100·0
Wales	61·0	28·9	10·9	100·0
Scotland	74·0	19·2	6·8	100·0
Great Britain	62·4	29·3	8·3	100·0
Girls:				
London and South Eastern	58·3	29·2	12·5	100·0
Eastern and Southern	60·1	29·3	10·6	100·0
South Western	59·5	28·1	12·4	100·0
Midlands	67·9	23·7	8·4	100·0
Yorkshire and Humberside	68·6	24·0	7·4	100·0
North Western	66·0	26·8	7·2	100·0
Northern	69·0	22·9	8·1	100·0
Wales	61·9	22·5	15·6	100·0
Scotland	75·3	16·9	7·8	100·0
Great Britain	65·2	25·1	9·7	100·0

Source: Department of Employment.

aged 15. Then there is an intermediate category comprising the remainder of the English regions and Wales, where rather less than two thirds of entrants are of minimum school leaving age. Finally, Scotland stands on its own; three quarters of entrants of both sexes are aged fifteen. The proportion of older entrants is correspondingly much lower in Scotland than anywhere else in the country. There is a marked tendency for boys and girls in Scotland to start work at an earlier age and consequently a larger proportion of them will have acquired only the minimum formal educational qualifications at school.

When we turn to Table 10.16 it should be appreciated that regional variations in entry to different categories of employment depend to a certain extent on the nature of the industry of the region; and, as we saw in Chapter 4, Scotland's industrial structure is none too favourable. The large proportion of both boys and girls entering clerical employment in the London and South Eastern region is a reflection of the high level of white collar or office employment available in that region. The tendency observed for Scottish boys to leave school at an early age is offset by the fact that a higher than average proportion of them enter into apprenticeships leading to skilled occupations. On the other

Chart 12

full-time qualified teachers in education authority and grant-aided schools (including special schools) autumn of each year.

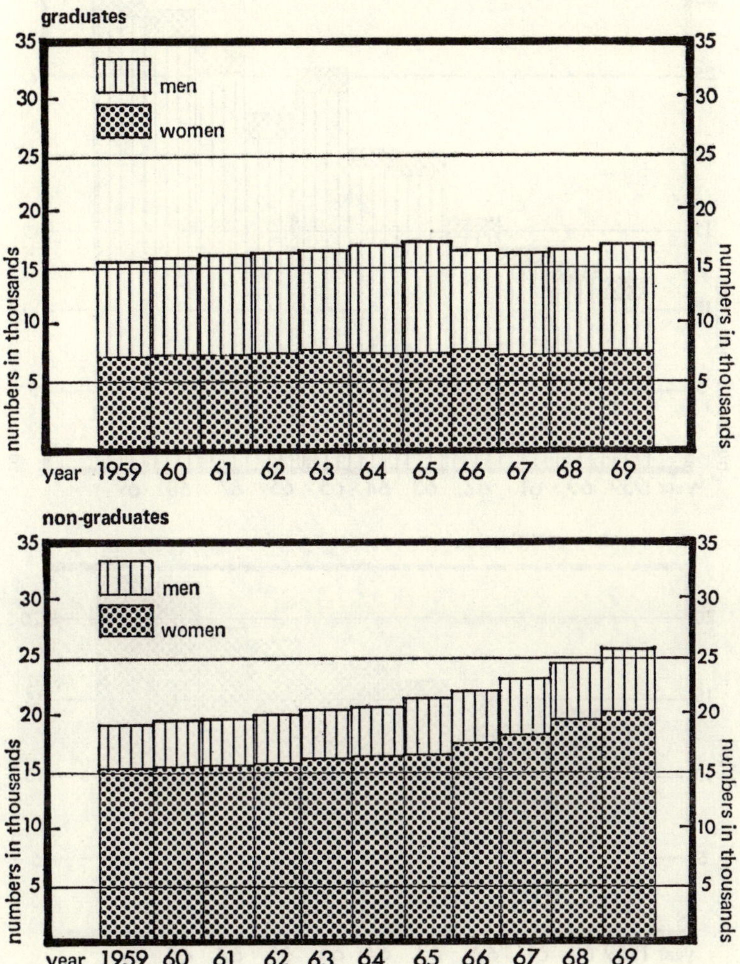

Qualified teachers who are not engaged in teaching, e.g. administrators, organisers, educational psychologists are excluded.

source: Scottish Education Statistics 1969

Chart 13

colleges of education
entrants to teacher training

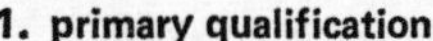

1. primary qualification

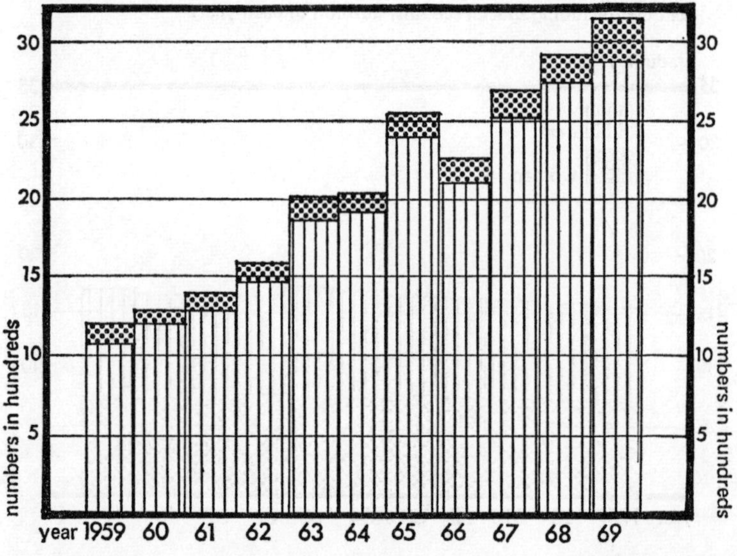

2. secondary qualification

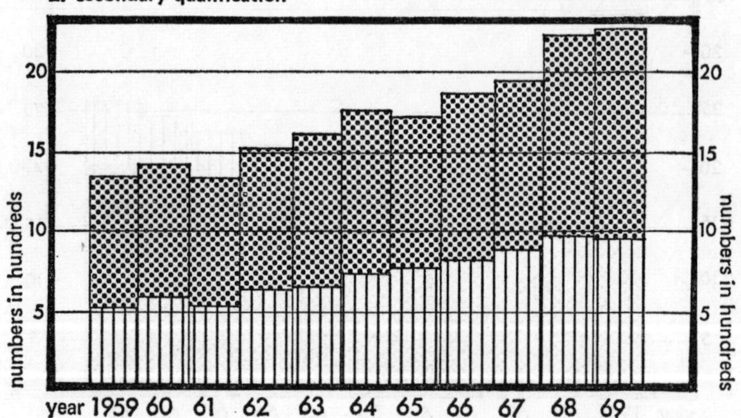

graduates

non-graduates

Students entering B. Ed. courses in 1965 and later years have been excluded from this chart.

source: Scottish Education Statistics 1969

hand, relatively few of them enter clerical employment, which may reflect a regional shortage of such jobs, or enter employment which offers systematic, planned training. As a result almost equally large numbers enter employment with no formal educational or training requirements as enter into skilled apprenticeships. Rather fewer than average girls in Scotland enter employment in the first four categories, but in this respect Scotland is similar to a number of English regions and certainly considerably better than Wales.

Table 10.16 Analysis of Boys and Girls Entering Employment by Type of Employment and by Region in 1969

	Percentages					
Boys:	1	2	3	4	5	Total
London and South Eastern	31·3	1·0	13·9	23·6	30·2	100·0
Eastern and Southern	41·2	1·3	8·9	16·4	32·2	100·0
South Western	40·1	1·2	5·6	19·9	33·2	100·0
Midlands	43·1	1·4	6·6	19·0	29·9	100·0
Yorkshire and Humberside	51·1	1·0	7·7	9·5	30·7	100·0
North Western	48·8	1·0	8·3	9·2	32·7	100·0
Northern	46·8	1·3	7·4	7·4	37·1	100·0
Wales	35·9	0·7	5·8	4·2	53·4	100·0
Scotland	46·6	1·7	6·3	4·0	41·4	100·0
Great Britain	42·6	1·2	8·3	14·0	33·9	100·0
Girls:						
London and South Eastern	8·2	1·1	52·5	13·3	24·9	100·0
Eastern and Southern	8·4	1·5	42·5	10·7	36·9	100·0
South Western	7·6	1·4	34·7	18·1	38·2	100·0
Midlands	6·7	1·8	36·3	21·0	34·2	100·0
Yorkshire and Humberside	6·4	2·7	34·7	16·3	39·9	100·0
North Western	7·3	2·1	41·8	14·7	34·1	100·0
Wales	5·1	1·9	28·2	8·8	56·0	100·0
Scotland	6·5	1·7	36·0	14·0	41·8	100·0
Great Britain	7·1	1·8	39·6	15·2	36·3	100·0

Source: Department of Employment.
1. Apprenticeship to skilled occupation.
2. Employment leading to recognised professional qualifications.
3. Entering clerical employment.
4. Employment with planned training.
5. Entering other employment.

While Scotland offers a higher proportion of university places, the critical question is whether Scotland is offering a commensurate proportion of employment and career opportunities to the graduates of her universities. Until recently, information on this important question was sparse, but the Appointments officers of the eight Scottish universities have recently completed an analysis of the career patterns of the 1968/69 graduates of Scottish universities. Medical, dental and veterinary graduates are excluded from the analysis.

5,860 students graduated with first degrees from Scottish universities in 1969. Of these, nearly 4,500, or three quarters of the total, were students who were normally domiciled in Scotland; of these Scots students, 932 or 21 per cent left Scotland for their first job or further training. In addition to the students taking first degrees, a further 782 students graduated with higher degrees. A lower proportion, 48 per cent, of higher degree graduates were of Scottish origin, and of these 30 per cent went out of Scotland for further training or employment. Putting these figures another way round, 80 per cent of first degree students and 70 per cent of higher degree students who normally lived in Scotland were successful in finding suitable training or employment opportunities in Scotland. The lack of comparable figures for previous years means that we cannot say whether these numbers have been rising or falling. When one bears in mind the very substantial increase in enrolment at Scottish universities through the 1960s, the data published by the Appointments Officers do reveal a high degree of absorption of native born graduates by industry, commerce, the public service and education in Scotland.

5 Mobility

Considerable mobility is required of workers in any developed modern economy, where the achievement of satisfactory economic growth means coming to terms with increasingly rapid industrial and technological change. Mobility may be broadly of two types: mobility between jobs and mobility between regions. Relatively little is known about mobility between jobs. It is estimated by the Department of Employment that more than 8 million changes of employer occur in Great Britain each year. Some people will have changed employer more than once in the course of a year, so that the figure does not represent 8 million different people on the move. The Department estimates that well over half a million employees—more than 2 per cent of the total—move from one of the country's ten administrative regions to another each year. Movement within regions runs at several times this level, and most geographical mobility is of this sort. Shorter distance moves are primarily motivated by reasons connected with housing, but a Labour Mobility Survey carried out by the Government Social Survey reveals that about 57 per cent of moves over 100 miles are made for job reasons. People with higher levels of education are more mobile than the rest, and men are more mobile than women.

There are considerable variations in mobility as between age groups and occupations. Young people, i.e. those aged between 20 and 44, change jobs most frequently, with a peak turnover in the age group 25 to 30. There is, however, an appreciable amount of movement of older workers, particularly those aged over 55. Unskilled people change job most frequently. Persons of managerial and executive status change jobs less frequently than those in other occupational status groups.

In a Labour Mobility Survey carried out for the Ministry of Labour, a comparison of the industrial distribution in 1953 and 1963 of all informants who had been in the labour force throughout the ten years showed that the proportion of men remaining in the same industry averaged between 65 and 75 per cent in the majority of industries. In mining, paper manufacture, insurance, banking, finance, professional and scientific services, it was more than 80 per cent and fell to 60 to 65 per cent in food, drink and tobacco, timber and furniture manufacture and miscellaneous services. In public administration and defence the proportion was only 42 per cent, but this reflects the high turnover associated with national service.

Motivation, distance, age, occupational status, sex and industry all have their influences on mobility, and should be borne in mind when we study the patterns of movement between Scotland and the rest of the country.

Data on mobility are sparse, but here we rely on data collected for the Sample Census of 1966. For the first time in a census, questions were asked about previous residence one year prior to the census and at the time of the previous census in 1961. While the information referring to the five year period 1961–6 may understate mobility by taking no account of changes of address in intervening years, it does nevertheless provide the best assessment to date of internal movement within Great Britain.

In the five year period 1961–66, Scotland gained just over 41,000 economically active persons by migration from England and Wales: over the same period, she lost 91,300. Overall, the loss totalled 50,000. For every 100 economically active persons Scotland gained from England and Wales, she lost 221. There are substantial differences in the character of this net loss when analysed either by occupational status or by industry. Looking first at occupational status (Table 10.17), we see that junior non-manual workers were the most mobile group, followed by skilled manual workers. Both of these groups showed losses in excess of the overall rate of 221:100. By far the greatest proportional loss was of semi-skilled workers, where Scotland lost nearly 4 for every 1 gained. The lowest proportional losses were among employers and managers in both large and small establishments and professional workers.

Table 10.17

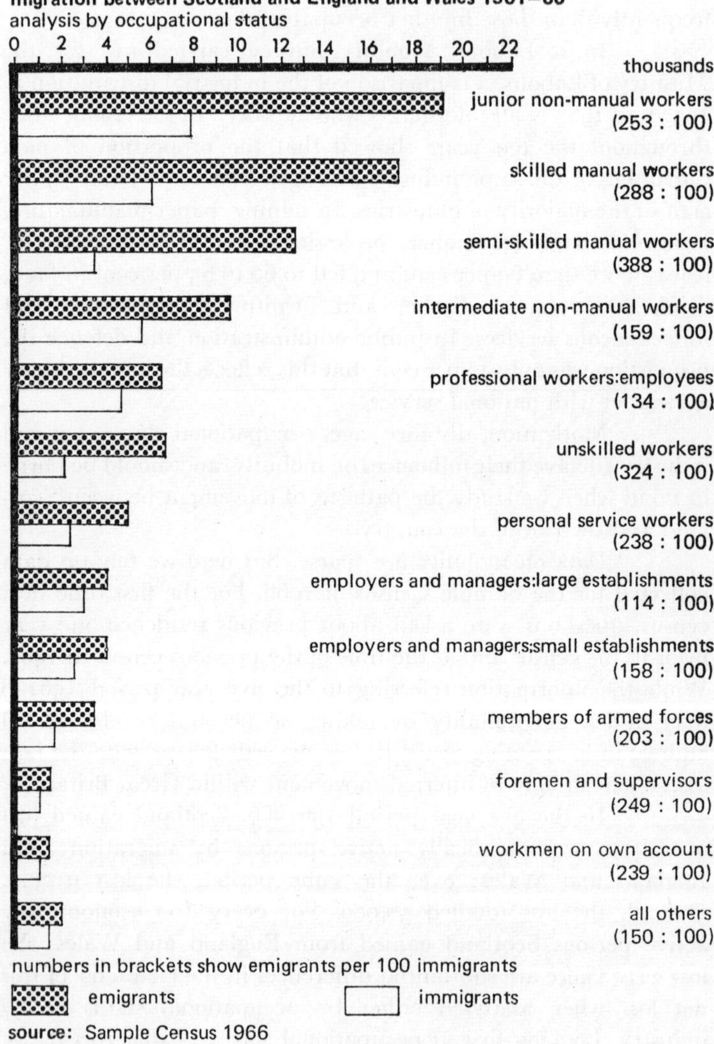

source: Sample Census 1966

When looking at the industrial analysis of migrants (Table 10.18) we see that workers in service industries are the most mobile. Among professional and scientific workers, Scotland

Table 10.18

migration between Scotland and England and Wales, 1961 – 66
analysis by industry

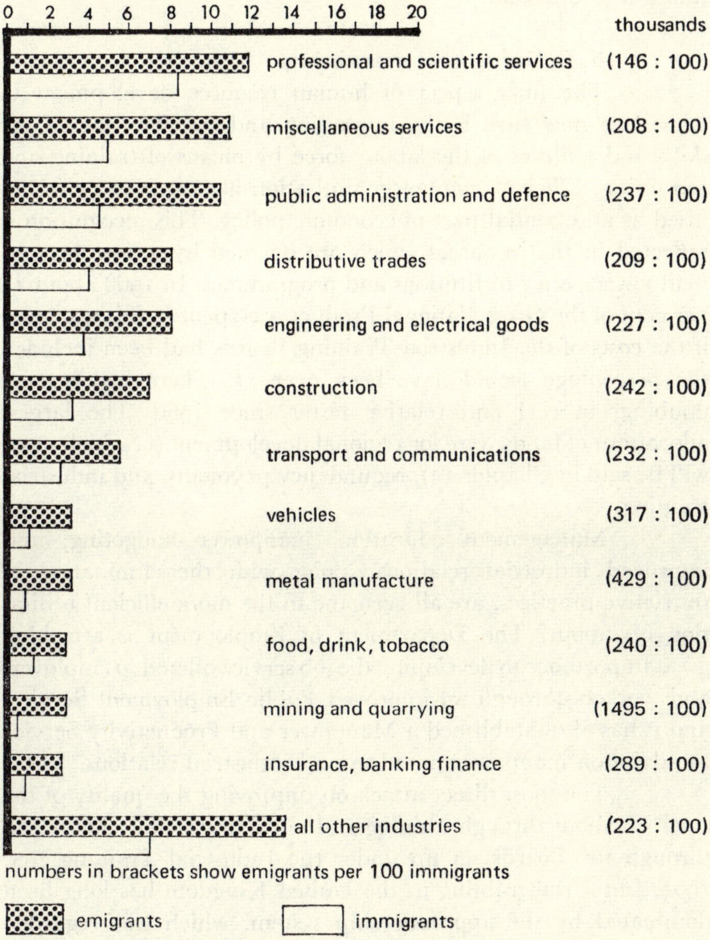

0 2 4 6 8 10 12 14 16 18 20 thousands

professional and scientific services	(146 : 100)
miscellaneous services	(208 : 100)
public administration and defence	(237 : 100)
distributive trades	(209 : 100)
engineering and electrical goods	(227 : 100)
construction	(242 : 100)
transport and communications	(232 : 100)
vehicles	(317 : 100)
metal manufacture	(429 : 100)
food, drink, tobacco	(240 : 100)
mining and quarrying	(1495 : 100)
insurance, banking finance	(289 : 100)
all other industries	(223 : 100)

numbers in brackets show emigrants per 100 immigrants

emigrants immigrants

source: Sample Census 1966

lost only a third more workers than she gained, the best performance in any of the main industrial groups. The very heavy loss of miners reflects the sharp contraction of employment in the Scottish coalfields in the 1960s.

The elimination of regional differentials in economic

development as a result of successful regional policies should have the effect of reducing the magnitude of migration flows. Identifying the characteristics and motives of migrants is one of the most complex problems facing regional economists. All we have been able to do in this section is indicate some of the more important orders of magnitude and features of recent migratory flows into and out of Scotland.

6 Training and retraining

The final aspect of human resource development to which we now turn is the upgrading and restructuring of the skills and abilities of the labour force by means of training and retraining. Efficient manpower utilisation has come to be recognised as an essential part of economic policy. This recognition is reflected in the resources which are devoted by government to manpower policy institutions and programmes. In 1968 about 1¼ per cent of the Gross National Product was spent in this way, and if the costs of the Industrial Training Boards had been included the percentage would have been over 1½. There had been a doubling in real and relative terms since 1960. The largest allocations of funds were for regional development (of which more will be said in Chapter 13), redundancy payments, and industrial training.

Management education, manpower budgeting, and improved industrial relations, along with the elimination of restrictive practices, are all germane to the more efficient utilisation of labour. The Department of Employment is attaching great importance to developing the job service offered to employers and workers through an improved Public Employment Service, and it has also established a Manpower and Productivity Service to advise on manpower practices and industrial relations.

The most direct attack on improving the quality of the stock of labour through training and retraining is now channelled through the Boards set up under the Industrial Training Act, 1964. Industrial training in the United Kingdom has long been dominated by the apprenticeship system, which was regarded very much as a form of industrial self-government. In recent years, however, both industry and the education services have questioned the system. The quality of training was uneven, too few firms were undertaking systematic training of their employees, and many firms were meeting their labour requirements by 'poaching' trained staff from other companies. It was against this background that the Industrial Training Act was passed. It provided for the establishment of Industrial Training Boards for appropriately designated industries or groups of industries, with powers to ensure that training is adequate in amount and quality and that the costs of training are spread evenly over the industry. The Boards typically operate levy and grant arrangements for these purposes. Each Board imposes a levy on its member firms which is then repaid in part or in full against evidence that the firm is undertaking or arranging training in the volume and of the quality stipulated by the Board.

By 1970 twenty-eight industrial training boards have been set up covering the greater part of industry. None of the boards has its headquarters in Scotland but seventeen of them have offices and training development staff located in Scotland. Three others have staff located elsewhere in the United Kingdom with special responsibilities for Scotland.

The progress made so far has been determined by the date of establishment of the various boards and the priorities which have emerged. Most boards have identified the development of training at the skilled level as a major priority and have concentrated on drawing up systematic training schemes for the main skilled occupations in their industries. Many schemes for the training of craftsmen include periods of broad-based training, given off-the-job by qualified instructors, followed by specialisation in particular skills. These methods are producing more flexible schemes and in many cases are enabling training periods to be reduced.

At the present time there are no centralised statistics collected by the various boards under the Industrial Training Act to show how much skilled training is being carried out in industry generally or in Scotland in particular. However, a survey of wages and salaries of employees in Great Britain conducted by the Department of Employment between September 1968 and March 1969 has produced as a useful by-product information on the number of trainees and apprentices in Great Britain. From this analysis it is estimated that there were just over 500,000 apprentices and over 800,000 other trainees in Great Britain of whom 80,000 in each category were in Scotland.

We have seen earlier in this Chapter that a greater proportion of young people in Scotland go into apprenticeships than is the case nationally. In recent years the number of young people entering industry in Scotland has been falling by around 6,000 per annum. Partly this reflects the fall in birth rate in the late 1940s and early 1950s and also the tendency for young people to stay longer in full-time education. Nevertheless, the proportion of boys under eighteen taking apprenticeships as their first jobs on leaving school has not only continued to rise since the introduction of the Act but in Scotland has continued to be above the national average.

Many training schemes have emphasised the importance of off-the-job training, under qualified instructors. Up to 31st March 1969 32,735 places had been made available for first year off-the-job training in Great Britain as a whole. In Scotland, the number of people registering for places in such schemes rose from 2,323 in 1967–8, to 2,915 in 1968–9. In the shipbuilding industry the percentage of first year trainees receiving off-the-job training in Great Britain rose from 24 per cent in November, 1965 to 45 per cent in May 1968. During the year to 31st March 1969, the Shipbuilding I.T.B. financed the provision of an additional 905 off-the-job training places of which 326 were in Scotland.

Government assistance with training costs as an instrument of regional policy is discussed more fully in Chapter 13. It can be noted at this point, however, that capital grants towards the cost of additional off-the-job training places for craft and technician trainees amounting to £398,000 were paid through industrial training boards in 1968–9, of which £174,000 was for places in Scotland. In 1969–70, an additional £12,000 was paid out as advances for 200 additional places, all of which are in Scotland.

364 applications for direct Government grants for training purposes were received from firms in the Scottish Development Area in the year ended September 1968 compared with 323 in the previous year. In the twelve months ended September 1969 £795,000 was paid out to firms in Scotland compared with £298,000 in the previous year. This large increase reflects partly the doubling of the weekly rates of grant payable in Development Areas after 16th October 1967. It is estimated by the Department of Employment that about 12,500 workers per annum are now being trained for new jobs in Scotland with the assistance of these grants.

As well as providing financial assistance for off-the-job training places, the Government also operates Training Centres for the retraining of unemployed or redundant workers. There are ten such centres, located mainly in the Central Belt with a total capacity of around 1,500 places.

It is still too early to make any firm assessment of the work of the Boards. In the early years there has been a tendency to concentrate on changing the traditional practices associated with apprenticeship training. This is understandable, given the origins of the Act. But there is a growing interest in the wider aspects of training and retraining for all manpower, consistent with the theme of this Chapter that human resources constitute an essential part of any active programme for promoting economic growth.

Summary

Human resource development is a subject of many and fascinating facets. We have only been able to look in the course of this Chapter at some of them. While it is impossible to draw any hard and fast conclusions, the high overall level of development of Scotland's human resources does suggest reasonable grounds for optimism for the future. On the other hand, the changes which have been made in the educational system in recent years have not been fully matched by a strong shift on the part of Scotland's young people away from the abnormally high propensity to leave school early. This is no doubt associated with the comparatively unsatisfactory structure of production in the Scottish economy which we have discussed earlier. It may be, of course, that industrial training can provide a means of bridging the gap between early school-leaving and the needs of production, though this remains to be seen.

We cannot afford to be too sanguine or self-satisfied, despite Scotland's long tradition of education. In the words of Alfred Sauvy, the leading French demographer, 'the national income of tomorrow will depend for each country on the qualifications of its active population, and this can be practically measured already in the school rooms where youth is at work, and from the kind of education that each receives'.

References

F. Harbison and C. A. Myers, *Education, Manpower and Economic Growth*, McGraw-Hill, 1964.

Alfred Sauvy, *General Theory of Population*, Weidenfeld and Nicolson, 1969.

H. Lind, 'Regional Distribution of Educated People in Britain', *Scotland*, October 1969.

J. Nisbet (ed.), *Scottish Education Looks Ahead*, W. and R. Chambers, Edinburgh, 1969.

Committee on Higher Education, Cmnd. 2154, H.M.S.O., 1963.

Employment and Productivity Gazette, May 1970.

'Mobility between Industries and Jobs', *Employment and Productivity Gazette*, July 1966.

Labour Mobility in Great Britain 1953–63, Government Social Survey.

Manpower Policy in the United Kingdom, O.E.C.D., 1970.

Minutes of Evidence of the Select Committee on Scottish Affairs 1969–70, esp. pp. 366–477, H.M.S.O.

Chapter 11
Financial Institutions

In the theory of income determination, a great deal of importance is attached to decisions to save and decisions to invest in new plant and equipment. We have seen how difficult it is to quantify investment in the Scottish economy, even when it is financed in several instances out of public funds. In this Chapter, we shall seek to identify some of the characteristics of the financial intermediaries in the economy which play such an important part in harnessing funds for investment. The role of financial institutions which provide a channel for savings is well recognised in the literature of economic growth and development. It was Francis Bacon who remarked 'Money is like muck, not much good, except it be spread.' What are the significant financial intermediaries which help to spread money around?

In our examination we shall find that some, the commercial banks, for example, have had a long-standing and intimate involvement with the growth and development of the Scottish economy. Others, such as the building societies, are almost entirely alien (i.e. English) in character, the Scottish-based building societies providing only a small proportion of the funds for house purchase in Scotland. Then there are the merchant banks which have developed very late and on a small scale in Scotland; and the Scottish investment trusts which control a large part of the national investment trust funds but which have tended to look beyond Scotland for their investment opportunities. Since the monetary system of the United Kingdom is a sophisticated complex of inter-related institutions, the reader will appreciate why it is possible to isolate only some of the broad features of the Scottish-based financial intermediaries. We are still a long way from establishing, for example, whether Scotland's requirements for capital are met wholly or even partially from her own institutions or whether Scotland is an importer or exporter of capital.

1 Scottish Banks

a) Their History Scottish banking has a long and interesting history. In certain areas of banking practice and principle the Scots bankers have been true pioneers. The Bank of Scotland, for example, was founded in 1695 for the express purpose of the promotion of trade, unlike most other banks of its time, including the Bank of England, which were established in order to support the credit of governments. In the creation of a branch banking system, the Scottish banks may be said to have led the world. By as early as 1826, when England did not possess a single joint stock bank and only very few branch offices, the Bank of Scotland operated sixteen branches and the British Linen twenty-seven. A testimony to the maturity of Scottish banking came in the middle of the 19th century with the Bank of England Charter Act of 1844; this Act confined the right of note issue in England and Wales to the Bank of England but the Scottish banks were permitted and have retained the right to issue their own notes.

Economic historians, for example the late Professor Henry Hamilton of Aberdeen University, attach great importance to the contribution made by the Scottish banks to the economic development of 19th century Scotland. The combination of the system of widespread branch banking and the payment of interest on deposits brought into active use the available savings and capital of the country. The uniquely Scottish, but now almost defunct, system of cash credits enabled the Scottish banks to lend at keen rates but with minimal risk to the emerging entrepreneur. At all times, the Scottish banking system seems to have been responsive to the needs of the economy and to have established a high degree of confidence with the Scottish people.

At the beginning of the 20th century the average Scottish bank was a relatively large institution. The ten Scottish banks had average deposits of £10·7 million compared with the sixty-seven English banks with average deposits of less than one million pounds. By 1918, however, the number of English banks had fallen to twenty and their average deposits had risen to £98 million; there were then eight Scottish banks with average deposits of £35 million. The 'Big Five' of English banking—Barclays, Lloyds, National Provincial, Westminster and Midland—had emerged by the end of World War I; they were to dominate English banking until in recent years by further amalgamations they have been reduced to three main groups.

Faced with the emergence of the English giants the Scottish banks could react by seeking or accepting affiliation with

Table 11.1 How the Banking Groups have formed

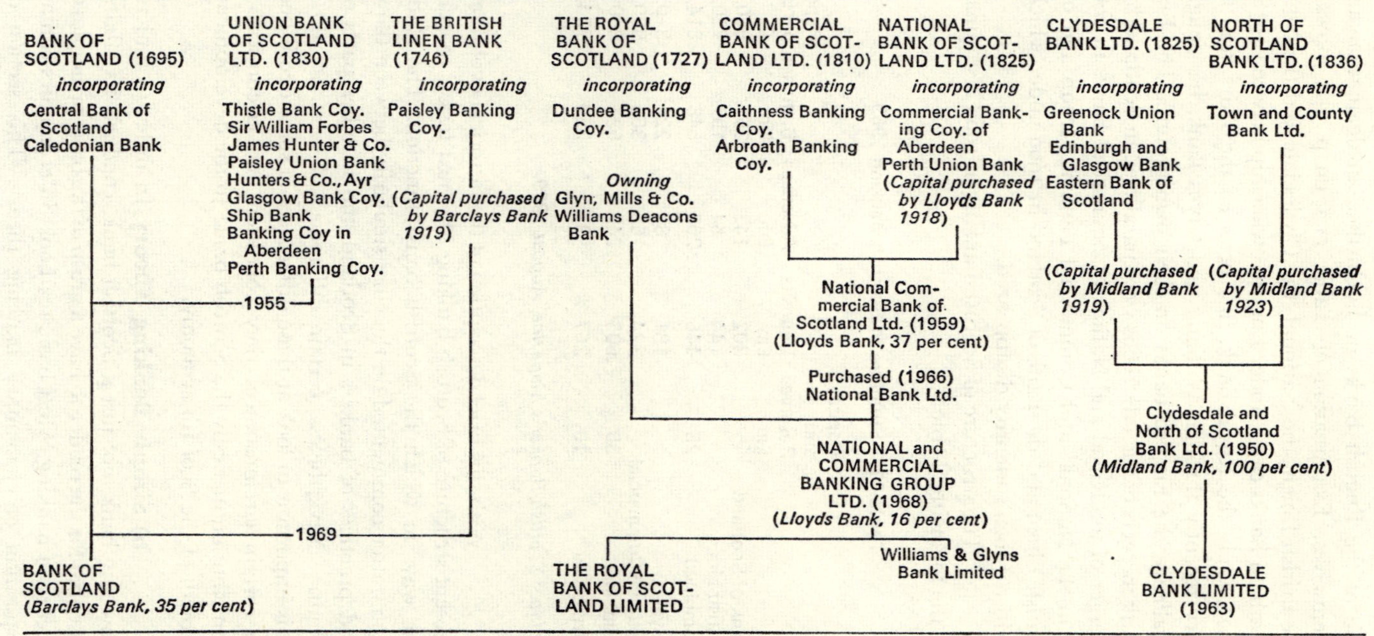

Source: Institute of Bankers in Scotland.

one of the English banks or by further amalgamation among themselves. Examination of Table 11.1 on p. 255 shows that the British Linen, the National, the Clydesdale and the North of Scotland Banks came under English ownership between 1918 and 1923. Only the Royal Bank, first between the Wars, and again very recently through Williams and Glyns Bank, has sought to challenge the English banks on their own ground. The English bank mergers of the late 1960s were paralleled in Scotland by the merger of the Royal and National Commercial Banks in 1968 to form the National and Commercial Banking Group and of the British Linen and the Bank of Scotland in 1969 under which the British Linen's identity disappeared.

The structure of Scottish banking in 1969 is summarised in the following Table.

Table 11.2 Structure of Scottish Banking 1969

	Capital and Reserves £m	Deposits £m	Advances £m	Branches No.	Deposits per Branch £
Bank of Scotland		302	142	351	860,000
British Linen		144	64	197	720,000
Combined	28	446	206	548	814,000
Royal		181	87	224	810,000
National Commercial		324	155	363	900,000
Combined	30	505	242	587	860,000
Clydesdale	13	267	97	350	734,000

Source: Scottish Banker's Magazine, August 1969.

With this brief description of the historical evolution and present structure of Scottish banking, the next task is to examine the ways in which the Scottish banks function. The Radcliffe Committee commented on the close similarity between the views and practices of bankers in Scotland and in other parts of the country. Nevertheless, certain differences of substance do exist. It is important to look at these differences in some detail because in certain circumstances they condition and circumscribe the contribution made by the Scottish banks to the development and growth of the Scottish economy.

b) Simple Banking Theory In order to understand how any bank, not just a Scottish bank, conducts its affairs it is essential for the reader to have a grasp of the basic principles of the theory of banking. Most basic textbooks in economics contain an exposition of elementary banking theory. This section draws heavily on *The Economics of Money* by A. C. L. Day (Oxford University Press, 1968).

There are two main kinds of banks, commercial banks and central banks. Scotland has no central bank of her own and our interest in this chapter is with the Scottish commercial banks. The most important feature distinguishing banks from other financial institutions is that their debts are used as money. Bank money is of two main kinds—bank notes and bank deposits. Whereas in England bank notes are issued solely by the central bank, the Bank of England, in Scotland all the commercial banks issue their own notes. The implication of this feature of Scottish commercial banks will be examined shortly. The other kind of money is bank deposits. These are the debts of a bank to its customers (depositors) which are recorded in the bank's accounts. Deposits are of two kinds, demand deposits, also known as current account deposits, and time (or term) deposits, also known as deposits on deposit account. Generally speaking, a depositor can call on or transfer his demand deposit at a moment's notice; with time deposits an agreed period of time must elapse, usually one to three weeks, before any transfer can be made out of a time deposit. Although it has not always been the case in Scotland, a further distinction between demand and time deposits is that nowadays time deposits are interest-bearing while demand deposits are not.[1]

The fact that the debts of banks are used as money accounts for the central importance of banks in the financial mechanism. Whenever a bank increases its total debts, the total amount of money in circulation increases or, to put it another way, banks act as creators of money. If, for example, a bank lends to a member of the public, creating a deposit in his favour, the amount of money in circulation rises. The whole basis of banking operations rests on the confidence on the part of the general public. The use of bank notes to settle debts depends on confidence in the institution which has issued the notes. So far as Bank of England notes are concerned the question of confidence hardly arises, because the Issue Department of the Bank of England can be regarded as the equivalent of a government department. For the Scottish banks, the question of confidence is critical if their notes are to be accepted freely, at least in Scotland. Confidence is also

[1] The distinction between demand and time deposits is arbitrary. Generally speaking, current and deposit accounts are regarded as money and any slight difference in liquidity between them is ignored. In Table 11.6 on p. 262, current and deposit accounts are both regarded as demand deposits, while deposits with other financial institutions such as building societies and finance houses are regarded as term deposits or 'near money'.

important to ensure freedom of transfer between bank deposits by means of cheque. A depositor will always want to be sure that he can convert his deposit on demand into the most acceptable form of money, notes and coin. Although it is nearly a century since the last bank failure in Scotland, experience in the United States and in Europe as recently as the 1930s underlines the importance to a bank of maintaining the confidence of the public.

In order to retain confidence, a commercial bank should always maintain sufficient reserves of cash to meet any likely withdrawals by depositors. In addition a bank should also possess sufficient reserves of assets which can easily and readily be turned into cash without appreciable loss. The need to maintain adequate reserves means that banks are very concerned with the form in which they hold their assets. Money held in the form of notes and coin is one form of asset; so too are deposits held at the central bank which can easily be converted into the notes and coin of the central bank. While prudence dictates that a bank will hold part of its assets in liquid form, the desire to earn profits will oblige a bank to hold its assets in their most profitable form. Notes earn no interest at all and generally speaking interest rates on short-term liquid assets are much lower than on long-term non-liquid assets. Banks will hold substantial quantities of government bonds maturing in series over ten years and also very small quantities of bonds issued by private firms which will generally earn more interest. Banks are also deeply involved in lending to private firms and individuals. Although in principle such loans would be regarded as being repayable at short notice, in practice many bank loans are of indefinite duration.

The conflict which a bank has to reconcile, is between making as large profits as possible and maintaining sufficient liquid assets to be able to repay debts on demand. In England, it is considered that cash reserves should be equal to 8 per cent of total deposit liabilities, and that reserves of liquid assets (cash, loans at call and at short notice to the discount market and bills) should not normally fall below 28 per cent of total deposit liabilities. The remaining 72 per cent of assets is made up of holdings of government bonds and of advances to customers.[1]

c) Trends of Deposits in Scotland The preceding elementary exposition of banking principles indicates that a rise in deposits enables a bank to increase its lending. The amount of

[1] The Bank of England has recently proposed major changes in the way in which banks will hold their reserves in future. These changes are discussed more fully on page 267.

deposits a bank can attract has obvious implications for its commercial viability. In the 19th century, the ingathering of deposits was regarded as one of the great distinguishing features of Scottish banking. Such was the success of the Scottish banks in attracting the unused liquid balances of the public that in the middle of the 19th century commercial bank deposits per head of population were certainly higher in Scotland than in England and Wales.

Table 11.3 Bank Deposits per Head of Population

	Scotland	England and Wales
	£	£
1901	24	21
1938	65	55
1951	146	141
1961	156	161

Source: 'The Scottish Banks: A Modern Survey', M. Gaskin.
Note: The figures show gross deposits which probably overstate the Scottish position. The distinction between gross and net deposits is explained by Gaskin, *op. cit.*, pp. 66–9.

While the Scottish banks have historically had a high level of bank deposits per head of population the indications are that for some considerable period of time the growth of Scottish bank deposits has been lagging behind that of English bank deposits. Growth in Scotland was particularly sluggish in the 1950s, but picked up considerably in the 1960s.

Table 11.4 Trends in Bank Deposits 1938–69

1952 = 100

	Net Deposits		Gross Deposits	
	Scottish Banks	London Clearing Banks	Scottish Banks	London Clearing Banks
1938	—	—	43	37
1948	—	—	99	97
1952	100	100	100	100
1955	104	105	102	106
1960	106	117	108	119
1963	112	128	118	131
1966	128	148	133	154
1969	150	167	155	174

Sources: 'The Scottish Banks: A Modern Survey', M. Gaskin; Financial Statistics.

Throughout the country as a whole there has been a fall in the amount of money held in the form of bank deposits. As was pointed out by the Radcliffe Committee, in 1945 the public was holding unusually large amounts of liquid and short-term assets.

The period of rationing which followed meant that people were not able to convert these assets into consumer durable goods as quickly as they might have wished. It was not until the late 1950s that the proportion of money held in the form of bank deposits to national income had returned to something like its pre-war level. While this analysis offers some explanation for the relative decline of the share of bank deposits in national income, it does not provide the whole answer. If it could be assumed that the public would hold in the future some constant proportion of their incomes in the form of bank deposits, the growth of national income would of itself generate an increase in bank deposits. An analysis of the ways in which the public are tending to hold their funds suggests that such an automatic increase in bank deposits need not necessarily take place.

Both within banking itself and over a wide range of financial institutions substantial changes have been taking place. There has been a marked shift out of liquid to less-liquid but more remunerative forms of deposits. Within the banking sector itself there has been a move away from demand deposits (non-interest bearing) to term deposits (interest-bearing).

Table 11.5 Cash and Deposits 1951–69 in the United Kingdom

	1951		1959		1969	
	£m	per cent	£m	per cent	£m	per cent
Cash	1,291	10·7	1,969	12·5	2,914	10·9
Demand Deposits	9,448	78·5	9,955	63·2	13,453	50·2
Term Deposits	1,302	10·8	3,833	24·3	10,452	38·9
	12,041	100·0	15,757	100·0	26,819	100·0

Source: Financial Statistics.

Throughout the 1950s current account balances in the English clearing banks rose by less than 1 per cent and actually fell in the Scottish banks. With the disappearance of the excess liquidity of the 1950s, there has been a recovery in the fortunes of bank deposits. English clearing bank deposits rose by 48 per cent during the 1960s and those of the Scottish banks by 37 per cent. The preference for less-liquid deposits is clearly demonstrated in England where time deposits rose by almost 80 per cent while Scottish bank time deposits rose by only 42 per cent. However, time deposits still account for a higher proportion of total deposits in Scotland.

This change in public preference for less rather than

more liquid assets is further illustrated by the growth in deposits of other institutions in the financial sector. Here, too, the difference between low (or non) interest and high interest bearing deposits is marked as is shown in Table 11.6. Whereas ordinary deposits in the Trustee Savings Banks rose by 5 per cent in the 1950s and by 25 per cent in the 1960s, the Special Investment Department of the Trustee Savings Banks recorded a gain of 227 per cent in the 1950s and of a further 300 per cent in the 1960s. Over the whole range of financial institutions, term deposits trebled in the 1950s and doubled again in the 1960s. Demand deposits, on the other hand, rose by only 5 per cent in the 1950s and by 40 per cent in the 1960s.

Bank deposits nationally have been forming an increasingly smaller part of national income. In part this may be explained by an increase in the velocity of circulation, so that bank deposits are being worked harder. Other factors have been at work to retard the growth in Scottish bank deposits. The nationalisation of such industries as coal and railways, for example, has led to an amalgamation of bank balances, not always in Scotland; the growth of chain stores most of which have accounts in London has resulted in a daily transfer of takings out of Scotland; most building societies and financial houses operating in Scotland have head offices in England. Three other factors have impeded the growth of deposits in Scotland. First, the Scottish economy has been growing at a slower rate, and this by itself would tend to produce a slower rate of deposit creation. Second, the proportion of deposits held in interest-bearing accounts in Scotland has always tended to be higher than in England and Wales; it is therefore only to be expected that the growth in Scotland of such deposits would be somewhat slower. Finally, the strength of the Trustee Savings Bank movement in Scotland has tended to divert to it funds which might otherwise have been lodged with the Scottish banks. With rather less than 10 per cent of the population of the United Kingdom, Scotland has 21 per cent of the total Trustee Savings Bank deposits; there is a Savings Bank office for every 19,000 people in Scotland as against one for every 45,600 in England and Wales.

The banking theory presented on pp. 256–258 suggested that it was by expansion of deposits that banks can expand loans and advances. If, therefore, bank deposits are growing at a relatively slow rate and are being subjected to strong pressure from other types of financial institutions, it might be reasonable to expect that banks, and particularly the Scottish

Table 11.6 Cash, Demand Deposits and Term Deposits—in the United Kingdom

£ millions

Year	Currency	Clearing Banks Current Accounts	Clearing Banks Deposit Accounts	Scottish Banks Current Accounts	Scottish Banks Deposit Accounts	P.O.S.B. Ord. Accounts Balance	T.S.B. Ord. Accounts	Building Socs. Deposits	Total Demand Deposits	T.S.B. Special Deposits Balance	Building Socs. Shares	Finance Houses Deposits	Treasury Bills	Total Term Deposits
1958	1,905	3,769	2,442	314	353	1,646	823	198	9,545	343	2,269	133	743	3,488
1959	1,969	4,064	2,431	331	371	1,679	859	220	9,955	380	2,518	192	743	3,833
1965	2,483	4,869	3,292	384	411	1,822	1,033	295	12,106	997	4,849	654	162	6,662
1968	2,838	5,334	4,177	446	488	1,589	1,046	335	13,415	1,311	7,453	612	86	9,462
1969	2,914	5,249	4,363	461	503	1,499	1,031	347	13,453	1,368	8,376	636	72	10,452
Per cent increase 1958–69	53·0	39·3	78·7	46·8	42·5	−8·9	25·3	75·3	40·9	298·8	269·1	378·2	−904·0	199·7

Source: Scottish Bankers' Magazine 1960; Financial Statistics.

Table 11.7 Assets Structure of the Scottish Banks

£ million

Year	Gross Deposits	Currency	Balances with B. of E.	Non-cover Cash	Balances with other Banks	Money at call and Short Notice	Treasury Bills	Other Bills	Gilt-edged Securities	Other Securities	Total Advances	Special Deposits	Fiduciary Issue
1963	846·0	144·7	1·6	23·2	42·5	81·7	25·1	9·8	193·8	26·9	—	—	1·3
1964	891·6	149·7	1·6	26·0	48·3	81·3	18·9	12·1	197·9	30·4	454·1	—	1·4
1965	931·2	153·1	2·0	28·3	53·8	91·8	20·7	12·2	157·4	31·4	507·6	3·0	1·4
1966	977·2	158·2	2·3	30·3	55·9	103·3	21·6	13·6	164·6	32·5	514·1	7·1	1·5
1967	1,024·7	160·3	1·7	29·2	56·8	109·4	24·0	15·5	199·7	34·6	503·0	10·2	1·4
1968	1,105·8	168·3	1·8	30·9	69·4	109·8	28·0	15·7	237·8	33·9	519·7	11·0	1·1
1969	1,142·0	175·7	0·7	32·0	80·3	109·1	6·6	19·5	251·2	33·5	548·4	11·4	1·3

Source: Financial Statistics.

banks, will only be able to achieve correspondingly modest increases in their lending. In fact, while Scottish bank deposits have risen by 53 per cent from £744·4 million in 1951 to £1,142 million in 1969, advances have risen by over 150 per cent from £217·3 million in 1951 to £548·4 million in 1969. This apparent discrepancy between relatively slow growing deposits and much faster growing advances brings into prominence two associated features of Scottish banking which distinguish it from English banking. The first is the assets structure of the Scottish banks and, second, the operation of government control over the supply of money via the mechanism of cash and liquidity ratios.

It was only in 1958 that banks in the United Kingdom were freed from all the restraints which had been imposed upon them at the beginning of World War II. At various times since then, however, the banks have been subjected to controls on their lending activities as part of overall economic policy. Between July 1958 and July 1961, advances by the Scottish banks rose by £167 million or 77 per cent. To put it another way, one third of the increase in Scottish bank lending since 1951 took place in this three-year period. Sixty-five per cent of this increase in lending was financed by selling securities, the remainder by a rise in deposits. It is here that we find the reason why Scottish bank advances have been able to rise so much faster than deposits. Between 1951 and 1969, the investments of the Scottish banks fell by £110 million. Indeed by 1965, investments had fallen by over £200 million on their 1951 level but have risen again by £100 million over the last four years as a result of the imposition of credit controls. The Scottish banks have been able to finance a substantial proportion of their increased lending by selling securities.

The reason they have been able to do so dates back to the period between the wars. Prior to 1914, Scottish banks lent nearly two thirds of their deposits in the form of loans and advances to customers. The ratio of investments to deposits stood at 30 per cent, compared with 18 per cent for the English banks. In supporting government monetary policy during World War I by buying government securities Scottish banks had by the early 1920s much higher investments than in 1914, and this investment ratio fell little during the 1920s. As a result of the economic depression of the 1930s bank advances fell throughout the British banking system. The effects of the depression were more severe and long lasting in Scotland and had their attendant consequences on bank advances. From a level of 54 per cent of deposits in 1930, advances fell to just over 30 per cent in 1935 and to 18 per cent in 1945. As a bank's assets are held principally in the form of advances or investments, there was a corresponding rise in the investments of the Scottish banks to offset the fall in advances. Investments, to a large extent, are a residual so far as banks are concerned; if an insufficient number of borrowers of the required status present themselves, then the bank will invest the surplus funds, probably in gilt-edged securities. But as advances normally yield a higher return than securities, investments will be sold when an expansion of advances becomes possible.

The Scottish banks emerged from World War II with a very high level of investments and a correspondingly low level of advances. By 1951, they had been able to increase advances to 30 per cent of deposits and the ratio remained around 27 per cent for the rest of the 1950s. By contrast, the English banks had not experienced nearly such a severe fall in advances and therefore not the same increase in investments. In 1938, for example, English banks' investments were 28 per cent of deposits compared with 57 per cent for the Scottish banks. By virtue of their proportionally much larger holdings of investments, the Scottish banks have been able to finance a large part of their increase in lending by selling securities. The question now is to what extent the Scottish banks will be able to support further increases in advances in the future.

d) Cash and Liquidity Ratios The banking theory on pp. 256–258 showed that a commercial bank will be careful to maintain certain minimum holdings of cash and liquid assets. In part for prudent banking reasons and in part by requirement of the Bank of England, the English commercial banks maintain a minimum cash ratio of 8 per cent and a liquidity ratio of 28 per cent. If the commercial banks are in a 'fully lent' position, with cash and liquidity ratios at a minimum, and if the Bank of England wishes to effect a reduction in bank lending, it can do so by means of 'open market' operations. The Bank of England will offer for sale through the Government Broker government securities which will be bought by customers of the commercial banks; the banks' holdings of investments will rise and their holdings of cash will fall. As the banks' cash ratios will now have fallen below 8 per cent, they will require to restore this position by converting their most readily liquefied assets into cash; their liquidity ratios will now have fallen below 28 per cent and will have to be restored by the restriction or the recalling of advances. The extent to which advances will be reduced will depend on the intensity with which the Bank of England wishes to apply its monetary policy. The fall in advances will be a multiple of the reduction in the cash or liquidity ratios as is shown by the following simple example:

If the Bank of England sells £16 million of government securities on the open market and if the commercial banks are maintaining a strict cash ratio of 8 per cent, the effect will be to reduce commercial bank advances by $16/8 \times 100 =$ £200 million, assuming all other things remain equal.

Alternatively, if the banks are maintaining a strict 28 per cent liquidity ratio, the effect on advances will be a reduction of $16/28 \times 100 =$ £57·1 million.

Normally, of course, 'open market' operations would be reinforced by other monetary measures, e.g. raising of Bank Rate, the introduction of Special Deposits, request to the banks to restrict their lending and so on. But the Bank of England can exercise a direct control over the lending activities of the English banks by operating on their cash and liquidity ratios. No such control is exercised over the Scottish banks for the reason that cash and liquidity ratios are concepts which have a rather different meaning in Scotland. One of the distinctive features of Scottish banking which has already been noted is the retention of the right of note issue. While this right may be regarded by some as a quaint anachronism and by the Radcliffe Committee as a rather tiresome complication, it is now appropriate to look at the implications of this note issue in the light of its consequences for monetary policy.

e) Note Issue of the Scottish Banks The fiduciary issue of the Scottish banks now stands at £2·7 million but the Scottish banks have the right to make further issues against 100 per cent cover in Bank of England notes. At the present time, the issue of Scottish notes amounts to some £147 million. For every £1 note of their own which they issue over and above the fiduciary issue, the Scottish banks are required to hold a Bank of England £1 note. The circulation of Scottish notes has risen more or less in line with total currency circulation in the United Kingdom. Scottish notes constitute approximately 6 per cent of total currency circulation, and within Scotland Scottish notes may account for around two thirds of the currency in circulation. In recent years, the Scottish note issues have averaged around 11–13 per cent of the Scottish banks' notes plus deposits, an increase over the early

1950s when the ratio was around 9 per cent. Their power to issue notes has the effect of enabling the Scottish banks to hold a greater quantity of assets than would be the case if they did not issue notes. This extra quantity of assets cannot be smaller than the volume of the note circulation. When a note is passed into circulation it is given either in exchange for an asset, e.g. as part of an advance to a customer, or for an equal reduction of a bank's deposit liabilities when a customer draws on a credit balance. In the second case, of course, assets do not increase but the composition of a bank's liabilities changes.

The principal use the Scottish banks make of their own notes is as till-money in their own branches. Only Scottish notes which are issued require to be covered by an equivalent holding of Bank of England notes. Their own notes provide the Scottish banks with an economical means of keeping their branches stocked with notes to meet day-to-day over the counter transactions. The Scottish banks aim to keep their branch holdings of Bank of England notes as small as possible and at a level sufficient to meet the demands of people who express a specific preference for Bank of England notes. By statute the Scottish banks are required to hold their note cover at the Bank of England or in two specified branch offices.

The cash ratio which determines the lending and investing activities of a bank is known as the operative cash ratio. For the Scottish banks this is not the ratio of total cash to deposits since this contains the large and passive holdings of Bank of England notes required to cover the note issue. At the present time, the Scottish banks' holdings of Bank of England notes as note cover amount to some £145 million. The operative cash ratio for the Scottish banks is the non-cover cash which has tended to average around 3 per cent of deposits compared with a ratio of 8 per cent in England.

This should not be taken, however, as implying that the credit-creating powers of the Scottish banks are greater than those of the English banks. The lower liquidity ratios in Scotland are a reflection of the greater length of time taken by the Scottish banks to settle with each other and with the English banks. Also, if deposits are being encashed a Scottish bank's reserves to meet such a contingency are mainly its own unissued notes. Cover for excess issue of its own notes does not have to be provided immediately by a bank since it is based on the average amount in issue on four successive Saturdays. The Scottish banks, therefore, require less cash in their branches and less in money market assets because they have more time in which to meet losses of deposits. They require less first line reserves (cash) and less second line reserves (call money and bills), but this is compensated for by holding more third line reserves (investments).

There is no minimum liquidity ratio to which the Bank of England can ask the Scottish banks to adhere, although it has on occasion requested the Scottish banks to observe their 'usual' liquidity ratios. In times of severe credit restraint, these rather gentlemanly requests may be reinforced by calling for special deposits or by imposing ceilings on advances.

f) New Measures of Credit Control At the time this book went to print major changes were under consideration with respect to the institution of new measures of credit control. In May 1971 the Bank of England issued a paper in which it set out its proposals to move away from the exercise of control over the banks through 'ceilings' on advances towards a system of control through the variation of interest rates, supported by calls for Special Deposits. A second objective of the Bank's proposals is to create conditions in which the various types of financial institutions involved in the attraction of deposits and the lending of money, i.e. Clearing Scottish, Merchant and Overseas Banks, Discount and Finance Houses, to compete on more equal terms. The proposal is that all banks should:

(i) hold not less than a fixed percentage of their sterling deposit liabilities in certain specified reserve assets;
(ii) that this reserve ratio should be uniform between banks and should be established at 12½ per cent of the relevant deposit liabilities;
(iii) the banks should place with the Bank of England such amounts of Special Deposits as the Bank deems appropriate to prevailing economic circumstances.

The assets which will constitute this reserve will be cash at the Bank of England and certain assets which the Bank will normally be prepared to convert into cash, e.g. balances at the Bank of England, Treasury Bills, money at call in the London Money Market, British government securities with less than one year to run to maturity, local authority bills eligible for rediscount at the Bank of England and a yet to be specified proportion of commercial bills eligible for rediscount at the Bank.

These are obviously far-reaching proposals aimed at achieving greater uniformity of treatment between the banks and other financial institutions and also at removing the policy of control by edict with which the banks have been unhappy.

At the time of writing, discussions are still proceeding between the Bank of England on the one hand and the Clearing and Scottish banks and other financial institutions on the other. It is, therefore, difficult to say with any degree of certainty what the precise implications of these proposed changes are for the Scottish banks.

The differences pointed out earlier in this chapter in the size and composition of the liquidity ratios of the Clearing and Scottish banks will disappear as will the differential in the level of Special Deposits. There may well be a modest increase in the Scottish banks' holdings of short term assets and a corresponding reduction in their investments. The net effect, however, should be to increase the lending capacity of the Scottish banks. Speculation as to the future of Scottish bank notes appears to be premature and these are still likely to continue to serve their function as till money.

g) Scottish Bank Lending British banks have traditionally avoided a policy of long-term lending. Their preference has been for short-term lending of the 'self-liquidating' type. Bankers regard themselves as being properly engaged when they are financing working capital, providing 'bridging' loans and financing on a temporary basis fixed capital development. The Scottish banks have been intimately involved in the economic development of Scotland, as the origins of the British Linen Bank testify. Scottish banks have followed, indeed have helped to mould, the traditional British policy of essentially short-term lending. Certain English banks allowed themselves to be heavily and rather painfully involved in the capital reconstruction of the cotton and steel industries between the wars, but there is little evidence that the Scottish banks allowed themselves to be committed in this way. Questioning of Scottish Bank General Managers by the Radcliffe Committee did establish that Scottish banks were and are prepared to lend for longer term than their English counterparts. This is particularly the case so far as agriculture is concerned. The provision of an overdraft is the principal means by which bank loans are made. Although technically an overdraft can be recalled on demand, in practice this may often prove not to be feasible. *De facto*, therefore, bank lending may prove to be of longer term than might appear to be the case.

Until recently no separate analysis has been published of advances made by the Scottish banks. Since the war, statistics of bank advances have been published by the British Bankers' Association, but these have contained no regional breakdown. In 1967, however, the Bank of England began to publish a quarterly series of advances showing the London clearing banks, the Scottish banks and the accepting houses, overseas and other domestic banks as three separate groups. The breakdown shows the type of activity being financed, analysed so far as is possible by the Standard Industrial Classification. A possible source of distortion in the figures is that they relate to the source of the advance and not to where the funds are being spent. Branch firms particularly may well have their advances organised for them by their head offices in England through one of the English banks for expenditure to be undertaken in Scotland. To the extent that this happens the figures will understate the amount of bank lending actually being spent in Scotland. There may also be movements of funds in the opposite direction, although the amount of Scottish bank advances being spent outside Scotland is likely to be relatively small. Apart from one set of figures published in the early 1930s, it is only very recently that it has been possible to analyse the figures of Scottish bank lending. We take this opportunity to present them here in some detail.

The quarterly figures of advances for the years 1967, 1968 and 1969 have been averaged to produce annual figures which in turn have been averaged to produce an average of advances of the three years. The advances to each Order Number of the Standard Industrial Classification have been expressed as a percentage of the total advances to primary, manufacturing, construction and service industry. Omitted from the analysis are the advances to the personal sector, the financial sector and to overseas residents. For the London clearing banks these advances averaged £1,219 million, or one quarter of all their advances between 1967 and 1969, and for the Scottish banks £111 million, or one fifth of Scottish bank advances over the same period. In order to establish whether the pattern of Scottish bank advances to industry has followed the pattern of the advances of the London clearing and other banks, a comparative analysis has been carried out on the basis of the distribution of employment in Scotland and in the rest of the country. The percentage figures for the distribution of employment have been divided into the percentage figures for the distribution of advances and the resultant ratios multiplied by 100. A ratio of 100 indicates that the bank advances to a particular industry are in exact proportion to its size as measured by employment.[1]

The first feature to notice is that within the broad categories of manufacturing, other production and service industry, the distribution of Scottish bank advances is basically similar to that of the other banks. Both groups of banks are relatively heavily committed to the other production and manufacturing sectors and under-committed, in employment terms, to the service sector. Within these broad categories, however, there are some interesting differences. The Scottish banks' long standing commitment to agriculture is very marked. With only just over 3 per cent of employment, agriculture, forestry and fishing account for nearly one fifth of advances. Less than 10 per cent on the English banks' advances go to this sector, although agriculture represents their heaviest relative commitment. Only one half of one per cent of Scottish bank advances go to the mining and quarrying industries, presumably a consequence of nationalisation. Advances to the construction industry are relatively low in Scotland and just above par in the rest of the country. A possible explanation may lie in the allocation of advances between the public and private sectors of the economy. The basis of the analysis is by industry irrespective of ownership (i.e. private, local authority or central government). For example, where a local authority obtains bank advances to finance house construction this will be shown under the heading 'Construction'. In Scotland, where a very much higher proportion of housebuilding is financed by local authorities than is the case in England and Wales, this could result in some overstatement of advances to the private construction sector and a corresponding understatement of the public sector. However, as advances in Scotland to the construction industry are relatively low and relatively high to local government this possible distortion does not offer a plausible explanation.

Scotland is one of the major centres of shipbuilding in the country and as shipbuilders have been chronically short of funds for a number of years it is not surprising to find that within the manufacturing sector the heaviest relative commitment is to shipbuilding. What may be surprising is that the English banks have an even greater commitment than the Scottish banks. In addition to the lending by the banks, the Shipbuilding Industry Board has also provided considerable sums to finance yard

[1] An employment measure may not be particularly satisfactory, but in the absence of up-to-date statistics on the value of gross sales or net output by industry employment figures are the best available.

Table 11.8 Analysis of Scottish Bank Advances 1967–9

	Average advance (£m)	As per cent of Total Advances	Average level of Employment (000)	As per cent of Total Employment	Per cent Advance / Per cent Employment x100
Food, Drink and Tobacco	37·8	9·1	107·3	5·1	178
Chemical and allied Industries	12·8	3·1	33·3	1·6	194
Metal Manufactures	10·6	2·6	49·1	2·3	113
Electrical Engineering	8·7	2·1	50·2	2·4	88
Other Engineering and Metal Goods	38·3	9·3	166·1	7·9	118
Shipbuilding	20·6	5·0	48·2	2·3	217
Vehicles	4·4	1·1	39·9	1·9	58
Textiles, leather and clothing	17·6	4·3	130·2	6·2	69
Other manufacture	24·9	6·0	130·1	6·2	97
Total Manufacture	175·7	42·6	754·4	35·9	119
Agriculture, Forestry, Fishing	78·7	19·0	67·6	3·2	590
Mining and Quarrying	2·1	0·5	50·4	2·4	21
Construction	28·8	7·0	197·4	9·4	74
Total Other Production	109·6	26·5	315·4	15·0	176
Transport and Communication	17·5	4·2	154·4	7·3	58
Public Utilities and National Govt.	7·6	1·8	79·5	3·7	49
Govt. Services	14·6	3·5	77·3	3·6	97
Distribution	23·3	5·6	210·2	10·0	56
Other Distribution	25·5	6·2	65·7	3·1	200
Professional, Scientific and Miscellaneous	39·8	9·6	451·3	21·4	45
Total Services	128·3	30·9	1,038·4	49·1	63
Grand Total	413·6	100·0	2,108·2	100·0	

Source: Bank of England Quarterly Bulletin.

modernisation. The main elements of the Scottish vehicles industry, i.e. British Leyland, Chrysler and Rolls Royce, are all externally owned and will almost certainly conduct the greater part of their banking business with English banks. This will explain the Scottish banks' relatively modest involvement with the vehicles industry compared with the English banks. Within the

Table 11.9 Analysis of London Clearing Banks and other Bank Advances (excluding Scottish banks) 1967–9

	Average advance (£m)	As per cent of Total Advances	Average Level of Employment (000)	As per cent of Total Employment	Per cent Advance / Per cent Employment x100
Food, Drink and Tobacco	262·6	5·5	724·7	3·6	153
Chemical and allied Industries	206·6	4·2	484·7	2·4	175
Metal Manufacture	169·2	3·5	546·9	2·7	130
Electrical Engineering	297·1	6·2	867·8	4·3	144
Other Engineering and Metal Goods	500·9	10·4	1,834·9	9·0	116
Shipbuilding	88·6	1·8	149·8	0·7	257
Vehicles	292·1	6·1	783·1	3·8	161
Textiles, Leather and Clothing	242·9	5·0	1,138·8	5·6	89
Other manufacture	325·7	6·8	1,537·9	7·6	89
Total Manufacture	2,385·7	49·5	8,068·6	39·7	125
Agriculture, Forestry, Fishing	433·6	9·0	356·4	1·8	500
Mining and Quarrying	90·8	1·9	459·6	2·3	83
Construction	340·6	7·1	1,390·6	6·8	104
Total Other Production	865·0	18·0	2,206·6	10·9	165
Transport and Communication	164·7	3·4	1,454·6	7·1	48
Public Utilities and National Govt.	65·9	1·4	918·5	4·5	31
Govt. Services	99·7	2·1	756·7	3·7	57
Distribution	340·2	7·1	1,793·8	8·8	81
Other Distribution	396·6	8·2	744·3	3·7	222
Professional, Scientific and Miscellaneous	499·0	10·3	4,404·7	21·6	48
Total Services	1,566·1	32·5	10,072·6	49·4	66
Grand Total	4,816·8	100·0	20,347·8	100·0	

Source: Bank of England Quarterly Bulletin.

service sector, 'other distribution' stands out as a category with which the English and Scottish banks are heavily committed. This sector covers much of the stockholding activity of the country, in which the banks have always had a major interest.

h) Future Trends in Scottish Banking During a period in which industrial and commercial units are increasing in size, there must be some concern at the ability of the Scottish banks to compete with their much larger English rivals. Sharing the accounts of larger firms is one solution which even the English banks have had to adopt. The recent mergers which have formed the Scottish banks into three main groups was a move without which the Scottish banking system would have been labouring at an even greater disadvantage.

Scotland has traditionally had one of the most intensive branch banking systems in the world. Even so, there are wide variations in banking densities between different types and sizes of towns. Generally speaking the smaller towns with populations under 20,000, with stronger agricultural connections and proportionately larger numbers of professional and commercial inhabitants, have the highest banking densities. In the larger industrial towns and cities banking densities are much lower and the use of banks by working class people seems much less fully developed. Over the United Kingdom as a whole, 27 per cent of the adult population have personal current accounts, whereas only 16 per cent in Scotland have. There is undoubtedly scope to foster more 'middle class' attitudes to banking, particularly in the larger towns. Extension of the system of paying wages by cheque rather than in cash should foster the banking habit; whether all or part of this market will be lost to the Post Office 'Giro' with its greater density of offices and longer opening hours remains to be seen.

2 Other Financial Intermediaries

Besides the banks, other institutions exist to provide capital, sometimes for highly specialised purposes, to support economic growth in Scotland. As we have seen the banks have moulded their practices and procedures to match the needs of the Scottish economy. There is undoubtedly a close relationship between the social and economic structure of a country and the financial institutions which have grown up to serve it. In particular the way in which income is distributed and the way in which wealth and assets are held will influence the type of financial institution into or through which savings and wealth are channelled. In Chapter 6, for example, we saw that the comparative lack of a middle class, along with a considerable volume of savings among the low income groups, has meant that in Scotland there is disproportionately heavy investment in low interest, liquid, Government savings media. In particular, the Post Office and Trustee Savings Banks acquire funds which might otherwise go to the commercial banks or to industrial investment.

Although the insurance companies, building societies, investment and unit trusts, merchant banks and Government savings media are presented separately on the following pages, it is essential to realise that important relationships exist between them. All of them are in more or less direct competition for investors' funds. Changes in the performance of one type of institution may, therefore, have important implications for the others. Rates of interest, security, ease of withdrawal and convenience of opening hours are all factors which determine their relative performance.

a) Insurance Companies Insurance companies fall into two main categories, 'life' companies and 'general' companies, the latter being principally concerned with fire, accident and marine insurance. Insurance companies rank in the first order of importance among British financial institutions with assets totalling nearly £15,000 million in 1968. Their assets have been growing at 9 per cent per annum over the past decade and currently are valued at more than £15,000 million.

The insurance companies are regarded as institutions of the greatest importance by the monetary authorities, particularly in relation to their role as large investors of funds. When an insurance company sells a life assurance policy, it is entering into a commitment to repay a fixed, or substantially fixed, sum at some date many years ahead. This would lead to the conclusion that insurance companies should seek to invest their premium income in long-term securities of the appropriate maturity. However, as many policies are sold 'with profits' and as policy-holders have become increasingly inflation-conscious, insurance companies have become increasingly large purchasers of equities. During the war, the insurance companies were placed under considerable pressure to invest all their accruing funds in government bonds which has been a further reason for their desire to reduce their holdings of fixed interest securities. There have been substantial changes in the composition of the assets of insurance companies, as is shown in the following table.

Despite the fact that the insurance companies' holdings of British government securities have fallen from a third of their assets in 1951, to around 15 per cent at present, insurance companies' holdings of government stock amount to over £2,000 million. As insurance companies have little interest in holding Treasury bills or short-dated stock, their holdings of long-term government securities may account for as much as one third of the marketable securities which make up a large part of the National Debt. A further measure of the size and importance of the insurance companies can be gauged from the fact that in 1957, they had funds available for investment of £300 million, equivalent to 19 per cent of the total required to finance all net fixed capital formation (public and private) in the United Kingdom in that year. Eleven years later, in 1968, the annual sum available to them for investment had risen to £1,000 million, equivalent to 27 per cent of net fixed capital formation in 1968. The life funds of insurance companies have been growing much faster than national income. Whereas national income at current prices rose by 70 per cent between 1958 and 1967, life funds trebled from £528 million to £1,640 million.

Table 11.10 Assets of Insurance Companies in the U.K. 1937, 1951, 1956 and 1968: per cent

	1937	1951	1956	1968
Mortgages	11·4	9·2	12·3	13·4
Loans on public rates to local authorities	3·1	1·0	1·3	2·2
British government securities	21·6	32·5	23·7	13·7
Commonwealth and foreign government securities	11·6	8·7	7·6	5·3
Debentures	16·2	10·8	13·4	15·9
Stocks and Shares (preference)	8·3	7·7	7·1	2·6
Stocks and Shares (ordinary)	9·8	11·8	16·1	25·0
Land and Property	5·5	6·7	7·8	9·4
Cash	2·1	2·8	2·1	2·7
Agents' balances, etc.	3·3	5·9	6·0	9·8
	100·0	100·0	100·0	100·0

Source: Radcliffe Report; Annual Abstract of Statistics.

There are seven major life insurance companies in Scotland—Standard Life, Scottish Widows, Scottish Amicable, Scottish Provident, Scottish Life, Scottish Equitable and Scottish Mutual—and one major composite company—General Accident, whose head office is at Perth. In 1969, the assets of the Scottish life companies totalled £1,825 million, around one eighth of the total funds controlled by insurance companies in the United Kingdom. In the 'Times Review of Industry' league table of 1967, Standard Life ranked third, Scottish Widows tenth and Scottish Amicable seventeenth among the top twenty-five British life insurance companies. Among the general companies, General Accident ranked third behind the Royal and Commercial Union groups.

A significant element of the British insurance movement

is located in Scotland and the brief outline given in this section of the importance of the insurance companies in the hierarchy of financial institutions applies with equal weight to the Scottish-based companies. Edinburgh, in particular, is the second most important centre in the country as regards the control and deployment of life assurance funds.

b) Building Societies Building societies hold an important though specialised place in the market for capital. Their liabilities, principally in the form of shares and deposits held by the public, total over £8,000 million. They provide finance for about two thirds of private house-building, a large and sensitive part of total net investment. Building societies are among the fastest growing channels of new savings as was shown in Table 11.6 on p. 262. The recently introduced SAYE scheme, in which the building societies are active participants, may well provide further impetus to the flow of funds into the movement. In the spring of 1968, the Building Societies Association commissioned a survey of the savings and investment habits of adults aged 16 and over.

6·2 million people, or about one person in six, holds a building society account, an increase of 42·5 per cent over 1965

Table 11.11 Savings and Investment Habits of Adults aged 16 and over, in the U.K. 1968

	Per cent of population aged 16 and over	Number Millions	Per cent change 1965–8
Government methods:			
Post Office Savings Bank Accounts	37	15·0	−0·8
Premium Bonds	37	14·8	−7·4
Trustee Savings Bank Accounts	18	7·3	−1·5
National Savings Certificates	15	6·0	−16·7
National Development Bonds	1	0·4	−57·1
Commercial Methods:			
Commercial Bank Deposit Accounts	23	9·6	n.a.
Building Society Accounts	15	6·2	+42·5
Stocks and Shares	9	3·6	+27·8
Unit Trust Holdings	3	1·1	+57·1
Other Savings:			
Life and Endowment Assurance Policies	65	26·1	+8·4
Pension or Superannuation Schemes	20	8·0	+19·1

Source: Building Societies Association.

when a similar survey was carried out. There is, however, substantial regional variation in the popularity of saving via building societies. This form of saving is most popular in Yorkshire and Humberside, but in Wales and Scotland relatively few people save with building societies, although individual holdings of building society deposits are higher in Scotland. Part of the reason why building societies are not favoured by the Scots as a channel for savings may be due to the competition from other institutions. We have already seen, for example, that the Trustee Savings Bank movement is strongly entrenched in Scotland. A more positive reason, however, may lie in the failure of a native Scottish building society movement to develop.

Why should it be that Scotland, a well-developed country so far as banking, insurance and investment trusts are concerned, has not seen a comparable development of building societies? Large English building societies such as the Halifax or Abbey National each do more business in Scotland than all the Scottish-registered building societies put together. Three factors probably account for the retarded development of an indigenous building society movement. First, a policy of rent control until the late 1950s had the effect of creating artificially low rents, thereby eliminating much of the incentive for owner-occupation. Second, there is a very much higher proportion in Scotland of house building by local authorities; since the war over 40 per cent of new housebuilding in England has been for private owners, compared with less than 15 per cent in Scotland. Third, there has been a reluctance among societies to lend on the Victorian tenements which characterise much of urban Scotland.

The twenty-eight building societies registered in Scotland handled only one tenth of the business done north of the border. In 1969 their lending amounted to £6·5 million out of an annual rate of £70 million by all building societies in Scotland. As building society lending is currently running at levels substantially in excess of £1,000 million per annum, the Scottish societies account for around one half of one per cent of total lending. Table 11.12 summarises the financial position of Scotland's twenty-eight societies in 1966. Half of them are insignificant institutions whose activities scarcely impinge on the housing market. Of the dozen or so which have any pretensions to size, by far the largest is the Dunfermline, whose assets account for half the total of all Scottish building societies. Yet, in comparison with the English giants, the Dunfermline Building Society is a very small institution. In 1969, the Investors' Chronicle ranked it

Table 11.12 Financial Structure of Scottish Building Societies in 1966

Scottish Building Societies: summary of financial statements

	Total Assets £	Increase on previous year £	Percentage Increase	Mortgage Assets £	Reserve Ratio per cent	Liquidity Ratio per cent	Advances Number	Advances Value £	Advances Average £
The Top Half									
1 Dunfermline	14,896,942	1,260,257	9·2	11,782,966	1·7	18·8	1,077	2,371,777	2,202
2 Paisley	3,041,563	363,603	13·6	2,634,046	4·3	12·8	331	690,578	2,086
3 Scottish	1,962,153	285,325	16·8	1,714,827	6·2	12·0	281	501,819	1,786
4 Dunedin	1,840,636	259,715	16·4	1,495,434	4·3	17·5	208	381,545	1,834
5 Inverness	1,774,085	121,110	7·3	1,573,707	3·9	9·9	195	344,283	1,766
6 Edinburgh	1,392,572	230,785	19·9	1,211,876	3·8	12·5	124	351,859	2,838
7 Century	1,380,002	118,319	9·3	1,105,385	6·6	19·5	135	269,405	1,996
8 Prudential	984,562	117,946	13·3	857,496	4·7	11·6	178	280,006	1,573
9 Kilmarnock	490,967	86,164	21·3	400,232	2·8	18·5	45	99,339	2,208
10 Galashiels	440,917	75,725	11·3	365,192	5·4	17·2	73	94,340	1,292
11 Govanhill	412,347	36,572	8·9	385,432	6·7	6·4	73	114,721	1,571
12 Peeblesshire	377,611	26,701	7·6	317,606	6·9	16·5	39	46,815	1,200
13 Farmers' and General	266,652	32,559	13·9	216,233	3·0	18·9	63	47,325	751
14 Stirlingshire	215,761	33,359	18·3	155,989	3·2	27·2	25	43,050	1,722
	29,476,770	3,048,140	11·8	24,216,421			2,847	5,636,862	1,980
The Bottom Half:									
15 Wishaw	162,900	4,332	2·8	142,110	0·9	12·0	22	32,475	1,476
16 Clydesdale	147,346	−1,004	−6·8	125,992	5·9	13·8	5	14,750	2,950
17 Huntly	116,817	20,626	21·4	112,837	3·6	3·4	15	22,200	1,480
18 Kirriemuir	107,048	−283	−0·3	36,844	nil	62·3	5	4,625	925
19 Permanent Scottish	98,593	6,398	6·9	87,750	4·7	11·0	11	13,350	1,214
20 Banffshire	89,189	15,406	20·9	82,055	9·6	7·2	15	24,236	1,616
21 West of Fife	47,052	−4,041	−8·6	38,150	nil	14·9	6	5,125	854
22 Elgin	46,890	−1,067	−2·2	31,113	5·8	32·3	nil	—	—
23 Leith	42,382	−596	−1·4	18,884	46·1	45·3	2	1,400	700
24 Bo'ness and Carriden	30,635	−2,947	−8·8	22,920	6·0	22·9	6	3,390	565
25 Hamilton	28,386	−128	−4·5	16,168	32·5	41·6	1	3,000	3,000
26 Fourth Dundee	12,010	37	0·3	4,540	11·2	62·2	nil	—	—
27 Phoenix	7,183	354	5·2	5,936	18·7	17·4	nil	—	—
28 Forfar	3,363	−38	−1·1	140	45·9	95·8	nil	—	—
	939,794	37,049	3·9	725,439			88	124,551	1,451

forty-fourth among British building societies with assets of £19·6 million. When compared with the Halifax with assets of £1,470 million or the Abbey National's £1,116 million, it can be seen that the Scottish societies must be regarded as relatively unimportant.

c) Merchant Banks There exists in the City of London a large number of firms known loosely as 'merchant banks'. Broadly speaking, their activities begin where those of the joint stock banks leave off. The joint stock banks' traditional reluctance to involve themselves in long term lending and their desire to provide capital primarily on a temporary or bridging basis have already been noted. The merchant banks exist to provide a wide range of financial services beyond those which the commercial banks normally offer.

Until recently, merchant banking in this country was confined almost entirely to the City of London: in Scotland, there were only two small and not particularly active merchant banks, both based in Glasgow.

Increasingly, however, in recent years has come the realisation by both bankers and businessmen that more fully developed merchant banking services in Scotland would be of mutual benefit. The essence of merchant banking is the knowledge and awareness of suitable commercial opportunities. The large London banks, with much international business on their books, were seen to be too remote and insufficiently aware of local conditions. Changes in company legislation have been forcing more and more Scottish family businesses to go public, thereby providing profitable new issue business for merchant banks. Scottish companies periodically accumulate substantial cash balances which the highly competitive interest rates of the merchant banks can do much to attract.

The last few years have seen a modest upsurge in merchant banking in Scotland. The two original Scottish merchant banks were the British Bank of Commerce, founded in 1935, and Glasgow Industrial Finance, founded in 1946. The British Bank of Commerce was reformed and enlarged in 1960 and in the last five years its pre-tax profits have more than doubled. It is associated with Samuel Montague & Co., one of the leading London banks. Glasgow Industrial Finance was set up in 1946 as an issuing house by a number of Glasgow and Edinburgh investment trusts. Between 1946 and 1964, it conducted £26·4 million of new issue business. In 1964 it was taken over by the Industrial and

Commercial Finance Corporation (I.C.F.C.)[1] and renamed Scottish Industrial Finance.

In chronological order, the new Scottish-based merchant banks are Edward Bates and Sons, now owned by a Scottish investment trust, which set up a Scottish office in 1963; its special interest is in portfolio management. In 1965, National Commercial and Schroders was formed by the National Commercial Bank of Scotland and Schroders, another London-based merchant bank. Also in 1965 came Scottish Financial Trust, a subsidiary of First National Finance Corporation of Birmingham, formed in 1959 by a group of businessmen and institutions in Birmingham to provide equity and loan capital for companies not yet ready to go public. Finally, in 1969, with backing from a number of Scottish investment trusts the Edinburgh-based bank, Noble Grossart, was established; and the London-based merchant bank, Singer-Friedlander, also opened a Scottish branch.

The advantages to Scotland of a more fully developed indigenous merchant banking system should be fourfold. First, it will tend to retain interest-bearing bank deposits within Scotland; second, it is developing within Scotland a cadre of financial experts who will spread a greater awareness of financial techniques; third, the financial advice offered will be more directly geared to the requirements of local industry, and fourth, the influence of Scottish merchant banks in the field of rationalising industry by merger and take-over could be significant.

d) The Stock Exchange The Stock Exchange is the market place for the buying and selling of securities: it provides the link between the savers and the users of capital. It is on the Stock Exchange that both government and private industry raise large parts of their capital requirements: it is via the Stock Exchange that the large institutional investors—banks, investment and unit trusts and insurance companies—as well as the small private investor regulate and augment their investment portfolios. The London Stock Exchange is by far the largest in the country and is one of the major international exchanges. By comparison the volume of business transacted on the Scottish Stock Exchange is small but the Scottish Exchange has a number of distinguishing features.

The two sets of figures in Table 11.13 are not directly

[1] I.C.F.C. was set up in 1946 with funds provided by the Bank of England and the English and Scottish Banks to provide credit for businesses for which the existing sources of finance are not readily available.

Table 11.13 Stock Exchange Transactions

ALL TRANSACTIONS	1965	1966	1967	1968	1969
Scottish Exchange:					
Total Turnover (£m)	236	234	359	422	431
No. of Transactions (000)	245·5	225·6	268·9	320·1	274·1
Average size of transaction (£)	961	1,037	1,335	1,318	1,572
London Exchange:					
Total Turnover (£m)	20,847	21,590	35,956	31,976	30,391
No. of transactions (000)	4,361	4,145	5,006	6,523	5,788
Average size of transaction (£)	4,780	5,209	7,183	4,902	5,251
Scottish Turnover as per cent of London	1·1	1·1	1·0	1·3	1·4
ORDINARY SHARES ONLY					
Scottish Exchange:					
Total Turnover (£m)	158·0	152·0	244·3	328·1	300·8
No. of transactions (000)	197·5	174·7	213·4	258·6	214·3
Average size of transaction (£)	800	871	1,145	1,269	1,404
London Exchange:					
Total Turnover (£m)	3,479	3,566	5,804	9,118	8,713
No. of Transactions (000)	3,417	3,119	3,891	5,313	4,539
Average size of transaction (£)	1,018	1,143	1,492	1,716	1,920
Scottish Turnover as per cent of London	4·5	4·3	4·2	3·6	3·5

Source: Financial Statistics.

comparable. The figures for the London Stock Exchange represent the sum of both purchases and sales by stockbrokers, the transfer of a security from one client to another being counted as two deals. The figures for the Scottish Exchange treat a transfer between two Scottish brokers as one deal. There is therefore an unknown element of duplication between the two series. The table does, however, bring out a major difference between the two Exchanges, apart from size. London is predominantly a gilt-edged market, under a fifth of its business being in ordinary shares in some years, while Scotland is predominantly a market for ordinary shares.

Table 11.14 The Scottish Stock Exchange

	Members	Firms
Aberdeen	10	4
Dundee	8	4
Edinburgh	60	10
Glasgow	110	27
Paisley	2	1
Stirling	2	1
	192	47

This is because almost the whole of the gilt-edged business is in London and the government broker deals only on the London Exchange. As a result total turnover in the Scottish Exchange represents only one per cent of the national total, although around 5 per cent of transactions in ordinary shares take place in Scotland.

On 1st January 1964, the amalgamation took place of the four main Scottish exchanges, thereby making it possible for brokers to operate between Glasgow, Edinburgh, Aberdeen and Dundee, as though across a single floor. The result of this amalgamation has been to allow Scottish brokers to place more of their business locally, increase their commission earnings and invest in modern equipment and research. Investment in research is becoming increasingly important for stockbrokers. Scientific evaluation of the performance of public companies, thereby ensuring that funds are channelled to the most efficient companies on the cheapest terms, is a discipline which stockbrokers are becoming increasingly obliged to adopt. Such research is an expensive investment for brokers and for many is a relatively recent innovation.

The average size of a Scottish stockbroking firm is small compared to a London firm's. In 1964 the average Scottish firm had 3·3 members compared with 9·6 in London; by 1968 the average Scottish firm had risen to 4·1 members, but the average London firm had risen to 13·3 members. A large number of amalgamations have taken place in Scotland: whereas there were 62 firms of stockbrokers in 1964, presently there are only half that number. A corresponding reduction in the number of London firms has meant that the Scottish firms have been able to make no impression in terms of relative average size. In terms also of average turnover per member there is a substantial size gap between the London and Scottish Exchanges which on the basis of recent evidence does not appear to be closing.

Table 11.15 Average Turnover per Member (Ordinary Shares in brackets)

		£000		
		Scottish	London	Scottish per cent of London
1965	1st Half	589 (415)	2,635 (540)	22 (77)
	2nd Half	579 (366)	3,435 (499)	17 (73)
1966	1st Half	665 (477)	2,918 (651)	23 (73)
	2nd Half	532 (297)	3,634 (430)	15 (69)
1967	1st Half	824 (485)	6,163 (677)	13 (72)
	2nd Half	965 (178)	4,923 (1,102)	20 (62)

Overall, turnover per member on the Scottish Exchange is only about one fifth of the turnover per member on the London Exchange. When allowance is made for the large volume of turnover in gilt-edged on the London Exchange, turnover per member in Scotland is still no higher than three quarters of the level in London. There is undoubtedly an important job to be done by a Stock Exchange based in Scotland with its more intimate knowledge of local needs and conditions. With increasing sophistication in investment analysis, the question is whether Scottish stockbroking firms can achieve the size which will enable them to support the necessary research facilities.

e) Investment Trusts Investment trusts are not trusts in the real sense of the word; they are ordinary companies which own funds rather than factories. Their assets are held mainly in the form of shareholdings in other companies, which they buy and sell in what they believe to be the best interest of their shareholders. Investment trusts are themselves financed by ordinary and preference shares which can be bought and sold on the Stock Exchange at prices which vary with supply and demand. The market value of the holdings of investment trusts in the United Kingdom at the end of 1968 was £5,421·3 million, a sum almost double their 1963 holdings of £2,753·2 million.

The 196 largest British investment trusts held portfolios totalling £5,134·7 million in 1969; of this sum £1,705·1 million, or exactly one third, was held by investment trusts based in Scotland. Investment trusts originated in Scotland in the 1870s, the movement having its roots in Dundee and Edinburgh. The largest British trust, Alliance Trust with a 1969 portfolio of £136 million, is based in Dundee.

Table 11.16 Size and Distribution of Scottish and U.K. Investment Trusts in 1969

	Number of Trusts			
	Scotland		United Kingdom	
Portfolio (£m)	Number	Per cent of total	Number	Per cent of total
0–20	25	49·0	119	60·7
20–40	9	17·6	37	18·9
40–60	8	15·7	21	10·7
60–80	6	11·8	9	4·6
80–100	1	2·0	2	1·0
100 and over	2	3·9	8	4·1
Total	51	100·0	196	100·0

Source: Investors' Chronicle.

Half the Scottish trusts had portfolios of under £20 million compared with over 60 per cent of all British trusts; the average size of portfolio of a Scottish trust was £33·4 million, compared with a national average of £26·2 million. Despite this apparent difference in size, it is not possible to say in a strict statistical sense that the average Scottish trust is typically larger.

There are four main centres of trusts in Scotland—Edinburgh, Dundee, Glasgow and Aberdeen. Edinburgh is by far the largest, controlling funds of over £1,100 million. Dundee ranks second with £260 million of funds, ahead of Glasgow with £200 million and Aberdeen with £100 million.

As the Scottish managed element of the British trust movement is so large, we may well ask if there is evidence of any appreciable difference in the characteristics and performance of the Scottish trusts. In particular, we shall look in this section at their dollar portfolios, gearing, management rating and yield.

Investment trusts' holdings are almost entirely in equities; their holdings of preference shares and loan capital form only a very small part of their total holdings. For both Scottish trusts and U.K. trusts generally, their holdings of equities are not confined to British securities. Of the trusts' 1968 holdings of £5,420 million, just under £2,000 million or 37 per cent was held in overseas stocks and shares. Traditionally, the Scottish trusts have been large investors in North America; the names of many of the trusts reflect their strong transatlantic associations. For all trusts, their dollar portfolios account for 31 per cent of their holdings; the Scottish trusts' holdings of North American securities account for 37 per cent of their portfolios. However, as with the difference in average size, it is not possible to say that there is a statistically significant difference in the size of the Scottish trusts' dollar portfolio.

Gearing is often considered to be one of the prime functions of trust management and can provide a significant boost to successful investment policy. Gearing is the relationship between the sum of assets attributable to equity holders and the total of other capital such as preference shares and debentures. If the assets of a trust were £1 million, financed by means of £100,000 of preference capital and £150,000 of debentures, equity assets would total £750,000 and prior capital £250,000. The gearing ratio would be £750,000/£250,000 or $\frac{1}{3} = 33\frac{1}{3}$ per cent. Gearing exaggerates market fluctuations. In this example, equity assets will rise or fall by $33\frac{1}{3}$ per cent more than the fund as a whole. If assets increased to £1·3 million or 30 per cent, equity assets would rise to £1·05 million or by 40 per cent. There would be a proportionately greater fall in equity assets if the value of the fund were to fall. Investors, therefore, have a better chance of appreciation in the market value of their investments if they are holding higher-geared equities. Given a continuation of inflation gearing will benefit the ordinary share-holder over the long term. Gearing is normally expressed in the form of a ratio such as 1:1·25 which indicates that if total invested assets appreciate by 10 per cent, then the net asset value should appreciate by 12½ per cent. Gearing ratios varied widely in 1969 from as high as 1:1·45 to 1:0·82. The overall gearing ratio for all trusts was 1:1.09 and the Scottish trusts had exactly the same ratio.

Investment is becoming an increasingly complex and sophisticated activity and the financial press plays an important role in assessing the management performance of companies and institutions. One such method of assessment has been devised for investment trusts by the 'Investors Chronicle'. It is reached by comparing on a year-to-year basis the rise or fall in a trust's total assets, after allowing for capital changes, with the general trend of markets as measured by a widely based standard index such as the Financial Times—Actuaries All-Share Index. The Investors Chronicle 5 year average management rating in 1969 was +2·5 for all trusts and +2·25 for the Scottish trusts. In statistical terms, there has been no significant difference in the performance of Scottish trusts as against all trusts, when measured by this method of assessment.

As with ordinary public companies, an investment trust's capital is subscribed in the form of ordinary or preferred stock. Trusts pay dividends in the normal way and the yield can then be calculated. The yield, i.e. the ratio of the dividend to the current market price, is one of the most commonly used means of assessing a company's status. Generally speaking, the lower the yield, the higher is the opinion of a company held by the stock market. The average yield in 1969 on all trusts was 3·3 per cent, although some were yielding as much as 7 per cent and others as little as 1·6 per cent. The average yield on all Scottish trusts was 3·2 per cent, almost identical to the overall average. Confirmation of the yield as a good measure of management performance can be obtained by correlating the 'Investors Chronicle' management rating index and the yield and finding that for all trusts and for Scottish trusts there was a very close relationship between them. Whatever differences may have existed in the past between Scottish and English trusts now seem to have all but disappeared. Whether this has been achieved by the English trust conforming more closely to the practices of the Scottish trusts or vice versa, is a matter which perhaps only national pride can decide.

f) Unit Trusts A popular and, on the evidence of Table 11.11 on p. 276, perhaps the most rapidly growing form of saving is through unit trusts. Funds controlled by unit trusts have risen by four times from £370 million in 1963 to over £1,400 million in 1969. Unit trusts differ from investment trusts in that there is no fixed number of units in circulation. Units are bought and sold from the trust company and the number issued varies according to demand. The issue and repurchase prices of the units are calculated daily according to the actual value of the underlying shares.

It is much more difficult to identify the Scottish based element of the unit trust movement. Certain unit trusts are managed by investment trust companies; others are managed part in Scotland and part in England. Changes in management and changes in the names of trusts also make identification of the purely Scottish difficult.

The Scottish unit trusts are confined almost entirely to Edinburgh. The largest, Scotbits Securities Ltd, has funds of nearly £120 million and is managed by a large Scottish investment house. Other Scottish based unit trusts include Barclays Unicorn, Crescent Funds, Jascot Securities, Target Thistle and, in Glasgow, Clyde General and Clyde High Income, both owned by the M and G group. Funds controlled by Scottish based trusts at the end of 1968 totalled £146 million, around 10 per cent of the national total.

g) National Savings In addition to the various institutions in the private sector, the public sector also provides important channels for savings. The Post Office and Trustee Savings Banks are both long-established institutions; the introduction of Premium Bonds in the 1950s was a major innovation. As Table 11.17 shows, National Savings are typically the savings medium of the young, small investor.

The entry age into one of the National Savings schemes is substantially lower than for any of the commercial methods, as is the size of holding. Two thirds or more of all National Savings holdings are of less than £100. Table 11.11 on p. 276 also showed that National Savings is becoming a less popular channel for savings.

Table 11.17 Age and Size Distribution of Savers in the U.K. in 1969

		Age people start saving				
		Age Group				
	Numbers of savers in million	Under 20 (per cent)	Under 30 (per cent)	Under 40 (per cent)	41+ (per cent)	Median Entry Age
Post Office Savings Bank Account	15·0	64	21	7	8	16 years
Premium Bonds	14·8	17	19	22	42	20 years
Trustee Savings Bank Account	7·3	35	23	20	22	25 years
National Savings Certificates	6·0	48	19	16	17	25 years
Commercial Bank Deposit Accounts	9·6	33	33	16	18	32 years
Building Society Account	6·2	19	26	18	37	34 years
Stocks and Shares	3·6	7	28	34	31	35 years
Unit Trustholding	1·1	4	10	31	55	41 years

		Size of Savings				
		Distribution of Holdings				
	Per cent of population having	Up to £100 (per cent)	Up to £250 (per cent)	Up to £500 (per cent)	Up to £1,000 (per cent)	£1,000+ (per cent)
Post Office Savings Bank Account	37	87	9	3	1	—
Premium Bonds	37	94	4	2	—	—
Trustee Savings Bank Account	18	68	16	13	2	1
National Savings Certificates	15	64	17	11	6	2
Commercial Bank Deposit Account	23	45	26	18	6	5
Building Society Account	15	28	22	21	15	14
Stocks and Shares	6	33	18	13	9	27
Unit Trust Holdings	3	42	21	21	11	5

Source: Building Societies Association.

Over the last five years withdrawals from National Savings have been greater than the sums deposited with the result that the amount remaining in National Savings (including accrued interest) has been growing very slowly when compared with other forms of saving. Within the National Savings movement, only the Special Investment Department of the Trustee Savings Bank has been meeting the challenge from the building societies, unit trusts and other forms of saving. On p. 261 it was noted that the Trustee Savings Banks were more firmly established in Scotland than throughout the country as a whole. This is further borne out by the analysis given in Table 11.18 below of different forms of National Savings per head in Scotland and the United Kingdom as a whole.

Table 11.18 National Savings per head in £s

	1964	1965	1966	1967	1968	1969
Scotland:						
Balance Outstanding						
Trustee Savings Bank:						
Ordinary	37·0	37·9	37·5	37·7	37·0	35·7
Special Investment	34·3	37·2	40·9	44·2	47·8	50·2
Deposits						
Post Office Savings Bank	3·7	3·8	4·3	3·9	3·8	3·7
Purchases						
National Savings Certificates	3·4	2·3	7·7	5·9	4·6	4·1
Premium Bonds	0·8	0·8	0·8	0·9	1·1	1·1
United Kingdom:						
Balance Outstanding						
Trustee Savings Bank:						
Ordinary	10·3	18·9	19·6	19·2	19·5	19·4
Special Investment	14·7	17·0	18·8	20·7	22·5	24·1
Deposits						
Post Office Savings Banks	10·3	10·4	10·5	11·2	10·5	9·7
Purchases						
National Savings Certificates	2·8	3·0	2·3	7·2	5·7	4·2
Premium Bonds	1·4	1·7	1·8	1·6	1·8	2·3

Source: Annual Abstract of Statistics; Digest of Scottish Statistics.

The banking services offered by the National Savings movement, i.e. the Trustee Savings Bank, Ordinary and Special Deposit and the Post Office Savings Bank are much more intensively used in Scotland than elsewhere, whereas the more speculative aspects of National Savings, particularly Premium Bonds, are much less favoured by the Scots investor.

Most forms of public saving are more popular in Scotland than throughout the United Kingdom as a whole. This provides further confirmation of the point which emerged from the examination in Chapter 6 of holdings of wealth, that as well as being thrifty the Scot is also conservative in his saving habits.

Summary

A complex picture emerges from our study of financial institutions in Scotland. In the monetary field perhaps more than in any other aspect of economic activity, London exerts a dominant influence. London is still a major international financial centre. It is against such a central dominance that the Scottish financial institutions must be viewed. With the head offices of a number of investment trusts, insurance companies and banks, Edinburgh ranks as a major, perhaps the major, provincial financial centre in the country. Indeed, Charlotte Square in Edinburgh is reputed to be the richest square in the United Kingdom.

Yet despite the undoubted financial talents which exist in Scotland, there are some curious anomalies. The commercial banks have tended assiduously their 'ain kail yard', but the investment trusts have generally looked outside Scotland. While the commercial banks have by tradition drawn very definite lines governing the scope of their activities, until recently there has been little interest on the part of other institutions, particularly merchant banks, to step in where the commercial banks leave off. The reasons may lie in a lack of sufficient opportunity in Scotland for the specialist type of financial institution; or it may be that the proximity of London and its comprehensive range of financial services have prevented full development in certain fields.

While financial institutions are important for promoting economic growth, it is not possible to establish any clear relationship between their quantity and quality and the performance of the Scottish economy. Nor would it be appropriate to assess Scottish financial intermediaries on any narrow national grounds. There is little virtue, for example, in suggesting that Scottish investment trusts should redeploy their portfolios and invest a higher proportion of their funds in Scottish enterprise. If we take the efficient use of scarce resources as our benchmark, any such redeployment could well involve a less efficient overall use of scarce funds. The important point to take out of the actual deployment of funds is that investment trusts and other intermediaries would obviously invest more within Scotland if they saw that it was more profitable to do so. We saw in Chapter 4 that the structure of production in the Scottish economy has not been transformed at a sufficiently rapid pace. Private investors may therefore be unwilling to risk venture capital in Scottish firms until they see the reality of buoyant growth. The disquieting paradox, however, is that the rate of industrial change could well be stepped up if more private investment funds were to flow into, or remain in, Scotland as a complement to the public resources which are being ploughed into infra-structure investment and the like. We shall see this public activity at work in Chapter 13 in particular.

Recommended Reading

The Scottish Banks: A Modern Survey, M. Gaskin, Allen and Unwin, 1965.

Banking in Scotland, F. S. Taylor, Institute of Bankers in Scotland, 1956.

History of the Modern Banks of Issue, C. A. Conant, Pertnem, 1909.

Banking in Britain, Central Office of Information, 1968.

Report of the Committee on the Working of the Monetary System, H.M.S.O., Cmnd. 827, 1959.

'The New Face of Scottish Banking', *Scottish Bankers' Magazine*, August 1969.

'The Future of Bank Deposits', F. S. Taylor, *Scottish Bankers' Magazine*, Vol. LII, p. 200.

'The Scottish Banks: Where to Look for Deposits', F. S. Taylor, *The Banker*, April 1966.

'Scottish Branch Structure 1951–61', M. Gaskin, *Scottish Bankers' Magazine*, Vol. LIV, p. 29.

'Scottish Banks Under the Microscope', J. A. Macdonald, *The Banker*, April 1960.

'Scottish Banks in the 20th Century', F. S. Taylor, *The Bankers' Magazine*, January 1952.

'The Small Fry' (Building Societies), *Scotland*, June 1966.

'A Very Ordinary Business' (Investment Trusts), *Scotland*, February 1967.

'The Quiet Revolution of Merchant Banking in Scotland', *Scotland*, July 1967.

'The Changing Trade' (Stock Exchange), *Scotland*, February 1968.

'Competition and Credit Control', F. S. Taylor, *Scottish Bankers' Magazine*, August, 1971.

'The Scottish Stock Exchange', I. M. Fyfe, *The Three Banks Review*, June, 1971.

Part 4: Regional Issues and Policies

Chapter 12
Regional Economics

In recent years a whole new branch of economics has evolved in which the focus of interest is the economy of a region. Regional economics tries to take account of space or location, to recognise explicitly that all economic activity cannot take place in one location and that different locations impose difference costs on the entrepreneur. In this Chapter we bring together some of the analysis of Parts 1 and 2 of this book in terms of some of the more important elements of regional economics.

First we ask how a region is to be defined, then ask what types of problem occur in a region. In section 3 of the Chapter we examine the calculus of costs and benefits that determine the location of economic activity in a region, and look at location theory, transport costs, and the other determinants of location that have been discussed and tested in regional economic theory and policy. The concepts of growth points and the regional multiplier are then examined, and in the final section we look at an assessment of regional economies which takes the level of unemployment in a region as the benchmark for determining whether the region is one in which the level of aggregate demand is deficient.

Although we use the phrase 'regional economics' extensively in this Chapter in many ways it implies too restrictive a definition. An important feature of the study of regional economics is its inter-disciplinary character. Sociology, demography, geography, physical planning and history are all disciplines which have a contribution to make, at least as important as that of economics, to a subject which might more properly be known as 'regional science' or 'regional analysis'. Indeed, it is through the study of regions that the closest and most fruitful co-operation between these disciplines has been achieved. In Scotland, we have perhaps made as much progress in this direction as anywhere in the world. The studies of the Lothians, Falkirk-Grangemouth, the

Central Borders, North East Scotland and Tayside have achieved a harmony and unity of purpose between social scientists and planners which might otherwise never have existed.

1 Regional definition

What is meant by a region? The economist may not be as concerned as the geographer or physical planner with the precise delineation of a region, but the use of the term 'regional economics' does imply that the economist is now interested in examining areas which are smaller than the national whole. It is possible to define a region in one of three ways, according to certain characteristics. First, a region may be defined on the basis of the homogeneity of one or a combination of its physical, economic, social or other characteristics. Within the United Kingdom, Scotland or Wales may be regarded as large homogeneous regions because they are defined by reference to some common ethnic, historical, cultural or legal characteristic. The people who live in Scotland are called Scots, they share a common heritage and are subject to the same Scots law: therefore, Scotland may be termed a region. In much the same way, it is possible to define the Breton region of France or the Basque region of Spain. Within Scotland, the Highlands may also be defined as a region on the grounds of homogeneity, this time because of a common physical characteristic.

Second, a region may be defined in terms of its relationship with a node or pole. A large city will act as the node or pole for its surrounding region. The factors linking a region to its node are complex, but will include such elements as reliance on it for employment, for major shopping, social and cultural activities, for higher education and for specialised business and commercial services. Often the circulation area of a city's newspaper or the reception area of a local television service provide a useful measure of the size of the region. The boundaries of such regions may be indeterminate and there may be considerable areas of overlap between them. The London area is the prime example of a nodal or polar region in this country and, indeed, most capital cities have their own clearly established regions. Within Scotland, the main cities of Glasgow, Edinburgh, Dundee and Aberdeen act as the nodal points for their respective regions.

Finally, a region may be defined in terms of its programming—or policy-orientation. By this is meant that a region may be defined in terms of its political or administrative boundaries. These boundaries provide the political or administrative framework within which programmes or policies for regional development may be implemented. This type of region is most commonly found in countries which are organised along federal lines, e.g. the United States or West Germany. While the federal legislature may provide the means of co-ordination and implementation of regional measures, arbitrary political or administrative boundaries may cut across regions which might more properly be defined in terms of some homogeneous physical or economic characteristic. By virtue of the considerable devolution of Government departments, Scotland may be defined as a region in this third sense as well. Indeed, certain of the measures of regional development, particularly in the field of infrastructure investment, are administered by Scottish-based departments. Even so, there are areas, particularly the Eastern Borders and Northumberland, which share common economic problems but are administered separately from opposite sides of the Border.

Defining administrative regions has been a major problem in England, since the creation of the regional economic Planning Councils and Boards in 1965.[1] Before then, the collection and publication of much of the demographic and economic data essential for regional planning had been based on a set of standard regions whose origins were mainly those of administrative convenience. The change to Planning Regions and the attempt to achieve a greater degree of regional homogeneity brought considerable changes in boundaries, particularly in the North of England. Successful implementation of regional programmes requires the creation of some form of regional identity or coherence which has by no means been firmly established in England.

2 Types of Regional Problem

If the definition of a region falls under one or more of three possible characteristics so too does the type of regional problem studied by regional analysts. Regions may be classified broadly into three types. First, there is the region which has a large primary or agricultural sector. Improvements in productivity on the land release factors of production, particularly labour, for employment in other sectors of the economy. If the region is not to suffer excessively from outward migration, its problem is then to provide alternative employment in the manufacturing or service sectors for workers displaced from the primary sector. Southern Italy and some of the Northern parts of Scandinavia are European

[1] For a fuller discussion of these bodies see Chapter 13.

examples of this type of region which is essentially suffering from under-development.

A second type of regional problem is to be found in older industrial areas. Here the original industrial structure has gone into decline, due either to the exhaustion of a basic raw material, e.g. coal or to an increasing obsolescence in its pattern of output. Many regions which developed at an early stage of the Industrial Revolution have increasingly found themselves in the 20th century with an outdated industrial structure. Allied to the industrial problem is linked invariably an environmental problem. Coal bings, waste tips, pollution from industrial effluent, sub-standard housing and social capital generally are to be found to a greater or lesser extent in these areas.

Scotland's regional problem is generally conceived in such terms. As we have seen in Chapter 4, Scotland's industrial structure developed from an early stage of the Industrial Revolution. This development was based on a few staple industries—coal, iron and steel, heavy engineering and textiles. When Britain's economic power was at its zenith in the 19th century, Scotland benefitted considerably from her early development. But this commitment to a few staple industries meant that Scotland failed to develop new specialisms on any substantial scale, so that with changing technology and changing patterns of demand, Scotland has found herself with a structure of industry which has become increasingly less appropriate to 20th century conditions. Scotland has not been alone in this respect. Within the United Kingdom, North East and North West England and South Wales have experienced essentially the same type of problem. Overseas examples of this type of region are to be found in certain areas of northern France, in the Belgian coalfield and the Appalachian region in the United States.

Finally, a third type of regional problem may arise as the result of rapid, perhaps even excessive growth, thereby creating problems of congestion within the region of growth and problems of imbalance in other regions of the economy. The solutions applied to this type of regional problem vary between countries. In the United Kingdom, for example, where London and the South East has for the greater part of this century been the fastest growing region, the answer has been effectively to extend the boundaries of the region by constructing a ring of New Towns around London. The current strategy for the South East envisages major expansion at a number of already established towns and cities but all of them within the sphere of influence of

London. In France, by contrast, the policy has been to counteract the growth of Paris by the creation of a number of 'metropoles d'equilibre' in major provincial centres. Over time, these centres will develop the industrial, social and educational facilities to lessen the country's massive over dependence on Paris. In Holland, it has been recognised that the major port and industrial developments on the west coast are leading to a regional imbalance in the eastern and northern regions which it is now intended to counterbalance.

Elements of all three types of regional problem exist in Scotland. With its heavy dependence on primary industry and its comparatively small manufacturing sector, the Highlands can be seen as an underdeveloped region exemplifying the first type. It is only with the establishment in 1965 of the Highlands and Islands Development Board that an effective regional development organisation has been created in the Highlands.[1] The regional problem which predominantly characterises Scotland is however, the second type, that of a mature industrialised region which requires a substantial measure of diversification in its industrial base. At several points in this book, and particularly in Chapter 4, we have seen the extent to which the former domination of the Scottish economy by coal mining and heavy industry has been lessened in recent years. This process of transformation is by no means complete. The second half of the 19th century saw the rapid growth and development of the metropolis of Glasgow: the second half of the 20th century will see its planned reduction and dispersal. All the features of the third type of regional problem—over-rapid and over-intensive development—are to be found in Glasgow. Its aftermath has been appalling and will require the largest voluntary migration of people ever seen in this country to rectify. A main reason for the building of New Towns in Scotland has been to create communities in which a large proportion of the population which is being overspilled from Glasgow can be housed and employed.

3 Factors Influencing Location

The first systematic attempt to take account of locational factors was the work of a German, von Thünen, writing in the 1820s about The Isolated State. He developed an analysis of the spatial distribution of agricultural production in relation to a large town situated in the middle of a fertile plain. From his simple but rigorous model he developed propositions about cost

[1] The H.I.D.B. is discussed in Chapter 13.

in relation to distance from the market, and he expounded a theory of economic rent based on differences in situation and transport cost. The first comprehensive attempt to set up a general theory of industrial location had to wait, however, for another century, and was the work of another German, Alfred Weber. He sought to explain location of industry on the basis of transport and labour costs. With a given set of markets for its produce and fixed sources of supply of labour, a firm would locate at a point which minimised its transport costs. Whether this point of minimum transport cost was nearer the source of raw materials or nearer the market would depend on the nature of the product and whether it gained or lost weight in the process of production. With Weber's assumption that the locations of the supply of labour were fixed, a firm might have to locate away from its point of minimum transport cost in order to be as close as necessary to the supply of labour. The more heavily dependent the firm was on labour, the closer it would locate to the source of supply and the higher might be the divergence from its point of minimum transport cost.

There were a number of weaknesses in Weber's approach. First he claimed that transport and labour costs are the only general factors determining location. We shall see shortly that there are a whole range of factors which firms may take into account when making decisions as to where to locate. Weber also presented his analysis exclusively in terms of the effects of location on a firm's costs. He did not appreciate that a particular location may also affect a firm's revenues. In a study of locational factors which we shall be discussing shortly, there is evidence that certain firms have in the past chosen not to locate in Scotland because of a fear that their revenues might be adversely affected. *The optimum location for a firm need not necessarily be the point of minimum cost: it should be the location at which the difference between the firm's costs and revenues is a maximum.* In this sense, the theory of optimal location may be compared with the theory of the firm, where the firm will seek to produce a level of output at which its profits are a maximum. There is only one level of output which satisfies that condition and there is only one location which is optimal for the firm. Recently, however, economists have argued that profit-maximisation is rather too restrictive an assumption and that businessmen may seek to achieve only what they regard as a satisfactory level of profit, which may fall well short of a maximum. So too with location, businessmen may be perfectly happy to arrive at a satisfactory location which does not impose unacceptable costs of production or where their revenues are not adversely affected, although there may be other locations which, in theory at least, they ought to prefer.

The problem can be illuminated by examining some of the empirical work on location which has been carried out. Theories of industrial location have been formulated in the context of a market economy, i.e. that each firm is free to choose its own location. In the United Kingdom since 1945 a system of control has been exercised over the location of industry by the use of Industrial Development Certificates (I.D.C.).[1] Any firm wishing to expand or relocate its premises by more than a specified minimum (ranging at various times between 3,000 and 10,000 sq. ft.) must obtain an I.D.C. from the Government before it can do so. By witholding I.D.C.s from firms wishing to expand in the prospering regions and only granting them if the firms undertake to relocate in Development Areas, the Government has been able to effect a considerable redistribution of industry over the last twenty-five years. That firms have relocated away from their own chosen locations and that they have continued in existence means, at the very least, that the costs incurred at their new locations have not been penal. There has in fact been a considerable amount of financial assistance offered to them by the Government to meet the costs of relocation.[2]

In a major study of industrial location in the United Kingdom, W. F. Luttrell concluded that the great bulk of manufacturing industry in the United Kingdom was footloose in the sense that it could operate satisfactorily in any of the major centres of the country. His estimate was that about two thirds of British manufacturing industry employing about six million people is potentially mobile in this sense.

Further evidence that the Government's I.D.C. policy has not had an inhibiting influence on industrial location is given by a study undertaken by the Board of Trade in 1966. Between 1958 and 1963, 4,934 I.D.C. were approved in the South East of England; 452 were rejected but of these 174 were subsequently approved. 278 applications or 5·3 per cent of the total were completely rejected. Of these 278 rejected applications the Board of Trade were able to analyse the subsequent behaviour of 239 projects. A number of solutions were adopted by the firms concerned but in only 10 per cent of cases was the project completely abandoned. 92 firms, accounting for nearly half the factory space

[1] The I.D.C. system is discussed more fully in the next chapter.

[2] The various forms of regional financial incentives are discussed in the following chapter.

concerned, decided to move to a new location; a further 92 accounting for one third of the factory space decided to develop by other means at or close to their location in South East England: the remaining 22 firms overcame their shortage of accommodation either by reorganising into larger groups or by arrangements unspecified to the Board of Trade.

Of the 33 projects which were abandoned, 8 were entirely speculative in character and were bound to be abandoned once an I.D.C. had been refused; of the remaining 25, all but 7 were influenced by factors other than the rejection of their I.D.C. In only 7 projects accounting for 1·7 per cent of the factory space, was there evidence that abandonment of the project was due principally to the refusal of an I.D.C.

92 firms decided to move to a new location and of these 65 were to locations acceptable to the Board of Trade on distribution of industry grounds. Not all of these firms moved outside South East England; 18 went to London overspill towns and 13 to less congested parts of South East England. 26 firms underwent what might be regarded as long distance moves to government assisted areas. 6 went to Scotland, 6 to Merseyside, 5 to North East England, 3 to South Wales and the others were distributed to a variety of locations in the United Kingdom. Four of these 26 had closed down their Development Area factories by 1966 so that the net result of these moves from the South East to a number of Development Areas was the construction of around 2 million sq. ft. of factory space and the provision of some 8,000 jobs. The Board of Trade analysis does not indicate whether mortality increases with the distance moved, so that we do not know if there were fewer closures among firms moving shorter distances.

As we shall see in Chapter 13, significant changes took place in regional policy between 1958 and 1963; the intensity with which the government has applied its I.D.C. policy has also varied over time, as have financial aids. Because of this, at best one can say that the evidence is that I.D.C. policy has had a very small absolute deterrent effect on industrial development, it has achieved a considerable measure of relocation, although it may be questioned if a more rigorous policy would have achieved an appreciably greater measure of redistribution. Suffice it to say that the factors confining a firm to a specific location do not appear to be particularly strong.

What, then, may be said about the factors which do influence the location of industry? Transport costs are one obvious element and a great deal of formal theory has been constructed on this basis. In its simplest form this theory says that a firm will locate at a point which minimises the sum of (a) the costs of producing the product and (b) the costs of distributing the product to its markets. Transportation costs do not necessarily increase in direct proportion to distance. Generally speaking, costs per mile are lower for longer hauls. Then there are terminal costs, i.e. the costs of loading and unloading. Different forms of transport have different terminal costs: or indeed, the same form of transport may have different terminal costs at different locations. The variations, for example, in port charges and in the efficiency of cargo handling equipment may make terminal costs lower at certain ports rather than at others.

A particular form of terminal costs, transhipment costs, may have major implications for Scotland in the future. Many cities have grown as a result of being transhipment centres for bulk cargoes. London, for example, is a transhipment point for many commodities—tea, sugar, coffee, wool and others. These commodities are brought by sea to London, landed, graded and processed, exchanged in specialised markets and finally distributed to their ultimate markets.

For certain commodities, particularly petroleum and mineral ores, tremendous reductions in transport costs have been effected in recent years by the construction of super-tankers. The charter rate per dead weight ton for a tanker of 300,000 tons deadweight is approximately half the rate for a tanker of 50,000 tons and there are further reductions for tankers going up to 500,000 tons. A consequence of the increasing size of tanker is that fewer and fewer ports have the depth of water to accommodate vehicles of 250,000 tons and upwards. Because of the shallow depth of the English Channel and the North Sea access by super tankers to the ports of Western Europe is becoming increasingly difficult. Scotland enjoys a unique advantage in possessing on her western seaboard, and particularly in the Clyde estuary, deep-water inshore anchorages to accommodate such large vessels. The implications of this unique natural resource were emphasised in a recent report entitled 'Oceanspan'. This envisages Scotland becoming a major transhipment and processing area of bulk commodities, not only for the rest of the United Kingdom but for North West Europe as well. Major developments in internal communications and in sea and air linkages with Europe would be necessary to allow this strategy to achieve its full potential.

Very little evidence is available about the incidence of transport costs on industrial location in Scotland. One study was carried out by the Toothill Report in 1961. From a sample of both indigenous Scottish firms and of immigrant firms, it appeared that the majority had transport costs of less than 2 per cent of sales. For only 5 per cent of Scottish firms and 15 per cent of immigrant firms did transport costs exceed 5 per cent of sales. The immigrant firms were further asked to compare their transport costs at their Scottish location with transport costs at their parent location in the south. 64 per cent found their transport costs higher in Scotland, 26 per cent found them the same and 10 per cent found them lower. Overall, the Report's conclusion was that transport costs were relatively unimportant so far as new industry coming into Scotland was concerned.

Of the 100 or so U.S. firms which have come to Scotland since the war[1] a substantial number have come to take advantage of Scotland's unique transport facilities. In no other part of the United Kingdom, nor indeed anywhere in Europe, do major east and west coast port facilities lie within 30 miles of each other as is the case in Central Scotland with the ports of Grangemouth and Leith in the east and Glasgow in the west. In addition, at Prestwick, Scotland has the country's second largest air terminal which is now handling a rapidly increasing volume of air freight. One major U.S. company in Scotland is on the record as saying that Scotland is now a more logical location from which to serve world markets for its product than its parent location in the United States.

Cameron and Reid have taken a more general view of the factors influencing industrial location in Scotland. In a study of a number of companies which examined sites for a new location in Scotland but eventually located elsewhere in the United Kingdom, they identified sixteen factors which might have been of importance to companies in their decision to select a site. These factors are listed below in order of the frequency with which they were mentioned by the companies interviewed.

They found themselves in agreement with the Toothill Report that most companies would find suppliers at competitive prices in Scotland and that high value or easily transported goods would not create severe incremental distributive costs for companies choosing to locate in Scotland. Few of the companies approached by Cameron and Reid were worried about increased costs as a result of being at a greater distance from their main suppliers. Most of them were large companies able to enforce favourable rates on their suppliers.

[1] See Chapter 4.

Table 12.1 Factors in site selection

Ranking	Factor
1	Supply of trainable labour
2	Accessibility to main markets
	Local authority co-operation
4	Transport facilities for goods
5	Good local management/labour relations
	Fully serviced site
	Ready built factory
8	Accessibility to linked producers
	Factory rents
	Attractiveness of local environment for transferred key workers and executives
12	Transport facilities for personnel
	Accessibility to main suppliers
	Local technical educational facilities
	Co-operation from local locating agencies
16	High productivity of local labour
Not mentioned by any firm	Low local labour rates

Source: Cameron and Reid: 'Scottish Economic Planning and the Attraction of Industry' University of Glasgow Occasional Papers No. 6, 1966.

Where they did differ from the Toothill Report, was on the grounds that the Toothill emphasis was entirely on transport *costs*, while Cameron and Reid found in most of the companies they interviewed concern that company *revenue* might be affected adversely by locating in Scotland. There are companies which, although they probably never thought of it specifically in these terms, anticipate a significant change in the elasticity of demand for their product as a result of locating in Scotland. In other words, by moving to Scotland, these companies would expect to lose certain customers; this, of course, may be offset by gaining new customers as a result of a move.

A second point of criticism was that although in *absolute* terms it can be accepted that the incidence of transport costs in Scotland is low, what is important are the *incremental* transport costs of a location in Scotland as compared with a location in another Development Area. If transport costs amount to only 2 per cent of sales in Scotland but to only 1 per cent at a location in, say, the North of England, then the incremental transport costs in Scotland are 100 per cent greater. These are important analytical points which can readily be identified in the marginal analysis economists use.

What Cameron and Reid did establish is that there are other factors to which firms would give at least equal weight in arriving at their decision. Although from Table 12.1, labour costs do not seem to figure in their calculations, the availability of trainable labour is rated as an extremely important factor. In Chapter 3 and elsewhere we have noted the existence of above average reserves of labour in Scotland as evidenced by high unemployment and low activity rates, particularly among females. Care must be exercised in interpreting such figures because what the unemployment figures do not reveal for example is the quality of people registered as being available for employment. A survey of the unemployed carried out in 1964 by the then Ministry of Labour suggested that only one fifth of the unemployed in Scotland at that time would have no difficulty in getting work; a quarter would have difficulty because of lack of local opportunity to match their qualifications; and over half would have difficulty in obtaining work on personal grounds such as age, physical or mental handicaps, prison record and so on. As we shall see later in this chapter measuring the demand for labour by comparing vacancies with numbers unemployed can be misleading unless care is taken in interpretation. Generally speaking, however, most firms coming to Scotland have found adequate reserves of trainable labour, although shortages do exist in certain key trades. A major part of regional policy, as we shall see in the next chapter, has been to assist directly and financially with the training and redeployment of surplus labour in Development Areas.

Much of the growth of employment in Scotland in recent years has been among female workers. The potential supply of female workers is difficult to measure as the female unemployment records of the Department of Employment considerably understate the numbers of women who are available for employment but who are not registered as unemployed. There is no effective way in which this potential can be measured except by detailed surveys in particular areas. One such survey revealed that in the county of Midlothian the number of women at work had risen by 25 per cent between 1961 and 1966 and that a further 30 per cent of women not currently working have a definite interest in employment, most of them on a part-time basis.

The availability of a site and/or a factory has been an important locational factor. Many firms, having made the decision to relocate, wish to get into production as soon as possible. A high proportion of footloose industry is of such a nature that its requirements for factory space can often be met by the provision of standard multi-purpose factories following an orthodox pattern of layout and design. An important element of British regional policy has been the construction of what are known as 'advance' factories, i.e. factories built in advance of demand and which are immediately available for a prospective tenant. Individual local authorities and New Town Development Corporations have authority to build advance factories as well as the Government.

We can conclude from this examination of the factors which affect location that a wide range of factors, many of them highly subjective, will enter into a businessman's locational decision. Location theory has sought to formalise these decisions by means of transport and production costs. While there may be occasions on which transport costs are important, perhaps critical, to a location decision this does not happen sufficiently frequently to serve as the basis of a general theory. It follows then that policy may have no precise basis in accepted theory. Two stories, perhaps apocryphal, may serve to illustrate the point. The first concerns a study of New England in which it was found that a firm in Worcester would clearly have been better off in Boston: the reason for its location in Worcester, it was discovered, was that the owners' mother-in-law lived there and his wife insisted on living in the same city. The second relates to an American firm now located in a town in the North East of Scotland which claims that it floated into that town on the tide of the provost's whisky!

4 Growth points

The concept which perhaps bridges the gap most successfully between location theory and regional economics is the growth pole or growth point. The basic idea of growth points is that economic activity tends to concentrate round a small number of focal points. The stronger the nodal characteristic of a region, i.e. the stronger the relationship of a region to its nodal point, the higher its growth rate and level of social and economic development is likely to be. In this situation, regional plans will tend to be more successful if they reinforce the natural nodal characteristics already in evidence in a region. The exception to this general approach is where the nodal centre is already so large and congested that further growth will tend to produce severe diseconomies.

Credit for evolving this concept is generally given to the French regional scientist, François Perroux. As early as 1951, however, a committee under Professor (now Sir Alec) Cairncross examining industrial problems in Scotland advocated that the relief of unemployment should not be the exclusive aim of regional policy but that attention should be paid to the stimulation of growth at selected points offering the best prospects for growth. This view was reiterated in 1961 by the Toothill Report which again made the case for the Government concentrating its resources in a limited number of growth areas. These areas are characterised by industries with a high degree of concentration, high income elasticity of demand for their products, and an advanced level of technology and expertise. In order that these areas should attain their growth potential the Toothill Report argued that the Government should concentrate infrastructure investment to provide the communications, housing, educational facilities, environmental standards and so on necessary for industrial growth. The Government responded in 1963 by designating eight such areas in Central Scotland—the five new towns of East Kilbride, Cumbernauld, Glenrothes, Livingston and Irvine plus the Vale of Leven, North Lanarkshire and Falkirk/Grangemouth. The new towns are obvious focal points of new industrial growth to which it is important to give every inducement to expand; the Vale of Leven, which lies between Dumbarton and Loch Lomond, has attracted a considerable amount of U.S. investment since the war; North Lanarkshire is the site of the major part of the Scottish steel industry including the steel strip mill at Ravenscraig and of a number of major industrial estates, and Falkirk/Grangemouth is the home of a major petro-chemicals complex as well as Scotland's aluminium rolling and castings industries. In a number of sub-regional studies carried out in Scotland in recent years, for example in the Central Borders and the North East, the principal recommendation has been for concentration of effort at one or a limited number of selected points.

The growth point concept endeavours to provide an explicit reasoned basis for regional policy, through concentrating public resources into an area which is then intended to become a focus for private location of economic activity. As we shall see in Chapter 13, the growth point policy adopted in 1963 has not been followed consistently. Policy has wavered between spreading the jam thinly and giving the growth points the lion's share of the resources and the incentives.

5 The Regional Multiplier

A tool of economic analysis which should be familiar to all students of economics is the multiplier. This was outlined in Chapter 1. Originally designed as a means of measuring the final effects at the national level of an initial injection of money, economists are increasingly turning their attention to measuring the size of the multiplier at the regional level.

In the simple form of the multiplier which we discussed in Chapter 1 there is assumed to be only one leak from the initial injection of funds—the savings leak. People can either spend or save their additional income. The greater the proportion they spend, the greater will be the multiplier effect. Conversely, the greater the proportion they save, the smaller will be the multiplier effect, i.e. the greater will be the leak. It is worth repeating here the formal version of the concept.

The multiplier is expressed as either (a) the reciprocal of 1 minus the marginal propensity to consume, i.e. $\frac{1}{1-\text{M.P.C.}}$ or (b) the reciprocal of the marginal propensity to save, i.e. $\frac{1}{\text{M.P.S.}}$

Where the marginal propensity to consume is high, say, nine tenths, the multiplier will be correspondingly large, in this case $\frac{1}{1-0{\cdot}9} = 10$ or $\frac{1}{0{\cdot}1} = 10$. The final increase in income will therefore be 10 times the size of the initial injection of money into the system. With a lower marginal propensity to consume, say two thirds, the value of the multiplier would be 3.

More advanced multiplier models take account of other leakages from the system in the form of direct taxation and National Insurance contributions, indirect taxation, imported consumer goods and the decline in transfer payments which would arise from the rising level of income.

When seeking to measure the size of the regional multiplier, the various leakages of a national character must be allowed for. In addition to these, other leakages will arise at the purely regional level which will have the effect of reducing the size of the regional multiplier below that of the national multiplier.

The main factor affecting the size of the regional multiplier will be the amount of capital and consumer goods which are imported into the region from other regions as a result of the initial injection of funds. If the injection of funds takes the form, say, of the construction of a section of motorway in a particular region, the additional capital equipment in the form of bulldozers, earthscrapers and so on may well originate outwith the region. Even if local people are employed on the project, their additional purchases may be of goods which are produced outside the region. The larger and more diversified the region, the smaller this form of leakage is likely to be, but undoubtedly some of the additional expenditure will leak outside the region.

There is a considerable amount of agreement among the various estimates of regional multipliers. Professor G. C. Archibald has put them in the range 1·2–1·7 with a 'best guess' of 1·25 for a typical standard region of the United Kingdom. Professor A. J. Brown estimates a value of 1·28 for the Development Areas as a whole against a national multiplier of 1·46. K. J. Allen (whose Scottish multiplier we shall examine shortly) estimates a figure of 1·4–1·5 for Scotland, and M. A. Greig has recently estimated a multiplier for the pulp and paper mill at Fort William of 1·44–1·54. There are differences in method and assumption between these estimates but they all produce regional multipliers of the same order of magnitude. Moreover, the smallness of the size of the multiplier indicates the magnitude of the leaks at the regional level.

Allen's estimate of a multiplier for Scotland takes the following leaks into account.

1. Savings (s)
2. Payment of taxes (direct and indirect) and National Insurance (t)
3. Purchases of goods produced in other regions and countries (p)

The regional multiplier thus becomes

$$k_r = \frac{1}{s+t+p}$$

Allen estimates personal income for Scotland in 1961 at £1,919 million (see Chapter 6 for methods of estimating personal income in Scotland). The two categories of leaks from this income are those which reduce personal income and those which are a function of Scottish expenditure on purchases from outside Scotland. Because of insufficient data, Allen estimates these leaks by applying United Kingdom or British data on a Scottish scale.

On a first round application of rather crude and inexact ratios and proportions to Scotland, the following set of leaks are estimated

	£ million
Direct taxes	189·9
National Insurance contributions	90·2
Indirect taxes	174·4
Imports from abroad	142·4
Savings	160·2
Imports from other regions	128·9
	886·0

Of a Scottish personal income of £1,919 million, £886 million, 46·2 per cent, leaks. For every £100 injected into Scotland only £53·8 would remain on the basis of these assumptions. The value of the multiplier derived from this data is 2·2. By applying a number of refinements to the elements in his initial assessment and by estimating the amount of its output that Scottish industry buys outside Scotland in the form of raw materials and components, Allen finally estimates the Scottish multiplier to be of the order of 1·4–1·5.

The fact that regional multipliers, not only the Scottish one, are low means that the leaks are correspondingly high. Trying to solve a regional problem in this case is like filling a bath with the plug out. Much of the expenditure in Scotland may spill over into regions which are already experiencing inflationary pressure. Nevertheless, the regional multiplier is an important analytical and forecasting tool which has had insufficient attention in Scotland. A more detailed understanding of the size and nature of a Scottish multiplier could have important lessons for regional policy in Scotland.

6 Unemployment and demand deficiency

In Chapter 1, we saw that there was a certain analogy between the flows of trade on an international scale and the flows between regions. A region could be regarded as having a balance of payments deficit in exactly the same way as a nation. However, while a nation must sooner or later find some means of correcting a balance of payments deficit, a region can remain indefinitely in such a situation. A region with a balance of payments deficit will experience depressed demand and high unemployment. In this section, we look a little more closely at conditions in Scotland to establish whether Scotland is experiencing a deficiency of demand which would be consistent with a balance of payments deficit. In carrying out this appraisal, much use has been made of a study of regional problems in the United Kingdom undertaken by the National Institute for Economic and Social Research.

The regional statistics which are available do not allow us to measure directly whether or not Scotland is experiencing a balance of payments deficit. At best, we can study certain of the features of the Scottish economy to assess if they are consistent with Scotland having such a deficit.

A characteristic of a region with an adverse balance of payments is that, as a consequence of the imperfect mobility of labour, it will experience a relatively high level of unemployment. As we have seen in Chapter 3 one of the main features of the Scottish economy for many years has been a level of unemployment substantially higher than the national average. We must now examine the nature of Scotland's unemployment rather more closely to see if it does indeed reflect a deficiency in the demand for labour.

Variations in the level of unemployment can arise from seasonal factors or from changes in the level of economic activity at different stages of the business cycle. Once these factors are identified, the basic or underlying rate of unemployment can then be measured. This has been done by economists working at the National Institute of Economic and Social Research, and their results are presented in the following table.

Table 12.2 Components of Male Unemployment, 1958–67

Region	Total Unemployment Rate (per cent)	Seasonal Rate	Cyclical Rate	Basic Rate	Basic as per cent of total
North	3·27	0·30	0·77	2·20	67·3
Midlands and Yorkshire	1·32	0·14	0·39	0·79	59·8
East and South	1·37	0·23	0·26	0·89	65·0
London and South East	1·29	0·15	0·29	0·86	66·7
South West	1·87	0·31	0·31	1·25	66·9
North West	2·24	0·15	0·57	1·51	67·4
Wales	2·77	0·32	0·56	1·89	68·2
Scotland	3·62	0·31	0·60	2·71	74·9

Source: National Institute Economic Review: November 1968.

While for most regions except the Midlands and Yorkshire, the basic rate of male unemployment has been around two thirds of total unemployment, in Scotland the basic rate is considerably higher at three quarters the total rate. A similar pattern emerges for female workers where although the absolute levels of unemployment are lower in all regions, again the basic rate in Scotland at 77·3 per cent of the total rate is the highest for any region.

A further refinement of this approach developed by the National Institute has been to compute what they have called 'structural plus frictional' unemployment. To do this they calculated the level of unemployment which might be expected to exist in each region if the numbers of unemployed and the numbers of unfilled vacancies were equal. The ratio of unemployed to unfilled vacancies can be taken as a measure, though not a particularly satisfactory one, of the level of demand for labour.[1] If the number of unemployed exceeds the number of vacancies then demand may be said to be low and vice versa. By attempting to compute a level of unemployment at which the numbers of unemployed and vacancies are equal, the National Institute calculated what might be described as the zero level of deficiency (or excess) of demand for labour. This level of unemployment will reflect only frictional unemployment, i.e. unemployment originating from people in the process of moving between jobs and structural unemployment, i.e. unemployment which is a function of the structure of industry in the region. Table 12.3 presents this data.

Table 12.3 Structural and Frictional Unemployment and Average Unemployment 5 (per cent)

	North	Midlands	Yorks. and Lincs.	East and South	London and South East
ural and frictional ployment (1)	1·62	0·90	1·01	1·18	1·04
ge unemployment (2)	3·52	1·31	1·60	1·33	1·28
a per cent of (2)	46·0	68·6	63·1	88·8	81·2
en:					
ural and frictional ployment (3)	1·24	0·79	0·86	0·92	0·86
ge unemployment (4)	1·99	0·72	0·81	0·65	0·55
per cent of (4)	62·3	109·7	106·1	141·5	156·3

	South West	North West	Wales	Scotland
ural and frictional ployment (1)	1·23	1·28	1·77	1·68
ge unemployment (2)	1·74	2·33	2·67	3·75
a per cent of (2)	70·7	55·0	66·2	44·8
en:				
ural and frictional ployment (3)	1·10	1·10	1·52	1·73
ge unemployment (4)	1·05	1·26	2·02	2·46
per cent of (4)	104·7	87·3	75·3	70·3

e: National Institute Economic Review, November 1968.

From the table it can be seen that for the period 1962–5, the structural and frictional level of male unemployment was below the average level of unemployment in all regions. The two

[1] This is because employers may not notify vacancies to the Department of Employment or, if labour is in short supply, they may considerably overstate their vacancies in the hope of recruiting a sufficient number of workers.

most nearly approached equality in the East and South of England and in London and the South East. In the North and North West of England and particularly in Scotland, the divergence was at its greatest. This means that in these regions was to be found the greatest 'deficiency' in the demand for male workers. A similar pattern emerges for female workers although the greatest deficiency of demand was in the North, Scotland being second. In a number of regions and again in the East, South, London and South East, there is evidence of a substantial 'excess' demand for female labour.

Evidence of demand deficiency may also be presented in terms of regions *per capita* income and gross domestic product. In order to appreciate how this may be done, it is necessary to recall from Chapter 1 the various ways in which national income may be expressed. The particular form in which we are interested is

$$Y = C+I+G+(X-M)$$

where Y = gross domestic product
C = consumers' expenditure
I = gross domestic capital formation
G = public expenditure on goods and services
X = exports
M = imports, so that $(X-M)$ = net exports.

Rearranging this equation it is possible to estimate 'non-consumption' expenditure, i.e.

$$Y-C = I+G+(X-M)$$

In a simple Keynesian model, it is this 'non-consumption' expenditure, i.e. $I+G+(X-M)$ which can be taken as determining the level of income. The equilibrium level of income is where 'non-consumption' expenditure equals savings. If savings can be assumed to be approximately the same function of income in each region,[1] then it could be expected that 'non-consumption' expenditure per head of population would bear a positive relationship to the pressure of demand and the fullness of employment. To put this in another way, these regions which have a high level of gross domestic capital formation per head, a high level of public expenditure on goods and services per head, and a high level of net exports per head will also be the regions where the pressure of demand is greatest and the level of unemployment is lowest.

Again, we turn to the National Institute study of regional

[1] In Chapters 6 and 11 there is presented evidence that both the volume and form of savings in Scotland differ considerably from the national pattern.

problems for confirmation of this hypothesis. If we classify the regions of the United Kingdom into one group with above average levels of unemployment and a second group with below average levels the pattern shown in Table 12.4 emerges.

Table 12.4 Regional distribution of expenditure, personal incomes and gross domestic product at factor cost in the United Kingdom, 1961

Region:	(1)	(2)	(3)	(4)	(5)	(6)	(7)
South East	1·0	502	177	331	111	109	116
North Midlands	1·1	465	196	276	102	120	97
Midlands	1·1	489	188	285	108	115	100
East and West Ridings	1·1	453	180	270	100	110	95
South West	1·4	400	108	283	88	66	99
North West	1·6	449	171	267	99	105	94
United Kingdom	1·6	454	163	285	100	100	100
North	2·5	411	163	244	91	100	86
Wales	2·6	401	130	244	88	80	86
Scotland	3·1	389	132	238	86	81	84
Northern Ireland	7·5	293	39	208	65	24	73

Source: National Institute Economic Review: November 1968.

(1) Regional unemployment: per cent.
(2) Gross domestic product: £ per head of total population.
(3) Non-consumption expenditure: £ per head of total population.
(4) Personal income after net transfers to public sector: £ per head of total population.
(5) Index of gross domestic product per head: U.K. = 100.
(6) Index of non-consumption expenditure per head: U.K. = 100.
(7) Index of personal income per head after net transfers to public sector: U.K. = 100.

Generally speaking, although the South West of England is an exception, regions showing below average levels of unemployment in 1961 also showed above average levels of *per capita* gross domestic product, non-consumption expenditure and personal income. Certainly, there is a very marked disparity in the North of England, Wales, Scotland and Northern Ireland. Although the relationship between the level of unemployment and regional per capita G.D.P., non-consumption expenditure and income is not completely perfect, it is strongly suggestive of a deficiency in effective demand in a number of regions, of which Scotland is one. The evidence which the National Institute has brought together in its major study of the regional problems of the United Kingdom leads inexorably to the conclusion that whether viewed from the side of unemployment, gross domestic product, non-consumption expenditure or personal income, Scotland is a region with most of the symptoms of an adverse balance of payments.

Summary

We have looked in this Chapter at the types of region which may be relevant in the setting of the Scottish economy, and seen the main types of economic problems which exist in regional analysis. It is clear from the discussion in Section 3 of the factors which determine location that a wide range of factors may influence a businessman's decisions. The growth point concept attempts to provide a rationale for a blend of government regional policy measures and inducements to private enterprise in order to prepare an environment which businessmen will find attractive in considering 'choice of location'. We shall see in the next Chapter that a whole battery of regional policy measures has been deployed in this setting. Finally, the application of simple income determination analysis to a region, suggested that Scotland is an area which may be suffering from a *deficiency of demand.* We cannot, however, conclude from the discussion in this Chapter that regional economics has now provided us with a completely new set of concepts and tools which we may apply to understanding and solving the problems of a region. Perhaps it is because of the complexities of regional problems that the policies that have been worked out to deal with them have proved so varied and so variable.

The future of regional policy in the United Kingdom must be seen against the background of the prospective entry of Britain into the European Economic Community. At the time of going to print, the Government had just published its White Paper, 'The United Kingdom and the European Communities', which set out the case for entry into the Common Market. By the time this book appears in the bookshops, the decision for or against entry will have been taken.

A number of member countries of E.E.C. pursue active regional policies, for example Italy, France and Belgium. It is recognised within the Community that regional policy has a vital and continuing role to play in economic development. It is argued in the White Paper that membership of E.E.C. will not inhibit the continuation and further development of vigorous regional policies which are necessary both on economic and social grounds. The anticipated acceleration in the rate of growth of the British economy after entry into the Community will, it is claimed, enable the Government to deal more effectively with the problems of regional development.

References

G. McCrone, *Regional Policy in Britain*, Unwin University Books, 1969.

H. W. Richardson, *Regional Economics*, Weidenfeld and Nicolson, 1969.

J. R. Meyer, 'Regional Economics: A Survey' in *Regional Analysis*, L. Needleman (ed.), Penguin, 1968.

W. Alonso, 'Location Theory' in *Regional Analysis*, L. Needleman (ed.), Penguin, 1968.

O.E.C.D., *Regional Factor in Economic Development*, 1970.

P. A. Samuelson, *Economics*, McGraw-Hill, 1967, Part 5.

Alfred Weber, *Theory of the Location of Industries*, University of Chicago Press, 1928.

W. F. Luttrell, *Factory Location and Industrial Movement*, NIESR, 1962.

Select Committee on Scottish Affairs, H.M.S.O., 1970, Appendix 7.

Oceanspan, Scottish Council (Development and Industry), 1970.

Report on the Scottish Economy, Scottish Council (Development and Industry), 1961.

G. C. Cameron and G. L. Reid, *Scottish Economic Planning and the Attraction of Industry*, Oliver and Boyd, 1966.

The Esk Valley, Midlothian County Council, 1970.

F. Perroux, 'Note sur la notion de pole de croissance', *Economie Appliqué*, 1955.

Local Employment in Scotland, Scottish Council (Development and Industry), 1951.

A. J. Brown, 'Regional Problems and Regional Policy', *N.I. Economic Review*, 1968.

G. C. Archibald, 'Regional Multiplier Effects in the United Kingdom', *Oxford Economic Papers*, March 1967.

A. J. Brown and others, 'The Green Paper on the Development Areas', *National Institute Economic Review*, May 1967.

K. J. Allen in *Regional and Urban Studies*, Orr and Cullingworth (eds.), Allen and Unwin, pp. 80–96.

M. A. Greig, 'The Regional Income and Employment Effects of a Pulp and Paper Mill', *Scottish Journal of Political Economy*, February 1971.

Chapter 13 Regional Policy Measures

The purpose of this Chapter is essentially to describe the various strands of regional policy as these have been drawn out in British regional policy since the war. We concentrate on measures which have been significant in tackling the regional problems of the Scottish economy. For example, we leave aside a discussion of measures in the 'grey areas', since these have not been particularly relevant to Scotland. In general, the review of regional policy measures throws up two distinctive features. First, policy has in general become more positive, moving away from an emphasis on the relief of chronic unemployment to more comprehensive objectives, of which the reduction of unemployment is only one, though of course none the less important for that. Second, policy has been highly variable, and in the ten years from 1960 to 1970 one can discern at least four major shifts in policy and in the content of regional development measures.

At different stages of this book, the reader's attention has been drawn to divergences in the level of economic activity between Scotland and the United Kingdom as a whole. Different measures of economic activity have been identified—gross domestic product, income per head, industrial output, growth of employment, unemployment, activity rates, emigration and so on. In almost every case we have observed a disparity between Scotland and the country as a whole; in almost every case the level of economic activity, however measured, has been lower in Scotland than nationally. It is this disparity which government policy has over the last twenty-five years sought to reduce. Scotland has not been the only area of the United Kingdom to suffer from such problems. Large areas of the North East and North West of England, Wales, particularly South Wales, and the South West of England have shared the same problems to a greater or lesser extent. They, too, have been designated as areas requiring Government assistance.

In recent years the emphasis of Government policy has changed. Until the early 1960s the primary objective of policy was the relief of unemployment; the types of measures adopted and the areas to which they were confined, were essentially employment-creating in a rather restricted sense. Nowadays, regional policy is conceived in much broader terms. While obviously still seeking to reduce regional disparities and bring into use human and other resources that would otherwise be idle, regional policy is now an important element of national economic policy. National inflationary pressures can be reduced by redistributing demand in such a way as to reduce pressure in certain 'overheated' regions, without penalising excessively regions where pressures of demand are lower. Experience has shown that when excessive demand pressures have built up in the more prosperous regions, and counter-inflationary measures have been taken, the effect on the less prosperous regions has been more marked, particularly in terms of high rates of unemployment. Losses of output and of earnings occur which would be much smaller if the discrepancies between the regions could be reduced, thus making management of the national economy much easier.

A feature of post war economic development in the United Kingdom has been the recurrence of pressures on the balance of payments. Periods of more rapid growth have been followed by periods of considerable restraint on the growth of incomes and output. Since the mid 1950s, 'stop-go' type policies have dominated national policy. Pressures of demand have built up rapidly in certain areas like London, the South East of England and the Midlands and the steps taken to damp them down have had their greatest effects in areas like Scotland and the North of England. With a more even spread of demand, the necessity for 'stop-go' policies might not be so pressing.

This is, however, an argument which should not be pressed too far. Many Western European countries, the United States, Canada, developing and under-developed countries have regional problems of the kind discussed in the previous chapter. All have pursued policies in the post war period with the same basic objective of reducing or eliminating regional differentials in prosperity. Not all countries have been faced with problems of the same character or magnitude. In certain countries only marginal regional problems exist; in others, the gaps between the prosperous and the less prosperous regions have led to large scale migrations of people out of the depressed and into the prosperous regions.

Into which category does the regional problem in

Britain fit? Is it marginal or is it substantial? One answer is provided by J. G. Williamson. In a study of regional inequalities in a number of countries, he comes to the conclusion that the regional variations in income levels in the United Kingdom were among the smallest in the world and second only to the Netherlands in Western Europe around 1959–60.

So far as Scotland is concerned, there has been since then a slight widening in the differential in income *per capita* from the national average (see Chapter 6). The scale of the regional problem in the United Kingdom is, by international standards, a modest one. The scope for improvement in management of aggregate demand at a national level by reduction of regional differentials in income per head is correspondingly limited.

Generally speaking, therefore, we are considering the problem of effecting modest changes in the levels of economic activity in the less prosperous regions of the United Kingdom. This should be borne in mind when considering the nature and scale of measures which have been introduced to deal with the regional problem.

2 Policy measures 1945–60

A systematic regional policy has developed in the United Kingdom only since 1945. Before the war, many parts of the country experienced prolonged and excessively high levels of unemployment as a result of the Great Depression. Most badly affected were the areas whose industrial structures were based on coal-mining, shipbuilding, iron and steel, textiles and other heavy industries. Scotland, the North of England and Wales were the most severely hit regions. Limited and piecemeal measures were introduced in the 1930s, including Commissioners for Special Areas (Development and Improvement). Small sums of money with restricting conditions were made available to these Commissioners, whose achievements were correspondingly modest. Towards the end of the 1930s trading estates were established in North East England, Scotland and South Wales and these subsequently have made a substantial contribution to employment creation. Measures whereby firms in Special Areas were exempted from certain taxes, and received assistance towards the payment of others, were introduced. This experiment in regional fiscal differentiation was not to be repeated until 1963. An Industrial Transference Board was set up to finance and facilitate the transference of workers, usually out of the Special Areas. It is difficult to assess what was achieved by these various measures as there was an upsurge in economic activity in the late 1930s in anticipation of World War II.

The foundation of post war policy was the Distribution of Industry Act of 1945. Modified by the Distribution of Industry Act of 1950 and the Distribution of Industry (Industrial Finance) Act of 1958, it remained the principal statute for regional development until 1960. In Scotland, the areas known as Development Areas defined by the act were the Clyde basin, including Glasgow, Dundee and the Inverness/Dingwall areas. The act was administered by the Board of Trade which could build factories in Development Areas, make loans to industrial estate companies, provide basic services such as gas, water and electricity for industrial sites, reclaim derelict land and give loans or grants to assist industrial undertakings on the advice of and with the consent of the Development Areas Treasury Advisory Committee.

The Distribution of Industry Act was reinforced by two further measures. The control of factory building was enforced initially by means of building licences but from 1950 onwards by a system of Industrial Development Certificates (I.D.C.) administered under the Town and Country Planning Act of 1947. This act makes it compulsory for any industrial building of more than a specified size (it has varied between 3,000 and 10,000 sq. ft.)[1] to obtain a Board of Trade certificate before planning permission will be granted. This system, which still operates, has been used consciously as a means of directing expanding firms to Development Areas by withholding or threatening to withhold an I.D.C. in cases where the Board of Trade has felt that a firm could reasonably expand or locate in a Development Area.[2]

The building of new towns was the second measure reinforcing regional policy under the Distribution of Industry Act. Faced with the problems of slum clearance, excessively high urban densities and the restoration of war damage, the Government embarked on a policy of developing completely new towns to relieve the urban pressures on a number of Britain's large cities. In Scotland the new towns of East Kilbride, Cumbernauld, Glenrothes, Livingston and Irvine are examples of this development. To give these new towns an economic as well as a social framework large numbers of factories were built in or near them

[1] On 7th December 1970, the government announced that the exemption limit for I.D.C. would be raised from 5,000 sq. ft. to 10,000 sq. ft. except in the Eastern, London and South Eastern, and East and West Midland regions where the limits would be raised from 3,000 sq. ft. to 5,000 sq. ft.

[2] See Chapter 12 for a discussion of the effectiveness of I.D.C. policy in the South East of England.

to provide employment for their immigrant populations. Many of these new towns were still building up during the 1950s and it has only been in the 1960s that the importance of their work as an instrument of regional policy has been fully recognised.

The principal reason behind the introduction of the post war legislation on regional policy had been the fear of the recurrence of large scale unemployment. By the early 1950s, it had become clear that this had become an extremely remote possibility. Levels of unemployment in the Development Areas, although considerably higher than the national average, were a mere fraction of their pre-war levels. The big upsurges in factory building and in government spending under the Distribution of Industry Act were allowed to subside as was the intensity with which the I.D.C. policy was applied.

From a peak of £12·8 million in 1947/48 Government spending under the Distribution of Industry Act fell to less than £3 million in 1957/58. Whereas in 1945/57, the Development Areas, with 20 per cent of the population of Great Britain, received over 50 per cent of all new industrial building, by 1954 their share of new industrial building had fallen to a strict population share. By the mid 1950s employment in Board of Trade industrial estates in Great Britain totalled 185,900, equivalent to 5 per cent of the insured employees in the Development Areas.

In Scotland, under the Distribution of Industry Acts of 1945 and 1950, £5·8 million was made available as loans and grants to firms in Scotland between 1945 and 1958. Under the Distribution of Industry (Industrial Finance) Act of 1958 a further £2 million was made available of which £0·9 million was for new enterprises. From 1945 to 1960, 49 million sq. ft. of factory building for manufacturing industry was completed in Scotland. Of this, 11 million sq. ft. was financed by the Government. 75,000 people or 3·5 per cent of the labour force were employed in Board of Trade factories in Scotland by 1959.

By the late 1950s, a number of major Scottish industries began to face problems of contraction. Coal mining, shipbuilding, textiles and others began to shed workers on a large scale. Of necessity, regional policy was resuscitated. In 1960, the Distribution of Industry Act was replaced by the Local Employment Act. This renamed and redefined the areas in which assistance would be made available. Development Districts, as they now became, were extended to include all areas in which a high rate of unemployment existed or was imminent and likely to persist. In practice, areas which had a level of unemployment of 4½ per cent or more could generally expect to be scheduled as Development Districts.

3 Growth Points

It was becoming apparent by this time, however, that tinkering with the geographical boundaries within which regional policy was applied was no longer sufficient. The inheritance of industrial blight and decay which typified large parts of Wales, the North of England and Central Scotland, the need to transform essentially 19th century industrial structures into 20th century terms, the deficiencies in communications and infrastructure generally, were problems which could no longer be tackled in piecemeal terms by a regional policy which had only limited and restricted objectives. Political and economic pressures built up especially in Scotland and the North of England which found their ultimate expression in the Report of the Committee of Enquiry into the Scottish Economy (the Toothill Report).

Commissioned by the Scottish Council (Development and Industry) an independent body representing industry, commerce, local authorities and trade unions in Scotland, this report challenged the whole philosophy of regional policy in Britain. The use of unemployment alone as the criterion for applying regional policy, it argued, was no longer sufficient. The emphasis should be placed on the creation of areas of growth—areas which by virtue of their geographical location, communications facilities, development potential or established industrial base, offered the best prospects for generating economic growth. These areas should be given priority in terms of location of new industry and of government spending on housing, roads, gas, water, electricity, schools, colleges and so on. The growth thus generated in these 'growth areas' would absorb the workers displaced in outdated industrial areas and provide the base for expansion in the future. In advocating this policy, the Scottish Council was restating the views it had expressed ten years earlier in the report of the Cairncross Committee mentioned in Chapter 12. The Toothill Report also criticised the non-specific and discretionary nature of the financial assistance to industry under the Distribution of Industry and Local Employment Acts.

The years between 1960 and 1963 saw intensive debate as to whether or not this country should follow a conscious regional policy. Certain economists argued that no steps should be taken to impede or divert the flow of resources, particularly manpower, from areas where demand was relatively low to areas where demand was high. By allowing free movement of resources a final position of equilibrium would be reached in which the demand and supply of resources in different parts of the country would be equated. Others argued that because not all factors of production are fully mobile, the existence of under-utilised resources in certain parts of the country represented output foregone and that it was in the national interest to ensure that these resources were fully employed. In the event, political factors played an important part and 1963 marked a significant watershed in the character and tenor of regional policy in the United Kingdom.

The main events of 1963, so far as regional policy is concerned, were the publication of government White Papers on Central Scotland and North East England in November and a major restructuring of the Local Employment Act in April.

The concept of the growth area was firmly accepted in the White Paper on Central Scotland. Eight such areas were designated in Central Scotland—the new towns of East Kilbride, Cumbernauld, Glenrothes and Livingston plus Irvine (now also a New Town), the Vale of Leven, North Lanarkshire and Falkirk/Grangemouth. The reformulated provisions of the 1963 Local Employment Act were to apply in these areas regardless of the level of unemployment. An expanded programme of public investment in Central Scotland was outlined whereby its share would rise to 11 per cent of the national total.[1] Improvements in infrastructure in these growth areas were proposed as were improvements in communications between them. The same philosophy was applied in the North East of England.

The criticisms of the financial provisions of the Distribution of Industry Acts and the 1960 Local Employment Act, namely that they were too imprecise in their character and too slow moving in their operation, were met by major revisions of the Local Employment Act. In addition to loans and grants offered at the discretion of the Board of Trade, firms expanding or locating in Development Areas were now eligible for standard grants of 10 per cent, in respect of investment in plant and machinery, and 25 per cent for industrial buildings. In addition firms in Development Areas were given the freedom to depreciate their new investment in plant and machinery at any rate that suited themselves. This free depreciation provision was equivalent

[1] See Chapter 9 for a discussion of infrastructure investment in Scotland since 1963.

to an interest-free loan from the Inland Revenue and as such proved to be a popular and effective scheme with industry.

4 Industrial Development Act, 1966

In 1965, the new Labour Government introduced far-reaching changes to the whole structure of company taxation. The previous system whereby companies claimed allowances of different kinds against their capital investment was replaced by a system of investment grants. Also the system of levying taxes on companies by a combination of income tax and profits tax was replaced by a Corporation Tax. The provisions of the 1965 Finance Act were incorporated into regional legislation under the Industrial Development Act of 1966.

The plant and machinery grants and free depreciation of the 1963 Local Employment Act were abolished and replaced by investment grants. Nationally, an investment grant of 20 per cent of the cost of new plant and machinery was payable, but in Development Areas this was increased to 40 per cent.[1] The initial allowance for industrial buildings was raised from 5 per cent to 15 per cent and the 25 per cent grant payable under the 1963 Local Employment Act was retained. As a new feature, however, the Board of Trade was permitted to offer a building grant of as high as 35 per cent to firms setting up new projects a long distance from their existing undertakings.

The changeover from the system which operated under the 1960 and 1963 Local Employment Acts to the system of the 1966 Industrial Development Act was undoubtedly complex. A comparison of the two systems of incentives as they operated before and after 1966, shows very little difference between them in overall value to firms in Development Areas. The precise value of the incentives depends on the accounting practices adopted by firms, particularly the rates of depreciation and of discount. Using one set of assumptions as an illustration, the amount of cash recovered by a firm by means of grant and tax allowances for every £100 invested in plant and machinery would come to £51·3 under the pre-1966 system compared with £52·8 under the system which existed until October 1970. On industrial buildings the recoveries would total £41·5 under the previous system and £39·7 under the system obtaining until October 1970.

In addition to making these major changes in the

[1] As an inducement to higher investment the investment grants were increased to 25 per cent nationally and to 45 per cent in Development Areas for 1967 and 1968.

nature of regional investment incentives, the 1966 Industrial Development Act made sweeping changes to the boundaries within which these incentives would apply. In Scotland, for example, the only areas not to be scheduled as part of the Scottish Development Area, were the Employment Exchange Areas of Edinburgh, Leith and Portobello. Similarly, large geographical areas of the North, North West and South West of England as well as Wales were scheduled as Development Areas. The emphasis had now moved away from defining Development Areas solely on the basis of the level of unemployment to creating large areas which had similar economic problems; the 1963 growth areas were relegated to the status of *primi inter pares*.

This departure from a policy of concentration on growth areas does in principle mean that businessmen have a wider choice of location in determining where they will set up shop in a region which enjoys the benefit of regional incentives. But there is a subtle change. The growth area concept recognised that social investment was a prerequisite of private investment, that businessmen might only be attracted to an area which had been given the appropriate infrastructure of roads, houses and other services. It recognised that one of the problems of past dereliction had been the rundown of social capital, and it also accepted that private economic calculations do not necessarily take account of the social costs of activity. Government had to set the scene, and then induce industry to come.

5 Regional Manpower Policy

Regional policy has been progressively strengthened from 1966 onwards by the introduction of measures which either contain a substantial measure of regional differential, e.g. Selective Employment Tax, or are entirely regional in character, e.g. Regional Employment Premium. Also, the regional element of national manpower policy has been developed considerably in recent years.

Selective Employment Tax (S.E.T.) was introduced in 1965 ostensibly as a means of diverting labour from service industries into manufacturing industries where shortages of labour were felt to exist. Initially all employers paid S.E.T. in respect of all their employees. Employers in manufacturing industries, however, received their tax contributions back some three months later plus an additional sum of 7s 6d per week for adult male workers and lower rates for female and juvenile workers. Subsequently, the 7s 6d refund was withdrawn for workers in manufacturing industries, but retained for workers in these industries in Development areas.[1]

In 1967, the Government introduced the Regional Employment Premium (R.E.P.). Firms in Development Areas are paid a certain sum (£1.50 a week for adult male workers and lower rates for female and juvenile workers). The theory is that this sum thus enables firms in Development Areas to reduce prices, increase sales and generate more employment. Guaranteed by the Government for a minimum period of seven years,[2] R.E.P. and the S.E.T. refund mean that for every 100 male workers over 18 employed, a firm in a Development Area receives £9,750 per annum and correspondingly smaller sums for female and juvenile workers. As we have seen in Chapter 1, the introduction of R.E.P. can be regarded as a means of restoring comparative cost advantage for the Development Areas.

The Department of Employment has stepped up considerably the assistance it now offers to firms in Development Areas, both in terms of cash and in terms of practical advice and assistance. The assistance offered by the Department falls under two headings—financial assistance and direct assistance.

a *Financial assistance*

1. Where an employer provides training for workers to fill new jobs, the Department will pay grants at the following weekly rates.

	men	women
Aged 18 and over	£10	£7
Aged under 18	£5	£4

Grants are not normally paid for training periods of less than 2 weeks or where the total cost involved would be less than £200. The maximum period for which a grant is paid is 52 weeks and is designed to ensure that a trainee of average ability has sufficient time to acquire the basic skills and knowledge required for the job.

2. Where managerial, supervisory or professional employees are sent on courses needed as a direct result of a firm's expansion, half the cost of tuition fees approved by the D.E.P. will be refunded.

3. If a temporary training school or training premises

[1] In the Budget of March, 1971, the S.E.T. rates were reduced by 50 per cent, as a first step towards the introduction of a Value Added Tax in 1974.

[2] In October 1970, the Government announced that R.E.P. would end in 1974.

are established in rented accommodation in a Development Area, pending the occupation of a factory in a Development Area, the D.E.P. will meet half the cost of rent and rates for a limited period and also half the cost of adapting such premises to training purposes.

b *Direct Assistance*

1. A firm which requires assistance with the training of new workers in semi-skilled engineering work may have the free assistance of specially trained instructors from the D.E.P.

2. Firms may interview and recruit trainees undergoing training at a Government Training Centre. If places are available a firm's employees may be trained at a Government Training Centre.

3. If a firm's expansion calls for training in supervisory skills, such staff can attend special D.E.P. Courses without payment of course fees.

4. The Department of Employment also provides training in instructional skills at a number of centres which can be attended free of charge by firms undergoing planned expansion.

5. The work of the Industrial Training Boards has already been referred to in Chapter 10. In Development Areas, special schemes are now run by the I.T.B.s to promote craft and technician training. Grants are available to employers who provide additional off-the-job training places for apprentices, technicians, commercial and administrative trainees. These grants which are additional to the normal grants payable by I.T.B.s take one of two forms:

(1) a capital grant towards the cost of providing additional off-the-job training places which will be used for training for at least five years. The grant will amount to 60 per cent of the costs incurred.

or (2) a *per capita* grant of £100 for each additional trainee may be paid annually until 1973.

Finally the I.T.B.s may pay grants of 70 per cent of the cost of new machinery and 50 per cent of the cost of second hand machinery installed by firms to create additional training places in their own training centres.

6 Policy Changes, 1970–71

One of the first measures introduced by the Conservative Government on its return to power in 1970 was major changes in the field of regional policy. It was concerned that the investment grants scheme was involving a high level of public expenditure without achieving its objectives. Moreover, it claimed, investment grants benefit firms whether or not they are making profits and can therefore result in uneconomic investment and lead to a waste of resources. It was also felt that the scheme discriminated against service industries and was expensive to administer. The following changes were introduced from 26th October 1970.

1. Investment grants are withdrawn and are replaced by a system of depreciation allowances for expenditure on plant and machinery. In the first year of expenditure 60 per cent[1] of the cost may be written off for tax purposes and a standard rate of writing-down allowance will enable 25 per cent of the reducing balance to be written off annually in later years. For expenditure on plant and machinery of £100 the allowances now are:

For year in which expenditure was incurred = £60
For first complete year of asset use 25 per cent of £40 = £10
For the following year 25 per cent of £30 = £7·5
For the next following year 25 per cent of £22·5 = £5·625 and so on.

2. In Development Areas, a system of free depreciation is introduced.[2] This means that firms will be free to write off expenditure on plant and machinery for tax purposes at any rate to suit themselves, subject to earning a sufficient amount of pre tax profit to enable them to claim the full allowance. For example, if a firm has made a profit of £100,000 before charging depreciation, but has incurred during the same period expenditure on plant and machinery of £150,000, it can only claim against tax allowances amounting to £100,000. The remaining £50,000 may be claimed the following year, provided the firm makes at least £50,000 in pre-depreciation profit. The advantage of free depreciation is that it gives tax allowances much earlier and improves firms' cash-flow.

Other measures introduced include improvements in the assistance already available under the Local Employment Act in Development Areas.

(i) rates of building grants in Development Areas increased by ten percentage points to 35 per cent and 45 per cent.

(ii) increases in the limits regulating the amount of assistance to be made available in relation to the additional employment expected to be provided.

[1] In the 'mini-budget' of July 1971, the depreciation allowance was increased to 80 per cent.

[2] Such a system operated between 1963 and 1966. Under the present system a somewhat wider range of assets will qualify.

Table 13.1 Financial Incentives in Development Areas

Development Areas (1)	Special Development Areas (2)	Intermediate Areas (3)	Non-Assisted Areas (4)	
1. Investment grants at the rate of 40 per cent for expenditure on new plant and machinery for use in manufacturing construction, civil engineering and extraction of minerals.	As Column (1)	As Column (1) but at the rate of 20 per cent	As Column (3)	
From 26th October 1970 Tax allowance in first year of expenditure of 60 per cent plus free depreciation. Investments grants withdrawn. *From July 1971* Tax allowance in first year of expenditure of 80 per cent	As Column (1)	Tax allowance in first year of expenditure of 60 per cent plus annual tax allowance of 25 per cent on reducing balance.	As Column (3)	7
2. Ministry of Technology factories for rent or sale (in certain cases the first two years may be rent free).	As Column (1) except that the rent-free period may be five years.	As Column (1) As Column (1)	— —	
From 26th October 1970 Now administered by Department of Industry and Trade, otherwise no change.	As Column (1)	As Column (1)	—	
3. Building grants at rate of 25 per cent of eligible cost (in certain cases, the rate may be 35 per cent)	As Column (1)	As Column (1)	—	
From 26th October 1970 40 per cent initial allowance on industrial buildings due to be terminated on 5th April 1972, now to continue indefinitely. Building grants to continue as before.	As Column (1)	As Column (1)	Present initial allowance of 30 per cent on industrial buildings to be reduced to 15 per cent from 5th April 1972.	
4. Loans towards capital needs (but not towards balance of buildin costs when a building grant is being made).	As Column (1) but with addition of loans towards building grants even when building grant is being made	—	—	

	Operational grants of 10 per cent per annum of cumulative expenditure on buildings and plant and machinery in each of first three years of operation of project.		
7. Assistance towards transference of key workers.	As Column (1)	As Column (1)	—
8. Regional Employment Premium of £1.50 for adult male workers in manufacturing establishments (lower rates for other workers).	As Column (1)	—	—
From 26th October 1970 Regional Employment Premium to be withdrawn in 1974.	As Column (1)	—	—
9. Selective Employment Premium: refund of S.E.T. plus additional sum of $37\frac{1}{2}$p per week for adult male workers in manufacturing establishments (lower rates for other workers). Hotels in certain parts of Development Areas also receive refunds.	As Column (1)	S.E.T. refunded to manufacturing establishments	As Column (3)
10. Training assistance from D.E.P. in the form of grants and provision of training Courses.	As Column (1)	As Column (1)	—
11. Training assistance from I.T.B. to finance additional training.	As Column (1)	—	—
12. Loans from Development Commission to tourist projects in certain rural areas.	As Column (1)	—	—
13. Loans and grants from Highlands and Islands Development Board (Highlands only).	—	—	—
14. Hotel development grants at the rate of 25 per cent subject to a ceiling of £1,250 for each new additional bedroom.	As Column (1)	As Column (1) but at the rate of 20 per cent and subject to a ceiling of £1,500.	As Column (3)
15. —	Payment of 30 per cent of eligible wage costs for first three years of operation of new project	—	—

Source: Ministry of Technology in Minutes of Evidence to Select Committee on Scottish Affairs pp. 520–1, H.M.S.O., 1970. Investment Incentives Cmnd. 4516, H.M.S.O., 1970.

(iii) more flexible use of powers to provide loans under the 1960 Local Employment Act.

(iv) wider use of existing powers under the Local Employment Acts for grants towards the cost of providing infrastructure services and clearing derelict land.

(v) a grant of 30 per cent of eligible wage costs for the first three years of operation of a firm new to a Special Development Area.

Industrial training programmes in the Development Areas are to be intensified and further limited schemes of assistance to tourism in the Development Areas will also be introduced. This package of measures was accompanied by an announcement that the rate of Corporation Tax has been reduced from 45 per cent to 42½ per cent for the financial year 1969 onwards.

The Treasury estimate that by 1974–5, the present scheme should result in a net gain to the Exchequer of £150 million (at 1970 prices) made up of

Estimated gross savings from ending investment grants	+£725 m.
Reduction of Corporation Tax	−£105 m.
Additional capital allowances	−£470 m.
Total net gain to Exchequer	+£150 m.

There now exists a comprehensive list of measures designed to promote growth in the Development Areas which it may be useful to summarise (see Table 13.1). The Development Areas are classified under three types: (1) the Development Areas proper; (2) Special Development Areas, i.e. areas within Development Areas which are deemed to be in need of additional assistance—these are mainly old coalfields;[1] and (3) Intermediate Areas, i.e. areas which are adjacent to Development Areas and, whilst not requiring the full range of Development Area facilities, are deemed to merit some measure of assistance—Leith is the only such intermediate area in Scotland.

7 The Flow of Funds

What has all this meant for Scotland? The injection of public funds into the Development Areas generally and into Scotland in particular has risen greatly in recent years. It is not possible to put a precise monetary value on all the elements of

[1] Since January 1971, the greater part of West Central Scotland has been designated as a Special Development Area in an attempt to combat increasing redundancy and rising unemployment. In August 1971, Glenrothes and Livingston New Towns were also given S.D.A. status.

Table 13.2 Financial Assistance to Scotland Under Local Employment Acts

	1963/4 (£m)	1964/5 (£m)	1965/6 (£m)	1966/7 (£m)	1967/8 (£m)	1968/9 (£m)
Act: Section 2						
ies on industrial estates	1·6	6·4	2·7	3·9	4·5	2·9
Act: Section 3/1963						
ection 2						
ng grants (at 25 per cent of cost)	1·3	3·4	6·0	8·2	7·2	6·6
Act: Section 1[1]						
and machinery grants						
per cent of cost)	0·8	1·7	2·1	2·7	0·8	0·1
Act: Section 4						
al purpose loans and grants:						
	10·5	3·7	4·6	4·7	4·5	7·0
s	0·2	—	0·1	0·1	0·6	0·7
under above Sections of Acts	14·4	15·2	15·6	19·5	17·6	17·4
nd as per cent of Great Britain	47·7	37·4	36·8	35·3	38·0	31·6

e: Digest of Scottish Statistics.
rceded by Investment Grants from 1966/7.

present regional policy but for Scotland a number of items of expenditure can be identified. First, we indicate expenditure under the 1960 and 1963 Local Employment Acts. Although parts of these acts have been superceded by subsequent legislation, financial assistance may still be offered under certain sections of these acts.

For the year 1969/70, government assistance to all Development Areas under the terms of the Local Employment Acts was £84 million of which Scotland's share was £18·4 million.

Table 13.3 Government Assistance to Industry 1968–9

	Scottish Development Area (£m)	Total Development Areas (£m)
Investment Grants[1]	58·4 (25)[2]	190·8 (84·3)[2]
Regional Employment Premium	40	100
S.E.T. additional payments	10	25
Local Employment Act, grants, etc.	17·4	54·9
Other[3]	2·5	3·5
Total	128·3	374·2

Scotland as percentage of Great Britain = 34 per cent.

Source: Scottish Office: Minutes of Evidence to Select Committee on Scottish Affairs 1970, Appendix 20.

[1] Total investment grant payments were £60m in Scotland and £429·9m in Great Britain.

[2] Figure in bracket is the extra 20 per cent payable in Development Areas and is included in main figure.

[3] Includes S.E.T. refund by hotels, D.E.P. training assistance and payments by Highlands and Islands Development Board.

Scotland's share of such assistance fell from nearly half the total in 1963/4 to just over one fifth in 1969/70.

With National Income at a level of £34,907 million in 1969, this means that rather more than 1 per cent of the nation's resources are now being applied to regional policy measures. Scotland's share is of the order of one third of one per cent.

8 The Machinery of Planning

At the same time as the financial incentives outlined in the sections 6 and 7 have been evolving, there has also developed a completely new approach to regional planning. The first coherent statements of Government policy for particular regions of the United Kingdom were published in 1963 in the White Papers on Central Scotland, the North East of England, and the South East of England, but it was not until after the publication of the National Plan in 1965 that an attempt was made to provide a national framework into which regional plans could be integrated.

The election of a Labour Government in 1964 brought with it a major change in the organisation of government. The hegemony of the Treasury in matters of economic policy was challenged by the establishment of the Department of Economic Affairs (D.E.A.).[1] It was intended that the Treasury should confine itself primarily to short-term matters of policy and that longer term planning and policy should be the concern of the D.E.A. The National Plan, produced and published by the D.E.A., was an attempt to specify targets in terms of growth of output, changes in productivity, growth of employment, capital investment and so on for the period up to 1970. These overall targets were translated wherever possible into regional terms. This integration of regional with national planning was an important step. In the event, unforeseen changes in economic conditions overtook the National Plan shortly after its publication, but, nevertheless, it represents a landmark in its attempt to specify regional and national objectives.

To implement the regional aspects of national policy, the country was divided into a number of planning regions. Scotland and Wales are separate planning regions and England is divided into eight regions. For each region an Economic Planning Board and Economic Planning Council were established.

The Planning Board is a body of civil servants drawn

[1] The Department of Economic Affairs was disbanded in 1969.

from Ministries and Departments having an interest in the activities of a region. Originally, a typical English or Welsh Planning Board had representatives of such departments as the D.E.A., the Board of Trade, the Department of Employment and Productivity, the Ministry of Housing and Local Government, the Ministry of Technology, the Ministry of Power or such other departments as were appropriate.[1] The Scottish Planning Board does not have representatives of the D.E.A. or Ministry of Housing and Local Government, as the activities of these departments are carried out by the ubiquitous Scottish Office.

The Economic Planning Councils are advisory bodies whose membership is drawn from industry and commerce, local government, trade unions and the universities. The members of the Planning Councils are appointed by the Government as private individuals and not as representatives of particular bodies or organisations. The chairman is normally drawn from the membership, except in Scotland, where the Secretary of State for Scotland is chairman of the Scottish Economic Planning Council.[2]

The Planning Boards and Councils were charged with the responsibility for producing reports and studies for their regions which could be considered within the overall framework of national policy. One of the first to appear was the White Paper on the Scottish Economy in January 1966. Taking the National Plan's forecasts as its starting point the White Paper then forecast changes in the levels of output and employment by 1970. Output was expected to rise by 4·8 per cent per annum in Scotland between 1964 and 1970 against a national rate of 4·5 per cent. Employment was expected to rise by 60,000, the result of a gain of 134,000 jobs and a loss of 74,000. (The discussion in Chapters 3 and 4 indicates just how far short of these forecasts, the actual performance has been.) The overall objectives of the Scottish White Paper were to obtain faster rates of growth in output, higher productivity and more employment opportunities in the expanding sectors of the economy. By this means the existing reserves of labour could be more fully deployed, unemployment reduced, higher activity levels achieved and the necessary reduction in outward migration achieved.

[1] The changes in Government structure announced in October 1970 resulted in changes in the names of certain departments, e.g. Department of Industry and Trade combines the former Ministry of Technology and Board of Trade.

[2] The word 'Planning' has now been dropped from the name of the Scottish Economic Planning Council.

The White Paper also carried out a number of preliminary studies in the Borders, North East, Highlands and South West of Scotland to establish the nature and extent and the demographic and economic problems of these areas. The need for more intensive study was apparent and a number of sub-regional studies were commissioned from Scottish universities. Edinburgh and Glasgow Universities co-operated to produce studies of the Lothians (in support of the development of Livingston New Town) and of Falkirk/Grangemouth (in support of the growth area proposals for the sub-region). Edinburgh University on its own produced a study of the Central Borders, in support of the White Paper proposal to introduce an additional 25,000 people into the Central Borders by 1980. Aberdeen University has produced a long-range study of the North East of Scotland, and Dundee University one of Tayside. The Tayside study differs in character from the others, being one of three studies undertaken to assess the feasibility of introducing large population increases into the estuarial regions of Humberside, Severnside and Tayside. Finally, Heriot-Watt University produced a study of the Esk Valley area in Midlothian in anticipation of future growth in that area.

The diversity of the problems of the regions under consideration and the diversity of approaches adopted has inevitably resulted in variations in the types of policies and solutions recommended in these reports. Generally speaking, however, they have recommended concentration of effort at a limited number of points, often incurring the wrath of excluded local authorities. To that extent, they have advocated a conscious application of the growth area concept.

Three areas of Scotland have not been intensively examined in this way, namely the South West, Central West and the Highlands. A study limited to assessing the tourist potential of the South West has been carried out by Strathclyde University. A Government study is currently underway of West Central Scotland, the most densely populated sub-region. In the autumn of 1970, proposals were announced by industrial and local authority interests in the area to set up a body to promote industrial development in West Central Scotland and to carry out the necessary supporting studies.

9 The Highlands

The Highlands and Islands have been the subject of a unique form of regional policy. The Highlands and Islands Development Board (H.I.D.B.) was set up in 1965 to assist the

people of the Highlands and Islands, i.e. the counties of Argyll, Caithness, Inverness, Orkney, Ross and Cromarty, Sutherland, Zetland to improve their economic and social conditions and to enable the region to play a more effective part in the economic and social development of the region. To achieve its objectives the Board has been given wide-ranging powers including the power
(i) to acquire land, compulsorily if necessary
(ii) to erect buildings (usually industrial or commercial) on land and engage in their management, hire or maintenance
(iii) to acquire, carry on, set up or promote directly or indirectly businesses or undertakings which in the Board's opinion will contribute to the economic and social development of the Highlands and Islands.
(iv) to provide advisory, training, management, technical accountancy and other services to businesses and organisations in its area
(v) to provide financial assistance by loans or grants or both
(vi) to undertake the carrying out of research, investigations and enquiries necessary for the execution of its functions.

The Board's expenditure rose from £106,000 in the first year of its operation to £2·95 million in 1969–70. Of its current budget £1·8 million is for grants and loans, £0·5 million for projects and developments, £0·25 million for research, development and publicity and £0·4 million for administration. Up to 31st May, 1969 the Board had received 1,805 applications for financial assistance. Just over half, 992, were approved, 293 were rejected and 412 were withdrawn. The amount of assistance the Board has approved to May, 1969 was £5·2 million of which £3·7 million was in loans and £1·5 million was grants. The financial assistance available from the H.I.D.B. is complementary to the assistance firms may be given by the Board of Trade. The purpose of the financial powers of the Board is to give special grants over and above the Development Area grant and loan assistance, so that the Board may have an 'edge' over other Development Areas with which it is in competition and which, geographically, may be better placed. The maximum amount which the Board may give, without prior reference to the Scottish Development Department, has been increased from £25,000 to £50,000 but the Board feels there are grounds for allowing it greater discretion in this direction.

The Board's strategy has been to support development in the three main sectors of primary industry, manufacturing industry and tourism. Forestry is seen as one of the three great hopes for a more secure Highland economy. In the 1966 White Paper on the Scottish Economy the Government announced that it would increase the planting programme in the Highlands to 20,000 acres a year after 1969 and in 1967 it was further announced that the government intended to increase Scotland's planting programme to 50,000 acres a year by 1976. The Board has been extremely active in the promotion of fishing and allied processing industries. Its initial scheme to finance the construction of 25 new fishing boats at a cost of £750,000 by 1971 has been increased to 35 boats. It has acquired and is running the former Herring Industry Board factory at Stornoway and considerable sums of money have been invested in factories in Shetland. Up to 1970, the Board had approved over £1·5 million of assistance for fisheries projects including the purchase of 119 new or second-hand fishing boats, 15 seaweed collection boats as well as to shipbuilding yards, processing firms and fish farming projects.

It is through the promotion of manufacturing industry that the Board believes it can do most to stem the drift of young people from the region as a whole. The major project to come to the area since the Board's inception has been the aluminium smelter at Invergordon, which comes into operation during 1971. In the last five years, the Board has given financial assistance to 166 industrial projects, 30 of which are new to the Highlands. Industry has received £1·3 million of financial assistance and it is estimated that 1,145 new jobs have been created.

The Board has also been active in the field of tourist development where its efforts have already borne results. Over 1,800 extra bedrooms have been provided as a result of its grant and loan assistance to hotels and boarding houses in the region. A major scheme costing £1 million to build up to five major hotels in the West Highlands and on the islands is under way and the first of these hotels on Mull will open during 1971.

The Board's chairman during its first five years was the eminent planner, Professor Sir Robert Grieve. Under his guidance, the Board undertook a tremendous variety of studies of the development potential of the Highlands and Islands. Geographical, geological, industrial, tourist, social and economic studies were all set in hand. The Board's long-term strategy also emerged, envisaging three major growth areas. The first of these is based on the Moray Firth and stretches in a loop from Inverness through such places as Beauly, Dingwall, Alness and Evanton to Invergordon. The second is based on the Atomic Research Establishment at Dounreay and encompasses the Wick/Thurso area. The third is the Fort William area based on the woodpulp mill at Corpach. Each area has a major industrial development associated with it which the Board hopes will form the basis of substantial long-term growth.

10 Evaluation

Regional policy in the United Kingdom has passed through several cycles in the last twenty-five years. From an immediate post war surge of interest, there came a virtual hiatus in the mid 1950s; from 1960 there have been four major changes in legislation and the present Government has indicated that it is currently undertaking a major review of the whole character of regional development policy.

It is not easy to appraise this array of measures which successive Governments have paraded through the regional policy field. One of the most striking features, to which attention has already been drawn, is the frequency with which policy has changed, particularly with regard to capital investment incentives. More precisely, we may ask how far policy has endeavoured to identify the wellsprings of growth which students of the subject, such as Denison have highlighted.

In the growth point concept there was clear recognition that public investment had to set the scene for private efforts at promoting the transformation of the structure of the economy. The two were seen as complementary, with the public sector carrying the weight of social costs, and seeking to provide an environment in which firms could reap the benefit of external economies. Apart from the continued emphasis on the New Towns, and in the Highlands, this growth point policy has become somewhat diffused and submerged by a blanket strategy.

The need to stimulate private investment directly by offering various kinds of subsidy or grant has been recognised. But this policy has suffered from two deficiencies. First, the nature of the inducements has changed far too frequently. The literature of economics has long recognised how important businessmen's expectations are for investment decisions, and frequent change may well induce uncertainty and defer investment decisions. Second, it has by no means been established how sophisticated businessmen are in their investment calculations, and how responsive they are to different forms of investment incentive.

Manpower as a source of growth has been increasingly recognised in recent regional policy. This has taken three forms, (a) the provision of employment subsidies to employers through

S.E.T. and R.E.P., (b) direct grants to individual workers with a view to improving the quality of skills in the labour force, and (c) the expansion of training facilities, both in educational and training establishments.

It has not always been clear which had priority, the various attempts to promote investment and make industry more capital-intensive or the various labour subsidies, which presumably make industry more labour-intensive. There has been no systematic and sustained effort to alter the Labour/Capital ratio, but for particular firms the range of inducements is presumably wide and attractive enough to give them an opportunity to determine for themselves how they propose to alter, if at all, the mix of their factor inputs.

Perhaps the above considerations suggest that policy has deliberately chosen, despite its many changes, to provide a range of incentives. This may make sense for two reasons. First, we have seen in the previous Chapter that business firms may well be influenced by a number of subjective considerations in determining their choice of location. Recent and present policy does at least provide a number of levers which they can clutch and pull. Second, it has been made clear throughout this book that Scotland is very diversified in its regional structure and problems, and the various sub-regions may well need different types of treatment. The Highlands are only one such region, and the sub-regional studies show how varied the problems are throughout Scotland.

Unfortunately, this variety of measures and their variableness make it very difficult to quantify the effects of policy for the regions. It is still an inexact science.

References

G. McCrone, *Regional Policy in Britain*, Unwin University Books, 1969.

Report on the Scottish Economy, Scottish Council (Development and Industry), 1961.

The Scottish Economy: A Plan for Expansion, Cmnd. 2864, H.M.S.O., 1966.

Minutes of Evidence to the Select Committee on Scottish Affairs, H.M.S.O., 1970.

J. G. Williamson, 'Regional Inequality and the Process of National Development' in L. Needleman (ed.) *Regional Analysis*, Penguin, 1969.

Report on the Scottish Economy, Scottish Council (Development and Industry), 1961, Appendix 38.

H. W. Richardson and E. G. West, 'Must We Always Bring Work to the Workers?, *Lloyds Bank Review*, 1964.

L. Needleman and B. Scott, 'Regional Problems and the Location of Industry Policy in Britain', *Urban Studies*, 1964.

Central Scotland: A Programme for Development and Growth, Cmnd. 2188, H.M.S.O., 1963.

The North East: A Programme for Regional Development and Growth, Cmnd. 2206, H.M.S.O., 1963.

Recoveries from Investment in a Development Area, Minutes of Evidence to the Select Committee on Scottish Affairs, 1970, Annex C.

The United Kingdom and the European Communities, H.M.S.O., Cmnd. 4715.

Chapter 14
Conclusions

1 Retrospect

When we look back over the analysis of the various themes taken up in this study it is clear that we have sought to appraise Scottish economic performance by reference to the kind of analytical framework which was marked out in the first Chapter. The criteria which have come to the surface, time and time again, have concerned such primary considerations as the growth of real *per capita* income, the rate of growth and mix of output, and secondary indicators of success such as the growth of employment.

We are of course perfectly aware that a society may have other goals besides the economic. Many Scots may wish for nothing better than a quiet life, or a beautiful countryside, and the preservation of a certain style of life and culture which are long-established. We recognise also that economic growth involves costs, and that one of the most valuable fruits of a successful economic policy may be the possibility of enjoying greater leisure. What we most certainly cannot afford, however, is a nostalgic hankering for past days and glories; one of the main lessons of this book has been the recognition of interdependence in economic activity. If we fail to keep pace with other areas and countries in the efficiency with which we use resources we must expect our relative position and our comparative advantage to deteriorate.

Judged by the indicators of the rate at which she uses her scarce resources, Scotland clearly lags. She is at a relative disadvantage to the United Kingdom as a whole in employment, incomes, the adjustment of her production structure from old and to new technologies, the balance of population flows, the evidence about her balance of payments, and so on. There is also considerable and suggestive evidence to indicate that she has not been enjoying any major economies of scale, or the external economies that are often associated with growth policies for regions. It is also clear that there are considerable disparities between areas within Scotland. This is not to deny that there has been marked change in the face and content of Scotland's economy in recent years. New investment has been attracted, new jobs found in new technologies, and the scale of Government economic action significantly raised.

So far as policy measures are concerned, it seems clear that no strong gains have been made through seeking to manipulate the level of total demand in the national economy in such a way that it favours particular regions. Monetary policy is notoriously difficult to operate in such a fashion. Fiscal policy holds out more promise, and certainly there has been plenty of action on the Government spending side of its own budget. But British policy has not been particularly adventurous in manipulating tax bases and tax structures as a method of affecting regional demand flows in practice.

We have seen that Selective Employment Tax and the Regional Employment Premium are discriminatory measures that have been used to help disadvantaged regions. But it is far from clear what their effect is on the demand or spending side in the economy. Regional Employment Premium can, for example, be passed on to consumers in the form of lower prices; it can be paid out to workers in the form of higher wages, and in that sense could conceivably help to raise the level of spending in the region in which the workers are employed and spend at least part of their incomes; it can also become in part an earnings component for the employer receiving it. Apart from the wage increase possibility, however, there is no guarantee that the Premium will actually promote the level of spending in the region in which it is being disbursed. The regional multiplier concept may perhaps help to shed light on these ramifications.

If we look next at direct tax systems, it should be possible in principle to discriminate personal taxation in favour of regions where demand is low, with a view to raising disposable incomes in them. For example, taxes on personal income could be levied at lower rates in Scotland than in other parts of the U.K., and Scottish-based companies might suffer a lower rate of corporation tax. The familiar objections to such proposals are that it is difficult to establish domicile for persons as a tax base, and that the concept of Scottish-based companies is a very diffuse one. Further, it can be argued, we can have no guarantee that any increase in disposable incomes which such discriminatory taxation achieved would actually be spent within Scotland and contribute to raising the level of demand in the region.

Indirect tax discrimination suffers from additional difficulties. First, persons who pay indirect taxation are in one sense volunteers, since they must make a purchase before the tax becomes liable. Even more fundamental, however, is that there is no guarantee that the output which is being favoured by such a discriminatory rate structure of indirect taxation is being produced in Scotland, and that the Scottish economy would benefit in its output from taxes which sought to help it in this way.

Nevertheless, despite these difficulties associated with manipulating tax rates to help an area, there is clearly scope for further analysis and also experimentation with tax measures that do endeavour to influence the size and regional flow of aggregate demand in the economy, in addition to the direct flows that stem from Government spending itself.

Undoubtedly, regional policy has tended to concentrate its efforts *vis-à-vis* private resources on measures which influence their supply. This fits well with the discussion set out in Chapter 8 on the sources of economic growth. Measures have sought to quicken the transformation of the production structure, and the analysis of Chapters 4 and 5 showed how critical this is for enhancing demand and incomes in the economy.

Regional measures have sought to stimulate capital formation, to affect both the quantity and quality of labour supply, and technological advance has been pursued through the efforts that have been made to promote the growth of such new industries as electronics. All the measures deployed with a view to influencing the regional supply of factors have demonstrated an interest in seeking to improve Scotland's resource position and her comparative advantage. We have identified and tried to quantify them in this study. Nevertheless, disquieting questions have kept recurring as we proceeded. Why has the tempo of change not been more rapid? Why is Scotland still out of step with the national average? If we are still in a period of transition, we may well ask when, after the early promise and subsequent disappointments of the decade of the 1960s, we may reasonably expect to make this transition and transformation the subject of a final rather than a series of interim reports?

Obviously, we must not fall into the trap of thinking that the economic problem can be resolved once and for all. There is no finality, in the sense of an absolute level or stage in our economic well-being which we can claim creates an optimum, a maximum, or even a Land fit for Lotus Eaters. Nevertheless, our interim reports are disturbingly tentative, and not overly optimistic. Why should this be so?

Two themes spring to mind. Have the objectives of regional policy been clearly stated, and consistently pursued? And has there been a systematic set of policy instruments? The two themes, or questions, are of course not completely separate. As policy objectives change, so the means may alter. For example, the growth point concept as an objective had harnessed to it a much more concentrated package of measures than the later more diffuse approach.

If we consider, first, the objectives, the most persistent has been the relief of unemployment. Both the Cairncross and Toothill Reports cited in the preceding Chapters suggested that policy objectives should be construed more positively, and we suggest below that the relief of unemployment is an important welfare objective but no more than a secondary economic objective. More recently, emphasis has been shifting away from the elimination of high unemployment to the more positive objective of raising *per capita* incomes nearer to the national average. In part, the Regional Employment Premium and Selective Employment Tax have been intended as income supplementation devices. The growth point concept, which the Cairncross and Toothill Reports saw as the main priority, has been watered down in recent years through the measures outlined in the last Chapter. Migration policy has been a continuing concern, but one which has suffered from inadequate data about the flows of people, and from a mixture of fatalism and chauvinism. We say more about migration policy as an objective in a moment.

We also have to recognise that one of the aims of regional policy has been the rearrangement of the balance of activity *within* Scotland. The establishment of the New Towns, overspill housing agreements, infra-structure investment, even the growth point concept itself, have all been conceived, at least in part, as means of alleviating the problem that is Glasgow. The objective of redistribution within Scotland has certainly had its positive economic thrust, but it has frequently been couched in terms of social distress and the negative characteristics associated with the concentration of heavy industrial activity around the Glasgow area. On the whole, the policy has also been equitable in intent; while relieving congestion we have also been seeking to help stagnating and under-developed areas which needed some rejuvenation. The various sub-regional studies, for example of Tayside, the North-East and the Borders, have argued the economic and the equity case for revitalisation of these parts of Scotland.

As to the second theme, the coherence of the policy instruments, it is clear that one component, Industrial Development Certificates, has been partly a *negative* instrument when viewed in a national setting. Attempts have been made to control development in congested areas such as the South-East of England. But there is a vast difference between being told that one cannot develop at A, and having a positive zest about going to B. This is precisely why negative measures have been supplemented by positive measures. These have been clearly specified in favour of regions to which Governments were seeking to attract resources and also retain existing resources in them. The first point, which emerged with striking clarity in Chapter 13, is that these positive inducements have been enormously variable. Inducements to invest have changed in form and content with great frequency. How easy is it for businessmen to respond to such incentives, and how easy is it for the student of policy to measure their response, when change follows fast on change?

A separate, but related consideration is that certain parts of the package of public investment, especially in infrastructure, can only be expected to pay off after the passage of a considerable period of time. What is not clear is, when we are entitled to stop being optimistic, waiting for the take-off that is around the next corner, and ask for the hard evidence of successful elimination of strong regional disparities? This leads to a more explicit consideration of the role of Government in the regional economic setting.

There is no doubt that regional policy is almost synonymous with Government action. By and large, it is the deficiencies of the private mechanisms for using resources which regional policies are criticising and endeavouring to eliminate. The public sector has to supplement the private. Indeed, we can put the matter more strongly. Public policy has had to eliminate many of the past external diseconomies in (say) housing and dereliction caused by the coal industry, as well as set the new scene through social capital formation which is intended to make an area a hospitable one for private industry. Of itself, the very fact of Government involvement may, at least in the British political system, explain some of the short-term changes in course. Equally, however, in the setting of policy objectives, we are entitled to draw attention to two desirable characteristics of the commitment by Governments to assisting certain regions.

First, there is a strong case for having more stable measures over a period of years, so that we may have some decent prospect of separating out and assessing the effects of policies that are intended to have their incidence and effects on one factor, say capital formation. Since we are so lamentably uncertain about the investment inducement measures that do attract firms to an area it would at least be helpful if Government measures did not change too frequently. Put another way, we still know surprisingly little about the hard core of forces that really influence the positive choice of location by industry, and Governments do not help to promote such understanding when they change horses in quick succession. Governments can of course retort that, as we suggested at the end of the previous Chapter, a blanket approach may be the best to adopt when our precise knowledge of investment responses is so deficient. And economists are of course fair game for the accusation that their pleas for stability are simply professional special pleading to make the regional economy into a controlled economic policy experiment. Nevertheless, economists will remain puzzled when it is not clear from policy measures whether they are seeking, for example, to change Capital/Labour or Capital/Output ratios.

Second, the need for a more analytical approach by Government to the resource-use it controls is fairly pressing. The case for a more explicit attempt to associate Government spending with particular programmes emerged very clearly from the analysis of Government spending in Chapter 6 and of Government capital formation in Chapter 9. While we accept that it may not be possible to allocate the defence budget in any unobjectionable manner, more explicit 'programme budgeting' by Government would illuminate such vexed questions as 'Scotland's share' of the public budget and resource use.

One of the paradoxes of the heavy Government involvement in regional policy measures is, however, that the more public the approach which is adopted, e.g. in infrastructure investment, the more difficult it becomes to identify the precise benefits and beneficiaries. Almost by definition the public programmes are much more than economic in their emphasis, and the opportunity cost calculus is both less urgent than in private resource use and also less relevant. Social objectives, very properly, loom large in Government action. Even within the economic calculus as well, there are frequently quality as well as quantity gains to be aimed at and, it is hoped, achieved and identified. Migration provides an excellent example of this multi-objective nature of Government regional measures. Very comprehensive action may be needed, embracing industrial, social, educational and housing measures, if a pay-off in migration behaviour is to be achieved. As suggested earlier, there may also be an inordinate time-lag before the outcome of certain of the more social types of regional policy undertaking can be assessed. Educational investment provides another good example of action which has an economic justification with long-term economic consequences, but which is also part of the total commitment of society to the way in which it seeks to implement the Parable of the Talents.

It then follows that there is a strong case for not changing public policy measures too frequently or abruptly if these are intended to affect private decision-making. It follows too that there may not in fact be a short time-scale for assessing the success of policies. This was vividly brought out in Chapter 4. What we do have to recognise, all the same, is that regional policy is not simply a matter of economics. It is a social and political issue, and Governments are often impatient for success and for the goodwill which may stem from an apparent positive relationship between what their policy measures try to do and what actually happens.

It is worth saying a further word about some of the objectives and indicators of success. One of the indicators of successful regional policy which is most frequently cited is employment gains, or additional jobs or, putting it negatively, the reduction in unemployment. This is of course a perfectly reasonable welfare criterion to keep in mind in considering all aspects of economic policy. The ultimate intention is to help people enjoy a better quantum of economic well-being. *But we cannot be satisfied with employment gains as a comprehensive measure of success*. We need look no further than the graphic experience of post-war agriculture in Scotland to sense what a misleading indicator of economic efficiency the number of jobs in an industry is. The wider criterion must be efficiency, judged by the competitiveness of the products, by profitability, and, above all, by the outcome in terms of people's incomes.

The same point applies to capital formation. We cannot be content to measure success by X,000 sq. ft. of new factory space. Moreover, it may not always be the case that the investment decisions which are made as a result of tempting grants or investment allowances are necessarily the most appropriate for the longer-term productivity of the economy. If it requires major subsidies to make certain projects even marginally viable, the disquieting question that remains is, whether such a channelling of resources really will make a significant contribution to the kind of transformation which Chapter 4 analysed. This comment may fit rather well with the disturbing feature that immigrant investment in Scotland has often taken the form of subsidiaries. It is obviously easier and cheaper to withdraw such experimental outposts from the scene than to have to abandon major projects. This again draws attention to the fundamental problem of time-scale and of public versus private action. Governments may have to give the lead, to adopt the 'big bang' approach, to show that the temperature of the economy is rising, and hope that major commitment of private investment will follow.

As we have repeatedly stressed in this book, neither employment nor investment is by itself a satisfactory indicator of reviving vitality in the economy. What is happening to one factor input cannot be the test of success. Factors are inter-dependent, and the efficient use of scarce resources has to be judged by the outcome in terms of productivity and incomes.

Let us take another of the policy objectives and the way in which its success is to be measured. We have seen that considerable efforts are being made to curb net migration from Scotland. Yet in an inter-regional setting it may make perfect sense for Scotland to be an educator *and* exporter of people. We in Scotland have always claimed that the quality of our education is 'second to none'. On comparative-advantage grounds, therefore, it could be argued that the Scots should provide one of the major educational reservoirs for the country as a whole, if we are as good at educating people as we have long claimed. This is of course dangerous ground for an economist to tread, because the human resource question is so much more than an economic one. National heritage and nationhood are subtle and complex phenomena. Even within the economic framework, too, it is important to bear in mind that firms which it is hoped to attract to Scotland may be discouraged if they have reason to believe that manpower, particularly of the more qualified kind, is likely to be in short supply. All that we are entitled to conclude about the manpower scene is that there has to be a broad balance of demand and supply, while recognising the problem of geographical and occupational imbalances.

2 Prospect

If we now look ahead to the broad sweep of likely economic development in Scotland, we can outline four important themes for consideration. First, there is the matter of the supply of resources of labour and capital. We noted in Chapter 8 that the labour force in Britain is likely to grow slowly in the decade that lies ahead of us. This means that when the overall level of national economic activity is high we must expect that the prosperous areas and industries will be willing and able to draw labour away from the lagging sectors and regions. Policies for redressing the net migration flows out of Scotland are therefore likely to be pulling against the collar, unless the positive attractions for employment in Scotland can be significantly increased. So far none of the direct and indirect inducements to labour has succeeded in reversing the heavy engine of migratory flow out of Scotland. We have also seen that the stock of capital is low in Britain, and additions to it are relatively slow as well, because of our low investment ratio. This does not provide the most favourable environment in which to seek to divert the flow of new capital into areas such as the central belt of Scotland. Given the scale of resources already committed to regional policy, and the competing claims of other policies, it is doubtful whether any major shift of additional resources for regional purposes can be contemplated in the foreseeable future.

Second, there is the problematical question of British entry to the Common Market. There is no doubt that this would involve a significant change in the frame of reference by which regional prosperity was assessed. The benchmarks of average performance would have to be widened, to take account of the major regional disparities that exist within the present European Community, between the south and the north of Italy, for example, and between the poorer agricultural and rich regions of the individual member countries and of the Community as a whole. There is great variety in the regional policies which are practised at present in Europe, and we could certainly expect that our particular regional issues would be given explicit recognition. Nevertheless, there is no doubt that Scotland would be on the periphery of the Community to an even greater extent than she is peripheral to Britain. Imaginative concepts such as Oceanspan, which envisage Central Scotland as a bridge between North America and the ports of the North Sea, could no doubt ensure that a centre of gravity was maintained, indeed enhanced, in the wider setting of Western Europe. But until the issues of British entry are resolved we cannot avoid the disquieting reflection that the networks of transport and communications in the United Kingdom would not be redirected automatically in Scotland's favour if Britain does join.

Thirdly, it would be most helpful to our assessments of regional policies if we could bear in mind the following tests of success of regional policy:

(1) The structure of production in the Scottish economy should be changing at a faster tempo. This need not mean that it must change in such a way as to mirror that of the U.K.

(2) For migration, we can aim for a reasonable long-term balance out and in; but that is not to say that it would be appropriate to try to establish complete equilibrium of demand and supply of labour in Scotland either in the short or long run.

(3) We can seek to make incomes in Scotland move closer to the national average, and regard this as a much more fundamental test of performance than simple and secondary indicators such as employment and investment.

(4) The question of economies of scale and external economies requires much more systematic appraisal, particularly if Governments are to make sustained commitments to growth point policies, as against a blanket strategy of providing sustenance for all.

Lastly, we return to a theme which was raised in the first Chapter, the inadequate statistical data available for intensive analysis of Scottish economic activity. We have to be realistic here and repeat the point already made, namely that the generation of statistical data is an economic activity, which costs resources. We can also add, however, that there is a danger in seeing Scotland as a special statistical case. More than in any other region of the national economy, the discussion of Scottish economic performance is concerned with the political implications, for Nationalism, Federalism, of a retention of the present political and administrative arrangements within the U.K. We have to recognise this special purpose which underlies the cry for more statistical information. Still, that in itself is no excuse for seeking to discourage statistical gleaning.

Our labours in producing this book were just coming to an end when the first issue of the new 'Scottish Economic Bulletin' was published in July 1971. It contains information that is new and important for an intelligent appreciation of the performance of the Scottish economy. With the hot breath of our publisher on our necks we have been able to take proper account only of its estimates of Scottish gross domestic product. Undoubtedly our kit of economic tools has been considerably enlarged by its publication.

At the risk of being labelled ingrates, however, we

would suggest that there is a modest shopping list of additional statistical information which could aid the analyst, and would also be beneficial for policy discussions. It would be helpful if more comprehensive data could be published about production, and if data could be made available more quickly. A bigger sample of incomes in Inland Revenue and Family Expenditure studies would provide a firmer foundation for regional and inter-regional analysis of developments in incomes. This is particularly important when it is borne in mind, as we have pleaded it should be, that income data in the end provide the most comprehensive single test of how resources have been used in a productive setting. We would also like to see more explicit programme budgeting being developed by Governments, not only at the national but at the local authority level. As a token of our realism we may perhaps add that it is unlikely that we can expect any rapid progress towards separating out the Scottish balance of payments and trade. The statistical difficulties of disentangling trade and payments flows are formidable, and rapid progress is not to be expected.

Regional policies can only be as good as the diagnosis of the problems of a region permit. We have seen in this study that we can go a long way towards identifying and analysing the Scottish economic problem. We like to think that one of the fruits of economic progress will be that this analysis, in time, will become easier for all who have an interest in Scotland and her economic well-being. Whether this analysis is used to make the case for any particular political status for Scotland is not our concern here. We saw in Chapter 7 that the appropriate question to ask about the Scottish economy as an independent entity is not whether she could 'go it alone'. The real issue is, how the scarce resources would come to be redeployed as the comparative advantages of Scotland changed and her resource endowments adjusted to a new situation. The purpose of economic analysis is to elucidate these and other problems of scarce resources: and it has, too, been the purpose of this book.

Index

D

E

F

G

M

N

O

P

R

S

T

U